psychological

solutions

to social problems

An Introduction to
Social Technology

SOCIAL PSYCHOLOGY

A series of monographs, treatises, and texts

EDITORS

LEON FESTINGER AND STANLEY SCHACHTER

psychological solutions to social problems

An Introduction to Social Technology

JACOBO A. VARELA

Montevideo, Uruguay

ACADEMIC PRESS   New York and London   1971

ACADEMIC PRESS, INC.
111 Fifth Avenue, New York, New York 10003

United Kingdom Edition published by
ACADEMIC PRESS, INC. (LONDON) LTD.
Berkeley Square House, London W1X 6BA

LIBRARY OF CONGRESS CATALOG CARD NUMBER: 70-137626

PRINTED IN THE UNITED STATES OF AMERICA

To my wife
HELENA

*a wonderful companion who
was the first to make me see
that what to me was a series of
independent solutions actually
formed a social system*

contents

preface

We are constantly surrounded by social problems. They stem from our interactions with others, and may range from the mildly irritating to the violently destructive. The issues cover broad areas, ranging from such trifles as persuading a spouse as to the best location of a piece of furniture in the home to international crises. We are also faced with the challenge of how to keep our explosively expanding technologies within bounds. Any one of these issues can become a social problem because of the involvement of persons of different backgrounds, interests, education, personalities, and abilities. These seemingly irreconcilable differences often make us despair of solutions.

This book is directed to all who, through their contacts with others, may suffer or cause others to suffer hardship. It includes all those whose primary concern in life, be it in their work situation, politics (both national and international), education, club, etc., is peaceful coexistence. The methods used were devised so that goals could be attained without sacrifice of personal integrity.

Since a major portion of this work was carried out in business organizations (merely because they were available and willing to put these new solutions to test), many of the examples given are taken from such settings.

However, participants have stated that the principles and solutions work just as well in other situations—home and family are those most frequently cited.

The book was planned for ease of assimilation. Principles are introduced through the use of examples, a procedure it is hoped will lead to greater clarity. In the last chapter all preceding material is integrated.

The work related in this book is a result of well-conducted scientific research. The solutions are not based on religious, political, or philosophical beliefs. It is quite possible that the reader may find himself saying: "Why this is exactly what I have been preaching all along!" Many beliefs are founded on "common sense" psychology. In a scientific work, however, the applications are of a more general nature. There is, for example, a technical solution for paving street surfaces so that rainwater will drain properly be they streets in Montevideo, Berlin, Paris, Moscow, or Washington. Similarly, the social solutions presented in this book are equally applicable and valid irrespective of the prevailing ideologies because they are derived from fundamental human behavior patterns.

This book differs from most books on "human relations," "personnel psychology," "salesmanship," "making friends," etc., in several respects, one of which stems from comparisons between pure and applied research. Pure research has as its goal the understanding of nature for its own sake; the applied researcher, on the other hand, strives for immediate results.

As Melvin Kranzberg (1968) stated in a penetrating analysis:

> The technologist's problem is to create a new and useful thing—a product, device, machine, or system. The problems are invariably complex. Having the idea for a new design, he usually must consider related problems of material, energy, information, and control. He must think about things that are already produced by other technologies that are possibly competitive. He must have the mathematical and scientific knowledge necessary to his various tasks and the completion of his design. . . . Scientists, on the other hand, have a preference for the small manageable problem. René Dubos tells us that the biologist, who decides as a student to study man, soon narrows to the study of an organ, then to the single cell, then to the cellular fragments, then to the molecular groupings, the individual molecules and atoms and,—if he knows enough— perhaps to the elementary particles. . . . On the other hand, the technologist, who must make his work meet some social need, cannot pursue such fragmented knowledge or bury himself too much in detail. He must keep the end-product constantly in mind, with all the many variables which enter into its making and use. Thus, all good engineering, from time immemorial, had been systems engineering insofar as it must take account of many parameters of a total practical situation.

No formal research is reported in this work, rather it is a collection of solutions applied to everyday problems, particularly those encountered in work situations.

Perhaps a more concrete and familiar example will help demonstrate more clearly the difference between "pure" science and technology. Let us consider the electric refrigerator. It is a combination of a series of marvels derived from many different areas of knowledge. While working on their own research projects, scientists in different laboratories contributed enormously to the development of the modern refrigerator, often without the slightest notion that they were doing so. Thus, an engineer designing a refrigerator today has at his disposal a large body of information derived from research in many areas. It is the coordinated application of *all* this knowledge that makes it possible for the engineer to produce a product we later so much admire.

As in the physical sciences, the technological designs for the solution of social problems presented in this book are based on certain principles derived from a variety of research areas. Solutions to social problems probably rank among the least understood phenomena of our times. If this book creates an interest in the application of the solutions discussed, in improving them, and in creating others, its main purpose will have been accomplished.

I am deeply indebted to many people. Among them are the supervisors and employees of many public and private organizations who were willing to apply or be subjected to schemes that seemed utopic and even outlandish, and who let me continue until results were eventually produced. It is unfortunate that space limitation does not permit even a partial listing of all those who have at different times enthusiastically and intelligently cooperated and contributed to the successful solution of many problems.

I am also particularly grateful to those social scientists who have at different stages provided encouragement and moral support. Among these I cite Dr. Ross Stagner, whose book *Psychology of Industrial Conflict* (Wiley, 1956) probably first started me on the course of applying social science findings to the solution of conflict, and who has shown interest and encouraged me in my work; to Drs. Leon Festinger and Stanley Schachter, who, when we first met in 1963, showed a lively interest and enthusiasm for the type of application I was attempting and at whose urging these experiences have finally been recorded; to Dr. J. P. Guilford who immediately understood the nature of the work and gave moral and maerial support by sending tests derived from his *Structure of Intellect Model;* to Dr. Norman R. F. Maier from whom I learned a great deal about group problem solving and who has always given me his moral support; to Drs. Mason Haire and George A. Miller for reading the manuscript and giving invaluable advice. Others who have understood and have therefore, at different times encouraged and helped: Anne Anastasi, Finley Carpenter, Barry Collins, Claude Faucheux, Harold B. Gerard, Carl Hereford, John T. Lanzetta,

William J. McGuire, T. M. Newcomb, Bertram Raven, Aroldo Rodriques, B. F. Skinner, Morris Stein, Henri Taifel, and Philip G. Zimbardo.

The last paragraph of Dr. John Paul Scott's book *Aggression* (University of Chicago Press, 1958) has greatly influenced me. I quote it in full: "Ours is a dangerous age in which the race between creative knowledge and destruction is closer than ever before. Destruction has not yet arrived, and knowledge still has a chance. Those of us who have scientific training and ability should do everything in our power to speed up creation and slow down destruction." This book is a determined attempt at following Dr. Scott's admonition.

I must also express my appreciation to all those who have systematically resisted the new innovations described here. Their opposition has been a powerful incentive to seek to improve them.

I wish also to express my great appreciation to Miss M. Dubitszky for what must be qualified as a superb job of editing. Further excellent editing by the competent staff of Academic Press has helped produce a more polished product. The assistance so willingly given by Academic Press has been of such high caliber that it is quite fair to say that without it this book would probably never have seen the light. Finally I wish to thank my assistant Mrs. Cristina Vásquez de Iruleguy for her constant support and cooperation in many phases of my work.

JACOBO A. VARELA

psychological

solutions

An Introduction to
Social Technology

to social problems

1

*Whenever I make an appointment,
I usually create ten malcontents
and one ingrate.*
Louis XIV

a common irritating
problem

Louis XIV voiced a problem that plagues many modern managers and supervisors in both private and public institutions. It is a problem that often delays the making of appointments because of the fear of negative reactions from those not appointed. Since this issue may have directly affected the reader either because he was the one who had to make such a decision or because he was the one expecting an appointment, we shall consider it as our first problem to be analyzed and solved by the application of social science findings.

First, we must study why an appointment generally causes such strong resentment among those who were not chosen. It is therefore necessary to start by explaining some of the findings resulting from the theory of cognitive dissonance devised by Leon Festinger (1957), the social psychologist. The name of this phenomenon, although it may sound unfamiliar, refers to a very common occurrence. It has probably happened to the reader today, and he will most likely experience it several more times while reading this book.

1

COGNITIVE DISSONANCE

The phenomenon characterized by the state in which a person finds himself when he receives two simultaneous and contradictory bits of information is called cognitive dissonance. For example, we expect a phone call from a friend, and the call does not come. The two cognitions or bits of information are:

- My friend was going to call.
- My friend did not call.

Dissonance refers to the incompatibility of two statements, which leads to a feeling of displeasure. Let's consider a musical analogy: When we hear sounds that are too dissonant, we feel they are unpleasant and may therefore turn off the radio, ask the singer, who may be out of tune with the piano accompaniment, to be quiet, or even get up and walk away. In other words, musical dissonance has a motivating force that makes us want to avoid it. In the same way, cognitive dissonance, defined above, is an unpleasant state, and we seek to avoid it as well. Festinger began this research on how human beings act to avoid dissonance, and it has been continued by many scientists, until we now know quite a bit about it.[1]

One of the first experiments, performed by Yaryan and Festinger (1961), was concerned with what happens when a person prepares for an event and finds out that there is little chance that the event will take place. The individual is consequently in a state of dissonance. The knowledge that he prepared for an event is dissonant with the knowledge that there is little probability that the event will occur. In this particular experiment, the subjects were made to memorize lengthy lists of symbols and their definitions for a forthcoming examination. Other subjects were merely asked to look over the lists, since the lists would be available on the examination day. Note that the first group was made to work hard for the special event, while the other group was not. Later, the experimenter told both groups that only 50% of the people would be examined because this was a new type of examination that the University was trying. He gave the impression that the decision as to which subjects would be tested had been made sometime before. Let us examine the position of both subject groups with respect to cognitive dissonance. First, the group that had worked very hard had two cognitions which were dissonant or incompatible:

---

[1] In the following sections, the reader will probably recognize his own behavioral processes as well as those of others.

- This professor made me work hard memorizing a list of symbols for an exam he said would take place.
- The same professor now tells me that there is only a 50% chance that I will have to take the exam.

From prior considerations, Festinger had predicted that the only way to eliminate the dissonance here was for the subject to *change* one of the cognitions. The first cognition could not be changed since he had already worked hard to memorize the list; his only alternative was to change the second cognition. He could easily do this by persuading himself that although only 50% of the group would be examined, he would surely be included in the chosen half. In order to test this hypothesis, the subjects were asked to indicate on a questionnaire whether they thought they would be one of the examination students. The results turned out exactly as expected: Those who had made the greatest effort at memorizing were much more likely to believe they would be tested than were those who had made little effort. It can be easily seen that those who had made little effort were not in a state of dissonance and hence had little dissonance to reduce.

At some time the reader may have waited in line, or experienced considerable discomfort and expense, to buy tickets to see a highly touted entertainer. If the show turned out to be mediocre, he would be in a state of dissonance: The knowledge that he had gone through considerable expense and discomfort—efforts usually justified only by first-rate performances—is dissonant with the realization that the show was second rate. Since it is now impossible to alter the cognition that he went through such expense and discomfort, the individual's only alternative is to persuade himself that the show was not really that bad, a common rationalization.

Another hypothesis based on the dissonance theory is that if our showgoer experienced great dissonance, he would seek social support in trying to reduce it. In other words, he will try to find others to support his rationalizations. For example, he may try to talk to many people and tell them how good the show was. However, if he tries to persuade someone who saw the show on *television*, without going through the trouble and without experiencing the subsequent dissonance, he will probably get nowhere.

With this background material on dissonance, we can return to the person who expected an appointment or promotion and analyze his thoughts and expectations in an actual case study. XYZ is a family-owned, commercial organization in which one member of the family, Fields, is the chief executive. He has several managers under him, who oversee the Sales, Purchasing, Administration, Financing, Market Research and Personnel Departments. The Administration Department, which concerns us here, is headed by Adams and is divided into several sections, each of which is supervised by a Section Head.

SECTION	SECTION HEAD
Accounting	Blake
Auditing	Clark
Office Services	Davis
Wage and Salary	Ellis

Adams is an old-timer. He has been talking of retiring for more than two years but never seems to make up his mind. He is very capable and runs a good department. His assistants are all devoted to him and have been quite cooperative: Blake is a very able chief accountant, although somewhat shy. Clark is an excellent auditor, very scrupulous with detail, but not very imaginative. Davis does a fair job. His work is rather complex because it embraces a hodgepodge of things. Ellis is rather new on the job. He has had prior experience, but he has not yet fully adapted to the new job, although he has made tremendous progress in a short time. He was hired at a salary slightly higher than what would normally correspond to his job evaluation because of his exceptional, overall abilities.

Over the years, Fields has maintained a policy of good relations with his personnel. This has meant encouraging them, praising them when they do something well, and inciting them to work for improvement. He has often told Blake and Clark, for instance, that their work is good and that there is a good future for them in the company. Similarly, Ellis was originally told that he would be on the wage and salary angle for some time but that there would be a future for him in the organization. At the time Fields made these statements, he was thinking of certain expansions planned in his commercial operations, although none of these men had the slightest inkling of those plans. Perhaps an organizational chart (see Fig. 1.1) will help show the overall picture.

Let us study, for a moment, the anticipated hopes each of these men

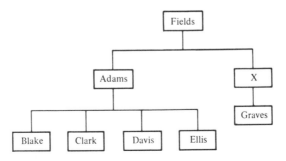

Fig. 1.1. Organization chart of XYZ business executives.

experienced after hearing Fields' encouragement. Each one perceived the statement regarding the possibility of having a future in the company as a promise of being appointed as Adams' successor, when he retired. Since each one had considerable contact with Adams in the course of his regular activities, each tended to see Adams' job as primarily concerned with his own particular line of work. Blake, for example, noted that every time he went to see Adams, Adams would drop everything else and instruct his secretary not to interrupt him. This gave Blake the impression that Adams considered his work extremely important and that therefore the main part of Adams' job had to do with accounting. (It should be added that Adams knew a lot about accounting, having once been Chief Accountant of the company.) It was therefore very natural for Blake to conclude that Adams' job would virtually be his after Adams' retirement. In fact, once, after a particularly encouraging meeting with Fields, Blake told his wife that night that he thought his promotion was almost certain. Ellis felt the same way. Wage and salary administration were a matter of great concern to Adams. Moreover, since he had also been told that he had a future in the company, it was quite easy for him, like Blake, to think that Adams' job would eventually be his. Clark and Davis were similarly convinced.

Unknown to all these men was the fact that Fields had actually been trying to find an outside replacement for Adams, since he did not feel that any of the subordinates mentioned could possibly cover the whole of Adams' job, in view of the proposed future expansion of activities. Not being able to find an outside man who would know enough about the inside workings of the company, he finally decided that it would be best to promote Graves, a very able man in the Finance Department, who knew the company well and who was experienced in all the relevant areas. He therefore immediately announced the appointment. It is interesting to analyze, in terms of the cognitive dissonance theory, the thoughts of some of those who felt cast aside.

Let us consider Blake first and note his two dissonant cognitions:

- Fields virtually offered me the job when he said I had a future in the company.
- Fields now appoints Graves to the job.

Obviously, Blake experiences considerable cognitive dissonance. We could construct similar statements for Ellis and the others. This dissonance, as we have seen, must be reduced. One way in which this could be done would be for Blake to recognize that after all, he was not fit for the job, that is, he could change his first cognition. But this alternative would cause more dissonance with other cognitions about himself—his self-esteem, for example. His other alternative would be to question Graves' appointment. He could say that Graves is totally incompetent and that it has been a long time since he had been on those jobs. He could also say that there was favoritism and that Fields was irresponsible or actually wanted to hurt him. This is a much easier alternative and, therefore, a more common way in which this type of dissonance is reduced.

It is important to note that what counts is not Blake's actual fitness for the job. The important aspect is that *he saw himself as fit for the job*. The same holds for the others. Stagner (1956), in a penetrating analysis on perception and motivation in industrial conflict, states: "If we assume that these conflict issues derive primarily from 'real facts', we shall inevitably wind up blaming some villain for industrial conflict. But, if we keep carefully in mind that each person behaves in terms of the fact *as he sees them*, we can concentrate on the fundamental problem; why do the facts look that way to him; and is there another way of looking at the situation which will be equally satisfactory without leading to conflict?" Fortunately, social science findings have given us ways of looking at the situation that do not lead to conflict and that enable us to design solutions that virtually eliminate the aftermath of discontent.

An immediate reaction from those who felt passed over was the desire to quit the company. However, we know from experiments based on cognitive dissonance, that *any* decision, including the one to quit, involves dissonance. Take the example of a person about to buy a car. He is undecided between two models. Each offers advantages, but each has drawbacks. Eventually, he decides in favor of one, but the moment he does so, he will experience cognitive dissonance. The knowledge that he has bought model A is dissonant with the prior knowledge that A had certain drawbacks. Besides, by not buying model B, he is left without the advantages that B had to offer. This dissonance is usually reduced by rationalizing that after all, the drawbacks of the purchased car were really not very important and that the advantages of the other make were overrated. If the dissonance is great, as has been stated, the person will need to seek social support. This means that he will try to persuade others about how good his decision was. This is a commonly observed phenomenon. Quite often, a man who buys a car goes around telling everyone what a wonderful purchase he has made. The same holds for the man who has bought a home or has gone to a special place for his vacation. From this we infer that the more a person talks about the advantages of a major decision he has made, the less certain he is that he has done the right thing. The same holds true for a religious or political convert. The more he talks about how good his new belief is, the harder the conversion must have been for him. This is the reason why converts to a new religion, a program of training, public speaking, or a weight-reducing method often become the best proselytizers. They are not really as interested in the other person's well-being as they are interested in reducing the dissonance caused by having engaged in some rigorous training, a demanding public-speaking course, or a particularly obnoxious reducing diet.

To go back to our disgruntled employees: Once they say to themselves, "I quit," they immediately experience dissonant cognitions.

- I have been working in this organization for many years.
- I suddenly decide to go elsewhere.

If the employee decides to quit, this decision is dissonant with the fact that he has remained so many years at one place. Since he does not yet know where he is going, he invents a hypothetical organization, which of course must be better than the present one. Since the other organization is still hazy in his mind, he must, to reduce dissonance, find something in it which is a great improvement over the present one, perhaps higher salaries. Because this dissonance must be even further reduced, he will seek social support for his decision. In other words, he will look for some fellow workers who will agree with him. Since the others who were relegated are in the same fix, he will easily find social support from them. The whole group will be convincing one another that the salaries paid are really low. It is interesting to note that this occurs at all levels and in organizations with greatly varying pay scales. Many strikes for higher wages can be traced to the accumulation of cognitive dissonance, due to many different sources, which make most people in the organization seek social support from one another based on the belief that their salaries are low. Grove and Kerr (1951), for example, showed that employees who felt insecure about their jobs showed discontent with their rates of pay, which in fact were quite high. This will be discussed further when we consider the subject of "Judging People We Know" in Chapter 4.

What actually happened in this case study was that Fields was faced with a series of indignant supervisors who became quite antagonistic toward him and Graves. Graves had to work for a long time before he could get any real cooperation—a goal that was only partially accomplished when Fields gave substantial pay raises to Blake, Clark, Davis and Ellis. Even this, however, has not mollified them, and at present Ellis is looking for another job.

A SOLUTION

In contrast to the unresolved situation just described, we shall now present one of the many cases in which a promotion has been successfully made using social science findings.

"Standard" is a rather large commercial outfit that has branches in several South American countries. In the larger countries, there are as many as seven branches, one in each city. These branches each employ approximately 50 to 250 people. The central branch in each country, and some of the regional branches, handle purchases, sales, financing, administration, marketing, advertising, personnel, and other functions. The smaller branches handle only sales, some accounting, and their own personnel problems. There is a good deal of independence among all these branches, although there is a central organization to which they all respond. This central organization allows quite a bit of leeway in handling matters. It is satisfied with receiving periodic reports and with sending key people to make audits.

At one point, Branch A of X country was in trouble. The trouble was directly traceable to top management. Williams, the head of this organization employing over 200 people, was a very unstable individual and had grown worse as problems became more acute. This situation was having a very disruptive effect on the whole organization, and it was only after carefully analyzing the situation (explained in Chapter 3) that the conclusion was reached to replace him.

In studying the job requirements carefully, it was found that there was no one at Branch A who could even be remotely considered for the position. Williams had seen to it that no one ever had the chance to learn the whole operation. Although there were several capable people in the organization, not one of them had the total knowledge, experience, mental abilities, interests, or other requirements to fill the top job. After a thorough search, it was finally decided that someone had to be brought in from outside. On the whole, this constitutes a sad case, since it had not been possible to assist Williams nor had it been possible to find a replacement from within. Although this seldom happens now in well-run organizations, it can occur at any moment, anywhere.

There were several good candidates that could have been spared from other branches. The very ticklish problem, however, was: how to bring in a candidate from another branch and place him above everyone else, several of whom expected the job themselves. Everyone sensed that the organization would not tolerate Williams much longer; therefore, all sorts of rumors and expectations had started to circulate about which of the 200-odd employees would eventually be selected to succeed him. The fact that none of them had the remotest chance did not occur to anyone, nor did anyone for a moment contemplate the possibility that an outsider would be brought in. Besides, behind each "Joe" who considered himself a likely candidate, there were several subordinates who felt they could take over Joe's job, which would be vacant once Joe was promoted.

The final decision was to appoint a man named Sims, from another branch, to head Branch A. Sims had worked in Branch A until reaching a higher position; he had then been moved to Branch B and from there to Branch C, where he currently held the top position in sales and merchandising. At Branch A Sims had been well liked, but several years had elapsed. No one dreamed that Sims would come back to A and be Manager over some of those who had once been his supervisors. There were therefore two problems. One was how to get rid of Williams without breaking the man. This topic will not concern us here but will be dealt with in Chapter 8. The second problem, which is the concern of this chapter, was how Sims could be brought in without causing great dissonance among those who were to be his subordinates. A table in which the names of all those expected to experience dissonance was prepared. This table included (a) name of the person involved, (b) position held, (c) degree of dissonance expected upon not being appointed,[2] (d) probable reaction, (e) degree of dissonance upon seeing Sims appointed after each became convinced that he would not make it,[3] (f) action to be taken prior to Sims' appointment, and (g) date on which action should be taken. A portion of such a list is shown in Table I. The original table contained 25 names—those whose position actually warranted their being considered for promotion and all others who might conceivably have had hopes (however absurd) for such a promotion.

The Regional Supervisor handled the interviews. He had the full support of the Personnel Manager, who had helped him in appraising the various candidates (including those mentioned) and in preparing Table I.

Earl, the Regional Supervisor, decided to talk first with Abe, about one month before the announcement of the appointment, that is, on D-30. Abe had often complained to Earl about Williams' incapabilities, particularly related to his own area of work. It would therefore be easy to broach the subject. Earl asked Abe how things were going in his department, and as usual, Abe stated that he was doing the best he could under the circumstances but that he often found it impossible to do things because Williams created a block. The latter wanted to do things himself and then procrastinated; so nothing was ever done. Earl posed the hypothetical question: "In case we eventually decided to move Williams somewhere else, whom do you think could run this job?" After much hemming and hawing, induced in part by Earl's pointed questioning, Abe stated that insofar as his own area was concerned, he could run the job himself because that would give him a free hand and also because he felt he could supervise the others. Earl said that he was glad to see him so courageous and that he knew that if Abe had a free hand he would do a marvelous job in financing. He asked Abe whether he knew the full extent of Williams' expected duties. Abe said he had a fairly good idea. The conversation continues[4]:

[2] Scale of 1 to 5, with 5 the most dissonant score.
[3] Also scaled from 1 to 5.
[4] This dialogue was reconstructed about two months after the actual interview took place.

TABLE I

Name— position held	No appoint. disson.	Sims appoint. disson.	Probable reaction	Action to be taken	Date
Abe— Treasurer	4	2	Would feel hurt at not achieving top job. Probably lose interest in present job.	Show job description so he can discover how much he lacks.	D-30
Bill— Sales Manager	3	5	Had had serious rivalry with Sims in past. Fully expected job. In many cases, Sales Manager had been moved up to top job; this was a precedent for Bill.	Show job description to see how much he lacks. Show Sim's qualifications without naming him until committed to accept; only then reveal that it is Sims.	D-20
Carl— Administrative Manager	3	1	Would feel a bit disappointed at not getting job but will be glad it's Sims, not Abe or Bill (has been having considerable friction). Used to get along very well with Sims.	Show job description so he will discover his limitations; then tell him Sims is the choice.	D-10
Dan— Auditor	4	2	Hurt at not getting the job because of the prestige and seniority (he is oldest with the firm). Reasonably glad that it will be Sims.	Show job description.	D-5

EARL: Have you ever seen a job description of the job as we expect it to be run, not as Williams runs it?
ABE: No, I never have.
EARL: Would you like to see one?
ABE: Yes, I definitely would.
EARL: I have one here with me. Let's look it over together and see what you think.

Both men looked over the description. As Abe read it, he began to have a worried expression. He asked Earl if some of the functions described couldn't be delegated. It was obvious, however, that most matters related to merchandising, sales, purchases, complaints, contacts with clients, etc. couldn't be delegated.

EARL: Tell me, in Finance do you delegate everything?
ABE: Well, I delegate a lot except when things get really tough.

EARL: Do you enjoy doing the routine jobs in your department?

ABE: No! I certainly pass those on to subordinates. What I enjoy most and feel that I'm best at is negotiating a loan when the situation is difficult, and things like that.

EARL: Do you think Bill or Carl could run agency A without your help by delegating all that to your present subordinates?

ABE: I think some of the routine things might work for awhile, although they need someone to keep an eye on them, but I doubt very much if they could do some of the complicated financing deals I have to make. They've often told me so themselves.

EARL: Well, in running the whole agency, something similar happens. The man on top has to handle personally all the most difficult problems in merchandising, complaints, and sales, as well as giving the Treasurer a sympathetic and understanding ear to his problems. Would you be willing to take over all those complicated problems?

ABE: Well . . . to begin with, I don't know much about merchandising, but perhaps with the help of the people in the department . . .

EARL: But that's just it. The problem is: Can you solve the problem when they can't?

ABE: No, definitely not. Besides, honestly, that's not the side of the business that most appeals to me.

EARL: But it's a very important part of the business, and you would have to give this the major portion of your time and attention.

ABE: Look, if that's the case, you'd better look elsewhere. But whomever you put on that job, see to it that he is not a perfect ignoramus about financing. I don't want to be continually blocked as I am now.

EARL: Well, I'm not counting you out, but it's obvious we have to do something. Please don't talk to anyone about this yet because no one knows we are seriously thinking about making a change. You know how it is—this place would be a hornet's nest in no time. Oh! the only one that knows something about this is Fred, the Personnel Manager. You can talk to him about it.

As soon as Earl left, Abe made a beeline for Fred. One finding we already know from dissonance experiments is that a person who needs to reduce dissonance looks for social support. This is a commonly observed phenomenon. To return to a previous example, when a man has been undecided for some time about which of two cars to buy because model P has several advantages and disadvantages but model Q also has many good and some bad points, he is in a state of conflict (described in Chapter 3). When he finally decides to buy Q, he will experience dissonance. His decision to purchase Q is dissonant with the cognition that he is stuck with the drawbacks of Q and is without the advantages of P. He easily reduces the dissonance by persuading himself that the disadvantages of Q are of no consequence and that the virtues of P are overrated. But if the dissonance is very strong, he will pester friends, fellow workers and others trying to prove to them how good the car that he bought really is. Knowing this and knowing Abe's dissonance would be high even though he had freely committed himself to the conclusion that the job was not for him, Earl gave him an opportunity to seek social support from Fred, the Personnel man. This guidance kept Abe from seeking social support among people who were as yet unprepared to receive the news.

Abe talked to Fred for about two hours—something that had never happened before. Of course Fred was prepared for this, and he knew it to be a vital part of the dissonance reduction process, so he listened to Abe patiently without interrupting him. Abe spoke at length about how this type of organization was a sales organization, how it should always be run by people with considerable sales experience, and how the people in the financial end should think of moving up, not to executive positions in the branches, but to the more important financial positions in regional or general headquarters. The Personnel man had a beautiful opportunity to see the dissonance reduction process in operation. Abe did not seem to care what Fred actually thought, rather he appeared more concerned with "persuading" Fred. Basically, of course, he was really persuading himself.

Earl had a harder time reducing Bill's expected dissonance. Bill, the Sales Manager, was a high-strung individual who thought he knew everything about everything. The problem was further compounded because when Sims had been at agency A years before, he and Bill had never managed to cooperate on anything. Of course, Bill had then blamed Sims for the difficulties.

Earl's task here was divided into three stages. The first, similar to Abe's case, was to get Bill to rule himself out. This he managed to do in about $1\frac{1}{2}$ hours. Then, after learning from Earl that Abe and Fred knew about the situation, Bill spoke at length with both of them. Bill's new viewpoint was that a more well-rounded man was required for the job. This caused Abe to be a bit puzzled, since he had reduced dissonance by persuading himself that the man for the job should come from Sales, namely, Bill. Thus, Abe returned to Fred, who, knowing of Earl's conversation with Abe, asked a few pertinent questions. He learned that Abe felt Bill knew very little about finance and that he would therefore never be able to help him with his problems. When Fred asked what Earl had said concerning this point, Abe remembered Earl's statement that no one would be appointed who was ignorant of financial matters. This recollection amazed him and made him start to wonder who *would* be appointed.

A few days later, on D-10, Earl returned. He again talked to Bill, got him to repeat his affirmations that he was not fit for the job, and then told him that a candidate had been found. Step by step, without mentioning Sims' name, Earl gave the candidate's qualifications and got commitments from Bill to the effect that these qualifications jibed ideally with the job requirements. Earl eventually asked Bill whether he would like to work under a man like this. Bill, now fully committed, said he would be delighted.

Then Earl asked Bill whether the picture would change if it happened to be a person he did not like. Bill replied: "How could I not like a man like that?" Earl gradually got more commitments along these lines until he reached a point where all he had to do was to state that the man was Sims. At first Bill was flabbergasted, Earl, however, continued to build up commitments, now referring to the candidate by name. Again, Earl told Bill that only Fred was in the know, and Bill immediately went to see Fred. While Bill was talking to Fred, Earl told Abe the name of the future Manager, adding that only Bill and Fred knew. It was interesting to see how Abe gradually reduced his animosity towards Sims by repeatedly talking to Bill and Fred until he started to speak very positively of Sims. This process took about a week. Earl proceeded in a similar way with the other hopeful candidates.

In the meantime, it was known that Sims was worried about how he would be received at Branch A. The whole process was described to him, but not having been trained in social science technology, Sims was prepared for the worst. When he finally arrived, a dinner was held in his honor. Both Abe and Bill made very laudatory speeches, praising the company's decision to appoint Sims and asking for and pledging full support to him in his new position. Sims was astonished. He later said he would have expected to see the Regional Manager do a striptease act or to have 10 naked dancers appear but never to hear Bill deliver such a friendly and sincere speech. That it was sincere became obvious in the ensuing days when Bill and all the others showed the greatest degree of cooperation with Sims. Needless to say, Sims has since become an enthusiastic proponent of social science technology and is always eager to try out new solutions to old problems.

A PROCEDURE BASED ON SOCIAL SCIENCE FINDINGS

Based on the preceding case study, a general procedure has been designed for making and communicating appointments.

1. Make a list of all possible candidates for the job.
2. Prepare a complete job specification for the vacant position, including job description, trait requirements and other data that will establish what kind of person is needed for that job.[5]
3. Compare each candidate's attributes with those required by the job.
4. Make a decision about who should be selected.
5. Make a list of all those who conceivably might aspire to the job, however absurd this aspiration may seem to you.
6. Make a ranking of the amount of dissonance each of these candidates will experience if he does not get the job.
7. Contact each one about his work and lead him to express his aspirations about the future.

[5] The next chapter will detail how new social science data can be useful here.

8. When he does so, discuss the job description with him until you get a commitment that he does not feel he can perform the duties. *Do not force this.* It has to be a free commitment. Be alert to the fact that you may have made an error in your original decision. Since no one knows this, you still have time to change your mind if you find that you had underrated a candidate who was really well qualified.

9. Repeat this with all other potential candidates at different dates and times. Do not do all this in one day. If you have never had such conversations with your subordinates, start having them now to prepare for the future and to create better relations in the meantime.

10. Allow at least a month to elapse between the above action and the public announcement of your final choice.

11. Two days before the announcement, contact the same persons in order of ascending dissonance (determined by the ranking established in point 6), with the changes you may have made as a result of the conversation described in point 8.

12. Remind the employee of the prior conversation, obtain a renewal of the commitment, and then announce the appointment. Ask for secrecy, but give the names of those already "in the know."

13. Verify that dissonance reduction has proceeded as predicted by talking to those who spoke to the subjects.

14. Make your public announcement.

This procedure has become standard, with gratifying results, in several organizations. In these companies, the usual aftermath of discontent, which was to Louis XIV and is to many modern managers a natural consequence of every appointment, has been virtually eliminated.

In the following chapters we shall present solutions to other social problems. Since some of the material is borrowed from ordinary common sense, the reader may occasionally feel that he is treading on familiar ground. However, even if something seems familiar, there is always an added bit of data that changes things drastically. In other cases, the whole process will be entirely different from anything the reader has ever seen, and it may well arouse cognitive dissonance in his own mind. He can reduce the dissonance by adopting the methods or even by improving them; he can also refuse to believe that the material has any value at all. The reader can choose any course he wishes, but if he lays this book aside now, he might miss some intriguing ideas that will perhaps remind him of problems he is now experiencing and that could possibly help him to solve those problems. More important, however, is the fact that social technology may someday soon become a mature pursuit in which the reader may himself become an active participant.

2

There's place and means for every man alive.

Shakespeare

judging people we don't know

All of us spend a significant part of our lives judging other people. We evaluate politicians of both our own and other countries; we also evaluate businessmen, educators, workers, union leaders, managers, friends, relatives, and many others. Some of these comments and criticisms are simply harmless talk, which does not affect the persons involved. Consequently, it really does not matter whether our judgments happen to be wrong or whether they are based on hearsay or insufficient knowledge. An illustration of such an incorrect judgment is Mark Twain's description of the naming of Pudd'nhead Wilson.

Wilson, a young lad, had arrived in a small Midwestern town. He had just met some of the citizens, when a dog started to howl, yelp, and generally make himself obnoxious

> . . . whereupon Wilson said, much as one who is thinking aloud,
> "I wish I owned half of that dog."
> "Why?" somebody asked.
> "Because I would kill my half."

The group searched his face with curiosity, and even anxiety, but found no light, no expression that they could read. They drifted away from him as from something uncanny and gathered in privacy to discuss him. One said:

" 'Pears to be a fool."

" 'Pears?" said another. "*Is*, I reckon you better say."

"Said he wished he owned *half* of the dog, the idiot," said a third. "What did he reckon would become of the other half if he killed his half? Do you reckon he thought it would live?"

"Why, he must have thought it, unless he *is* the down-rightest fool in the world; because if he hadn't thought it, he would have wanted to own the whole dog, knowing that if he killed his half and the other half died, he would be responsible for that half just the same as if he had killed that half instead of his own. Don't it look that way to you gents?"

"Yes, it does. If he owned one half of the general dog, it would be so; if he owned one end of the dog and another person owned the other end, it would be so, just the same; particularly in the first case, because if you kill one half of a general dog, there ain't any man that can tell whose half it was, but if he owned one end of the dog, maybe he could kill his end of it and —"

"No, he couldn't either; he couldn't and not be responsible if the other end died, which it would. In my opinion the man ain't in his right mind."

"In my opinion he hain't *got* any mind."

No. 3 said: "Well, he's a lummox, anyway."

"That's what he is," said No. 4, "he's a labrick—just a Simon-pure labrick, if ever there was one."

"Yes, sir, he's a dam fool, that's the way I put him up," said No. 5." Anybody can think different that wants to, but those are my sentiments."

"I'm with you, gentlemen," said No. 6. "Perfect jackass—yes, and it ain't going too far to say he is a pudd'nhead. If he ain't a pudd'nhead, I ain't no judge, that's all."

Thus, the citizens' lack of humor led them to brand the stranger as ignorant—making the subsequent discovery that this "pudd'nhead" was actually a brilliant detective all the more dramatic.

Most of us may find Mark Twain's passage irresistibly funny because of the irrational "reasoning" followed by the townspeople in reaching a decision about that particular person. At the same time, we may be quite unaware that we ourselves frequently make equally irrational, although not such funny, judgments based on what we hear or observe about those around us. Furthermore, there are times in our lives when the personal judgments we make have far-reaching consequences for both us and the person judged. For example, people in positions of authority often must decide whom to select among several possible candidates for employment or whom to promote or fire. In the latter case, it may happen that a person who at first seemed admirably suited for a certain position later turned out to be unqualified. Such a complete reversal in judgment is a common occurrence. It would seem worthwhile therefore to look at what social science can do to help us minimize errors in interpersonal judgment in the area of personnel selection.

The concepts presented here deal mainly with judgments involved in the selection of persons for different jobs, as well as questions concerning promotion and appraisal. In addition, the principles to be discussed have also been found useful in making judgments about family members or close friends and associates—even such things as deciding whom to invite to a party or for whom to vote.

SOME MISCONCEPTIONS

As a rule, each of us comes into daily contact with many sorts of people, and each of us has, accordingly, developed his own system (accurate or not) of judging them. Sometimes the same system of interpersonal judgments is shared by members of the same group, but this does not guarantee the correctness of the concepts included. We may say, for example, that Joe is a very *cooperative* person, as if cooperation were an ingredient that we all possess to a greater or lesser degree and does not really vary from one situation to another. We do this quite oblivious of the fact that cooperation means working together to the same end. Thus, Joe's cooperation with me depends just as much upon how I act toward him as upon how he acts toward me. Similarly, a manager may find that his subordinate, Joe, is very cooperative, while Joe's colleagues may think of him merely as a vile flatterer or, following Jones' (1964) analysis of the subject, an ingratiator (a less pejorative term meaning essentially the same thing).

Social science, in the field of psychology, has long pursued the quest for accurate judgments about persons derived from observations of their behavior, from standardized tests, and from interviews and other instruments. In some areas, the advances have been great; in others, scientists still appear to be groping. Nevertheless, enough has been learned to allow us to make increasingly accurate judgments, particularly when it comes to personnel decisions.

One may object that scientific judgment is a more complicated process than judgment by intuition or casual selection, but this is necessary because people are very complicated. An engineer thinks nothing of writing several pages to draw up a specification for a turbine or a compressor that he wants to acquire. An insurance executive thinks it is his duty to write a lot of fine print to specify the exact conditions of an insurance policy. Yet, when it comes to hiring the man who will run the compressor, or the turbine, or the man to handle insurance policies, very little attention is paid to describing the type of person needed. People, however, are much more complex than turbines, compressors, and insurance policies. If the engineer and the lawyer have been able to master the principles of their jobs, there seems to be no apparent reason why they cannot also master the principles and the language that will enable them to talk intelligently about people. Before presenting the actual methods devised for making personnel decisions, however, some important basic concepts should be discussed.

These basic concepts fall into two general areas: The first, which is dealt with in this chapter, is the problem of judging people we don't know or with whom we have had little contact (when there are several applicants for a single job, for example). The second, which will be the subject of the next chapter, is the problem of judging people we know well, like the ex-applicant who has been on the job for some time.

HOW PEOPLE ARE

In Chapter 1 dissonance was defined as the state in which the person finds himself when he receives two cognitions that are incompatible. Let the reader be prepared to experience considerable dissonance when he reads the following material since many of the findings reported here are bound to clash with his preconceived notions of how people are. The writer can remember more than one lively discussion over the existence of the term cooperation, with the more frank managers stating: "You have destroyed one of my most firm and cherished beliefs, yet I refuse to believe that I could be so totally wrong." Unfortunately, if we are to become scientific in dealing with people, leaving aside methods comparable to alchemy or witchcraft, there is nothing else to do but accept the findings of serious research. One excellent way of reducing the dissonance involved is to have an open mind, a real interest in learning about people. The reader is probably quite receptive about new developments in the technical aspects of his job. He would also need a similar attitude toward these findings about people and a willingness to try the techniques recommended here.

CLASSIFICATION SYSTEMS

There are many ways in which people can vary, in the same way that there are many ways in which, for example, vehicles can vary. In order to be able to talk intelligently about vehicles, we should start by making a classification system. This will include trucks, trailers, motorcycles, scooters, etc. Then, within each of these major classes, we designate sub-classes. Trucks, for example, could be subdivided into dump trucks, tank trucks, trailer trucks, and vans. Each of these could again be classed as to model, make, year, loaded weight, etc. We cannot talk about varied and complex things unless we classify them according to logical criteria.

In the same way, we must classify the great number of possible traits according to which human beings can vary. For our purposes, we shall use only those traits that will be significant with respect to job requirements. Hence, we create an initial, major classification of traits into five groups:

- Physical traits
- Mental abilities
- Interests
- Personality
- Background

PHYSICAL TRAITS

There are many ways in which people can vary physically. Similarly, jobs vary greatly in their physical requirements. Some require people to be strong. Others need people who have full color vision. In others, what are called physical defects are unacceptable. It should be noted that it is impossible to speak of physical defects as such when we refer to jobs. Varicose veins may be a serious handicap for a person who has to stand all day or may bar a person from doing heavy physical work, but they have no bearing on his being a writer. Therefore, when we include health as a physical trait necessary for a given job, we are not referring to a general physical examination, but to the health requirements for the particular work involved. Accordingly, when we send people to the company doctor for a physical examination prior to their starting work, we should also send a job description so that the doctor can pay greater attention to those aspects of health that are necessary for the performance of that particular job. There is, therefore, no such thing as a general health standard or overall health examination in personnel selection.

Another quite overworked physical concept is that of manual dexterity. Based on the observation that there are obvious differences in the ability different people have to work with their hands, many manual dexterity tests have been designed and put on the market. Unfortunately, the results of these tests have not been promising. Commenting upon them, Anastasi (1968) has this to say:

> What can be said about the effectiveness of motor tests as a whole? The most important point to note in evaluating such tests is the high degree of specificity of motor functions. Intercorrelations and factor analyses of a large number of motor tests have failed to reveal broad group factors such as those found for intellectual functions.

A little later, after giving the results of some extensive factor analytic research by Fleishman and his associates (Fleishman, 1954; Fleishman and Ellison, 1962; Fleishman and Hempel, 1956) in which some major factors have been identified, Anastasi adds:

With regard to commercially available motor tests, the functions they measure are very simple and their validities against most criteria are not high. For this reason, such tests serve better as part of a selection battery rather than single predictors. In general, motor tests have been most successful in predicting performance on routine assembling and machine operations (Ghiselli, 1966). As the jobs become less repetitive, perceptual and intellectual factors come to play a more important part.

We will leave the subject of physical traits for the moment and discuss the second classification.

MENTAL ABILITIES

The quest for what we mean when we talk about *intelligence* has been a long one. Actual research was begun only after many years of philosophizing about the subject of intellectual ability. J. M. Cattell started in Wundt's laboratory in Germany almost 100 years ago. Thereafter, several workers, including Binet and Simon in France, were followed by Terman at Stanford University who prepared a revision of the latter's work which was called the Stanford-Binet Test. It was here that the unfortunate term "intelligence quotient," or I.Q., was coined. The term I.Q. is considered unfortunate because its apparent simplicity and widespread use led most people to the conviction that intelligence is a unitary attribute and that this attribute can be precisely measured; therefore people's minds are simple enough to be defined in terms of a single number. For the purposes of our work, nothing could be further from the truth.

Fortunately, L. L. Thurstone, through a complex mathematical technique called *factor analysis*, was able to prove that intelligence is *not* a unitary trait. Instead, it is composed of several largely independent abilities. Initially, the following aspects of intelligence were delineated.

VERBAL COMPREHENSION	Mainly a measure of vocabulary and the understanding of language.
WORD FLUENCY	The speed with which words can be emitted under certain circumstances.
NUMBER FACILITY	The speed with which simple numerical computation can be carried out.
SPATIAL ABILITY	The ability to visualize spatial relations in two or three dimensions.
MEMORY	The ability to remember numbers associated with words.

SPEED OF PERCEPTION   The ability to recognize rapidly differences or similarities between parallel col-
umns of numbers or names.

DEDUCTIVE REASONING   The ability to reason rapidly about simple
problems—the type of reasoning varying
from one problem to the other.

INDUCTIVE REASONING   The ability to find relations among apparently unconnected things. For exam-
ple, given a number series, the subject
must find the rule governing the series
and accordingly determine which number
should follow the one given in the initial
series.

One important by-product of Thurstone's work was that it reduced the
naive rivalry among persons concerning who has the highest I.Q. or, perhaps
more frequently, whose *child* has the highest I.Q. Those low in I.Q., in many
cases, have come to feel quite ashamed of their apparent inferiority. Parents
are seldom willing to resign themselves to the fact that their children have a
low I.Q. Similarly, many high I.Q. subjects act as if they were superior beings.
When the new mental abilities were discovered, it became hard to say who is
more intelligent than whom. Is the man who is exceptionally high in perception, number ability, and deductive reasoning but low on verbal and inductive reasoning more intelligent than the man who is low in perception and
number ability but high in verbal and inductive reasoning skills? Was Isaac
Newton more intelligent than Shakespeare, or were either more intelligent
than Bach? Thurstone's work made this type of question as meaningless as
the medieval metaphysical question of how many angels could stand on the
head of a pin. There is no such thing as intelligence. Rather, there are a series
of unrelated mental abilities, and since different jobs require these in different
degrees, personnel selection becomes simply a problem of finding who has
the abilities required for any given job.

It readily became evident that salesmen, for example, had to be high in
verbal comprehension and word fluency; whereas a cost accountant could be
low in these abilities but should be high in numerical ability and speed of
perception. Each can do an excellent job if he has the required abilities for
the tasks he must perform. If, however, these two individuals were to exchange jobs, the results for both would probably be very poor. When each
is assigned to his proper job, the supervisors would probably speak of these
men as intelligent. After an exchange of jobs, each would probably be considered not intelligent. Hopefully, this little example will help to illustrate

the relative nature of mental abilities, and the uselessness of the concept of general intelligence, which will have no further place in this book.

If this causes considerable cognitive dissonance to the reader, some comments are now in order: First, we cannot simplify people just because we have an earnest desire for people to be simple. Boilers, TV circuits, women's dresses, educational methods, cooking recipes, string quartets, and the many other things with which we daily deal are complex. Those who deal with them very closely would be indignant if someone were to propose that one single number alone could represent all the features of each one. They would insist upon the need for *many* factors to describe each unit, in order to distinguish it from another. People are much more complex than boilers, lathes and even computers, so we must resign ourselves to the fact that we simply cannot define all mental abilities by one number. It would be nice if our desire for simplicity fit the facts, but the inherent complexity of the human mind makes the attainment of this desire totally illusory.

In fact, the monumental work of J. P. Guilford, with his great insights into the classification of the human intellect, shows that the problem is even too complex to be handled by the scheme described by Thurstone. While working on the classification of mental abilities, Guilford came upon the rather disturbing discovery that there were, in fact, many more abilities than those originally discovered by Thurstone and that these were unrelated to one another. For example, he found a new spatial factor different from Thurstone's spatial visualization (Guilford and Lacey, 1946). This was termed *spatial orientation*. It was found that a person could be high in spatial visualization without necessarily being high in spatial orientation. The disturbing situation which evolved can be compared to a certain phase in the history of physics. There was a time when everyone was pleased that at last the electron and the nucleus had been discovered, and now everything in the atom could be tidily explained. Then new particles began to appear. Just when simple structure had been described, new particles kept cropping up. Today, the field of the physics of particles is almost chaotic because of the continuous discovery of new particles.

By the time Guilford had identified 20 mental abilities, the situation had become nearly as chaotic as that caused in physics by the proliferation of new particles. He did what any other scientist would have done under the circumstances; he tried to set up a classification scheme. He was not the first one to do so, but he was the first to be at all successful. He managed to develop a scheme that not only greatly clarified the whole situation but also proved very fruitful. It is very important to describe this scheme in detail because it has proved to be extremely interesting and useful in the study of persons and why they are as they are. Guilford's three-way classification scheme classifies mental abilities in the following manner.

Operation Performed.   There are five different *operations*.

Cognition.   The act we perform when someone shows us an object, say a bunch of keys, and asks us to tell him what it is, and we do so. This is just one type of cognition. Guilford has found that there are at least 24.[1]

Memory.   If someone shows us a bunch of keys, takes them away, then asks us to state how many keys there were, and we remember correctly, we are using our memory. Again, there are 24 different types of memory.

Divergent Production.   If a group of us suddenly find ourselves in trouble, and we have to find a way out, it is possible that some may have many *different* ideas of how to solve the problem, while others may have few ideas. Those who have many are high in divergent production abilities. Just as there are 24 kinds of cognition and memory, there are 24 different types of divergent production.

The reader may become a little irked at the repeated mention of 24 abilities under each operation without further explanation; perhaps some clarification is now in order. Suppose the problem is that we have promised to design a piece of furniture, say a night table. Someone in the group may be able to make a whole series of different designs, while others find themselves at a loss as to how to begin. On the other hand, if our problem was to write the text of an advertisement for a newspaper, one member of the group might be able to write several different texts easily, while the one who could design many types of night tables might not be able to think of anything but the simplest copy. Both would be exercising considerable divergent thinking ability, but each in a different area. The same holds true with respect to the operations of cognition and memory.

Convergent Production.   This is the ability to find the answer to a problem when there is only one correct solution. Suppose our TV set breaks down, and we appeal to a service man. The good service man will be able to find rapidly which is *the* component that is out of order. He will then either repair or change it, that is, if he is high in convergent ability. If he is low in convergent ability, he may tamper with all the parts of our set without finding the real cause of the trouble, and perhaps leave it even worse shape than it was before. The reader has probably experienced this sort of trouble with the servicing of a TV, a car, a washing machine, a camera or some other type of mechanical object. Perhaps his service man was low on convergent production ability and should never have gone into the field of servicing. This is not surprising since the area of convergent production has been little explored and, to the author's knowledge, has never been specifically used to select or guide people who should go into repair work.

[1] More will be said about these later.

Evaluation.   Recall that in discussing divergent production, we cited two cases: one was making several designs for a night table, and the other was writing several texts for an advertisement. But the job is not complete when the designs and texts are made. It is also necessary to determine which designs and texts are the most suitable, given certain criteria. In other words, which night table will best suit the person who asked for it and which goes best with the rest of his furniture? Which of the several advertisement texts, by carrying the message correctly, will appeal most to the persons we want to reach? The ability to select the best product is a form of evaluation. People who are very good at divergent production are not necessarily good at evaluation, that is, at deciding which is the best of all the proposed solutions. Hence evaluation ability is independent of divergent production ability.[2] In his "Essay on Criticism," Alexander Pope on satirizing critics says:

> Some have at first for wits, then poets, past,
> Turn'd critics next, and prov'd plain fools at last.

In these and in many other lines such as

> And censure freely who have written well

Pope makes a common error. He assumes that because great poets have the divergent ability to produce and the evaluative ability to criticize, therefore all would-be critics who are really evaluators should also have produced great works, that is, should also be high in the divergent production abilities. This we now know to be incorrect and many people are great evaluators though incapable of creating. This of course does not mean that there aren't many who not being high on evaluative ability *believe* themselves to be great critics and it is against these that Pope makes his justifiable and delightfully devastating attack. Again, there are 24 different abilities in evaluation.

Content Involved.   We have seen how there are five different types of operations. However, in the course of describing them, hints were given that the various mental abilities can also be classed on the basis of the *content* involved.

Figural.   This area comprises designs, drawings, etc. Figural ability would be quite essential for the person designing the night table.

Symbolic.   This area comprises codes, mathematics, data processing, numbers, etc. If we give the matter a little thought, we should be able to think of people we know who are very good at drawing or at remembering paintings, even the smallest details, but who are very poor with numbers, algebra, for example. We may also know a good accountant who is excellent

---

[2] As a matter of fact, all the abilities mentioned so far are independent of one another. A person may be high in several, medium in others, and low in still others. All sorts of combinations exist.

with numbers but who cannot recall even simple designs. This is of little importance to him since it has no bearing upon his job.

Semantic. This is the content dimension that has to do with language and meaning. We do not know whether Shakespeare was as good as Rembrandt was at drawing or as Leverrier, the discoverer of Neptune, was at calculating. However, we do know that Shakespeare was phenomenally good at using language and language concepts. Different jobs require the ability to use language concepts in different degrees. No one would ever be required to have the ability of Shakespeare, but obviously the person with good semantic skills would have less trouble writing a report or understanding a complex book on philosophy, than would a person low in ability in this area. Jobs must be analyzed in order to determine how much semantic ability is required. However, the type of semantic ability required is also important. According to Guilford's classification, people may be high in semantic cognition, or semantic memory, or semantic divergent production, or convergent production, or evaluation. For example, a person filing reports must be good at cognizing semantic classes since he has to file properly according to certain criteria. These reports must be classified well if they are to be retrieved rapidly without wasting time. On the other hand, the person on a filing job has no need for divergent production of semantic systems since the task does not involve this ability. A series of advertising texts to be published consecutively constitute a semantic system. The man writing these texts must certainly be very good at divergent production, although he may be low in the cognition of semantic classes.

Behavioral. This is the last content category and concerns the actions of people. For example, a person who is good at cognition of behavioral units is one who can instantly detect, from say, facial expressions, what is wrong with someone else. This would seem to be a very important ability for any supervisor, who must realize immediately from a subordinate's "long face" that something must be wrong, possibly with the work situation. Supervisors who are skilled in the cognition of behavioral units are generally able to avert trouble caused by dissatisfaction among employees. Others are unaware that anything is going wrong until there is an explosion in the whole department. Since this is a new group of abilities defined by Guilford, the present administrators of different institutions or organizations were probably hired without any consideration of their behavioral skills and tested only for symbolic and semantic abilities. Because some of these people may be low in behavioral abilities, they probably did not notice signs of smoldering conflict until the trouble erupted. Thus, not using behavioral skills in personnel selection has probably caused great discord, including strikes, in many areas. Supervisors who did possess behavioral abilities, would have quickly noticed trouble and would probably have been able to do something about it, particularly if they also ranked high in divergent production and evaluation in the behavioral area.

The cognition of behavioral *relations* is another important area, which again is independent of other behavioral functions. For example, we all know some persons who go to a cocktail party and are immediately able to notice a new relationship between two persons of opposite sexes. They do this by noting minute, almost invisible actions, while others see nothing.

Product Concerned.   By this time, the reader will have noticed that we are not merely content with classifying mental abilities according to the operations performed (cognition, memory, etc.) or the content involved. We need a third category, which Guilford has labeled *product*. Mental abilities can be classed according to which of six products are dealt with.

Units.   We have already seen what is meant by units in the discussion of certain behavioral units, that is, facial expressions. "Semantic units" might seem to be a rather pedantic way of referring to words. A person high in cognition of semantic units merely has a large vocabulary; but if he is low in divergent ability, he may have a hard time *using* these words in different ways on different occasions.

Classes.   These are categories, which contain more than one unit. We have seen that the person doing filing has to be good in the cognition of semantic classes. On the other hand, a person who *creates* filing systems has to be good at divergent production of semantic classes since he has to invent the different ways in which certain material can be categorized. In order to select the best way, he must also possess skill in *evaluating* semantic classes. The latter skill will help him select the method which best fits all the criteria concerning how and for what the system is to be used. Unfortunately, all these abilities are not generally found in the same person. Perhaps, we should say fortunately because jobs are varied, and we therefore need varied people to fill them. This fact not only adds spice to life but is very useful in group problem solving, which proceeds most efficiently when the people working together complement one another.

Relations.   We have noted that the person who entered the party and noticed a new relation between persons of opposite sexes was very good at cognition of behavioral relations. Having this ability may be important for a salesman or supervisor. Relations abilities also exist in figural, symbolic and semantic areas.

Systems.   A system is defined by Guilford (1967, p. 91) as "an organized or structured aggregate of items of information, a complex of interrelated or acting parts." A behavioral system, for example, is a short sequence of events that, connected together in time, have a meaning. For example, a worker makes an error, spoils some work, and hides the spoiled work; the Foreman finds it, and bawls him out. All this constitutes a behavioral system. Suppose the Department Head sees the situation. Suppose also that the Department Head has read this book and, after reading it, has decided that bawling people out accomplishes nothing.[3] If the Department Head is good at cognition of behavioral systems, he will need only two or three bits of data to grasp the meaning of the sequence of events that has taken place. If he is low in this ability, he will never see what's going on until the day he has serious trouble in his plant. The Department Head also needs some divergent production and evaluative ability in the behavioral area in order to know what to do about what he sees, that is, if he infers that something must be done. There are also figural, symbolic and semantic systems.

Transformations. This is an ability that is used in solving certain puzzle tasks, such as unscrambling letters given in a mixed-up order to form a hidden sentence. It is also the ability needed to notice rapidly that PEO PLEAR ECOM PLEX means: People are complex. There may be jobs which involve semantic figural or symbolic transformations, although it is difficult to readily name any. The ability to cognize *behavioral* transformations, however, is extremely useful, especially for the supervisor and the salesman. As a matter of fact, the salesman should be generally good in all the behavioral abilities mentioned so far, although there are many different types of salesmen requiring different abilities, which depend upon the products they sell, the type of client they contact, etc.

Implications. Given one situation, product, or condition, that product, situation or condition gives rise to or implies something else. Again, this concept is best explained by the use of examples. This skill is highly important in planning (Berger *et al.*, 1957). Let us suppose that a person has to decide between two courses of action. Skill in the cognition of implications means the ability to *plan*, i.e., to anticipate all the consequences that each of these courses of action implies. Some people can't think of the consequences until they see them after the events have actually happened. Others are able to foresee implications and can therefore take them into account when planning. Evidently, cognition of *behavioral* implications is very important in sales, personnel work, and public relations. Cognition of *semantic* implications is important for all sorts of planning, including data processing, writing, politics, diplomacy, and all strategy design.

Guilford has established a very useful code that simplifies the identification of each ability, and we shall henceforth use it when referring to them.

---

[3] That reprimanding is ineffective will be one of the most important conclusions drawn from later chapters. Concrete substitutes for reprimanding will also be given.

Operations

C = Cognition
M = Memory
D = Divergent production
N = Convergent production[4]
E = Evaluation

Content

F = Figural
S = Symbolic
M = Semantic[5]
B = Behavioral

Product

U = Units
C = Classes
R = Relations
S = Systems
T = Transformations
I = Implications

According to this code, CMU signifies Cognition of Semantic Units, i.e., the ability to recognize the meaning of different words; DSI stands for divergent production of symbolic implications, etc. This may sound a little complicated at first, but experience has shown that with a little practice supervisors are able to handle these code names and their concepts without any more difficulty than they face with the concepts and codes used in the rest of their work. The usefulness of Guilford's classification is that with only 16 concepts, we can analyze and describe as complex an entity as human intellect, which is, in turn, composed of 120 different abilities.

INTERESTS

Data regarding interests have been more diffuse than the material related to mental abilities. In the job context, *interests* refer to different persons' liking or disliking the performance of different kinds of jobs. The most common instruments used to measure this area are the Strong Vocational Interest Blanks of Men and Women (1943). These tests measure an individual's references for about 50 occupations. There is also the Kuder Preference Record (1953–1956), which gives scores on interests in 10 broad areas, such as

---

[4] Note: C has already been used to denote cognition.
[5] Note that again the S has already been used for symbolic.

mechanical, scientific, artistic, etc. There is a third important study by the U.S. Employment Service (1956) in which interests are defined as tendencies to become absorbed in certain activities and to continue with these activities, without a concomitant inclination to leave them. This work was based on Cottle's (1956) bipolar factors. One such factor is defined as the "preference for working with things and objects" versus the "preference for working with people and the communication of ideas." A second factor is the "preference for business contacts" versus the "preference for work of a scientific or technical nature." In our discussion of interests, we prefer to use a *mixture* of concepts derived from these other studies. For example, we use interest in mechanical things as defined by Kuder and business preferences as defined by the U.S. Employment Service report.

Difficulties in Discussing Interests.   One problem stems from the fact that interests may be affected by a difference in motivation or persuasion. Later, we shall see some of the techniques which have been used to make a person take a greater interest in a certain type of work. Therefore, interests are not nearly so stable as mental abilities. Besides, there is the problem of the *prestige* of occupations. In general, people rank the relative status of occupations in the same way, regardless of their age, sex, geographical region, size of place, or education (Reiss, 1961). This is true although there is "less than perfect concensus on the *amount* of prestige to be accorded occupations" (Reiss, 1961, p. 194). Consequently, variations in prestige may lead to variation in interests with respect to certain lines of work.

Another difficulty is the question of whether interests are related to the mental abilities required for the performance of a job. Guilford (1967) found very low but significant correlations between thinking-interest scores and thinking aptitude scores. Nevertheless, this finding applies to only *one* area of a job, and it is still possible that eventually a *multiple* correlation may be found between interest in performing certain types of work and the ability to do such work. Super (1957, p. 224) states that: "Interest is related to success in occupations only under special conditions, when the congeniality of the activity is crucial to application; when, as in most occupations, motivation from other sources such as status and income needs can suffice, interest in the activity itself is not related to success." Even Strong (1958) states that after 37 years of studying interests, he has learned something about them but little about satisfaction. He states: "We have made far more progress in measuring capacities than in ascertaining men's goals."

Our selection design incorporates interests only when it is obvious that such interests really contribute to success on the job and when these interests are ascertained in a well-conducted interview. For example, we may ask the person which of two types of work he would prefer, since we have two job openings at equal pay and with equal opportunities for future advancement. We then proceed to describe two jobs that differ only in terms of the interest factor required; that is, one may be mainly concerned with mechanical work and the other concerned with office work. When the person shows a preference for one, he is asked to explain why. To be convincing, his answer must include an enumeration of past events showing interest, how he persisted in the type of activity involved in spite of difficulties encountered, and so forth. These interest tests are very useful for vocational counseling purposes, but for personnel selection, the time needed for administration and interpretation does not warrant their use, particularly if the information can be obtained more rapidly in an interview.

PERSONALITY

This field is even more vague than the one of interests. There are several different theories of personality. Hall and Lindzey (1970) give a detailed description of about a dozen of these. From those theories it is seen that *personality* has a different meaning depending upon which theory we study. In personnel selection, the most useful theories are those based on *traits*. For example, Allport (1928) describes a personality trait called *ascendance–submission*, later altered to *ascendance–timidity*. There are some people who are more ascendant than others, which means that they are able to face unfamiliar situations without feeling discomfort. Others are very shy and would rather work at jobs that do not require contact with others. Is this difference due to an innate trait? Is it due to differences in behavioral abilities? Does it represent merely different habits? The spectacular changes in this dimension that have been produced, in some cases with adequately designed, programmed training, and the lack of success in others lead us to believe that even this single trait is complex. Nevertheless, when selecting a person for a job that requires ascendance, like selling, it is probably best to size up the person as he is *at the moment*. Between two candidates equal in all of the specification requirements, we should probably choose the one who is ascendant *now*. Perhaps the other one could eventually be trained to lose his shyness. But a job has to be done, and we simply do not have the time to initiate such training, particularly if we have ascendant candidates available *now*. People high in general activity are labeled dynamic. Some people are simply more dynamic than others. Guilford (1959) mentions the factor of *general activity*. For example, dynamic persons tend to do things fast or maintain a rapid pace —eat and walk rapidly, etc. In general, they exhibit energy and are happiest when involved in action. There is an old saying in Russia: "When you want to hire a man, put a meal in front of him and watch him eat. If he eats fast, he is a good worker; if he eats slow, he is a poor worker." This rather naive test (which would be affected by hunger as well as energy level) nevertheless points to a recognition of the relation Guilford found among various measures of activity level.

Smith (1969) has found evidence for a general activity syndrome. In a survey of eight Massachusetts towns and cities, 304 adults were interviewed and indices obtained in such diverse activities as membership in voluntary organizations, reading nonfiction periodicals, viewing active response to public issues as important, and others—all of which although diverse in character, imply activity. Although such variables as gregariousness, approval motive, and affiliative need may have somewhat contaminated the data, the general activity syndrome clearly emerges.

Traits Used in Personnel Selection. In our study of personnel selection, we researched the work of Cattell (1950, 1965), Eysenck (1947, 1953), and several others for material that could be useful in selection designs.

One personality trait that is finding wide application in these designs is the need for *approval* (Crowne and Marlowe, 1964). This signifies the degree to which a person's behavior is motivated by the desire to obtain approval from others. Approval motivation has been taken into account in the design of persuasions and in conflict resolution, as we shall explain in the appropriate chapters.

The need for approval may be temporary, depending upon the situation. If the person's life is unsatisfying and approval is not forthcoming in real life, he may escape into fantasy. Dr. Norman Maier (personal communication) offers a cogent theory regarding this situation. He feels that the whole outlook of modern psychiatry is wrong, since it tends to help man *find* himself. Dr. Maier believes that the main problem we must face today is to help people *forget* themselves and think more of others. The whole tone of this book follows Maier's dictum. If the reader can master and use all that is included here, he will be busy thinking of others and have little time left to think of himself.[6]

It should also be noted that great need for approval may interfere with certain important duties. For example, supervisors who are high on the approval motive scale tend to be too interested in themselves and to forget their subordinates' needs and problems. An interesting question that we have not yet been able to answer, due to insufficient data, is whether those high in need for approval are low in the behavioral abilities of the Guilford SI model. It is quite possible that a negative correlation will be found.

[6] John Stuart Mill stated in his autobiography that he believed only those who concentrate on any object other than their own happiness—particularly the happiness of others—can really achieve happiness themselves. If this is so, then whoever uses the designs set forth in this book may obtain not only practical results but a certain measure of happiness as well.

A very interesting study, which has shown great promise for the selection of supervisors, is that related to the *authoritarian personality* (Adorno *et al.*, 1950). The authoritarian personality has been described as a syndrome or collection of traits that tend to go together. The typical high authoritarian is a person who adheres strictly and inflexibly to conventional values. He feels anxious even if others threaten to violate these values; that is why he insists on having rules and regulations that treat everyone alike. But, the authoritarian is also submissive, although not in the normal sense of having respect for authority. Rather, he shows an almost irrational, exaggerated need to submit. He usually does as he is ordered and is lost if he does not have the rule book or a higher authority to guide him in case of trouble. When he feels hostile or frustrated, he evidences authoritarian aggression, which usually takes the form of "taking it out" on his subordinates or underprivileged groups. In other words, he is hostile only when it is safe for him to be so.

The authoritarian also disapproves of a free emotional life. He is usually very concerned about sex and becomes indignant and intolerant regarding the sexual misbehavior of others. He simply cannot live freely because he is basically very insecure; that is the main reason for his authoritarianism.

Still another characteristic of the authoritarian is his tendency to stereotype. People are either good or bad. If good, they are good in everything—good workers, loyal and good husbands, fathers, students, etc. If bad, they don't have a single redeeming feature. Authoritarian personalities have what is called intolerance for ambiguity. They cannot admit that Joe, who is sloppy in his work, can still be a very hard worker. If sloppiness is unbearable to the authoritarian and if Joe is sloppy, then there is nothing good at all in Joe, and the only thing to do is to fire him.

The authoritarian tends to be superstitious, believing that occult, outside forces have great bearing on his daily problems. This actually relieves him from the responsibility of making decisions; he would rather have the stars decide for him. Accordingly, he is relatively unable to accept blame. And, socially, the authoritarian sees relations among persons more in terms of power and status than in terms of friendship. For example, he tends to draw lists of guests in terms of rank rather than personal affinities. A very good summary of this material is given in an article by Sanford (1956), which is more accessible than the monumental work by Adorno *et al.*

Types. The authoritarian personality, as we can see, does not consist of a single trait defined in the trait theory we have been using. It falls more into the category of *types*. For a long time, social scientists shunned types and typologies for many reasons. Types were hard to define, and when they were defined, it was done by means of traits. Besides, a type description based on a certain group would seldom conform to other individuals. "Typical accountants" or "typical philanderers" were, it turned out, very different from one another.

Recent research by Stein (1966) has changed this. Stein based his work on a list of human needs originally defined by Murray (1938). Among these needs are the need for achievement, autonomy, order, play, affiliation with others, domination of others, etc. Altogether, there are 20 needs. Different persons vary in the degree to which these needs are relevant to them. Some have a great need for order, others for play, and so on. Stein asked his subjects to rate the 20 needs according to how important they were to him. He has subjected the data to (Q) factor analysis, a variant of the same mathematical technique devised by Thurstone to discover the primary mental abilities and used by Guilford to greatly expand the latter into the SI model. He has identified several different types of persons according to the way they rank their needs. Moreover, he has done this not only in the United States but also in Israel, Italy, Japan, and other countries. He has gathered additional experimental and test data that differentiate between the types. These results are sufficiently significant to suggest that he has found something of primary importance that can be used to detect the types of persons who are required for different occupations, as we shall see in the succeeding paragraphs.

The socially oriented.   This type of individual appears to be dedicated to other people. He enjoys being with and working with other people. In so doing, he finds his greatest satisfaction in assisting helpless individuals and in supporting, comforting and protecting others. A man of this type is also sympathetic. He avoids hurting others, so he is not critical or severe in his interpersonal relationships. He is not a hostile or an aggressive person. Compared to others, a person of this type is less autonomous and defers to authority. He can be dominated by others and is likely to accept restrictions placed on his behavior. Indeed, he strives to conform to others' wishes; when he knows what they want, he will try to fulfill their requests.

The intellectually oriented.   Members of this type also enjoy being with other people and working with them. Unlike the Socially Oriented type, however, they place greater emphasis upon achievement. In striving to attain their goals, these men are likely to follow internal frames of reference; they believe they know what is best. Therefore, if they and the authority figures for whom they work are not in agreement, conflict may develop. So long as agreement on ideas exists between them and their supervisors, these volunteers can be quite loyal and devoted subordinates. They are sensitive and are aware of both internal needs and external stimuli. Compared to the other four types, they are more likely to seek out and enjoy sensuous impressions and to enjoy aesthetic feelings. But since they are not very well organized, they may find themselves frustrated in constructively utilizing their aesthetic impressions. Left to their own devices, members of this type are likely to leave an unpleasant situation rather than cope with the difficulties they encounter and seek a new environment that would give them greater satisfaction.

The action oriented.   An individual of this type aims to get things accomplished. He enjoys working with others, but it is most important to him to be in control of the situation. Compared to the other four types, this individual is more involved with achievements and with dominating social situations. He sees himself as confident and as liking to influence others, but at the same time, he is aware of others' needs and can be quite nurturant and sympathetic. He is inclined to be systematic in what he does and accept responsibility. He is not likely to avoid situations because he might be blamed for his actions. This type gives higher priority to fulfilling goals than to satisfying his impulses in life. He is a doer and an achiever rather than a player. When he does satisfy an impulse, he will do so in a socially acceptable and approved manner, rarely overindulging himself because he does not like to appear inferior. He gives the impression that he will strive to be upright and sincere in whatever he does by following the code that he has been taught.

The unconventional.   A person in this group enjoys aiding helpless people with whom he can be supporting and comforting and from whom he apparently receives support and comfort in return. He is not very discriminating in his interpersonal relationships, and he is unlikely to reject others unless they try to dominate him. A member of this group likes to have others around him so that he can be seen and heard and can entertain and amuse. He enjoys playing and indulges his impulses. He will seek others who will provide him with sympathetic understanding and possibly some direction and leadership, but not domination, because he prides himself in not being abrasive or submissive to others. He is not very well organized because he sees organization as coercive and believes order does not allow freedom. Nor is he an achiever, because he regards himself as a free soul who is just as happy to see others go their own way. Underneath, he may be thankful that others are more organized because it is through their presence that he can indulge his own impulses. Finally, if others are kindly disposed toward him and provide him with leadership in a permissive atmosphere, he will, under these conditions, be able to develop and achieve goals.

The resourceful.   The resourceful type is oriented toward achievement and is not passive. He enjoys being with others but is not likely to be submissive to them. Indeed, in a situation where there is a choice between satisfying his own or others' needs, he will elect to first satisfy his own. He can be easygoing and relaxed and enjoys relationships with women. He feels under pressure if his freedom is interfered with or if his position of mastery is threatened. Under such circumstances he feels anxious, but he soon recovers his resources and finds new means of coping with his problems. Thus, a person of this type is rather flexible. He is also willing to accept momentary compromises, as he keeps his eyes on long-range goals.

BACKGROUND

From the preceding discussion, it has become quite obvious that human beings differ in many ways. It can readily be appreciated why the adjective "unfortunate" was applied to the I.Q. concept. If we are to study who is best fitted for a given job, we will not be very successful if we take into account only the extremely broad concept of general intelligence.

For this reason, therefore, persons who do personnel selection often rely on past experience. Presumably, if the applicant has done well elsewhere on a similar job, he will work well here. However, if a careful analysis of the present job is not undertaken, essential differences between the two situations may be missed, and this may lead to failure on the second job. If we go into a thorough analysis of the job and of the possible candidates, the chances of failure will be greatly reduced. But, in order to do this, we must use a systematic method that economically takes into account all of these factors.

Before going into the system that has been designed, however, it will be useful to present a summary of the five groups of traits discussed.

SUMMARY OF POSSIBLE TRAIT REQUIREMENTS AND THE METHODS OF ASSESSMENT

PHYSICAL TRAITS

Health.   Assessed by interview and medical examination. Never look for a general state of good health; rather, keep in mind that health requirements and tolerance for impairments vary from job to job.

Color blindness.   Assessed by color-blindness test (Ishihara, Dvorine Pseudo-isochromatic Plates, 1953).

Strength.   Assessed by physical observation in interview and questioning concerning past work.

Eyesight.   Insistence on 20–20 vision must be made only where necessary. Use an optometrist where this factor is crucial.

Hearing. Appraise at interview, unless the requirement is for very exacting position, e.g., a musician, in which case a test of absolute pitch may be necessary.

Voice. Assess at interview, if an agreeable and cultured voice is necessary as in the case of a telephone operator, museum guide, etc.

Size. Keep in mind whether the person has to work in cramped spaces or has to reach up to tall shelves, and how much of the time must be spent doing these things.

MENTAL ABILITIES

It is important to keep in mind the 15 key concepts.[7]

Operations. Cognition (C), Memory (M), Divergent Production (D), Convergent Production (N), and Evaluation (E).

Content. Figural (F), Symbolic (S), Semantic (M), Behavioral (B).

Product. Units (U), Classes (C), Relations (R), Systems (S), Transformations (T), Implications (I).

Where tests are not available, the only alternative is to try to assess the skills at the interview. More information will be given on the interview later in this chapter.

INTERESTS

Commercial.

Scientific.

Artistic.

Social.

Routine, concrete (possibly related to lack of divergent production).

Creative (possibly related to high divergent production).

Other special interests.

Although interest tests are available, the interview is more economical when large numbers of candidates have to be assessed. A well-conducted interview can yield considerable data on interests and inclinations.

---

[7] For many of these, tests are available at the Sheridan Psychological Services, P.O. Box 837, Beverly Hills, California, 90213. Tests in Spanish and Portuguese languages (translations made or supervised by the writer) will be available from the authorized distributor: Helena Reyes, Bv. España 2926 Ap. 401, Montevideo, Uruguay.

PERSONALITY

Ascendance.   Use Allport A–S reaction study or assess at interview.

Tendency to be dynamic.   Assess at interview.

Need for approval.   Use SD scale (Crowne and Marlowe, 1964) or assess at interview.

Authoritarianism.   Use California F. Scale (Adorno *et al.*, 1950) or assess at interview.

Type.   Socially oriented; intellectually oriented; action oriented; unconventional; resourceful. Use tests (Stein, 1966) or assess at interview.

BACKGROUND

Age requirements or limits.   Be careful with this point; do not rule someone out merely on the basis of prejudice. Some very young people can be quite remarkable, as can some people far beyond what is considered the maximum hiring age or even retiring age.

General educational level required.   Keep in mind not only the specific job needs but also the educational level required to keep up with the rest of the organization and to understand policies and the reasons for changes in them.

Miscellaneous requisites.   Special trade or knowledge, languages, etc.

Experience requirements.   Based on the preceding information, a system for a Personnel Selection has been designed. While looking it over, the reader may feel that he is seeing something that is already familiar. This is partly true, since some concepts and methods are borrowed from existing practices. However, the essence of this method and the final result are very different from what has been previously published.

PROCEDURES FOR PERSONNEL SELECTION

Since we have seen that human beings are so enormously complex and that there are so many possible factors to consider, we must first determine which are essential. To do so, we must define which tasks are to be performed, that is, we must have a job description. This is extremely important. We cannot determine which traits will be required in an applicant until we have a clear definition of what the person must do. The job description must include a statement of the *mission* of the job under consideration. If the mission is not clearly stated, the employee is sometimes given tasks quite unrelated to the purpose of his actual job and is then considered a poor employee because the main mission never gets accomplished.

A description of the complete design for personnel selection will now be given, together with illustrative examples. First, let us take the simplest case—the selecting of one person from several possible candidates. There is a position to be filled. It may be for a maintenance mechanic, a computer programmer, a salesman, a secretary, the Chairman of a Department of Psychology at a university, or any other position. Since, as stated above, we cannot decide whom to hire until we know very well what he has to do, we must first have a *description* of what his job contains. Even this cannot be done well, however, unless we know the *main objectives* of the job. We therefore proceed in steps.

JOB DESCRIPTION

State the Mission.   This is usually done in one sentence, which contains the ultimate objective of the job. It does not stipulate what the person does; rather what results are to be obtained. For example, the mission for a maintenance supervisor in a plant could be: "Assures that all equipment and installations are in correct operating condition at all times in order to avoid delays in production due to breakdowns." This definition of the mission gives us no clue about how the supervisor will carry out this mission. One man may sit in his office and use the phone to call outsiders to come in and do repairs; another may rush around and do it all himself; and a third may set up an organization with a machine shop, mechanics, electricians and helpers who will do the work under his supervision. Obviously, we would need three men, all quite different from one another in many respects, in order to achieve the same mission in these three radically different ways.

In the same way, we could attempt to state the mission of the Chairman of a Department of Psychology: "Assures that the quality of instruction and research conducted is of such a high caliber as to produce competent social scientists that will give the Department a high short- and long-term reputation." Again, this says nothing about how the individual will go about achieving this goal. It should be noted that the mission of a Psychology Department Chairman may vary from one institution to another. Very often, after a person has been on the job for some time, we berate him for poor performance, when the problem was that we had initially failed to write a clear definition of his mission.

Define the Tasks to be Performed.   Once we know what the mission is, we are in a position to state the acts that the person must perform in order to accomplish this mission. For example, some of the tasks to be performed by the maintenance supervisor might be:

(a) Sets up a schedule of inspection to note possible causes of breakdown so that action may be taken before these occur.
(b) Sets up a preventive maintenance schedule so as to replace parts before their useful life is consumed.
(c) Maintains adequate stocks of spare parts and replacements by placing orders on time so that there will never be a lack of these when needed.
(d) Assigns work daily to his subordinates according to the priorities given him by the Plant Manager.
(e) Maintains a competent work force by hiring personnel with proper qualifications.
(f) Trains his personnel in the specific aspects of the equipment to be repaired.

We are now in a position to decide which type of individual will best be able to perform the above job. Let us now define the specific tasks to be performed by the Chairman of the Psychology Department in a university. This list, which of course may vary widely from one university to another, might read as follows:

(a) Recruits highly qualified social scientists with varied backgrounds in order to have an eclectic Department.
(b) Sets adequate standards for admission of students so that the latter will be able to profit most from the staff and so that the staff will feel motivated by having persons to train who are able to keep up with their standards.
(c) Maintains harmony within the Department by conducting meetings in which his collaborators can discuss problems and arrive at unanimously satisfactory solutions. (This is very important in view of the high caliber of the persons involved and their need to participate.)
(d) Motivates his subordinates by taking a personal and an active interest in all the teaching and research activities conducted, the findings, and the problems involved.
(e) Assists his subordinates in helping to solve the many problems that will arise as a result of their teaching and research activities.
(f) Makes the necessary contacts and persuasions to obtain funds and material equipment necessary for his subordinates' activities so as to leave them free to spend their time in teaching and research missions.
(g) Balances the teaching and research activities of his subordinates so as to make the most equitable and efficient use of their varied abilities and interests.
(h) Conducts, promptly and efficiently, all the bureaucratic affairs related to the job, including required reports, requisitions, etc., so as to keep the Department up-to-date at all times.

(i) Maintains relations with professional societies and other institutions in order to establish interchanges of information and subordinates, to obtain lecture engagements from outsiders and for his staff, and to make committee assignments for his staff, etc.

(j) Maintains contacts with other institutions and organizations in order to help find openings for graduating students.

Trait Requirements. The above are lists of duties to be performed in order to accomplish the missions defined. Although only partial, they are sufficient to enable us to determine which personal qualities are required for the job at hand. We do this by analyzing the individual tasks and relating them to the traits we think will be needed. As each trait is named, a justification is given for its inclusion. The relative importance of the trait and the degree to which it is required are also stipulated.

The problem of validity. The preceding description of the selection process may meet with the disapproval of many social scientists, whether they are pure experimentalists or persons actually involved in industrial psychology, because at no point have the correlations among criteria for job success and the many traits mentioned been cited. It is true that most of the existing literature on personnel selection is based upon the scientific principle of validity, whereby a certain criterion for success on the job is established (tests, interviews, etc.) and the correlations are calculated between work success and the factor(s) mentioned. If these prove to be fairly high, then the same measures are related to job success in an entirely new group of subjects. The stability of the relationships obtained constitutes an index of validity for the measures used, which may now be administered to job applicants as predictors of success.

This method is a carryover from the method based on sound scientific practice that has been so successful in discovering relationships in social science. But technology is not always the same as science, and the method that works for one may not be as useful for the other. In many ways, social science technology is akin to engineering. Although engineering is largely based on scientific discovery, its methods are often quite different from those of the pure scientist. The pure scientist has to be very rigorous in his method if he wants to prove that he has discovered something. The engineer, on the other hand, has to get a job done. Similarly, in personnel selection the wide diversity of jobs in industry makes it exceedingly cumbersome and impracticable to try to adopt the research attitude. Besides, in personnel selection correlational studies are impossible because large samples are required, and we simply do not have enough people performing identical jobs in identical settings. Thus, the practical, everyday situation is far removed from controlled laboratory conditions.

This discrepancy is recognized in an apologia following the description of an experimental industrial design in "Emotional Disruption and Industrial Productivity," by Schachter *et al.* (1961). The authors state that the experiment was initially designed incorporating a series of methodological niceties. They add, however, that: "The problems of attempting to keep tight control of the experimental situation in the hubbub of a major industrial operation forced us to abandon many of these niceties if we were to have any experiment at all." After describing the considerable advanced planning necessary to avoid disruptions caused by the experiment itself, they note: "These experiments were carried out with superb cooperation from management but as with all such studies they are still subject to the disrupting chance factors characteristic of real life situations. In one way or another each of the three studies was plagued by difficulties of this sort."

Their insistence upon continuing to use laboratory methods in spite of the "disrupting chance factors of real life situations" has led some researchers to over-simplify the problem. Instead of analyzing the full complexity of jobs and the great number of components that lead to greater or lesser success, they try to define a *single* criterion of job success. Korman (1968) in an extensive review of studies predicting managerial performance, concludes that: "There seems little reason for thinking that we have learned much about the psychological variables indicative of managerial behavior insofar as these variables are determinable by objective personality inventories. There have been and continue to be many studies that attempt to predict 'managerial ability.' " Thus in monumental studies such as Laurent's (1962) in which 443 managers were lumped together in an attempt to discover what leads to managerial success, test scores were combined to give a single score, and such variables as position, salary, history and effectiveness rankings were combined to give an Overall Success Index.

Although the resulting correlation between these two measures is impressive and follows excellent research design, it still seems a formidable procedure to follow for every type of position. Moreover, although it is statistically significant for the sample studied as a whole, the correlation is still too low to be of practical use when a given decision has to be taken with respect to a single individual. For example, the more successful managers were shown to be relatively high in inductive and verbal reasoning abilities. Long before we knew about this and other similar studies, we were including the requirement of high verbal and inductive skills in our job specification for most supervisory positions. Depending on the type of supervisory job, the requirements were more or less stringent. We required a manager of a data processing department to be very high in inductive ability, although we would not be too strict with him in the verbal area. With a sales manager, the verbal requirement would be much more stringent. Similarly, a maintenance supervisor would have to possess good spatial abilities, while these would be unnecessary for the sales manager. These job specifications of course refer to Thurstone's primary mental abilities. If we considered all the abilities derived from Guilford's SI model and had to perform individual validity studies for each one with respect to each different job in a complex industrial operation, the task would be virtually hopeless.

The case is similar when an engineer designs a structure; he does not afterwards proceed to test every single beam, column, strut, or partial combinations of these. The initial studies that made the design possible were done under controlled laboratory conditions, but the designs themselves had to be based on the assumption that the different findings were applicable even when combined in new ways. When O. H. Amman designed the George Washington Bridge, he did not build a different one alongside it to test which was better, although several different designs had initially been contemplated.

So far, we have referred to predictor variables. A more profound problem refers to the criterion. As Blum and Naylor (1968) state: "The criterion is basic to all measurement in industrial psychology. Without adequate criteria, industrial psychology is ineffective and ceases to be a science." Nevertheless, these authors recognize that the search for the criterion has, in general, not been very successful, and they do, in fact, express some doubt about the possibility of even establishing such a criterion. They cite Dunnette (1963), who comments: "Investigators have been reluctant to consider the many facets of success and the concomitant investigation of the prediction of many success measures and instead persist in an unfruitful effort to predict the criterion. Thus, I say: junk the criterion!" In his paper, Dunnette bases his conclusion in part upon Thorndike (1960), who says: "Success is a many faceted thing, and we need to relate the predictions to the different facets of success. This is a complex task and one not easy of fulfillment."

Recognizing that the task was "not easy of fulfillment" long before Thorndike delivered his paper, we developed the personnel selection design described here. But the design described so far is only a part of a broader one. The rest will be described in the next chapter.

The interview.   At several points in this chapter, we have recommended the interview as a method of assessing traits for personnel selection. The interview as a tool of assessment has both its defenders and its detractors. Among the latter are Scott *et al.* (1941), who describe a case in which 13 industrial executives were asked to interview 12 applicants for sales jobs. They were asked to rate the applicants from best to worst. The results indicated such large discrepancies among the raters' opinions as to make all of them practically worthless.

A more recent and thorough research of the interview as an assessment device is given by Webster (1964). A series of experiments was conducted in order to determine whether certain candidates were fit for certain jobs. In some of the experiments, an interviewer made his decision, while an observer who did not intervene made his own. From this and other experiments, a generally negative conclusion was drawn. It was found that interviewers develop stereotypes of good candidates and try to match those interviewed to such stereotypes. Furthermore, biases are established early in the interview (unfavorable impressions produce a stronger bias than favorable ones), and interviewers tend to seek data that support hypotheses already formed.[8]

All these criticisms are true and acceptable if the object of the interview is to assess *the whole person* in terms of his fitness for a job. But as we have seen, this is an impossible task—whether we use an I.Q. test, a test for managerial ability, or an interview. However, when an interview is used to detect, one by one, *each* of the *several traits* stipulated in the job specification, it can be a very useful instrument. It is also important that persons be highly trained in the art of interviewing. As part of their training, interviewers should conduct post mortems on persons selected who did not turn out well in order to see why the prediction failed. Interviewers should also be trained *not* to make a decision until they have assessed every trait indicated in the specifications for each candidate, taken notes on each of these traits, and also taken the time to think about the whole person. In addition, he should discuss his impressions with someone else who has made a similar interview. It often happens that when these discussions take place, there is a difference of opinion regarding one or more of the traits judged. In this case, either a new interview should be made to reassess this trait, or a third party should be called upon to do a special interview in order to get an additional opinion on this trait alone.

Guilford (1959) cites several studies in which interviewers proved ineffective in assessing certain traits for which tests are available. He concludes that: "Where there is an alternative between assessing traits by means of tests and by interviews, the tests should have a decided preference." We heartily endorse this conclusion. We would not waste a minute in an interview trying to find out whether the candidate is high or low on cognition of verbal units, when we could administer 3-minute vocabulary tests with a reliability of over 0.90. Neither would we waste time trying to judge color-blindness when a few Ishihara plates can clearly detect this trait in a short time. However, if it is important to know whether a person is really interested in mechanics, it is relatively more efficient to interview him. It is not very difficult to get him to talk about his experiences, e.g., how a particularly strong interest helped him overcome obstacles in certain cases. There are additional ways of obtaining information in the interview that are quite reliable. However, a full consideration of the ways in which social science findings may be applied to the

---

[8] The author is reminded of the saying: "He uses statistics like a drunkard uses a lamppost, more for support than for illumination."

conduct of good interviews can be given only in a more advanced treatise on the subject.

A DESIGN FOR PERSONNEL SELECTION

We shall now present an example of a design for selecting a personnel manager, using all the principles described in this chapter.

Although this person has already been considered trait by trait, it must be recognized that this was done for the sake of convenience. It is most important, once all traits have been evaluated, to sit back and think of the whole person. (Bruner, Shapiro and Tagiuri, 1958.)

JOB DESCRIPTION

COMPANY: X

DEPARTMENT: Personnel

JOB: Manager

BASIC MISSION: Under the general supervision of the President of the organization, develops, interprets, coordinates and administers the company's policy with respect to personnel in order to maintain the best possible employee relations necessary to achieve maximum productivity and worker satisfaction.

SPECIFIC FUNCTIONS: Directs a staff of several persons. Performs personally some of the following duties, delegating others in accordance with his subordinates' abilities.

1. Maintains control of company's acts to assure compliance with legal legislation in terms of such things as work hours, rest periods, insurance, vacations, etc. Does so by keeping the necessary records enabling the company's overall situation, or that of any individual, to be known at all times.
2. Maintains personnel files on absenteeism, tardiness, records of especially good or poor performance in order to know any individual's standing at any time, as a basis for studying possible action.
3. Recruits personnel by advertising in newspapers, contacting employment agencies, secretarial, commercial, or academic schools, and utilizing other personal contacts.
4. Selects candidates to be submitted to supervisors by preparing job descriptions and specifications, interviewing, testing, and using other approved methods of assessment to see whether candidates meet present standards.

5. Aids supervisors in evaluating existing personnel as a basis for rewarding, analyzing promotion possibilities, helping to correct errors in performance, and discovering talent and unused abilities.
6. Processes admissions, transfers, promotions, and separations.
7. Assists top executives in formulating personnel policies.
8. Represents the company in collective bargaining, prepares memoranda illustrating the company's position, and explains it to labor.
9. Performs job evaluation studies based on job analyses in order to help establish adequate salary differentials among different jobs.
10. Coordinates training programs including personnel induction, helping supervisors spot training needs, preparing training plans and putting them into operation, and measuring and otherwise assessing the results of training.
11. Administers the company's social benefit program, which may include such items as a ten-year award, a bulletin board, and recreational or other social activities.
12. Continually assesses employee morale by analyzing absenteeism and turnover records, tardiness, resignations, by conducting exit interviews, and by interviewing employees periodically, in order to spot possible trouble areas.
13. Counsels employees with respect to their work or personal problems.
14. Supervises the trainees as they go about their job rotation assignments to assure continuance of the program and maintenance of trainee morale.
15. Coordinates management development programs whereby individuals to be promoted to supervisory positions, or those recently promoted, receive adequate instructions in the techniques of supervision.

TRAITS REQUIRED FOR PERFORMANCE

Physical Traits
1. Health.   Should have good health. Must not be continually absent because of chronic illness.
2. Voice.   Should have an agreeable voice free from speech impairments that may hamper communications with others.
3. Appearance.   Should have good appearance. Must inspire respect not only in company personnel but also in candidates for employment and others for whom he will probably be the only company representative.

Mental Abilities
1. Social content categories.   He should be high in social skills as follows.
   Cognition
   (a) Units (CBU).   Necessary in order to be able to size up emotional states of different persons as a diagnostic tool.

(b) Relations (CBR).   Necessary in order to diagnose problems in interpersonal relations, to assess attitudes of groups towards problems, and to maximize the efficiency of problem-solving conferences.

(c) Implications (CBI).   Very important in order to be able to predict outcomes of present situations in order to take adequate measures in case of possible undesirable outcomes.

Divergent Production

(a) Units (DBU).   Very important in interviews to convey different attitudes to those interviewed according to temperaments and situations in order to establish rapport, provide positive reinforcement, and do other things that will maximize the effect of an interview.

(b) Systems (DBS).   Must have the ability to imagine different systems of relations to be able to propose these to the several supervisors in order that they will be able to arrive at the best possible solutions for the organization.

(c) Transformations (DBT).   This is particularly important in interviews and in problem-solving conferences in such acts as reflecting. The ability to abbreviate and summarize is especially important in Maier's type of problem-solving conference. Also ties in closely with ability for production of semantic transformations (DMT).

Evaluation

(a) Must be good in all areas of social evaluation, in order to be able to judge situations and to instruct others in training situations, e.g., training in interviewing, counseling, group problem-solving.

2. Semantic ability

Cognition

(a) Should be high in cognition of semantic units, including ready command of a wide vocabulary and the ability to understand what is being said by others. Cognition of semantic classes is required in order to be able to classify jobs according to job-evaluation systems. Should be high in cognition of semantic systems to be able to write lucidly or otherwise communicate. Finally, should be good at cognition of semantic transformation in order to be able to understand ideas expressed in different terms. An ignorant laborer and a highly educated technician may find themselves in the same approach-avoidance conflict and express themselves in terms that are basically each a transformation of the feelings expressed by the other. Should also be high in semantic implications. This ability was first recognized in connection with planning abilities, and it is in this sense that this trait is essential to the job.

Divergent Production

(a) The Personnel Manager should be high in most of the traits in this area. In order to modify his language rapidly to adapt it to the person to whom he is talking, he will need to be high in divergent production of semantic units, classes, relations and transformations. His ability in divergent production of semantic systems will be very useful in conducting meetings, interviewing, and otherwise planning the considerable verbal material with which he deals.

Evaluation

(a) Should be very high in evaluation of semantic implications in order to understand the implications of the material he hears and reads, so as to take action without running the risk of taking incorrect action.

Interests

1. Should be interested in social work, as well as in scientific work. He has to look after the welfare of the workers and other personnel and help them with their difficulties, not only because he is personally inclined to do so but because he enjoys solving problems scientifically.

Personality

1. Ascendant. Should be ascendant rather than shy in order to be able to face up to many varied daily situations with persons of all types.

2. Emotionally mature. Should be emotionally mature and free from serious complexes or personality disorders that may cause friction when dealing with others.

3. Dynamic. Should be very dynamic. Must take care of many small problems and deal with them rapidly because these will occur frequently.

4. Intellectually oriented (Stein, 1966). Experience with a limited sample of five Personnel Managers who are very effective in introducing and keeping up the ideas set forth in this book has shown that all of them typed themselves in this category. The only statement they rejected was the last one in the description. This states that if left to their own devices these persons are likely to leave situations not to their liking. The opposite has been shown to be true of the five individuals studied.

Background

1. Experience. Must have at least five years experience in dealing in practical affairs, particularly in the type of organization in which he is to work, in order to have a general "feel" of how things are run. A Personnel Manager who is to work in industry will be more valuable if he has worked in another industry instead of an academic setting. The characteristics of industry, including the degree of urgency which exists in turn-

ing out products, may be so unfamiliar to him as to delay his becoming effective in such a new setting. These remarks, of course, refer to a person with five years' experience. A more experienced person who has seen different types of operations may be able to adapt quickly to a job in an entirely new setting.

2. Education.   Should have a college degree, but not necessarily in social science, and particularly not in social science research. If he has the latter training, he may tend to do research instead of carrying out social science technology.

3. Other knowledge.   It is important for him to have varied interests. He will come in contact with persons of very diverse interests and must be able to respond in some way to all of these.

4. A knowledge of the English language is necessary so that he can read the literature in which the latest findings are announced. Before too long a man who can also read Russian will be able to acquire information that may fit in with that published in English. Probably very good technological designs will be made by those who have access to both sources.

A COMMENT ON PROCEDURES FOR PERSONNEL SELECTION

As can be seen from the sample personnel selection design, there are nearly 30 different traits or type descriptions to be considered in selecting a Personnel Manager. Some of these will be demanded more stringently than others. For example, with respect to divergent production of semantic relations, we should not be too disturbed if the applicant fell only in the 50th percentile. This means more than one-half of the candidates would be acceptable on this score. If we accept as an average a 20-percentile range for each trait or type, all of which are assumed to be independent of one another, our chances of successfully filling the job would be $(\frac{1}{5})^{30}$. We would therefore need 2^{30} candidates in order to find one who will fill all our requirements. Since it is virtually impossible to obtain such an immense number of candidates, we shall probably not find the ideal man. Instead, we shall have to settle for the one who is most adequate in terms of the more essential traits and then *modify the job* to fit the candidate selected. The same will probably be true with all the other jobs in the organization. The result will be that instead of creating an organization and then fitting candidates to our inflexible scheme, we shall have to draw up an *approximate* organization and then *redesign* it according to the qualifications of the actual individuals whom we obtain through the use of these methods. It is to be noted that although the specification often refers to a "man," nothing in it precludes a woman from holding such a responsible job.

3

*All is offense when man has for-
saken his true nature and is doing
what does not befit him.*

Sophocles

judging people we know

Research in the area of judging people has its origin in the answer to a question that is seldom asked, or if it is asked, it is answered incorrectly. The question is: "Why is it that often we are at first very enthusiastic about a person but later judge him to be despicable, thus drastically changing our minds?" This sort of thing happens quite often in organizations. A person is selected for a given job. At the moment of selection he is considered an outstanding candidate. There couldn't possibly be anyone better. Yet, some time later—maybe months, a year or two, or ten years later—he is viewed as totally incompetent, unfit for the job, and full of all sorts of defects. He is therefore fired. The same holds true for friends, politicians we support, spouses, etc. Helen Rowland defined a grass widow as the angel a man loved, the woman he married, and the devil he divorced. Why is it that our judgments about people are so often subject to such violent reversals? Of course, we always rationalize by saying that it was the other person who changed, not us. Our judgments are never wrong. But we posed the question. Might not the answer lie, in part, in our changed perception, and if so, what can be done about this? In other words, might it not be that it was something in the

49

situation that changed and that perhaps we ourselves have caused this change?

We recognize two problems: One is the serious error we might actually have made to begin with and might have therefore avoided, thus saving ourselves and the candidate the future trouble. The other is even more personal. It regards the trauma we cause the person we at first praise and then violently reject. In more common terms, we are causing what would normally be called an injustice. We will see later that the concept of justice or injustice will have no bearing whatsoever on our work with concepts derived from social science findings.

PERSONNEL APPRAISAL

In the industrial and the organizational setting, this problem has been attacked by means of what is called *personnel appraisal*. There have been all sorts of schemes proposed, but in most of these serious weaknesses have been detected. As in Chapter 2, instead of starting with our procedure and then justifying it, the psychological foundations will be first explained. Our method for appraising others will arise from these foundations. Fundamentally, we shall have to base our techniques upon how people *are* and not on how we *wish* they were. This concept must be emphasized repeatedly because, in most cases, we become angry when other people do not act the way they were supposed to according to "logic" (our logic).

MOTIVES UNDERLYING OBSERVED BEHAVIOR

When we judge people we know, we generally do base our decision on what we *observe* of their behavior, that is, what they did and said, to whom and under what circumstances, what errors we believe they committed. We may praise or blame. In general, we are more prone to blame than to praise. Therefore, it seems best to take a close look at what is generally considered misbehavior. I will focus this discussion more on the work situation because it is there where we have systematized the method. However, experience has shown that those who learn how to judge according to social science techniques in the work situation will usually apply the same principles to other interpersonal relations, such as in the home, the club, etc.

MISBEHAVIOR

Let us assume that a supervisor directs a group of employees doing the several tasks required of his section or department. He notices, what to him, are several kinds of misbehavior: One person may make many errors; another comes in late; a third is frequently absent; and still another is belligerent in his attitude toward his co-workers. A fifth may show real signs of insubordination; a sixth may be totally apathetic; and a seventh may show no interest whatever in his work.

In most organizations, this kind of "misbehavior" is dealt with by using a rule book that establishes the kinds of penalties to be applied for every one of these misdemeanors. For example, it may be prescribed that arriving late more than a given number of times a month will make a person subject to a reprimand. Should the situation continue, there may be a severe reprimand. Further tardiness may lead to a suspension. Eventually, if this punishment does not solve the problem, the employee is summarily fired. The same procedure is used in coping with errors, absenteeism, insubordination, aggressiveness, etc.

There are two interesting things to be noted regarding this procedure: In the first place, it is a minor replica of the penal system that prevails in society as a whole. Crime, misdemeanor, and other unacceptable behavior is classed according to gravity and attenuating or aggravating circumstances, and punishment is pre-established for every such misbehavior. This type of thinking prevailed from before the time of the Code of Hammurabi. It is therefore quite natural that organizations, which are smaller sub-societies embedded in the larger one, should merely copy the philosophy and methods that prevail in the larger society. After all, the same people are involved. If they are legalistic in their affairs, they will tend to be the same on the job as they are at home and with their children.

The second interesting aspect is that labor unions, which have presumably been set up as labor organizations with the primary goal of defending the workers, quite willingly accept such rules and the corresponding punishment. The role of shop stewards is usually one of defense attorney, when a disciplinary measure is applied. Arbitration has been resorted to in many cases in order to decide definitely who is right. Notice the close resemblance between an arbitration procedure, in which the organization accuses a worker and the labor union defends him until the arbitrator decides whether the applied sanction was justified, with the judicial procedure, in which attorneys on both sides prosecute or defend a criminal until a judge or jury finally decides who is right.

Over the centuries in penal practice and over the decades in industrial practices, the severity of the penalties has decreased. Criminals or suspects were tortured, hanged, drawn and quartered, broken on the wheel, etc., less than 200 years ago. Workers were fired for trifles with no severance pay less than 30 years ago. Now the penalties are physically less severe, although they may be psychologically horrendous. Karl Menninger (1968) makes a strong case against the crime of punishment, referring chiefly to the penal system as it now stands. Many others have joined in decrying the present state of the penal system (Sachar, 1963). However, neither the unions nor the workers involved have started a movement against the profoundly disturbing results of the application of a similar system in organizations. There has been no reaction against a system in which there are less severe types of punishment but in which the actual number of cases is far larger. It is quite probable that the total impact upon society of the sum of the immense number of these minor cases far outweighs the effects of the blatant errors in the penal system. Such "minor cases" are also found frequently in educational systems that penalize students with low marks.

The material which follows will reveal that there is something basically wrong with the whole penalization system. The object of this chapter will be to study what can be done about misbehavior in organizations. The psychological bases will first be given and then followed by a procedure to deal with such problems.

THE APPROACH-AVOIDANCE CONFLICT

It is a very common occurrence for someone to say "I like baseball," or "I like spinach," or "I like Jane." Equally probable is that statements such as "I dislike baseball," "I dislike spinach," or "I dislike Jane," are made just as frequently. These statements assume that my like or dislike for Jane, baseball, or spinach is invariant. I simply like or don't like them. I may like or dislike more or less intensely, but my attraction or rejection is assumed to be fairly constant.

Nevertheless, research has shown that the attraction felt for a liked object is greater the closer we are to the object. For example, if I like baseball, but it is a Tuesday evening in midwinter, my attraction for baseball at that moment is rather limited because it is felt to be so far away. However, in the spring on a beautiful Saturday afternoon, with an important game being played which I may see, my attraction for baseball rises to a high pitch. Brown (1948) showed that this principle also holds for animals. He tested rats in a channel, attached a small spring scale to them, and found that the closer they were to where food was to be found, the harder they pulled, i.e., the greater the effort they expended to get the food.

We humans are not too different from rats in this respect. When vacation is several months away, we are mildly attracted to the thought, but two weeks before our vacations are due, we feel that a nervous breakdown will follow if anything interferes with our projected rest period. The same holds true for a loved one. The nearer we are to the person, the more attracted we are. Anyone who has a dog knows how much harder the dog will pull on the leash toward the door, when he is going out, the closer he is to the door. The phenomenon is quite universal. Our attractions are not constant. They increase or decrease as a function of the distance we are from the object.

When we feel rejection, the effect of distance is even more marked. The closer we are to a poisonous snake, a nasty looking spider, a decaying corpse, or a very disliked person, the greater the rejection we feel. This was also experimentally demonstrated by Brown in the paper cited. The gradient of rejection is much sharper than the gradient of approach. When something strongly repels us, say a red-hot steel plate, the repulsion is quite weak when we are far from the plate. If we are 50 feet away from the plate, we may look on with curious interest, and if someone tries to push us a foot closer, we may take this as a mild joke. But if we are three feet from the same plate, and someone tries to push us 6 inches closer, our reaction against being forced toward it may be very violent indeed.

At this stage the reader may start wondering: "How true! But so what?" The question may in part arise from an ingrained habit we have of making simplistic judgments about people; whereby we attribute their action to only one cause. "Why did Jane marry Sam?" someone asks, "for his money," or "for his looks," will be the probable answer. "Why did Joe quit his job?" "Because of the low pay," or "because it was too far away," may be the reasons given. Note that in every case, we expect to receive or be given *one* single reason for the action. The complexity involved is overlooked. It was Kurt Lewin (1935) who was probably the first to study what happens when the same object attracts us strongly for one reason and repels us strongly for another. Brown (1948), Miller (1948), and others have studied the effects of this sort of situation and have given us great insight about what can be expected. The situation occurs daily and is not really too far-fetched. Say a man wants to buy a car. He likes model A for several reasons, but there are also reasons that deter him from buying A. He may like it because it is flashy, and he likes flashy things. It has a powerful engine, and he loves power and speed. However, it may cost more than he can really afford, and his wife may highly disapprove of such a purchase. He therefore has certain attractions for the car, and at the same time, other aspects produce rejection. If the rejections are very great, he may hesitate when he goes into the showroom, and the salesman greets him, saying that he just wanted to have another look at the car. Later, far from the actual purchase possibility, when he sees another similar car on the street he may feel more attraction than rejection. The whole situation can be graphically represented in Fig. 3.1.

Figure 3.1 illustrates that at point *A*, at distance *a* from the object, the force of attraction is greater than the force of rejection. Therefore, the man feels attracted to the car. As he nears the showroom, although the attraction increases, rejection increases faster, as shown by point *B*, distance *b* from the

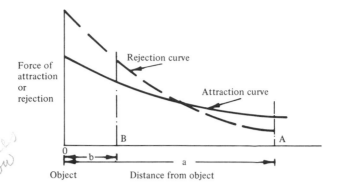

FIG. 3.1. Graphical representation of approach-avoidance conflict with respect to a given object.

object (which is closer than *a*). When he enters the showroom the rejections quite overpower his attractions. He therefore finds an excuse and goes out again, quite frustrated. The same holds true if a person is attracted to another person of the opposite sex, when both are working in the same office. Suppose both are married, have families, and realize that having an affair might have very serious consequences. Far from the other person, the fear of consequences seems remote, so plans are made for establishing some sort of informal contact. However, as the moment for meeting at the work situation draws near, the fears gain ascendance over the attractions, and the parties remain silent or merely talk about work or other neutral matters.

This type of situation occurs daily in all sorts of settings and with all types of subjects. The reader himself must surely have been in such a situation. It has been given the name *approach-avoidance conflict*. The important point, however, is not that the approach-avoidance conflict exists, but rather how we make a decision, take the plunge, and the conflict disappears and how, at other times, it is impossible to escape the situation. This in turn provokes great anxiety, which the person tries to reduce.

AROUSAL AND RETICULAR FORMATION

Before proceeding with the discussion of approach-avoidance conflicts and their consequences, it is convenient to consider what has been discovered with respect to a portion of our brains that lies where the spinal cord enters. This portion, about the size of the little finger, is called the *reticular formation* because it is highly reticulated, i.e., crisscrossed. Until a few years ago, little was known about this structure. Recent discoveries by Lindsley (1957), Hebb (1955), and others have linked it to the state of arousal in which we may find ourselves at any given moment. We have two extremes: at one end there is deep sleep; at the other extreme is agitation. In between, there are all sorts of arousal states. We may be dozing, mildly interested, rather interested, extremely interested, very excited, almost panicky, etc. Bindra (1959), in a penetrating analysis of arousal, shows curves initially suggested by Freeman (1940) relating level of arousal to efficiency of performance (see Fig. 3.2).

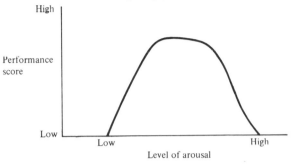

FIG. 3.2. Performance as a function of the level of arousal. [Adapted from Bindra (1959) by permission.]

According to Fig. 3.2, the performance score on a given task is a function of the level of arousal. For example, if the person has to copy drawings of print designs, thereby producing a very low level of arousal, a state of drowsiness may lead him to perform very poorly. However, if the person is over-excited, he may also perform poorly on this type of work. In between, there is an *optimal* level of arousal. It is at this point that the best results are achieved. We will see in a later chapter how this concept is used in the design of persuasions, in which the level of arousal is maintained at the optimum level for maximum effect.

Bindra (1959) has suggested that *frustration*, i.e., the kind of situation that exists in the case of approach-avoidance conflict, may lead to a high level of arousal. This frustration not only reduces the person's efficiency, but it also makes him react by engaging in that response which is strongest in the person's repertoire. For example, if a person has a tendency to be aggressive, the approach-avoidance situation, if very severe, can cause him to show his aggressiveness. If a person tends to rationalize, such a situation will make him tend to rationalize more. The same holds true for all sorts of what have been called *defense mechanisms*, which are employed in approach-avoidance conflict situations. Several of these will be described, with examples given of each.

DEFENSE MECHANISMS

Reaction. ~~Formation~~   This is the tendency of a person, in an approach-avoidance situation, to disguise a motive so completely that it appears to be the exact opposite of the original intent. An example will show how this works: Let us assume that a person feels attracted to his job because of the good pay, stability, and the status he derives from it, but he also feels very negative about it because he lacks certain important abilities. Suppose, for example, that he writes training manuals but is low in divergent production in the semantic area—a skill which is very important in such a task. Or suppose that he controls the quality of silk prints, a job which requires good color discrimination, and he is color-blind. Many color-blind people are often unaware of their deficiency and are quite distressed when this is pointed out to them (Pickford, 1951). It may be possible that the job requires evaluation of symbolic systems, as in computer programming, and he is low in that area.

If the employee has a natural tendency to work hard and is responsible, the arousal caused by such an approach-avoidance conflict will be alleviated by the use of reaction formation. Thus, instead of withdrawing from the job, he will tend to show great activity. He may run hither and yon, take piles of work home, stay overtime, and seem otherwise overly active. Nevertheless, the net results may be of little value. The excess activity seems to be a cover-up for the employee's deficiency. Of course, this response is completely subconscious. The person would be indignant if the underlying process were pointed out to him. As Pickford showed in the case of color blindness, this occurs when the lack of an essential mental ability is pointed out.

It would, of course, be not only senseless but even cruel to try to point out this inadequacy. It is important to realize that this behavior is a sort of cover to conceal a failing. Imagine a pretty girl who has a scar on her face. She has found a way to comb her hair so that a lock of it covers the scar. If this hairdo seems strange to someone, it would be very bad manners—indeed cruel, to tell her that her hair isn't becoming that way and, with a gesture, push it aside to show the scar. Her reaction would be ungrateful to say the least. The same thing happens when psychological failings, hidden by subconscious processes, are pointed out to the subjects. It is even worse if a test result is shown to prove the point, because it is tantamount to showing a certificate proving that the person is incompetent. If this is done with a sufficiently large number of people, they may, because of the anxiety provoked, seek others who are in the same position (Schachter, 1959) and conclude that the whole testing program should be scrapped. Telling a person the cause of his subconscious reaction to conflict, or even worse, proving to him that his incapacity is the cause of poor work results, is about the clumsiest thing we could do. No improvement can be expected. Instead, we will have a strong negative reaction in addition to the initial problem, and we will merely have added another problem to the existing one.

Displacement.   The person who responds in this way to an approach-avoidance conflict tends to transfer his aggressive feeling from its original object toward someone else. For example, he may like his work and feel secure, but have an overbearing boss who continually berates him in front of his fellow workers. He does not react against his boss directly but instead displaces his aggression toward others. Miller (1948) has shown in experiments performed on rats that this aggressiveness tends to be re-directed toward objects that are similar to the one causing the problem. Bennis (1964) cites a case in which an overbearing discussion leader left the room, and a member of the group who looked like the leader tried to take over. The group reacted against the new leader even before he had a chance to act. Thus, if the boss is the cause of his anger, the employee may become aggressive toward certain of his fellow workers, particularly those who look like his boss. He may become angry at clients or others who have nothing to do with the cause of his conflict. Here again the response is subconscious. If we tell the man that he is aggressive and that he must stop, he will probably deny his anger and instead feel hostile toward *us*.

Obviously, these two defense mechanisms, reaction formation and displacement, are really symptoms of the existence of an approach-avoidance situation. We must consider them as such. In this respect, they are similar to symptoms in medicine. A doctor examines a patient and finds, say, a very warm forehead; he takes that as a symptom of possible illness. He doesn't jump to an immediate conclusion about the cause or immediately start to prescribe a remedy. He must tie this factor in with other symptoms. The person may have a warm forehead because he has the flu, because he has pneumonia, or because he has been in front of a very hot furnace looking at molten steel. In the first case, the doctor would tell the person to go to bed and perhaps prescribe some medicine. In the second, he would probably order immediate penicillin shots as well as bedrest. In the third case, he would tell the person to simply cool off and probably have a drink of water. Note that *in not one of these cases would he prescribe putting an ice bag on the person's head.* Any doctor doing such a thing would be considered an incompetent quack, because he would be treating a symptom instead of trying to find and correct the *cause*.

In the same way, if a person shows a great deal of frantic but unproductive activity or if he is aggressive toward several people with no apparent reason, we would be social-science technological quacks if we were to call him in and bawl him out for the observed behavior. Knowing how approach-avoidance conflict works, what we have to do is ask ourselves the question: "What is the possible cause of this man's behavior? What rejection of the work (or family or social) situation causes him to act like this?" Then, instead of trying to correct the observed behavior, we would go about trying to correct the underlying cause. But there are still other responses to approach-avoidance conflict, which we will consider as symptoms not to be cured but rather to help us detect where the underlying cause lies.

Projection. The person who uses this device projects onto others the source of his conflict, thereby disguising the fact that he suffers from it. In a very interestingly designed experiment, Bramel (1963) showed that very masculine male subjects placed in a situation that led them to believe they had homosexual leanings tended to ascribe homosexuality to the other partner in the experiment. The conflict was thus softened by projecting the cause of the conflict onto someone else. This phenomenon is very common in daily life. A person who is rather disorderly in his habits, for example, tends to blame his low and sloppy output to the lack of neatness on the part of others on whom he depends. An untidy cashier will tend to blame the errors in his cash balances on the illegibility of the orders for payment. A severely sexually repressed man or woman will tend to project all kinds of lewd desires and actions onto others, perhaps lamenting that today's youth is corrupt, etc.

Again, when we see a person continually criticizing others for some particular fault, we must ask ourselves the question: "May it not be possible that this person is undergoing a serious approach-avoidance conflict which involves this fault and is subconsciously projecting this problem to others?" We have a symptom which cannot be cured by trying to treat the symptom but by discovering the cause that produces it.

Alcohol. A person in a severe approach-avoidance conflict situation may turn to alcohol. This is such a general response that it occurs not only in persons but also in animals. Masserman (1943) trained cats to eat by opening a box, an act that delivered a pellet of food. After they had become accustomed to this procedure, he connected a device that delivered a strong blast of air to the cat when it opened the box. Thus, he created an ideal approach-avoidance situation. There was attraction based on hunger but avoidance based on the extremely disagreeable air blast. The cats were then fed milk containing 5 % alcohol; whereupon they would approach the box and open it quite unconcernedly while receiving the blast of air. In fact, their reaction was similar to that of the man in the approach-avoidance situation with regard to the woman, which was previously mentioned. He loses his inhibitions and makes advances to her in spite of his previous avoidance, doubts and fears after he has had a few drinks at a cocktail party.

The trouble with alcohol is that although it reduces rejections and therefore frees the person to approach the object, the boldness lasts only as long as the alcohol level in the blood remains high. When this level returns to normal, the person finds himself in the same approach-avoidance situation he faced before, but without his defense mechanism. He therefore feels much worse. Detecting incipient alcoholism resulting from such conflict is rather difficult. When alcoholism takes on greater magnitude, it is usually no longer possible to eliminate this symptom by correcting the initial approach-avoidance conflict that started it. Usually by the time it becomes obvious to everyone, alcoholism is no longer a problem that can be handled by the normal supervisor or friend and must therefore be transferred to specialists—psychiatrists, Alcoholics Anonymous, or others who have the time, training, and experience.

Rationalization.   Since we know that man is a rational animal, we feel a need to find reasons for our actions even when these are irrational. Our behavior in approach-avoidance conflict situations often leads us to rationalization as a way out. If I detest making out expense accounts every time I travel, it is quite possible that when I am on a trip I will solemnly decide to make out my expense account just as soon as I get back. I am in an approach-avoidance situation because my sense of duty makes me wish to do it, but my disliking of the task deters me. However, on returning, the first thing that greets me is an interesting problem; so the expense account promptly leaves my mind (see Repression in the following section). If this goes on for days and if the accounting department complains about my negligence, I may tell them that I simply haven't had the time to do it, due to more important matters, that I lack some data, or that a bill I paid was to be mailed to me and has not arrived. Some people, knowing that this is untrue, will say that I am lying. They will therefore devise some punishment for me. The diagnostic approach that is proposed here has no place for the term "lying." I was merely rationalizing. What they must do is try to find out "why this man is rationalizing about his expense account." It may be because he lacks number facility, or perhaps he is not accurate in recording his expenses and finds that he loses financially every time he makes a trip.

A mechanic insufficiently trained in the use of a machine or lacking the abilities (good eyesight, etc.) for the job may blame his poor performance on the alignment of the machine. The maintenance people may align the machine perfectly, but the mechanic still complains that there is vibration. Many hours are lost trying to find defects in machines, systems, processes, and procedures that are merely rationalizations. These in turn are produced by an approach-avoidance conflict on the part of the mechanic. Our question must again be "what rejection causes this person to rationalize?" Rationalization is one of the commonest and easiest defense mechanisms to detect. If we prove to the mechanic that his rationalization is untrue, he may cease one form but adopt another one. Thus, we must stop destroying these rationalizations and diagnose the underlying cause.

Almost invariably, when we try to introduce the persuasion designs described in Chapters 4 and 5, the old-time salesmen will say: "This is very interesting, but it won't work for this market." If they are then told that it has already worked in this market, they will immediately say: "Well, it may have worked in this market, but it can't be applied to this line of goods." If it is shown that it has worked with that particular line, then the reply will be: "Well, it won't work with my clients." This can go on eternally. The salesmen are in an obvious conflict situation. Management has asked the consultant to tell them about the new sales designs. They want to comply with management's request, but having had long-time habits that are quite different from what is proposed, they will react against the new methods because it means relearning their occupation. We ceased long ago to approach the problem in this manner. Instead, we have designed an appropriate persuasion, described in Chapter 5, and the problem is minimized.

There is one very important aspect about rationalizations to be considered: People differ in their ability to invent good rationalizations. It would seem that those who are high in the divergent production semantic relations, systems, transformations, and implications abilities are capable of making such extremely convincing rationalizations that they may fool almost everyone. In such cases, the thing to keep in mind is not how true the objections sound, but how easily the person finds a new and equally valid-seeming objection after an answer has been found to each. One way to check is to ask a hypothetical question. If the salesman has said that the persuasion won't work in his market, one may ask: "Suppose we were able to find a way to make it work in this market, say by some miracle, how does this strike you?" If he now counters with another objection, he is rationalizing. This technique has not been proven through research, but it still constitutes social science technology. We are simply joining findings from Guilford's SI model to what is known about rationalization and the approach-avoidance conflict in order to develop a diagnostic method.

Repression.   This, like some of the other defense mechanisms, was first described by Freud. The person faced with an approach-avoidance conflict in which he is required to do something that is very distasteful to him, either because it is associated with a particularly painful experience or because he lacks the ability, training, etc., simply forgets to do it. The unconscious postponement of the expense account report just cited is one case in point. We are surrounded by people who "forget" to do things they should have done. We term this carelessness, and in many organizations this behavior is punished; the severity of the punishment is usually proportional to the damage caused by the person who forgets. Of course, if the person forgets again, he is punished more severely because he is no longer a first offender. If he continues to forget, he may eventually be fired for gross negligence, with his union concurring in the decision.

The position set forth in this chapter, or rather in this whole book, is quite at odds with such a philosophy. At the risk of tiring the reader with repetition, the crucial question will again be posed: "Why is it that this man, who seems to be such a good worker in so many other aspects, nevertheless, forgets a duty that is really important and that could eventually lead to his discredit or loss of employment?" As long as we persist in attacking the symptom alone, we will fail to solve the problem.

A recent development, proposed in many industries, has been given the name *zero defects*. The method consists in asking everyone in the organization to sign a commitment to the effect that he promises not to make any mistakes. Those who proposed this method were obviously acting on insufficient knowledge of what human beings are like. They overemphasized a very important statement in the second paragraph of the Declaration of Independence of the United States of America, "all men are created equal." As we saw in Chapter 2, all men are *not* created equal. We therefore cannot expect perfection from *all* of them at *all* jobs. We know of a case in which a worker erred in mixing colors in a printing establishment and was disciplined for it. We administered a color-blindness test, and not surprisingly the employee was color-blind. In another case, several workers had, for years, been doing good work to very exacting tolerances, but lately some of them had made serious errors. They were of course disciplined. After asking about the workers' vision, the reply was given that all had been given exacting vision tests when they were hired. Since it was now years later, the alert Personnel Manager asked whether vision could not change over the years. New vision tests were given, and all those who had made mistakes were found to have deficient vision that needed immediate correction. Appropriate glasses were prescribed and used, and the workers no longer make errors. Making these workers sign commitments to the effect that they would not make errors or punishing them when they do are about the least effective things one could do. Applying disciplinary measures to someone who represses or utilizes other defense mechanisms is equally senseless.

Many readers who are now in industry, or who are faced with problems such as these, are perhaps wondering: "All right, this diagnosis thing sounds fine and is all right when it comes to wearing glasses. But what are we to do if people continually forget or continually make mistakes after they *do* get the glasses? If we can't apply disciplinary measures, what in the world are we expected to do? Just sit back and watch them making mistakes?"

An analogy with medicine will provide a partial reply. When a doctor sees a patient, he takes three distinct steps: Based on questioning and on observation of the patient, he makes a preliminary diagnosis. He may feel that the patient has tuberculosis, ulcers, or some other disease. He then orders blood tests, urological analyses, X rays, etc., in order to confirm his preliminary diagnosis. When his preliminary diagnosis is confirmed by this second step, the doctor takes the third step and starts to prescribe cures. But the confirmed diagnosis does not necessarily tell the physician what to do. Diagnosing and curing are two entirely different acts. The second cannot be done without having gone through the first, but the first does not automatically imply how the second should be conducted. There are still many illnesses that can be diagnosed but about which nothing can be done. (Tetanus, advanced cases of hydrophobia, and many cases of cancer can be easily diagnosed, but doctors feel helpless because nothing has yet been found to cure these diseases.) Fortunately, many ills such as pneumonia, considered incurable three or four decades ago (although they were easily diagnosed) are now easily cured. But it has taken a long time between the discovery of how to diagnose an illness and the discovery of how to cure it. In many cases, no cure has been found. The problem of inevitability has been partly solved by the use of preventive medicine, that is, not letting the disease reach the patient. Such techniques include vaccinations as for smallpox and polio, treating the drinking water against typhoid fever, and so on.

These same principles hold for social science technology. We have been accustomed for many years to diagnosing and prescribing simultaneously. Penal codes, by making punishment automatically fit the crime, have led us into this dead-end. We must learn how to separate these into two distinct functions. This chapter deals with diagnosis. A later one will deal with a few of the cures we have been able to devise for psychological ills.

Regression.   This represents another Freudian insight. It means retreating to an earlier or more primitive form of behavior. In adults, it means behaving like a child. When a difficult problem is posed to someone which places the subject in an approach-avoidance situation, a possible reaction may be merely to sulk or say: "I don't want to be bothered." We usually refer to such acts as "childish behavior." Many people have been reprimanded and eventually fired for it. Good diagnosis might have discovered that there was a precise cause for this phenomenon. If it had been found and corrected, an otherwise excellent worker might have been retained.

Illness.   A very common reaction to severe approach-avoidance conflict is illness, especially if the person has a natural tendency to become ill. Let us take a simple example: A worker is attracted to his job because he loves the type of work and the environment, but he fears the lack of stability prevalent in the organization because he sees people continually being fired. Far from the job, on the weekend, he will remember the positive aspects, but as Monday morning comes, he suddenly contracts an unbearable headache or a really painful upset stomach. When the certifying doctor visits him, he may find that there is nothing basically wrong with this person. The employee may even be accused of faking illness. However, the headaches, allergies, and other such symptoms may be quite real.

Brady (1958) subjected pairs of Rhesus monkeys to a very interesting test situation, which yielded results relevant to this discussion. Both were seated in restraining chairs, that is, they had a certain liberty of movement but were restricted to a seated posture. Each had a brass bar on which his feet could rest. At intervals of 20 seconds both monkeys received an electric shock through the bar. This was disagreeable but not sufficient to cause lasting damage. Each monkey had, close at hand, an electric toggle switch. The difference between the two was that monkey A had his switch so connected that should the monkey push it down within the 20-second period, the shock would be avoided on that one occasion. Monkey B's switch was disconnected. A rapidly learned that he should push the switch down every 20 seconds in order to avoid the shock. B soon lost interest in the switch, since whatever he did with it, the shock continued. A was in a typical approach-avoidance situation. He wanted to count the 20 seconds accurately so as to avoid the shock, but obviously the task was just too much for him.[1] If A erred even once in his count, *both* monkeys would receive the shock. However, the one whose switch was disconnected did not feel the responsibility for avoiding the shock, that is, for solving this problem. However, the one who had learned how to avoid it, definitely devoted his full time and energy to this virtually impossible task. The shock situation continued for six hours. After this time, the apparatus was disconnected and the monkeys, particularly monkey A, could rest. Six hours later, the shock situation would start again for another six hours. This went on day and night. After a period of about three weeks, A, who was in the approach-avoidance situation, that is, who wanted to avoid shock but simply could not, died of a perforated, duodenal ulcer.

The experiment could not be more dramatic or illuminating. It is obvious that this is a totally subconscious process. Monkey A does not deliberately die. His organism has chosen illness and eventual death as a means of escape from an intolerable approach-avoidance situation. On a greater or smaller scale, this happens to human beings. Headaches, allergies, ulcers, coronary attacks, asthma, and many other illnesses can result from approach-avoidance conflicts. Of course, the supervisor, spouse, or relative must not jump immediately to such a conclusion and prescribe a change of job, using separate rooms, etc. Only when one comes across a symptom of illness for which the doctor can find no physiological cause, should we, as supervisors, spouses, parents, teachers, etc. immediately ask the eternal diagnostic question: "Is it possible that there is a strong avoidance in the situation that causes these somatic symptoms?" We once saw a remarkable case of allergy. A very

---

[1] It would probably be too much for a human being; if the reader does not believe this, let him try to count 20-second intervals for half an hour.

amiable accountant was placed under one of the most infuriating management consultants we have had the privilege of meeting. It drove the accountant to despair. But being a very amiable person, he tried to take the matter in stride. However, an allergy started to develop in his legs, which took the form of swelling and ugly, red-colored ulcers. It was a disgusting sight to see. The doctors tried everything but nothing seemed to work. The situation grew steadily worse until the accountant could barely walk and therefore had to stay home from work for several days. In a few days, there was some improvement, but on returning to his job, the condition reappeared with increased virulence. It seemed that it would take months before his legs would heal. However, when the consultant eventually withdrew, his legs healed and returned to normal in less than two weeks.

Experiments conducted in the Soviet Union have been able to reproduce virtually any kind of illness desired by submitting subjects to all types of stress situations. The results have been the creation not only of ulcers but also heart attacks, allergies, and all kinds of diseases.

Compensation.   Let us assume that a person who has very high abilities in one area is put on a job in which he has very little opportunity to use them. He will probably try to *compensate* by devoting his spare time to a hobby that will allow him to use his abilities to the fullest extent. An actual case is that of a person very high in divergent production of figural symbolic and semantic systems. He had been placed in one of the more routine jobs in the data processing department of a large company. He turned to painting in his spare time. As reported by those who know him, he was classed as merely a fair painter. Nevertheless, he devoted much energy and many hours to this pastime. When eventually he was appointed analyst and given full freedom to guide programmers in their work, thus putting to maximum use his divergent production abilities, he gave up painting and has become a remarkable analyst and programmer for a complex operation. He is a fountainhead of original and timesaving ideas.

Haire (1964), in an important book in which some of the principles expounded here are described, asks this important question: "Why does the boss often seem to work longer and harder than his subordinates, while a worker on the production line will go home at night to agonizingly build a perfect boat in a bottle?" Haire states that a large part of the answer lies in the fact that the job may mean a lot to the boss, in terms of ego-need satisfaction, but little to the subordinate. The latter therefore compensates by building boats in bottles. We venture to say that a more complete diagnosis may be necessary. Perhaps egoistic needs are important. However, it is also possible that the subordinate has great ability in cognition, divergent production, and evaluation of figural systems, which he has no chance of using on his routine production-line job. The full utilization of skills may be as important as the fulfillment of ego-needs.

Some time ago, we were asked to select the 10 best men, out of 100 who were doing the job by hand, to handle fork-lift trucks. The Guilford abilities were not then available; so the job was done using the Thurstone Primary Mental Abilities. The supervisors were trained in how to interpret the tests and on how to interview. A job description and specification were duly drawn up, and on the basis of this information, tests and interviews, the 10 best men were selected. However, it was pointed out that there was one man, Joe, who was very high in verbal ability, inductive and deductive reasoning. The interview also revealed that he was studying law at night and was fairly advanced. Since we had been asked a few days before to find someone to assist in the legal department, it was quite natural that we should suggest that instead of going to all the trouble, expense and delay in finding an adequate, outside man for the legal department, Joe should be given the job. Besides, it would have a good morale effect not only on Joe but on the rest of the personnel to see that the company was starting a policy of promotion from within.

The suggestion was received with an expression of incredulity on the part of Management. "How in the world could we do such a thing? Joe is the union representative on the loading platform. As such, he has created plenty of trouble. We've tried to fire him several times, but every time we made an attempt we got a terrific reaction from the union. It would be folly to put the union representative in our legal department." When approach-avoidance conflict was explained to Management, they saw that many of Joe's past reactions, which had caused considerable trouble, came from two fundamental situations: First, there had been extremely poor handling of the personnel on the loading platform. Second, Joe had abilities and knowledge far beyond those required for merely moving small cases by hand from one place to another, 8 hours a day. It was quite predictable from his high verbal and inductive abilities, that he would have to compensate in some way for being tied down to what to him was the most boring job on earth. It is interesting to note that Joe's fellow workers, whose mental abilities were very low, were quite content to work at moving boxes. They did not even want to try to run those "confounded new machines." (There was also a certain element of danger involved in using the fork-lift truck). Eventually, Management saw the light and Joe was offered a job in the legal department. He has been an excellent employee ever since, is very happy with his job, and has received several raises. He has also continued his studies. Obviously, once the avoidance element of the conflict was withdrawn, a person who was in danger of being fired, turned into a happy and efficient worker.

Absenteeism and Tardiness.   Very often this behavior can be directly traced to an approach-avoidance situation. If a person who was normally punctual starts to arrive late, we must again ask the crucial question: "Why does this person come in late when he realizes that by doing so he jeopardizes a job he seems to like so much?" The same is true for excessive absenteeism. When a person is in the midst of a very strong approach-avoidance situation, he tends to forget the highly disagreeable elements over the weekend and thinks only of the positive aspects of his job. As Monday morning arrives, however, the prospect of facing this unbearable situation makes him subconsciously magnify that slight headache or liver trouble. He therefore asks a relative or friend to notify the office that he is ill and can't possibly come to work.

Some time ago, the writer was approached by a very understanding and humane Personnel Manager of a company employing 400 workers. He said his problem was terrible. He was having 35% Monday absenteeism. The plant just couldn't operate under those conditions. Initially, absenteeism on Monday was not that bad, but Management had later decided to "do something about it." A rule was therefore adopted whereby anyone failing to come to work on Monday would be automatically suspended for one day, usually the following day. However this failed to correct the Monday situation; it also created the same absenteeism problem on Tuesday. Since matters became worse, the Board decided to increase the penalty. Anyone absent on Monday would automatically be suspended for 2 days, usually Tuesday and Wednesday. Now things had become so bad, with 35% Monday absenteeism, that the Board was on the verge of ordering that Monday absences would be penalized by a suspension of 3 days. It was at this stage that we were consulted about whether this drastic measure would really help to improve matters.

The Personnel Manager was instructed in the nature of approach-avoidance conflict, dissonance, and other social science concepts. Eventually, he designed what to the Board seemed to be a preposterous and dangerous solution. An announcement would be made that there would be *no* suspensions or sanctions of any kind for Monday absenteeism as of that date. Instead, he and two supervisors he trained would tour the plant and speak to 10 workers selected from the 130 who had failed to work the day before. Very kindly, one of them would approach a worker and say: "I didn't see you around yesterday. Anything wrong?" This was asked very kindly without the slightest hint of reproof. They got all sorts of answers: "had stomach trouble; my kid was very sick, etc." The replies were accepted at face value, although for the most part they were clearly excuses (really rationalizations). The supervisor then asked the employee how he felt today, or how the kid was today, etc. The answer was always "much better," as if the person was relieved at not having to go into further details.

On Wednesday, the same interviewers again toured the plant and asked the man with the presumably sick child: "How's your kid today?" The worker had often forgotten his rationalization and would ask rather baffled: "My kid—why?" "Because of his Monday illness you told me about yesterday." "Oh! he's fine, just fine, it turned out to be nothing at all." The interviewer expressed his satisfaction that things had turned out well. Similar procedures were followed with the other nine employees. The following week, 10 other persons were given the same treatment.

Eight months later, Monday absenteeism had dropped to less than 5%. More importantly, it was discovered that some people *were* having real trouble, and the company was able to help in these special cases. Other measures taken to improve relations also contributed, but the easing of tension was one of the major factors.

All of these symptoms allow us to diagnose the existence of approach-avoidance conflict. However, the presence of such a behavior does not necessarily indicate that there is such a conflict. As in the case of the warm forehead, the doctor recognizes that there may be many causes, some of which may be trivial. For example, a person may be irascible merely because he did not sleep well last night. If he is aggressive toward others, the cause is not necessarily an approach-avoidance conflict; he merely needs some sleep. However, if he is *often* irascible because in *general* he sleeps little, we again have a possible symptom.

DISSONANCE PROBLEMS AND THEIR CAUSES

Misbehavior in a work situation may also be caused by other factors. We saw in Chapter 1 how dissonance can cause a person to seek social support by talking to others and trying to persuade them to his point of view. Therefore, if we see a person vehemently arguing against the organization for which he is working, we gain nothing by calling this disloyalty and applying punishment for such outrageous and inadmissible behavior. He may instead be reducing dissonance because someone was appointed to the post he expected. There are many other dissonance-producing situations in organizations that may cause similar reactions. A few of the most common will now be discussed.

Concern about Stability. Let us imagine a person working for an organization who has two cognitions: (1) He feels that employment in this organization is secure. (2) One day he arrives at work and finds that two fellow workers have been fired, without an adequate explanation. He considers these employees to be on a level equal to his own. He can reduce the dissonance aroused by these two simultaneous cognitions by derogating the authorities responsible for the firing; he can also contemplate quitting and experience the same sort of routine described in Chapter 1 (demand more pay, etc.). His superiors would consider this behavior "unreasonable" since the employee had recently received a raise. Again, we have the problem of diagnosing why this person is behaving in such a manner.

Lack of Recognition for Work Done.   When presenting these cases to supervisors and other interested parties, this is the point on which we generally receive the greatest response. In other words, virtually everyone is familiar with what happens when someone is not praised sufficiently for an accomplishment. Here again we have two dissonant cognitions.

- A person does a special job for which he takes special pains. As he does so, he has visions of what the effect will be when he presents the finished job and of the recognition and praise he will receive.
- On presenting the finished product, the other party concerned, his supervisor, spouse, son, daughter, father, friend, etc., finds fault with what the person believes to be trifles.

The two cognitions are dissonant. A concrete case may be that of a man in the Cost Department who prepares a detailed and thorough analysis of the possible costs of several proposed expansions. Upon presenting them to his supervisor, he expects some positive recognition. Instead, the supervisor remarks: "Oh! You did this on plain onionskin paper instead of on the normal paper with the company's letterhead!" Another case may be a husband who goes to some trouble to get something for his wife and, instead of gratitude, receives criticism for a small detail.

The reaction to this kind of dissonance may be very violent indeed. In companies, we frequently hear the remark: "With the pay I get what does he expect!" Of course, the irate employee then seeks social support for this urging others to agree that pay in this company is indeed low. Such a person may soon be labeled an "agitator" who has "infiltrated" the organization to cause dissension. Poor diagnosis! And from such poor diagnosis it is highly unlikely that any resulting corrective action will be effective.

Exclusion from Meetings.   This case is very common. The two cognitions involved are:

- The employee believes that he is an important constituent of the work group, something that is a source of great satisfaction to him.
- A meeting is called to discuss a problem that falls partially within his area, and no one remembers to invite him to the meeting.

The dissonance-reduction may take the form of derogating the meetings: "Those meetings are useless, they take up a lot of time, nothing gets accomplished, and unknowledgeable people give opinions." When the uninvited person is heard attacking meetings as useless or acting in a childish manner toward them, we tend to label him as uncooperative, without diagnosing his actual problem.

Nonmaterialization of Expected Benefits. This is one in which many organizations commit the worst offenses. The two cognitions are:

- There has been considerable comment that there will probably be a special benefit awarded. This may be a salary increase, a special bonus, a holiday on a certain date, etc. The rumor has not been denied, although it seems obvious to everyone that the management is aware of it.
- The date arrives at which this benefit was expected, and the benefit does not materialize.

The cumulative dissonance caused by this kind of situation can be very great, principally because it tends to affect *everyone* in the organization. Since some individuals may be more vocal than others in their dissonance-reduction and social support-seeking, these will be labeled the "leaders" who have "infiltrated" the organization and who are responsible for the general state of unrest.

Derogation of Usefulness. Again two dissonant statements describe the condition.

- The person believes he is an important element in an organization or club (a belief held by everyone to a greater or lesser degree; and in organizations, *every* job is important).
- He hears someone in higher authority comment that his job is unimportant.

Here again we have a case in which dissonance-reduction will probably take the form of derogating the higher authority, finding that his own pay is inadequate, and, of course, seeking social support for his dissatisfaction.

Salary Inequities. These have, in the past, proved to be such a flagrant cause of dissonance that empirical methods have been established to cope with them. Bergen (1939) recognized that salary inequities are more potent sources of dissatisfaction than are the general levels of pay. The dissonance can be expressed again as follows:

- I work a lot, have studied a lot to be able to perform this job, and have needed a great amount of experience to be able to do it.
- X does a far easier job, which requires little knowledge and little experience, and he earns more than I do.

The result has been the proliferation of all sorts of job evaluation systems— their main purpose being that of establishing fair salary differentials between different jobs in order to eliminate these inequities. It is interesting to note that virtually everyone who has entered the field has wanted to create his own job evaluation system. This is typical when solutions are based purely on empiricism. Job evaluation, as now practiced, has in many cases attenuated the problem. Nevertheless, we cannot escape our feeling that much can be done to improve the existing solutions. There are two principal reasons. One of these is the dictum stated by Carpenter and Haddan (1964): "An operating rule that is founded in a well developed discipline, and which is carefully derived from adequate knowledge, is more useful than a rule which is less soundly based." Job evaluation, as presently practiced, is not based on a well-developed discipline derived from adequate knowledge. The difference between the two levels can be explained by comparing can openers and the calculation of the orbits of artificial satellites. There are probably as many different can openers as there are persons who design them. There is no well-founded, scientific theory backed by experimentation regarding can openers. On the other hand, whoever tackles the calculations of the orbit of an artificial satellite will get essentially the same result because there is a well-founded discipline entitled celestial mechanics by means of which orbits are calculated.

Job evaluation, as now practiced, is similar to the can opener type of procedure. One difficulty in such cases is that when trouble arises, there is a tendency to oversimplify. This tendency is shown in a recent report put out by the American Management Association (1969), which describes a conflict between what the job evaluation requires and what supply and demand dictate with regard to personnel in the area of preparing computer software. Instead of refining the existing method, the report seriously recommends reverting to more primitive and long-ago discarded systems. There is hope, however, for a major change in this tendency, because of the theoretical work being performed in this area. For example, Adams (1963a, 1963b, 1965) has done considerable theorizing and research work that is beginning to illuminate the subject of inequity in wage payments. These studies show that the subject is much more complex than had originally been assumed by those devoted to job evaluation. Besides, such discoveries as those derived from Guilford's SI model of mental abilities and others have vastly complicated the subject because they show the great number of relevant factors which must be taken into account.

In an analysis of the present status of dissonance theory, Aronson (1966) recognizes the increasing complexity, due to new factors, that continually occur. He states: "This added complexity should not lead us to throw our hands up in despair. Rather, it should lead us to a more careful analysis of the situations we are dealing with and perhaps with an even greater concern with individual differences."

There will undoubtedly be a profound change in job evaluation when all this work and further research results are considered. We are working hard at it but are not yet able to report a satisfactory working procedure. However, since a job must be done, we continue with the only thing thus available —the "can opener variety," that is, straight job evaluation. This is a common state of affairs in technology. If we were to wait until every aspect of a product had been tried by means of theoretical research, we would still be waiting to ride the first automobile, use the first phone, or fly the first plane. There is a real challenge for anyone with high divergent and evaluation ability in semantic systems and with the adequate scientific knowledge to create the revolution in job evaluation that most of us do not yet see as necessary, because of our complacency with the present system.

These cases of dissonance-producing situations are taken from Varela (1961). Many more instances can be cited. As a matter of fact, it is impossible to define and prescribe for every daily, dissonance-producing situation. The important point is that dissonance leads to attempts at reducing it and that these attempts will take the form of changing a cognition (rationalization), seeking social support, derogating the dissonance-producing source, etc. It is especially important to note that the dissonance effect under complete freedom of choice conditions is very great. It not only leads to a total change of attitude but also causes, under certain circumstances, complex physiological changes in the human body (Zimbardo, 1969).

FIXATION

Maier (1949) studied the problem created when rats were repeatedly frustrated. The rats were supposed to jump from a stand to one of two differently marked openings with light swinging doors. Behind one of these, food could be found. By repeatedly changing the position of the food, Maier made the rats become so frustrated that they would develop a fixed habit of jumping to, say, the door on the right. They persisted in this behavior even when the swinging door was screwed tight. The rat would still jump toward that door even if the act meant falling to the floor and receiving a strong punishment, i.e., the pain of falling. The behavior persisted even if the door to the left opening was withdrawn and the desired food was perfectly visible in the exposed opening!

Human beings, after undergoing prolonged and intense frustrations, often show a tendency toward fixation. They will continue to engage in a behavior that is damaging to them long after considerable evidence shows that another behavior would be much more advantageous. George Santayana defined this in a way when he said: "Fanaticism consists in redoubling your effort when you have forgotten your aim." At any rate, fixation is a serious problem that must be faced, not as a symptom to be treated but as something leading us to unravel the original cause of such intensely irrational behavior.

PSYCHOLOGICAL REACTANCE

A phenomenon recently investigated by Brehm (1966) is one he terms reactance, probably because of its similarity to electrical reactance. When a current is made to pass through a coil of wire, an electromagnetic field is established that opposes the flow of such a current. In the same way, when persons receive certain types of communications, the effect is to make them oppose the communication received. The communicator thus considers the individual stubborn and uncooperative.

An example adapted from Brehm will illustrate how reactance operates. Generally, we feel that we are free to perform certain acts. For example, a man may wake up in the morning feeling that he is free to go and play golf or to stay home and watch television. His wife, however, informs him that today he *must* play golf since she has some friends coming in to play bridge. The man immediately feels that his freedom is being curtailed. He experiences reactance, which stimulates him to reestablish his freedom. He therefore tells his wife that he particularly wanted to stay home and watch TV since there was a special show he wanted to see. He will probably stay and turn the TV set on a little louder than usual, simply to emphasize the fact that he can do as he pleases.

Brehm gives other examples that are easily applicable to the work situation. A secretary who frequently goes to the water fountain is told by her boss that she must no longer go there. Since she fears him because of the power he has over her, she can restore her freedom only by implication. One way of doing this is by telling *others* to go to the water fountain. She is in part regaining her freedom by getting others to perform the forbidden act. She may also engage in even more reprehensible behavior, e.g., doing her nails in the office when she should be typing reports. By engaging in another activity of this kind, she is also proving to herself that she has not lost her liberty.

If the boss should find her putting on nail polish, he might be infuriated. If he is familiar with social science technology, however, he will merely stop and think, "Why is this very good secretary engaging in such reprehensible behavior?" Eventually, knowing the reactance phenomenon, he may link the nail polishing to his lack of tact in telling her not to go to the water fountain. He might realize that instead of forbidding visits to the water fountain, he should have tried to diagnose: "Why is this very good secretary getting up and going to the water fountain so often?" [2]

[2] As we shall see in Chapter 4, concerning the design of persuasion, reactance can produce the opposite results from those desired even when convincing arguments are presented. The persuasion designs have been constructed so as to reduce or eliminate entirely the reactance phenomenon or else to use it in such a way as to enhance persuasion.

There are probably many different ways in which reactance can be expressed, some of which can be quite objectionable. But the solution is obviously *not* to punish or threat, as these will merely increase the reactance. The proper method is first to determine the etiology of the symptoms (undesired behavior) and then to choose suitable solutions based on the causes of the problem.

The reader at this point may feel a bit confused. He started out with a stable belief system regarding other people's errors, their absenteeism, insubordination, childish behavior, and so forth. According to traditional and long-accepted mores, these acts are to be countered by means of adequate punishment, perhaps including a mild verbal reprimand. Now, the reader may agree with a lot of what has been said, but at the same time, he may feel as if the rug has been pulled out from under him. He does not know where he stands or what to do about it. How does one go about making a really efficient diagnosis? (Let us leave the corrective measures for later.) How can one be sure that the diagnosis is being uniformly and correctly made in an industrial design. In the same way that doctors have established diagnostic procedures that can be used by individuals all over the world, without the presence of the inventor, a quite effective diagnostic procedure has been devised that can easily be replicated in any work setting. Again, the reader may find things that may seem familiar to him. This should not be surprising because where there are no social science data to guide us, we have merely resorted to the usual practices. The procedure has been improved as new discoveries have been made in the social sciences. It will doubtless be improved still further as new findings are made and as more experience is gained, but the present system has been in operation for over eight years in some organizations with very satisfactory results.

SUMMARY OF PERSONNEL BEHAVIOR

Before presenting the design of a specific solution to the diagnosis problem, we should summarize what has been presented so far. Each cause of trouble will be mentioned, along with the symptoms it manifests.

Approach-Avoidance Conflict.   The person feels attracted toward an object for one or more reasons and at the same time repelled by it for one or more reasons. The main characteristic is that when far from the object in time or distance, the attraction is felt more strongly than avoidance, thereby causing approach behavior to the object. Close to the object, however, the minuses outweigh the pluses, thereby driving the person away. If he cannot get away from this push-pull trap into which he has fallen or been made to fall, there will be a tendency to act in a manner that seems quite unrelated to the cause of the conflict. Among the observed behaviors which should be taken as symptoms of such conflict are:

Reaction formation.   Subject disguises the true motive by rushing and engaging in what is apparently almost frantic but ineffective activity.

Displacement.   Subject is aggressive toward others with no apparent cause.

Projection.   Subject tends to attribute to others the source of his conflict. An example is the worker who complains that everyone else around him makes errors in numerical calculations, when actually he himself is inept in an area that is an important part of his own job.

Alcohol.   Subject tends to find relief in drink from the conflict he can't handle. Drugs also belong to this class.

Rationalization.   Subject tends to find plausible sounding reasons which excuse his poor work. This is the familiar "sour grapes" reaction.

Repression.   Subject tends to repress or forget those aspects of a situation which are disagreeable to him.

Regression.   Subject tends to retreat to an earlier form of behavior, as when an adult behaves like a child or an adolescent.

Illness.   Subject tends to become ill as a means of escaping a severe approach-avoidance situation.

Compensation.   Subject tends to engage in another activity so as to compensate for the lack of opportunity to use certain abilities in his job.

Absenteeism-tardiness.   Subject tends to be late or absent in order to escape from disagreeable aspects of a job.

Cognitive Dissonance.   Complaints about pay and other conditions (except where the wages are really low).

This behavior may result from the worker's feeling of insecurity, a sense of being left out of meetings to which he thought he should have been invited, hearing that his job isn't important, feeling that his pay is low, etc.

Commenting to others disparagingly about the organization.   This signifies reduction by seeking social support, because of the same conditions just mentioned and also when benefits had been promised or expected, they later failed to materialize.

Fixation.   In cases of extreme frustration, fixation is the tendency to stick to a given idea or solution in spite of overwhelming evidence that such a solution is not viable.

Psychological Reactance.   This is the tendency on the part of an individual to restore a freedom to act as he pleases when he feels someone or something is threatening that freedom. Reactance may be produced by: (a) direct orders, (b) general regulations that he feels affect him, and (c) rule booklets that define allowable and forbidden behavior. The person will tend to restore freedom by: (a) insisting on engaging in the forbidden behavior, (b) inciting someone else to engage in such behavior, and (c) engaging in another behavior also considered reprehensible but not expressly forbidden.

A NEW PERSONNEL APPRAISAL DESIGN

The technological solution for all these personnel behavior characteristics will be known as personnel appraisal. However, it must not be confused with methods (mentioned earlier in this chapter) that are currently described by this title in books on industrial psychology. These procedures use rating scales, in which the individuals are rated on a series of attributes and a score is assigned to each. These scores are often added to provide a total score.

Since it was felt that this method was subject to all sorts of biases and errors (Blum and Naylor, 1968; Ghiselli and Brown, 1955; Maier, 1965; and Anastasi, 1968) other techniques have been proposed. Among these are the *critical incident technique* (Flanagan, 1954), the *ranking system*, the *paired comparisons*, the *forced choice*, the *in-basket* (Frederiksen *et al.*, 1957), among others.

All these methods try to solve the problem by changing the instrument involved. Not one of them makes use of findings from social psychology (cognitive dissonance, psychological reactance, etc.). Often the efforts have been concentrated upon the form itself or on training the supervisors how to use the form. In the author's opinion, the form seems to be the *least* important aspect of the total appraisal process. Rather, the most important element is an understanding of the psychology involved. This is what we shall now discuss.

DESIGN OF THE APPRAISAL SYSTEM

The first question to be asked is: "Why are we setting up an appraisal system?" Several goals have been proposed, not necessarily in their order of importance.

- To select persons who are eligible for promotion.
- To find persons with the necessary ability to be transferred to other work.
- To determine increases in pay as well as bonuses on the basis of merit.
- To discover unused abilities.

- To help determine training needs.
- To help distribute work according to the abilities of each employee.
- To help personnel improve performance by correcting behavior where necessary.
- To improve the organization by redistributing the work.

Initially the appraisal method to be described was first designed to help correct behavior when necessary, however, the system proposed has proved useful for all the other goals as well.

After asking the first crucial question, others resulted. For example, we found that it was important to ask: "Why does this person, who evidently needs his job, nevertheless fail in certain aspects of it?" "Why does this person work well with some people and not with others?" Finally, and most importantly: "What can we do about it?"

The method finally devised is as follows:

1. *Make up a job description and specification sheet.*   This is exactly what we did in Chapter 2 when we tried to judge people we didn't know. It is a trifle more difficult to do this without including biases created by our knowledge and attitude toward the present job-holder. The description must of course include the job mission, as well as a statement of each of the several tasks to be performed in order to carry out this mission.

2. *Describe step-by-step how the person being appraised performs each of the tasks.*   In this part, the appraiser, usually the supervisor working with an assistant from the Personnel Department, tries to forget what the person himself is like and concentrates on how the *work* is being performed. To promote objectivity, the person from the Personnel Department keeps asking the supervisor for specific instances to justify the latter's impression. For example, say the specification stated that one task is to "give information to other Departments when requested." Let us further suppose the supervisor feels the worker involved does this task poorly. The assistant would then ask the supervisor for specific instances. The latter must cite several, as the personnel man refuses to accept just one case as evidence. These instances are written down. Specifically, the appraisal may look like this: "*Fair.   Often unclear in giving information. Case of Brown invoice 5/5/67, Smith report 5/10/67, and Jones file 5/11/67.*" These remarks need not be extensive, although the supervisor must explain them thoroughly to the Personnel man. The written record merely notes the case references as reminders. On other items, the supervisor may find that the worker is excellent. This technique has proved to be a very good way of avoiding the halo effect, the tendency toward leniency, and other sources of bias.

The following is taken from an actual case of a maintenance supervisor.

Job description

A. Sets up inspection schedules so as to examine and replace parts before breakdowns occur.

B. Sets up preventive maintenance schedules so that parts can be serviced adequately and replaced before their useful life is over.

On appraising the worker with respect to Statement A, the supervisor states "Does an excellent job. Was able to avoid a costly breakdown on a vital stamping press by noting a crack in the crankshaft that would surely have led to failure and partial destruction of the machine at a critical time. Noted a small, but significant, leak in the air compressor gasket which was rapidly replaced, thus avoiding costly delay." However, regarding Statement B, the supervisor made the following comment: "Not very good. He relies more on his visual acumen than in setting up schedules. An example is the case of the diaphragm in the gasoline engine motor pump which should have been replaced every six months and which caused trouble twice because this precaution had not been taken." Here we have a case in which the supervisor recognizes that the man being appraised does one thing well, yet fails in another area.

The supervisor's major concern will now be to answer the question: "Why?—Why is it that this maintenance man can be so sharp at detecting imminent failure, yet never seems to be able to set up and carry out a workable preventive schedule?"

Note again that up to now the supervisor has limited his comments to the *results* of the work performed. He has as yet given no opinion on the person himself.

3. *The supervisor must now give the positive and negative aspects of the person involved.* It has been found that the halo effect now tends to disappear. Since the supervisor has had to recognize that as far as the *work* is concerned, some aspects are good and others are not, he can recognize that the maintenance supervisor appears to be very alert but somehow does not seem to be able to plan. The positive and negative aspects are written down.

4. *The supervisor must now diagnose the cause of the problem.* It is here that the vital question is asked: "Why is the person good in some areas and poor in others?"

The supervisors are of course highly trained in social science technology, as described in this book. Otherwise, they would be unable to diagnose. They would be like laymen examining a person showing apparently serious symptoms of illness. Supervisors not trained in these areas are apt to say that the employee "shows ill will, that the man wants to be fired in order to collect severance pay, that this is a case of negligence, that this illness is feigned," and so forth. All these are different names for what is observed—they are not explanations.

When, however, a supervisor is highly trained in social science technology, he can say, as the supervisor did in this case: "It looks to me as if this man is high in cognition of figural units but is probably low in divergent production of semantic systems." (A preventive maintenance plan is a semantic system, and there are probably several that can be set up.) The supervisor suggested that the maintenance man be tested in these areas. Fortunately, Dr. Guilford had recently sent the appropriate tests and these had been translated, given to outside groups, and percentile norms calculated. The supervisor's surmise was confirmed: the maintenance man was high in cognition and evaluation of units and classes but was low in divergent production of systems and implications.

Note the similarity between this and the doctor's diagnosis. The supervisor first made a preliminary diagnosis. He then asked for a test in the same way a doctor asks for an X ray, and the diagnosis was proved correct. Other cases are more complex. If approach-avoidance conflicts due to conflicting motivations appear, along with dissonance, reactance and lack of abilities all in combined form, the case may prove really complex and may require a problem-solving meeting among the supervisor, his superior, the Personnel assistant, and the Personnel manager. Fortunately, not all cases need that much attention.

However, a very important, fundamental point must be stressed. Because of the application of social science findings, the burden of improvement has shifted from the worker to the supervisor. Prior to the application of this method, the man would have been reprimanded the first time he forgot to replace the pump diaphragm. The second time he would have been severely reprimanded. A third such "crime" would have been countered with a suspension; a fourth would probably have brought a longer suspension; and finally, he would have been fired. The organization would have lost a man who obviously had abilities that were useful to the organization, and the man would have left with a feeling of utter failure. It is the author's contention that this whole procedure is not only inhuman but also stupid because it is bad business. Besides, the dismissal will have an unsettling effect on other workers who may have thought that employment at the firm was fairly stable. New symptoms of other kinds may arise elsewhere as a result of this incident, as we illustrated before, and the process will continue endlessly with disastrous results.

It may seem that this method takes more time and requires knowledge that is simply not within reach of supervisors. On the contrary, we feel very strongly that if a supervisor has the capacity to handle the technical aspects of his job, be it machine shop, printing, accounting, spinning, selling, teaching or whatever, he must also have the capacity for acquiring the technical knowledge needed for handling people. If he does not have the capacity, the time, or willingness to acquire this knowledge, then he has no business being a supervisor. We felt, when we first started doing this work, that if we had to do all the designs for an entire company, the results would be severely limited. However, if *every* supervisor in the organization were trained in the use of social science technology, then the total effect would be very beneficial.[3]

There have been a few cases of supervisors who have not been successful at mastering these techniques. The application of adequate tests has shown that these were either high on the California F Scale, that they were low in the Guilford behavioral abilities, or that they were low in some of the semantic areas. A lot has been learned now about what supervisors should be like. When the work currently being done in this area is finished, a paper will be published in an appropriate journal, telling all that has been learned. We know even now, however, that supervisors must be carefully selected and must have the ability to learn and to apply social science technology in order to make valid diagnoses. The importance of the supervisor's ability becomes apparent when we realize that, within the content of our view of job appraisal, the responsibility for improvement on the part of a worker, student, etc., must shift largely from the individual being judged to the person making the judgment.

As an example of how our system works, we shall now present a complete personnel appraisal, taken from real life.

JOB DESCRIPTION

TASK: Designer I—Apparel Company.

BASIC MISSION: Applies artistic and technical knowledge in order to insure that the prints which have been adopted will turn out to be a readily salable product in this market.

FUNCTIONS:

1. Enlarges, reduces, or otherwise adapts designs to fit the sizes of the print rollers or frames so that on repeating the design in the printing operation, the resultant total design, on the whole length, will give an impression of continuity.
2. Creates different color combinations for each design to be shown to the Chief Designer for his approval so that he can decide how many meters will be made of each color combination.
3. Selects colors, inks, pencils, pens, brushes, and other materials in order to obtain the desired results.

[3] Besides, should we disappear, the whole innovation would also disappear. We now feel quite safe that we can travel abroad, be ill, or otherwise be absent, and the supervisor will continue to diagnose correctly the causes of problems.

4. Creates new designs for special clients on request and follows instructions given by the Sales Department through the Chief Designer.
5. Makes studies of designs purchased abroad in order to adapt them to our market conditions and the possibilities of our equipment.
6. Occasionally may make an original design for a print.
7. Attends color-fixing meetings, giving opinions on the best combinations as well as on solid color fabrics, and makes the weekly color orders to the mill according to the final decisions taken at such meetings.
8. Cooperates with the Assistant to the Chief Designer, giving instructions to Designers II on how to proceed with their work.
9. Occasionally cooperates in the preparation of the Fashion Calendar.

PERSONNEL APPRAISAL 1

NAME: Maria Suarez   Date: 23 May 1969
TASK: Designer I   Date last appraisal: 10 May 1968
AGE: 25—Married   Years on job: 5

Results on Job

FUNCTIONS:
1. She is excellent at making the size modifications. She was very clever in adapting the chrysanthemum design so that it would fit on a difficult roll and yet managed not to make it look distorted. She was also very good in the antelope design in which she cleverly concealed the feet in grass, which was made to look as part of the landscape of the next scene.
2. Extremely neat and very good at combining colors that are really fashionable. This was particularly noted in the acetate collection six months ago, most of which she did and which has been widely praised by the clients.
3. Very good, being careful always to select the correct materials with very little waste.
4. She has been particularly good at adapting a design from a European creator to the needs of client XYZ. She has not had much chance to do more of this.
5. Very good at adapting designs purchased abroad that are rather difficult to reproduce without deviating from the original idea. She was particularly good at the op-art adaptations which proved quite difficult to print. Nevertheless, the changes she introduced made it possible to manufacture these easily without losing the typical op-art character.
6. Does this very well. She was particularly good in shirtings for the first part of the 1970 collection, although her designs fell off in quality for the second half.

7. Gives opinions with obvious good taste but is often rough in the way she does it.
8. Directs the new girls who have been admitted as Designer II but spends too much time with them.
9. Has been working on this for too short a time to be able to form an opinion, but she has not contributed much as yet.

PERSONNEL APPRAISAL 2

Personal Aspects, Diagnosis, and Solution

NAME: Maria Suarez

PERSONAL ASPECTS:

Positive characteristics.   She has very good taste and is extraordinarily neat and precise in her work. She is very ingenious at adapting designs to our equipment.

Negative characteristics.   She talks too much. She does not respect the opinions of others, although this is a condition that had not occurred before. She seems to have become irascible and indifferent; her originality has also declined.

PRELIMINARY DIAGNOSIS: She has recently lost a small nephew she loved very much. This has probably caused her to lose interest in her work. Confirm whether this is the cause by a well-conducted interview.

SECOND DIAGNOSIS: She is in an intense double approach-avoidance conflict with respect to her work and to the art school she is attending. She has had special privileges concerning hours to enable her to attend art school. However, as part of an effort to standardize hours of work for employees, this privilege has been withdrawn. She had wanted to become a portrait painter, but the full work schedule means that she must give up art school and abandon this career.

She has also experienced considerable dissonance, because another Designer I who entered the company the same time she had, has been given important tasks cooperating with the chief designer. She is therefore no longer consulted as much as she used to be. All this started some six months ago.

RECOMMENDED ACTION: In an attempt to reduce the conflict caused by having to abandon portrait painting, she will be given some creative work, such as selecting and designing dresses for fashion shows. The company should also try to get her more interested in the Fashion Bulletin and consult her more on fashion in order to erase the impression that she is being left aside.

If her great interest in art studies continues and her abilities prove to be adequate, it will be better to let her continue those studies as soon as she is financially able to do so without having to work for the company.

WHO WILL TAKE ACTION? _____

WHEN ARE RESULTS TO BE EXPECTED? _____

APPRAISAL MADE BY: _____

    Assisted by _____(from Personnel Department)

4

This is called practice, but remember to first set forth the theory.

Leonardo da Vinci

the design of
persuasions

Trying to persuade others is an important task for salesmen, lawyers, professors, buyers, politicians, diplomats, and many others. For them, persuasion is crucial to success, but being able to persuade correctly is also very important to the rest of us. Usually, our persuasions consist of presenting all the arguments supporting our position, possibly including some derogatory remarks about the opposite viewpoints. If the person we are trying to persuade holds a contrary opinion, he will very probably be trying to persuade us at the same time, using the same method. Such a discussion is common, but it generally achieves nothing. Each one listens to the other's arguments only to find flaws in the other's reasoning. He can thus prove how wrong the other person is and how right he is. This type of persuasion, which usually takes place among supporters of different political parties, different athletic clubs, or persons holding opposite views on major issues, seldom produces changes of opinion. Nevertheless, this fact does not deter us from using exactly the same procedure when we try to convince the next person we meet. Most books on salesmanship (an important and frequent form of persuasion) tell us how straight arguments can be presented most efficiently and dramatically. The fact that the more dramatic presentations have been more effective than straight arguing has convinced many that it is the best way to sell, that is, to persuade.

Social science research, however, offers a large group of findings that can be very useful in the design of far more effective forms of persuasions. Let us look at some of the relevant methods and findings.

ATTITUDE SCALES

In general, most research on attitude changes or persuasion has proceeded more or less as follows: Subjects are given a rating scale. This consists of a straight line marked with a certain number of divisions, whose two ends symbolize opposite, extreme positions. For example:

DEFINITELY   DEFINITELY
DISAGREE   AGREE

| | | | | | | | | | | |
|—|—|—|—|—|—|—|—|—|—|—|

The subject is given a statement, and he is asked to express his position on the statement by marking a corresponding point on the scale. A persuasion is then attempted, and the subject is later given the same statement with the same scale and again asked to mark his position. This procedure involves a large number of subjects, and averages of the results before and after the persuasion are obtained. If the persuasion was successful, then there must be a significant change in the average score from before to after, in the expected direction. There are appropriate statistical tests which make it possible to estimate the level of statistical significance for the differences thus obtained.

Besides scales like the one shown, there are other methods of making attitude measures. Paired comparisons and equal-appearing interval scales (statistical methods designed by Thurstone that will not be discussed here), for example, consist of statements that cover a variety of feelings in reference to a given object. For example, attitudes toward the Korean war (Hill, 1953) were measured by the following scale.

- I suppose the United States has no choice but to continue the Korean war.
- We should be willing to give our allies in Korea more money if they need it.
- Withdrawing our troops from Korea at the moment would only make matters worse.

- The Korean war may not be the best way to stop Communism, but it is the only thing we could do.
- Winning the Korean war is necessary whatever the cost.
- We are protecting the United States by fighting in Korea.
- The reason we are in Korea is to defend freedom.

When this scale was made, the Korean war was a major issue to many citizens of the United States. Note that these statements vary considerably along the favorable-unfavorable dimension. After judges have given their opinions as to how strong each statement is, there are mathematical methods for determining what the distance is from one statement to the next along the continuum. A subject indicates his attitude by picking out the item that best expresses his feeling, and a number can then be assigned to his attitude. Attitudes can therefore be expressed numerically for purposes of comparison.

Another method of measuring attitudes is the Likert scale (Likert, 1932). For each of a series of statements, the subject is asked to indicate his direction and the degree of affect by placing a $+3$ if he strongly agrees, $+2$ if he agrees moderately, and $+1$ if he agrees slightly. Negative affect is expressed by: -1, mild disagreement; -2, moderate disagreement; -3, strong disagreement. This is the method used in creating the California F Scale for authoritarianism, which was mentioned in Chapters 2 and 3 on judging people.

Sherif and Hovland (1961) have raised serious objections to these types of scales. These objections are based on methodological and psychological considerations and need not concern us here, but the crux of their objection was that attitudes reflect complex states of mind that cannot be expressed along a single dimension. Their solution was the creation of an entirely new type of scale in which a person's attitude toward a given object is assessed by measuring his so-called *latitude of rejection*. Before continuing what may seem to the reader a rather bewildering and disconnected introductory résumé of different measures of attitude, we must explain that all these remarks will be integrated and unified when we come to the actual design of persuasions.

The Sherif and Hovland scale contains a series of statements about the object in question. One such list is the following, which comprises statements regarding elections.

- The election of the Republican presidential and vice-presidential candidates in November is absolutely essential to the country's interests.
- On the whole, the interests of the country will be served best by the election of the Republican candidates for President and Vice-President.
- It seems that the country's interests would be better served if the

presidential and vice-presidential candidates of the Republican party are elected in November.

- Although it is hard to decide, it is probable that the country's interests may be better served if the Republican presidential candidates are elected in November.
- From the point of view of the country's interests, it is hard to decide whether it is preferable to vote for the presidential and vice-presidential candidates of the Republican party or the Democratic party in November.
- Although it is hard to decide, it is probable that the country's interests may be better served if the Democratic presidential candidates are elected in November.
- It seems that the country's interests would be better served if the presidential and vice-presidential candidates of the Democratic party were elected in November.
- On the whole the interests of the country will be best served if the presidential and vice-presidential candidates of the Democratic party are elected in November.
- The election of the Democratic presidential and vice-presidential candidates is absolutely essential to the country's interests.

This scale is administered by copying the above statements on four sheets and presenting them in the form of a booklet. The subject is asked on the first sheet to indicate which statement he prefers most. On the second sheet he is asked to state which other statement, besides the one indicated on the first sheet, he would be most likely to endorse. The number of statements accepted is called the latitude of acceptance. If he endorses three statements, then his latitude of acceptance is 3. The subject is now asked on the third page to indicate which statement he rejects most, and on the fourth page, which other statements he would also reject. The number of statements rejected is called the latitude of rejection. Suppose a person is a rabid supporter of, say, the Republican party; he would give the first as his most preferred statement and probably reject all the others. His latitude of rejection to the Democratic party would therefore be 8, since there are eight statements that he rejects. A mild supporter of the Republican party might endorse the third statement and would probably reject only the sixth, seventh, and eighth statements. Therefore, his latitude of rejection to the Democratic party would be only 3.

There is one aspect of the latitude of rejection, crucial to persuasion and therefore one of the most important aspects of persuasion designs, that has not been considered by the exponents of the theory. This aspect can best be illustrated as follows: Let us assume that a person has a latitude of rejection of 6, that is, he rejects 6 statements. Since there is one statement that was marked as *most* strongly rejected, it can safely be presumed that the others are *less* strongly rejected. Among these, one will be the least rejected of all. Those statements which are least antagonistic to the position initially held by the person are those which can be more readily assimilated. But the point to be noted is that *once these statements have been assimilated, the latitude of rejection changes and the person's position on the issue is now less extreme.* Suppose that the person had an initial latitude of rejection of 6 and somehow he assimilates one statement, say that closest to his initial position. Since this statement is no longer rejected, the person is left with a latitude of rejection of 5. Assuming that the latitude of rejection is a measure of antagonism towards the object in question, then the individual is now less antagonistic than before; also there is a *new* statement which is the least rejected and may therefore be more easily assimilated than the rest. If he can be persuaded to accept this statement as well, the latitude of rejection will be reduced to 4, with a further decrease in antagonism. In other words, as each item is assimilated, our subject changes in his whole general attitude; he becomes less antagonistic toward the issue and thus more susceptible to further change. In this theoretical context, we believe we shall be much more effective with persuasions on major issues if we treat them as gradual processes and not one-shot affairs, i.e., if we proceed by a method of *successive approximations.*

There has been a controversy in the literature on attitude change about whether a person will change his viewpoint most if the persuader asks for extreme change or if he asks for only a slight change in attitude. In an early experiment, Hovland and Pritzker (1957) concluded that communications which advocate a greater amount of change from the audience's viewpoint actually produce a greater change than a communication that asks for a change of position not much different from that initially held by the audience. Similarly, Sherif and Hovland maintain that "the greater the discrepancy between the subject's own stand and the position advocated, the greater the displacement away from the subject's position (*contrast effect*). When only a small discrepancy in position exists, there will be a tendency for displacement towards his own stand (*assimilation effect*)."

The discrepancy between these two positions, in both of which the same researcher (Hovland) intervened, is explained by Sherif and Hovland (1961) in terms of the content involved—the first study was conducted with more or less neutral issues; the second concerned an emotionally charged national election. Still, the controversy has continued because many of the findings from dissonance theory have led to the hypothesis that the greater the change advocated, the larger the magnitude of change in opinion (Zimbardo, 1960). Sherif *et al.* (1965) argue about this and cite several authors, including Moscovici (1963) who states that: "This is one of the most constant hypotheses of dissonance theory: people with the most extreme attitudes change most." Sherif *et al.* challenge this position and cite evidence, such as Elbing (1962), in which more extreme stands taken in role-playing produced relatively *less* change in attitude (contrary to what would be expected from dissonance theory). Janis and Gilmore (1965) and Rosenberg (1965) performed experiments in which the size of the incentive was varied and also obtained results opposite to those derived from dissonance theory. The controversy has been put to a thorough test by Carlsmith *et al.* (1966), one of the most carefully conducted experiments on the subject. They have finally demonstrated that dissonance reduction occurs best under conditions in which the subject makes a spoken commitment rather than a written one. This finding on spoken commitment will be most crucial to our persuasion designs.

The finer subtleties of this controversy will not concern us here because we are mainly interested in obtaining *results;* surprisingly, it has been possible to design persuasions using simultaneously what appear to be antagonistic positions. At first it seemed to some of us that we were being almost heretical in joining such discrepant positions, but it is not the first time in the history of science that apparently irreconcilable theoretical positions achieved harmony in actual applications.

REACTANCE

In trying to persuade, before moving to an actual example, let us consider another point that can be most easily assimilated—we may create *reactance* or resistance to further assimilation, or if assimilation does occur, it may be rather unwillingly. Reactance is discussed by Brehm (1966): "As the pressure to comply increases, the pressure not to comply also increases and the result and effect on the individual's final response is difficult to predict. In addition, where the magnitude of reactance is less than the pressure to comply, the individual will do what is suggested but less enthusiastically than if no reactance were experienced." Thus, reactance makes further persuasion difficult. The problem then is how we can obtain step-by-step assimilation without causing reactance. If we can achieve this, successive assimilations will make the person less negative to our viewpoint, and the gradual persuasion can proceed smoothly.[1]

PERSUASION DESIGNS

We know from dissonance theory that if we can somehow, without constraint, get a person to make a free and public commitment contrary to a

[1] Ironically, it has been possible to achieve this very type of persuasion by using reactance itself, as well as cognitive dissonance. Reactance will not necessarily be used in every case, but one example will show how useful it may prove in persuading effectively.

privately held belief, there will be a tendency for the person to reduce the dissonance so caused by changing his private belief in the direction of the publicly expressed opinion. The freer he feels in making this commitment, the greater will be the tendency to change the private belief. If we can therefore get the person to freely commit himself to the least rejected item on a particular scale, he will reduce dissonance by changing his private belief on this item. All this reasoning has led to a type of persuasion that combines the different and often apparently opposed principles based on dissonance, reactance, latitude of rejection, and the Thurstone and Likert rating scales. An actual case will be useful in showing how this can be achieved.

EXAMPLE 1—PERSUASION BY SUCCESSIVE APPROXIMATION USING REACTANCE

Statement of the Problem.   A middle-aged friend of ours is married and has two children. He is not wealthy and cannot afford much insurance, but he is the mainstay of his family whom he loves very much. He leads a strenuous life trying to make ends meet, thus limiting the time he can spend with his family. A former classmate, who leads a similar life, is now having serious ulcer trouble. Nevertheless, our friend is very negative toward doctors and medicine in general and refuses to have a medical checkup. Direct attempts by both his wife and a friendly couple to persuade him to see a doctor has produced reactance and made him even more negative. He has reached the point of even shunning dental checkups, something he used to do regularly.

Design of a Persuasion.   Our goal is to help him by designing a persuasion directed at getting him to see a doctor for a checkup. Straight persuasion could not possibly be used, since this was known to be useless.

The first step is to construct a scale that reflects our friend's attitude. We shall combine the Thurstone, Likert, and Sherif and Hovland scales. It will be noted that the Hovland and Sherif scales were symmetric about a neutral, center statement. We can make a similar scale that will measure the latitude of rejection using different statements that may be more or less related to the subject at issue. We start by writing the scale values first and then fitting statements that we feel our friend would judge to be equivalent to those scale values. For example, the statement "I should see a doctor now to get a medical checkup" would probably be rated -5; whereas "I love my family very much" would rate a $+5$. It is obvious that we must know our friend well before attempting to make such a scale. Good persuasion designs must be preceded by a good diagnosis.

In the case under consideration, the final scale adopted for the persuasion design is shown in Table I.

TABLE I

Statement no.	Subject's attitude	Content
I	+5	I love my family very much.
II	−1	I spend very little time with my family.
III	−2	My health is much worse now than when I was a young man.
IV	−3	I have not provided for my family's future.
V	−4	At my age, health problems arise which left untended may turn into something serious but which can be prevented by early detection.
VI	−5	I should go now and get a medical checkup.

As will be noted from what follows, a little ingenuity had to be used so that each item, upon being assimilated, would lead directly to acceptance of the following one.

Armed with this list, we approached our friend alone. In the following dialogue *X* will be the persuader, and *Joe* will be our friend. Certain preliminary amenities will be left out as well as incidental conversation not directly related to the course of the process of persuasion. This may detract from the reality of the intercourse, but it will make the essential parts more outstanding. Comments will be made as the dialogue progresses to show the principles involved.[2]

X: You know Joe, I don't think you love your family. (This initial statement will cause considerable reactance, which Joe will reduce by affirming the opposite. This will at the same time help reduce his negative reaction to Statement II when reactance is provoked on that item. His freedom to believe he loves his family has been menaced).

Joe: Why in the world should you say such a thing? In what way do I show it?

X: Well, I don't know too well. It may be just a feeling. But tell me, in what way do you think you show your love for them?

Joe: You surprise me. Honestly! I may not be remarkable, but I think I'm as good a husband to Mary as anyone can be. We're very good friends. I try to please her in any way I can, and I think she does me. I believe I provide for her wishes as much as is in my power. I give the kids the best education I can afford, and you know very well how much I have to work to make ends meet. Do you think me selfish in that? Of course I like the work I do, but it's really my wish to see Mary and the kids as comfortable as possible that makes me work as hard as I do.

X: Yes, I really guess you're right. I'm sorry for what I said. I guess I misjudged you. I must recognize that you do spend a good deal of time with your family. (Joe, who is now rather aroused and piqued, is ready to reestablish his freedom on this point, on which X again causes reactance. This item was a −1 up to now.)

Joe: No, there you're wrong again. That's just one of my main problems. I work so hard

[2] Notes taken down immediately after interview.

that I never seem to have enough time to be with Mary and the kids. I think they miss this because I don't see them nearly as much as I used to. (By creating reactance, the persuader has succeeded in getting Joe to commit himself to the effect that he sees little of his family. Joe reduces the dissonance caused by this commitment by changing his attitude. The item which would have been scored -1 a few minutes before has now become at least $+1$. This shift has been obtained without the type of reactance feared by Brehm.)

X: I'm sorry to hear that, but you seem to be working very hard. I think you're lucky that you can afford to do it, because your health certainly seems to be a lot better now than when we all were first married. (Here X provokes further reactance. Joe will try to reestablish his freedom to think as he wishes by denying X's assertion.)

Joe: There you're wrong again. I couldn't possibly do today the things I used to do as a young man. I couldn't dream of indulging in the rough sports I used to practice, and although I do believe my health is very good, it can't be compared to what it was then. Besides, I often feel tired and low. (We have another commitment which is much nearer to our final goal. Joe must now reduce dissonance by changing his private belief about his health. Note that his latitude of rejection has now been reduced to 3; therefore his antagonism toward the final issue is less than it was at the beginning.)

X: Well, even if you recognize that your health may not be as good as it was and that perhaps in the future it may continue to decline, working as hard as you do, anything that could happen to you would be very hard on your family sentimentally but not materially. You have provided very well for their future.

Joe: No X, unfortunately I can't say that. I haven't been able to save much. There's a mortgage on the house, and I just haven't been able to carry enough insurance. You know, at our ages premiums are pretty stiff. I've provided for accident insurance, which is cheap, because accident was what I felt might be more likely to happen to me, but I have nothing to cover me in case of disability due to illness. Maybe I should have spent more on that than on other things. (The persuader has achieved a great step. He has obtained a commitment to the effect that the family is not provided for in case of illness. Joe must reduce the dissonance he experiences between this commitment and his formerly felt belief that since nothing was going to happen to him, his family would never risk having economic problems. Joe must now change this latter attitude. At this point, Item IV has now become a $+1$, automatically raising Item III to a $+2$, and Item II to a $+3$. The latitude of rejection is now down to 2.)

X: You seem to be making too much of this. After all, at our ages it's rare for anyone to have serious health problems that can't be treated once the symptoms are detected.

Joe: Don't be too sure of that. Remember Bill and his bad case of ulcers. He had been feeling upset and jittery for some time. If he had taken care of that early, he wouldn't be in such bad shape now. (The persuader is now very close to his final goal. He has so far limited his action to getting commitments from Joe in such a way that Joe feels he has done so freely and without constraint. Dissonance reduction will proceed quickly as the latitude of rejection is further reduced. Remember that if latitude of rejection is a measure of attitude, a lower score means a less negative attitude.)

X: How in the world do you expect Bill to have detected that?

Joe: Should have seen his doctor. I guess we're all fools on that score. Another man I know, who is also working very hard, recently had trouble with his coronaries. Mary's been after me for some time trying to have me get a physical checkup, but I've been stubborn. I guess it's really unfair because if anything happened to me,

Mary would have to bear the burden in the same way that Martha is now having to do with Bill, who is sick with ulcers.

X: What do you think Bill should have done?

Joe: Gone and got a checkup long ago, and I guess that's what I ought to do now. (Joe would now rank at least +1 or +2 an item that prior to this persuasion would have been marked −5. The persuader has brought about a complete change in attitude.)

There are two things to be noted: First, the persuader has obtained a complete change of attitude in about 30 minutes by getting gradual commitments and allowing time for dissonance reduction. Thus, we appear to have been correct in viewing persuasion as a gradual process and not something to be achieved by merely presenting a series of arguments (as is done with most persuasions, whether in real life or in the laboratory).

Secondly, and even more importantly, a change in attitude does not necessarily mean that there will be a change in behavior. Joe may now place a +3 opposite the statement: "I should go now and arrange to get a checkup," but this does not necessarily mean that he will actually call the doctor. As Festinger (1964) has stated, ". . . it seems clear that we cannot glibly assume a relationship between attitude change and behavior." However, according to Insko and Schopler (1967), ". . . attitudes, cognitions and behavior are not necessarily consistent, but we will assume that there is a tendency towards consistency." They further add that: "In order for any tendency toward triadic consistency to operate, it is necessary that the individual perceive the relationship between his new attitude and some behavior. Just because an individual has a new attitude towards civil rights doesn't mean that he will perceive what he can do." In a study by Linn (1965) measuring attitudes and behavior of subjects towards having a picture taken with a Negro, it was found that individuals with either positive or negative attitudes did not necessarily act in accord with these attitudes in an overt situation. Similarly, Johnson (1968) showed that smokers who had announced a decision to quit smoking endorsed fewer rationalizations than other smokers. The data were congruent with the interpretation that the dissonance of the smoker can be reduced by his belief that he will discontinue smoking in the near future—a near future that, of course, may never arrive.

In view of these findings, the persuader must not feel triumphant because he has made his friend radically change his attitude. Quite often salesmen feel baffled because a client seemed sold; yet, later the same client failed to place the order. Accordingly, the persuader must continue after he has obtained attitude change until he gets action. He must use the same type of approach if he wishes to reach the final goal.

In the case we are considering, the persuasion for action after attitude change proceeds.

X: Well, it might not be a bad idea, but where are you going to find a doctor good enough to find anything wrong with you?

Joe: Look! A checkup doesn't mean that they'll find something wrong. Very often they confirm that you are fine and let you go on as you are. Sometimes they spot some little thing, and they tell you about it. But I don't know who I'd go to. I haven't been to a doctor in a long time.

X: How does this doctor that's treating Bill strike you?

Joe: Seems all right to me, maybe I ought to call him.

X: Do you know his name?

Joe: It's something like Smithers or Smithkin—I don't remember.

X: Do you think Martha knows?

Joe: Of course! She's calling him up all the time.

X: You're right. Why don't you call Martha and get his right name and number.

Joe: All right. I'll do that.

X: You better tell Martha what it's all about. She might get scared and think you are in trouble.

Joe: You're right. I wouldn't want to add to her troubles by making her think I'm sick too. (The persuader is getting Joe further committed to action by getting him to repeat his commitment to a third party, using as an excuse the argument that he should not alarm his friend's wife.)

Joe called Martha, got the name and number, and X saw to it that Joe called the doctor then and there to make an appointment. He then asked Joe whether this news would make Mary happy. When Joe said that that is exactly what Mary had been wanting for some time, X told him to go and see Mary and make her happy by telling her of his decision (a further commitment). By getting Joe to heavily commit himself, the persuader was avoiding the phenomenon of post-decision regret (Walster and Festinger, 1964; Walster, 1964). More will be said about this subject later.

Example 1 has demonstrated one way of designing and executing a persuasion by using a given set of principles. As was indicated earlier, reactance played an important part in getting the subject to commit himself to new beliefs. It is interesting to note that in a persuasion experiment by Cox and Bauer (1964), reactance was evidently obtained. The phenomenon was not understood and was misinterpreted. The authors comment that ". . . a systematic move counter to the suggested direction is also persuasion though possibly of a 'perverse' form." The authors label this phenomenon perverse simply because it is unfamiliar and possibly because they published their article two years before Brehm published his book on reactance. As usually happens in science, the new and unusual are often labeled in derogatory terms.

There are other ways of obtaining equally free commitments without using reactance. Illustrations of this will be found in the more complex persuasion subsequently presented.[3]

[3] As this book goes to press, the writer has been made aware that someone else had been thinking along similar lines simultaneously. In "Attitude Change," Kiesler, C. A., Collins, B. E., and Miller, N. (Wiley, 1969) state (p. 301) that Sherif presents a key to overcoming resistance to persuasion. The authors state that: "Persuasion will succeed

EXAMPLE 2—PERSUASION BY ANALOGY

An interesting study by McGuire (1960, 1960a), investigating some aspects of cognitive consistency with regard to attitude change, has been very useful in designing an entirely different type of persuasion. The first McGuire paper tests a hypothesis derived from Festinger's theory of cognitive dissonance. McGuire predicted that a dissonance-increasing message would produce less change on an explicit issue than a dissonance-reducing message but that the dissonance-increasing message would produce more change on a logically *related* issue. A concrete case of this is: If we tried to persuade Joe in Example 1 by telling him to get a doctor, which is dissonance provoking, there would be little change. We would merely get reactance. However, if we could find a logically *related* issue and persuade him on that, using the same type of reasoning, there would be a greater opinion change on the main issue. This hypothesis was supported by McGuire's experiments. Actually, this technique was used in a small way when a parallel was drawn between Joe's position and Bill's. Joe was quite willing at one stage to admit that Bill should have gone to a doctor, although he was not ready to take such a step himself.

The second McGuire paper makes more explicit the type of reasoning involved in actual persuasion. Two types of persuasion methods are described. In one, McGuire assumes that the subject holds a certain belief and that this belief is based on certain premises, in the form of a syllogism. For example, in the case of our friend in the previous example, a simple syllogistic scheme would be:

- People who are not ill should not consult doctors.
- I am not ill.
- Therefore, I should not consult a doctor.

According to McGuire, since the subject is very sensitive to the conclusion, persuasion attempts at changing that would be, as we have seen, unsuccessful. However, if we were able to persuade him on one of the premises, say that ill people are not necessarily the only ones who should consult

---

when it proceeds by small steps to be successful, each persuasive attempt must be modest. Presumably, when successful, the respondent's latitude of acceptance has been broadened." Curious over having missed an important point of which he was claiming authorship, the writer contacted the authors. Dr. Norman Miller, who was responsible for that part of the text in personal communication to the writer stated that he couldn't claim to have seen it in Sherif's work, but that it seemed such a logical conclusion that he had been teaching it in his class for years. The writer is glad to be the first to point out this coincidence. This has been common in other sciences and has often led to friction. There is no room for such absurd rivalries in the social sciences. The world is too full of strife for those who are engaged in social science to embark on futile debates over who had the idea first.

doctors, he would experience cognitive dissonance because his privately held conclusion would not follow from the changed premise. He would then have to reduce dissonance by altering the conclusion.

McGuire's second procedure is even more subtle. He constructs another syllogism on an unrelated issue, but one which embodies the same reasoning. Since the subject does not have an irrationally immovable position on the conclusion related to that issue, he will accept all the reasoning involved. But this acceptance will cause dissonance when he compares the reasoning in one instance to the reasoning in the other. Thus, he will have to reduce the dissonance created by changing his conclusion on the issue for which he had, until then, held a dogmatic position.

In the rest of this chapter, we shall combine the various types of persuasion we have considered. For example, instead of using just two-premise syllogisms, as McGuire does in his several experiments, we shall use *chains* of reasoning. The chain may be of the syllogistic type in which the conclusion of each syllogism becomes a premise for the succeeding one, or the sorites type in which all intermediate conclusions are suppressed, or a combination of these. The main point is that the subject initially holds a certain attitude toward a particular object. We wish to change this attitude, but if we attack his attitude directly, we shall surely cause too much reactance, which will militate against the desired change. The attitude is presumably based on a series of reasons. According to McGuire, we can direct the persuasion toward one of the premises and then let dissonance–reduction or need for consistency lead the subject himself to change his conclusion. An alternative method would be to apply the persuasion to a related issue—one which is not so emotionally important as the one at hand. He will then maintain cognitive consistency by applying the new reasoning to the original issue. The point to note here is that commitments are obtained without causing reactance. In other words, cognitive dissonance will operate even upon the premises to which the nonemotional issue is related. Again, an example will show how this operates.

ANOTHER TYPE OF PERSUASION

Statement of the Problem.   ABC is a company manufacturing recuperated leather. The process consists of shredding leather scrap, mixing it with a binder, and then rolling it into sheets that are allowed to dry. The resultant product is of very good quality, considering uniformity of thickness, lack of flaws, savings in scrap, etc., compared to the natural product. It has advantages for making insoles of shoes because natural leather comes in greatly varying thicknesses, shapes, and so on, and therefore cannot be used efficiently. Shoe manufacturers who have been using natural leather all their lives react strongly against any attempt on the part of the salesmen who try to persuade them to use recuperated leather. They are frequently unwilling to even give it a try. It is known that those who *have* tried are very enthusiastic about the product and have obtained real economies, as well as improvement in their product quality. Yet, there are some who are absolutely adamant. Consequently, a persuasion was designed to employ against a highly resistant individual, known as C.

Client C had always resisted using synthetic fiber clothing. He had had a bad experience years before with nylon shirts, when they first appeared, and had always worn wool suits, either heavy ones in winter or light ones in summer. However, circumstances had eventually led him to switch to synthetics, and he is now delighted with wash-and-wear clothing. An important reason for the change was the appearance on the market of really high quality synthetic fabrics for men's wear.

An important point must be first elucidated. There has been a good deal of criticism directed against experiments in persuasion on the grounds that these are conducted in a laboratory setting where the audience is captive. This, it is said, differs from the real-life situation, where the audience is not captive and can leave the field. This criticism is summarized by Cohen (1964): "The picture of the effects of persuasive communications that has emerged from correlation surveys indicates that few individuals are ever affected by communications. Research using experimental techniques, on the other hand, indicates the possibility of considerable modification of attitudes through exposure to communications." Cohen cites some reasons for this difference, of which the following are deemed to be the most important: The fact that in surveys a whole program is investigated, while in experiments only one variable is studied. The fact that in the experiment the time interval between the communication and its effect is very short, something that one does not obtain in field studies. Surveys reach the subjects in natural environments, where they are subject to the influence of others.

Sherif *et al.* (1965) stated the matter even more forcefully: "When a researcher gets a subject into the laboratory or classroom, he has achieved a major triumph. He can usually assume that the individual has consented to be present and will at least take notice of what is going on. The laboratory, classroom, and formal indoctrination session, omit, therefore, the first and crucial phase of most communication situations; the communicator must secure and hold an audience for his message."

There is, however, a very effective answer to all these objections. If the laboratory is so successful in obtaining good results from persuasions, all we have to do is to conduct our persuasions in laboratory settings. In other words, instead of taking the laboratory into the field, we take the field into the laboratory. In the persuasion by successive approximations presented as

Example 1, we can assume that the conversation took place in a quiet living room with no interruptions to break the process as it was designed. That was an essential element in obtaining the desired result. In the present case our recalcitrant client must first be persuaded to come into the showroom in which we can reproduce the laboratory situation. It was to obtain precisely this first goal that a persuasion by analogy was designed.

Design of the Persuasion. The design started out not with a premise but with a conclusion which C would readily accept, i.e., the superiority of synthetic over natural fibers. (Synthetic fibers and recuperated leather were to him both artificial as opposed to natural.) The client will be persuaded to commit himself to accept the reasons for which synthetic fibers are better for suits—these being the very reasons that should make him decide in favor of recuperated leather. Since he is rather sensitive on the subject of leather, an intermediate step is introduced in which he recognizes the general superiority of synthetic over natural products. Otherwise, he might rationalize that artificial materials are acceptable for suits only but not for shoes.

After having freely made these commitments, C will experience considerable dissonance in view of his unwillingness to try recuperated leather. He will have to reduce his dissonance by at least accepting an invitation to visit the plant where the artificial leather products are made. Since the first persuasion will be at the client's place of business, it will have to be done very quickly in order to reduce the probability of interruptions. The laboratory situation can be reproduced in his place of business for brief periods of time. The actual design is given in Table II.

Armed with this analogy, the persuader (represented by X) approached the client (represented by C) and held the following conversation[4]:

X: That's a very nice suit you have on. What material is it?
C: It's Brand. They make very good clothing.
X: So I see. Is it wool?
C: No! This is the Emtex cloth made of polyester fiber. It's really very good.
X: What's so good about it apart from the good looks?
C: Well, in the first place, it's washable. It's very tough. My brother has had several suits of the same material, and they never seem to wear out. Besides, I can wear it all day, and it never looks unpressed. I'm as neat at night as when I left in the morning.
X: Well it looks like you made a very good buy. But I bet it's expensive.
C: No, really. The suit actually costs less than a lightweight woolen suit, and besides I like it much better.
X: I don't blame you. I wonder how it is that they have been able to make cloth with such good qualities at reasonable prices.
C: Actually it's the result of all the new advances in the chemical laboratory.
X: Do you think that the synthetic chemical industry is able to make the fibers in your suit to very close specifications?

[4] Notes taken down immediately after interview.

TABLE II

Original reasoning on main issue	Reasoning on logically related issue	Generalizations inverted	Reasoning on main issue
Nature produces the best products. Natural leather has been used from time immemorial. Natural leather is used by all good shoe manufacturers.	*Conclusion:* My synthetic suit is the best buy in the market. *Premises:* Synthetics are manufactured under rigid, controlled conditions, therefore: Synthetics have properties that have been built into them by special processes —something be achieved in nature, therefore: Synthetics are more even in quality than natural products.	*Premises:* Synthetic manufacturing processes allow making products under rigid controls. In general, it is easier to build in desired qualities into synthetics than to find them in nature. It is possible to obtain stable qualities in synthetics. In general, synthetics are being applied more and more. *Conclusion:* Synthetics are, in general, preferable to natural products.	*Premises:* Natural leather comes in many different thicknesses, which complicates manufacturing. Natural leather has to be taken as it comes. Natural leather is very variable in its properties.
Conclusion: Natural leather is the only product I should use.			*Conclusion:* I should at least hear what these people have to say about recuperated leather.

C: Of course. The chemical industry could never have survived if they hadn't.

X: Do you think they make their fibers as even in length and thickness as the sheep make wool?

C: Much better. Haven't you seen how the wool exporters have to use classifiers to sort out the different kinds of wool? I don't think they have that sort of thing at the plant where they made this cloth. They make it properly from the beginning. Besides, they can make these synthetics with the properties they want. They can make cheaper ones that cause piling, those little balls that form on lower quality goods, or stuff that wears better. They can make things that hardly shrink. Almost nothing at all.

X: Do you think that the fact that it is a synthetic made under rigorous control conditions has anything to do with it?

C: Of course! That's the whole *hitch.*

The reader will by now have recognized the process involved. The client, without constraint, makes commitments supporting all the premises in the analogy previously drawn. Although, until now, C has probably never made these premises explicit, doing so requires him to reduce dissonance by persuading himself of the truth of these premises. Since it is by means of these same premises that he rejected recuperated leather, he now will find himself in a state of dissonance, i.e., he is applying one set of premises to one situation but not to a very similar one. Of course, C can easily rationalize that the premises hold true for suits but not for leather; leather is different. For this reason, the persuader must immediately generalize the premises.

X: Do you think then that synthetic products can be, in general, more uniform in quality than the natural kind?
C: Yes, in most cases it's probably true.
X: Do you think that manufacturing processes make it possible to build in qualities that a natural product cannot offer?
C: Of course. Nature is always variable and modern manufacturing is very precise. At least good manufacturing.
X: You think then that synthetic products are in general displacing the natural ones?
C: It would seem so.
X: Can you remember any other cases in which this happened?
C: Well, fiberboard has displaced the wood I had in the partitions here, and plastic has displaced wood in writing materials, pens, for example.
X: Do you think that this sort of thing is on the increase?
C: Yes. There's no doubt that we are in the age of great technological progress.
X: Would you let me invite you to visit our plant where you can see for yourself how we have been able to make recuperated leather under rigorous manufacturing conditions that give uniform and controllable quality that can be as useful to you as that suit you are wearing?

In every case that *this* approach has been tried, the client has acceded to this request and a date has been made. Of course, the approach was different with different clients, depending on the preferences of each. Thus, if we want to persuade, we must make a complete diagnosis before attempting our persuasions. According to Freedman and Fraser (1966), a person who has already acceded to a small request is more likely to comply with a larger one. Thus, agreeing to visit the plant has theoretically made A more likely to accept the larger request, that is, to actually buy the material offered.

The rest of the persuasion design that was used when the client visited the showroom at the plant and was exposed to a full persuasion will not be reported, except to note that it was highly effective. In Chapter 5 a similar case of complex persuasion in a showroom will be illustrated.

EXAMPLE 3—PERSUASION USING SOCIAL PRESSURE

Asch (1952) has extensively studied the effect upon a naive subject when a group of peers incorrectly judge the length of a line, and the subject is then asked to give his own judgment. Over one-third of the subjects, who were unaware of the deception, agreed with the majority, i.e., gave clearly incorrect judgments themselves. Among those who gave *correct* responses, a large number still became confused, doubt-ridden, and in various ways tried not to appear different from the majority. Crutchfield (1955) repeated the procedure using opinions on issues instead of line judgments. In one case, the statement "Free speech being a privilege rather than a right, it is proper for a society to suspend free speech whenever it feels itself threatened" was accepted by only 19 % of the control subjects compared to 58 % of those under social pressure in the Asch paradigm.

Social pressure thus constitutes a powerfully persuasive tool, under certain conditions. For example, the persuasion must be exerted by a minimum of four persons acting in concert. According to Asch (1958), the majority effect virtually disappears when opposition is reduced to one of two persons (there is only a slight effect), but the phenomenon is maximized when there is a majority of three. Beyond that, any increase in the size of the opposing majority fails to produce any greater effect. A subsequent study by Gerard *et al.* (1968) has cast some doubt about whether more persuasion can be obtained with a larger number of persons, but the results are not presently conclusive enough to justify not accepting Asch's conclusion.

Let us see how this can be used in actual persuasion: There is a retailer who sells neckties. He has a tendency to buy conservative styles because he is very conservative himself. A market survey has shown that the zone in which he has his place of business buys all sorts of ties. He is therefore losing considerable business because of his habit of buying only what *he* likes.

The retailer is invited to see a new collection of ties and to give his advice regarding whether the collection is stylistically well-balanced. However, he is also asked to bring his buyer, the head of the men's wear department, and another person, possibly his wife. (The important thing is to have at least four people. More than that will not be necessary, as shown by Asch.)

The client, Mr. Gomez, arrives with Mrs. Gomez, Mr. Diaz, his buyer, and Mr. Perez, his Sales Manager. The salesman first shows a conservative tie. Mr. Gomez says he likes this one, but the salesman also asks each of the other persons for their opinions. This is done in order to establish a certain equality between those present, i.e., to demonstrate that Mr. Gomez' opinion is not necessarily the most important. Then a slightly less conservative tie is shown. As the salesman talks about it, he scans the faces of the group, looking for signs of approval. There may be a slight head nod on the part of one, or other signs of approval and disapproval.

Disapproval is generally shown by a slight frown, pursing the lips, etc. In some recent research on the subject of unspoken language (Wiener and Merhabian, 1968; Merhabian, 1968; Merhabian and Ferris, 1967; personal communications from R. Keckley, and J. T. Lanzetta), it has been found, for example, that positive attitudes toward a communication are frequently accompanied by a posture of leaning forward. There is still, however, much research to be conducted on the subject before findings useful to persuasions can be obtained, since apparently there are many different cues that can be used to determine whether a subject has a positive or negative attitude. In the absence of other, more definite findings on this point, the persuader has to use his own judgment to decode nonverbal messages. It is very probable that this involves cognition of behavioral units, but although the existence of this ability has been predicted from Guilford's SI model, no objective test has yet been devised. It would be very interesting if some way could be found to do research that combines the nonverbal studies cited with the measurement of behavioral abilities. For example, if the Wiener and Merhabian type of study were to take into account Social Intelligence as defined by O'Sullivan *et al.* (1965) and the research currently in progress at the Aptitudes Research Project of the University of Southern California, interesting and perhaps unexpected findings would probably result.

To return to our case of the neckties: When the salesman shows the somewhat less conservative tie, Mr. Gomez frowns slightly, while Mr. Perez, his Sales Manager, shows more interest, say by leaning forward. Then the salesman will ask Mr. Perez *first* what he thinks of that tie. Mr. Perez will of course say that he likes it. The salesman will ask "Why?" He does this for two reasons: one is to get a full commitment from Perez; the second is to gain time in which to scan the rest of the group for signs of approval. He notes a sign of approval from Mrs. Gomez, say a very slight head nod as if acquiescing to Mr. Perez' comments. As soon as Perez stops talking, the salesman turns immediately to Mrs. Gomez and asks her how she feels about that style. Since she has already acquiesced in nonverbal terms, she probably will now verbalize her approval. The salesman asks her again to give support for her opinion, and as she does so, he scans the two remaining persons. Diaz had been rather neutral until then, but he now shows signs of moving toward approval. When asked about it, he expresses a positive opinion.

We now have a majority of three verbalized, positive opinions against Mr. Gomez' nonverbalized, negative attitude. The latter is now asked for his opinion, and he will very likely go along with the majority. The salesman is not content with that, but tries to get a further commitment from him. Since Gomez has now expressed an opinion contrary to his formerly held belief, he is in a state of dissonance, which he can reduce by finding that there are certain types of clients who would buy that tie—times are changing, some people will wear "anything," and he must cater to them. The salesman tries to get the greatest possible commitment which, having been made to him and to the three others, becomes very important. All this causes Gomez to reduce dissonance by finding that the tie was not so bad after all. This procedure is repeated with every new style presented. The salesman must be very quick to find out which of the four is the first to show approval and then continue the sequence in the order in which they do so—leaving for last the person who initially showed the most disapproval.

Incidentally, this type of persuasion can be very neatly combined with the two types described earlier (persuasion by successive approximation and persuasion by analogy). The subject must, of course, be one that concerns the four persons, used as conveyers of social pressure, and not just the recipient of the persuasion. When it is practicable, the persuader presents *generally* the crucial reactance-producing remark or pertinent question and then directs his attention toward the person who he feels will give him the answer he is seeking. He then continues with the rest of the group, as previously shown.

There is an important point to be noted with respect to individual differences in susceptibility to social pressure. Festinger (1957) predicted that persons high on the California F Scale, i.e., with high intolerance for ambiguity, should easily be able to reduce dissonance (through attitude change). This has been confirmed by Harvey (1965), who found that "concrete" subjects, people quite akin to high authoritarians, changed more in the direction of a communication opposite to their viewpoint when they thought it would be made public than did the "abstract" subjects. Malof and Lott (1962) obtained similar results. In another vein, persons high in the Ethnocentrism Scale (Adorno, *et al.*, 1950), another indication of rigidity, showed more tendency to conform in an Asch-type situation than persons low in ethnocentrism. Crowne and Marlowe (1964) found that persons high in the need for approval were much more susceptible to such social pressure and would therefore agree with the majority more often than those who did not require much approval from others. Crowne and Liverant (1963) had previously shown that persons with a high need for approval, and who are affected by others, possess relatively little self-confidence, and can elicit these through their own abilities and efforts, are high conformers in an Asch-type situation.

The persuader must know all this before attempting persuasions and will therefore, in general, get opinions from these conformers *last*, unless they show approval initially. A problem may occur when the person who is a high F-scorer, intolerant of ambiguity and high in the need for approval, is the boss. The others who agree with him are always used to looking to the boss before giving an opinion, to be sure they do not contradict him. Such a type of boss is particularly liable to surround himself with ingratiators. These will tend to use opinion conformity as an ingratiation tactic (Jones, 1964). We then have the apparently difficult, but very common situation, of a high authoritarian or need-for-approval person, who is quite ready to submit to social pressure but who is surrounded with ingratiators who in turn are always ready to conform the authoritarian's opinion. The way to deal with this in a persuasion where social pressure is to be used is to seat the persons in such a way the ingratiators will not be able to see the expression on the boss' face when an opinion is required. They will therefore be forced to give their own opinion, which is possibly discrepant with the boss'. The salesman, who is able to see all the expressions, will therefore be the only one to note this discrepancy, if the boss shows a nonverbal disapproval. But by continuing the social pressure tactic, he will finally get the boss to submit to the social pressure created by the opinions of his subordinates. Often this has resulted in situations in which the boss, giving his (conforming) opinion last, does so very forcefully, even giving new reasons that his subordinates had not mentioned! In such cases we are getting high commitment from the boss, which requires him to reduce dissonance still further. The above phenomena vindicates Moscovici's statement and Zimbardo's findings that people with the most extreme attitudes also change the most, although not necessarily in the exact way posited by these two researchers.

It seems almost unnecessary to add that when persuasion by social pressure is attempted, those who show signs of disapproval must under no circumstances be allowed to verbalize their disapproval until the approvers have had their say. Otherwise, social pressure works in reverse, since there is commitment to an opposite stand, which would subsequently be much harder to change.

OTHER PRINCIPLES OF PERSUASION DESIGN

COMBINED PERSUASIONS

The examples presented so far represent only simple cases of persuasion. Much more elaborate and effective designs have been made, for example, to aid in the presentation of new products. One such design for reestablishing confidence in business conditions and therefore increasing the tendency to buy in critical times has been reported by Zimbardo and Ebbesen (1969). This situation also includes the use of the successive approximation method for inoculating against counterpersuasion, which is an elaboration of the method of successive approximations previously described. Before giving a description of an even more complex persuasion, it is necessary to introduce additional basic concepts that make possible the most effective designs.

COMPLYING WITH SMALL REQUESTS

Brief reference has already been made to a finding by Freedman and Fraser (1966), which states that complying with a small request makes a person much more prone to comply later with a larger one. This phenomenon is extremely useful in persuasion. In the authors' original experiment, housewives were contacted by telephone, simulating a market research organization, and asked to give brief information on a product they were using. Later, they were again contacted and asked whether they would allow several men to enter their homes and make a detailed search (letting them go through cupboards, etc.) of all the products they used. All of those who refused to comply with the first request, also refused to comply with the second. Of those who assented to the first request, 53% let the men come to their houses. Only 22% of the control group—women who had not been previously contacted—agreed to such a preposterous suggestion. Thus, compliance with an important request is made much more likely if the individual has already complied with a smaller request in the same area. A further implication is that such compliance predisposes him to comply with an even larger request. In the same way that the method of successive approximations was used for reducing the latitude of rejection, successive approximations can be used to obtain compliance with increasingly larger requests. It is quite conceivable that if the second request Freedman and Fraser made to the housewives had been less preposterous, there would have been an even higher degree of compliance. The second request was to have 5 or 6 men come in and have full freedom of the house in order to classify all the household products used. If the second request had been to have an interviewer go to the house and ask questions and perhaps see the general layout of the house, it is quite probable that a greater percentage would have allowed it. *Then*, if the accepting housewives had been asked to have the more thorough survey made, they would probably have complied in larger numbers with this unusual request.

This technique is often used in interviewing. If, in a difficult interview, one begins by asking the person to tell the *main* problem he has, the individual will likely demur. But, if the problem is approached by successive approximations, in which the person is requested to tell a little more each time with positive reinforcement given for having revealed that much, he will probably describe his problem in full.

A start has been made in designing persuasions by means of successive requests. In one case, the first request was simply to let the salesman put up a small sign in the client's store advertising an aspect of a certain product. Nearly all the clients agreed to do so. The second request, to visit the salesman's headquarters, was accepted by 90% of those who had put up the sign. Furthermore, *all* those who went to the place of business were willing to look at the samples the salesman had to offer. Finally, when asked to buy, over 60% of those who had previously refused to buy, when approached by conventional means, now agreed to purchase the goods. This difference cannot be solely attributed to the sequence of complying with increasingly larger favors, since special persuasion techniques of the type described here were used in the final sale; however the favor-compliance sequence obviously helped. At least, a large number of clients who had not been previously willing to visit the salesman's place of business did so after complying with the small request (having the sign set up).

DISTRACTION

Allyn and Festinger (1961) reported an experiment in which it was shown that when people were forewarned regarding the content of a persuasive communication arguing *against* a position they held strongly, they tended to reject the speaker and were less subject to persuasion than if they had not been forewarned. The original explanation given for this result was that forewarned persons might be in a better position to marshall their defenses against the persuasive communications. Another explanation offered was that since the subjects who were not forewarned had also been given another task to do while listening to the speaker, they were possibly not in a position to present sub-vocal arguments against the speaker's stand and would therefore be more susceptible to persuasion. To test this possibility, Festinger and Maccoby (1964) had students see a film presenting a persuasion opposite to their stand on an issue. Another group of students heard the same persuasive sound track, but instead of seeing the original film, they saw a very funny film of the same duration. They heard the sound track present an argument against an opinion they held, which had nothing to do with what they were seeing on the screen. Those who saw the distracting film showed a significantly greater change in attitude, thus indicating the importance of sub-vocal arguments in resisting persuasion.

Based on this evidence, most of our persuasion designs start with distractions, and the client is not forewarned. He is invited into the showroom, and the conversation begins with a topic quite removed from what he would have expected. The persuader must plan the situation so that the distraction will eventually lead smoothly and effortlessly into the main subject. In this way, the client will be fully involved in the latter without being aware of it.

In a more recent reexamination of the distraction hypothesis, Haaland and Venkatesan (1968) examined the possibility suggested by McGuire that a learning-theory approach to the problem of distraction would lead to opposite results from those found by Festinger and Maccoby. Unfortunately, the replication was done using different themes. The Festinger–Maccoby experiment used attitudes toward fraternities, whereas Haaland and Venkatesan tried to persuade on the subject of reducing the voting age. It is possible that the difference in results may be due to a greater or a lesser degree of involvement on the part of the subjects. Another clue to the meaning of the difference between the results, one which proves useful for the design of persuasion, is given by the latter authors. They state that to the extent that persuasion involves *learning*, factors such as distraction should *inhibit* attitude change.

A lesson derived from this is that distraction should probably be used only at the beginning of the persuasion or when introducing each new theme, particularly if the persuasion involves learning new material, as is often the case. Baron and Miller (1969) have found that distraction is effective only in some cases and is related to source credibility, a reasoning not elaborated on here. However, in some cases of actual practice, there is little conflict between apparently irreconcilable findings. In the design of persuasion, it is best, following Festinger and Maccoby, to start with a distraction. Then, lead the subject to the persuasive material, information, etc., *without distraction*, using reactance, dissonance, and reinforcement theory.

EFFECTS OF EATING AND DRINKING

Janis, Kaye, and Kirschner (1965) report evidence that eating a free food while reading a persuasive communication facilitates a change in attitude. For this reason, the distribution of food and drink has been included in most persuasion designs. However, in a later study, Dabbs and Janis (1965) concluded that the consumption of food induces only a momentary compliance toward the donor. It is strongest at the time the food is being consumed, but it apparently drops in effectiveness after the food has been consumed. There is no contradiction here. Because of the reinforcing effect noted, the person being persuaded is given food at the start of the persuasion and then again when positive responses have been made. This food acts as a reinforcer, but it must be handled very tactfully.

LANGUAGE USAGE

With the exception of some general advice on the use of "effective selling words," derived from practice and found in books on salesmanship, very little has been done in the research of what is the best use of language for creating effective persuasions. It is quite possible that some conflicting findings derived from persuasion experiments may be due to differences in the language used. One of the few highly useful findings we have is that of Kanouse and Abelson (1967) who conclude that certain types of verbs and objects go well together. If the correct combination is chosen in a persuasive statement, it will be more effective in changing attitude. Verbs, for example, can be either *manifest* or *subjective, positive* or *negative*. Objects, on the other hand, can be *concrete* or *abstract*.

Manifest verbs. Those that express a relation which is directly observable and relatively delimited in time. Examples are: buy, sell, persuade, travel, report, break, build, destroy, produce, denounce, kill, and cure. These are all things that can more or less be observed and that, in general, the action represented has a beginning and an end.

Subjective verbs. Verbs that express an orientation of a person toward an object or another person or group of persons, which is difficult to observe directly and which is relatively enduring. Examples are: love, hate, fear, trust, admire, and covet. These are things that we cannot directly observe. We cannot observe someone's love, hate, or admiration, although we can see the *effects* these produce. For example, we can see the person who hates, strike someone. To strike is a manifest verb, but hating is really subjective because we are able to infer that hate exists from the act of the hater.

Positive and negative verbs. Both manifest and subjective verbs can be sub-classed as positive and negative. For example, among manifest verbs, buy, build, produce, and cure are considered positive verbs in the sense that they represent something positive or constructive. On the other hand, destroy, denounce, and kill are negative verbs. Among subjective verbs, love, trust, and admire are positive verbs; whereas hate, fear, and distrust are negative.

Concrete objects. Verbs often refer to objects which can be classed into concrete and abstract. Concrete objects are buildings, sparrow-hawks, india ink, chairs, and anything else that can be easily identified.

Abstract objects. These are less well-defined and refer generally to classes of objects rather than to the objects themselves. Typical abstract objects are sources of air pollution, food destroying vermin, figure-preserving foods, liberty-loving citizens.

Kanouse and Abelson (1967) found overwhelming evidence to prove that a communication that employs a positive manifest verb together with a concrete object is much more persuasive than the use of an abstract object. Similarly, if the verb is subjective and negative, the communication is much more persuasive if the object is abstract than if it is concrete. An example of each combination will illustrate these findings.

1. *Positive manifest verb with concrete object.* Shirts are stronger and wear better if the main seams are sewn with six-stitch machines than with four-stitch machines.
2. *Positive manifest verb with abstract object.* Shirts are stronger and wear better if they are put together by more efficient methods.
3. *Positive subjective verb with concrete object.* The fear of being generally considered a sloppy person is reduced by using shirts with six-stitch seams than if the four-stitch seams are used.
4. *Negative subjective with abstract object.* The fear of being generally considered a sloppy person is reduced by using clothes that are assembled by more efficient methods.

Perhaps the reader will get the feeling that Statement 1 is much more persuasive than Statement 2. Similarly, he may feel that Statement 4 is more convincing than Statement 3. If he is not fully convinced, he should give this a trial the next time he wishes to persuade someone. Perhaps, it can be recalled how often someone tries to persuade us of pending but undefined danger (subjective verb) and tries to do so by supporting his stand with a lot of concrete evidence. This seldom produces good effects. On the other hand, if generalities are used, they may make us much more prone to believe that the danger is real. A little thought about the type of argument used in persuasion with regard to real or imagined internal or external dangers used by effective demagogues will easily show how often this kind of language manipulation is used.

We have incorporated this finding into the design of persuasions. However, it often happens that the conversation with the client takes an unexpected turn. In such cases, those persuaders who are high in cognition and divergent production of semantic units, classes, and relations will have a decided advantage over those less gifted in these mental abilities.

CURIOSITY

The subject of curiosity and exploratory behavior—often called *purposeless* behavior—as a motivational factor has received considerable, recent attention. For example, Harlow (1950) found that monkeys investigated and manipulated puzzles in the absence of any motive other than what might be termed curiosity. Berlyne (1957), experimenting with humans, found that persons devoted more time to looking at strange and unfamiliar pictures (a bird with a head at each end) than at normal ones. The motive of curiosity has often been used by astute salesmen. When showing a set of samples, they will leave a few aside, as if they were not to be shown to the client. The client asks what they are, and the salesman says that those are samples that he just simply doesn't think the client will care for. The latter in many cases insists on seeing them. After looking at them and hearing the salesman repeat that he does not believe they are for him, the client experiences reactance, which provokes him to say he thinks they *are* good for him. The salesman has thus obtained a commitment from the client. This commitment reduces the negative feeling the client might have initially had against the goods in the first place. He reduces the dissonance created by actually changing his private belief. It can be seen that in an intuitive way, the motive of curiosity was being used at least in the beginning. Obviously, the rest of the process is easily explained in *terms of social findings*.

COMMENT ON THE USEFULNESS OF SOCIAL SCIENCE FINDINGS

The confirmation that this strategy is solidly based on social science findings may make some wonder why it is necessary to bother about social science research at all, if some people arrive at the right results through intuition. There are several replies to this. One is stated by Carpenter and Haddan (1964), in discussing the application of social science findings to education: "An operating rule that is found in a well-developed discipline, and which is carefully derived from adequate knowledge, is more useful than a rule which is not so soundly based." Adequate knowledge may confirm that a procedure based on trial and error is sound. This, however, is no excuse for continuing to use trial and error when there are research findings available that allow us to design methods derived from sound scientific knowledge. A second reason for so doing is that by trial and error and astuteness, a few people (some experienced salesmen) may be able to arrive at such techniques as manipulating curiosity. However, with well-designed, scientifically based methods, the processes are made available to others besides the gifted few. If, for example, we had to rely only on intuition equal to Edison's to make electric lamps, there would be very few of them available. Fortunately, methods were devised whereby many people could acquire the knowledge. Electric lamps have therefore become available to all.

A third reason for using scientific findings in design is that although an astute salesman may have discovered the idea described above, it would never have occurred to him to design persuasion by successive approximations combined with persuasions by analogy, using social pressure, the approval motive, etc. The writer has had ample opportunity to show these methods to social scientists and business men in many countries of North and South America. In all cases, there is complete surprise that these results could have been achieved. Evidently intuition and inspiration alone cannot do the full job. It is necessary that these ideas be communicated to others, with different backgrounds, who can apply more ingenuity and eventually design even better persuasions.

5

The object of all science, whether natural science or psychology, is to coordinate our experiences and to bring them into a logical system.

Einstein

the design of

complex persuasion

It is intriguing to note that Albert Einstein refers to psychology in the very first paragraph of "The Meaning of Relativity" (1950), which deals with a unifying interpretation of the physical world. Psychology, however, in trying to achieve unity, has generally created more division than coordination. A myriad of different "theories," dealing with any number of given fields, are constantly being published.[1] These books help to demonstrate the antagonistic, and sometimes virtually irreconcilable, positions held by the different proponents of those various theories. Insko, for example, gives an evaluation at the end of his presentation of each theory. In these evaluations, the merits of each theory are weighed against those of the theories proposed by others. For example, he says that Sherif and Hovland's Assimilation-Contrast theory is not a serious contender in the field of attitude change. (All this is, of course, presented at a strictly theoretical level.) La Fave (1969), in an interesting paper, reaches the conclusion that all different types of conflict can be reduced

---

[1] Typical of such books are "Theories of Personality" by Hall and Lindzey (1970), "Theories of Attitude Change" by Insko (1967), and "The Cognitive Consistency Theories" by Abelson *et al.* (1968).

110

to one, which varies only in degree, and that consistency theories, which underlie attitude change, could also be reduced to a single type.

In Chapter 4, however, we saw how material from the Sherif-Hovland theory could be linked with findings derived from the rival Festinger cognitive-dissonance theory to construct a useful application-persuasion by successive approximations. It is our contention that the coordination of all our knowledge and experience "in order to bring them into a logical system" will be achieved only when social science findings from all different areas are combined in practical applications, like the one described in Chapter 4. In that instance, there was no rivalry which made one theory a better contender than another.[2]

DESIGNS BASED ON INTEGRATED THEORIES

This chapter will describe persuasions based on combinations of various theories and findings. Eventually, it is to be hoped that as more and more findings are integrated into the design of effective solutions—for not only persuasion difficulties but other social problems as well, a comprehensive social science theory will emerge. For now, however, we shall be concerned only with *complex persuasions:* a person's attitude when results cannot be achieved by the simpler processes described in the preceding chapter.

Sometimes a person's negative stand on any subject may be a virtual fixation because of past frustrations. In other cases, it may be the result of ignorance or habits acquired over the years. When we encounter one of these complex situations, it will be very difficult to achieve persuasions by merely using successive approximations, persuasion by analogy, social pressure, or the other simple devices. It will be necessary to combine all of these, as well as findings derived from other sources, in order to devise a complex persuasion design. Many of these have already been designed, but generally, it takes time to prepare one because it requires careful diagnosis of the subject, his motivations at the moment, the situation involved, the problems he faces, his relations with the person doing the persuading, and so on. This situation occurs very frequently in salesmanship. A client may be in a serious approach-avoidance conflict with respect to some goods. He may like the manufacturer but dislike the price. He may consider the goods to be of good quality but unwilling to meet the payment terms. He may believe that the supplier gives very good service but is unreliable in his deliveries. He may feel that he gets many material advantages but that he is being dealt with in an overbearing

[2] Similarly, persuasion by analogy combined McGuire's inoculation theory with the dissonance hypothesis.

manner. Things in general are very complex. There is a great tendency to talk price, but as we have seen earlier, talking of money may be merely a symptom of dissonance-reduction, or it may be a rationalization resulting from an approach-avoidance situation.

Two cases will be presented, both taken from sales situations. There is a particular reason why the material on persuasion has been limited in this way: Complex persuasion designs tend to be expensive. Since all of the research reported in this book has been conducted with no financial assistance, it has been necessary to rely on commercial and industrial organizations who have been willing to absorb the expense of designing and staging these designs. As the work progressed and success followed success, the companies involved became more and more willing to invest in these designs; it was shown that these designs generally cost a fraction of 1.0% of the sales price of the goods involved. Thus, it has not been difficult to interest such companies in our methods.

The two cases involve very different situations: One concerns raising the prestige of goods that had become discredited because of several factors (most of which had already been corrected). The second involves the introduction of a new, expensive line of products by a company establishing operations in a market in which it was totally unknown. Both were considered extremely difficult problems—in one case because the existing image was felt to be so impoverished that it would require years to effect a favorable change and in the other case because there was simply no image at all, with the added disadvantage of entering a market against long-entrenched competition. Before going into the details of each of these persuasions, it is necessary to reiterate some material previously presented.

THE RETICULAR FORMATION

In Chapter 3 reference was made to the reticular formation. Recall that the reticulated system at the base of the brain determines the degree of arousal in which a person may find himself at any particular time. When we feel drowsy, the reticular formation is only slightly activated; however, as it becomes more and more activated, we become increasingly alert. We also showed that for different tasks, different levels of arousal are required. This is the reason why drafting rooms are generally quiet places, whereas stock exchanges give an impression of bedlam. The persons working at these different tasks are each most effective working at his optimum level of arousal, which may vary greatly from one situation to another. Too high a level of arousal may become obnoxious and reduce efficiency. Too low a level may lead to a damaging decrease in alertness.

The most notable quality of the reticular formation is that it keeps a person aroused at a given level not because the person receives more or less interesting or alerting stimuli but because of *changes* in stimuli. If we hear a fiery orator, we may feel tremendously inspired for the first few minutes, but after an hour of fiery oratory, our minds begin to wander. If our orator changes his tone to a more conversational style, however, we are immediately aroused. Soldiers in the battlefield have been able to sleep soundly through the roar of cannon and exploding shells, yet awaken suddenly when the firing suddenly ceases. In this case, the roar had become commonplace and the reticular formation had adjusted to it, making the soldier drowsy and finally driving him to deep sleep. But a change in the noise situation brings an arousal of the reticular formation, which immediately awakens the sleeping man. The same holds true even with things we like very much. We may go to a museum to admire a Rembrandt. We may even sit and admire it for quite a long time. But if we wander through the museum and see 50 Rembrandts, we may become so weary that when we encounter one of his greatest masterpieces, we may glance at it almost carelessly. Good playwrights, movie directors, theater and ballet directors have a sort of intuitive understanding of this phenomenon. They do not run five extremely funny scenes together. The scenes, alternate from light to dark, from funny to pathetic, sad to ironic to humorous, etc. This uncanny ability of Shakespeare, Moliere, Mozart, Beethoven and many others lies precisely in their perfect sense of timing— knowing when we need a change from funny to serious, or from major to minor.

The persuasions described in the previous chapters were too brief for us to be concerned about the phenomenon of reticular formation. However, a complex persuasion cannot be done in a few minutes. Therefore, if we want the subject's undivided attention for the duration of the persuasion, which may last from one to several hours, it is imperative that we keep his reticular formation activated to the optimum level at every instant during the persuasion. Otherwise, it is quite possible that his mind will begin to wander, and what we have planned will be lost. Fortunately, there are innumerable resources that can be used in order to achieve the aim of holding a persons' undivided attention. We must, however, be careful not to create so many changes that the clients are left dumbfounded (as occurred in some of our earlier persuasion designs). It is a matter of experience and a little practice. The creation of the activating changes should be entrusted to those who are high in the areas of divergent production and the evaluation of figural semantic and behavioral systems and transformations. All this will be explained in the examples which follow.

The reader is warned, however, not to copy the examples presented. He may use his ingenuity in creating his own designs made to fit circumstances that may be quite different from those described here. There are innumerable things he can manipulate—lighting intensity, position of the persuader, voices, and so forth. In addition, adjuncts may be used, such as charts, movies and models. The choice of factors to be manipulated depends upon the problem involved and the preferences of the persuader.

A PERSUASION DESIGNED TO IMPROVE
A DAMAGED PRODUCT IMAGE

XYZ is a large textile organization operating in a South American country. It has a very good reputation for the quality of goods it makes and for its general responsibility as a firm. The men in its Sales Department are highly trained in the application of social science technology to executing persuasions because most of them have been selected by means of the methods described in Chapter 2. They are therefore very high in cognition, divergent production, and evaluation of semantic and behavioral areas. Most of the members of the department score low on the California F Scale and are low on the Crowne and Marlowe MC Scale.

The General Situation.   One year ago, XYZ decided to introduce a new line of goods in which it had had no prior experience. At the same time that it sold the goods, it launched an advertising campaign designed to give a high-quality image to its new line (referred to here as "Jewel"). Unfortunately, the defects had not been completely removed from Jewel, and a sizable quantity of goods was delivered that turned out to be inferior in several ways. Public reaction was negative; retailers were especially annoyed. Jewel's image suffered accordingly; thus the situation for the 1969 season looked bleak. However, following the initial promotion program, even larger quantities of these goods had already been put into production for the next two years. Comparatively speaking, production for the first year was 40, with a figure of 90 planned for the second year (100 would be considered standard). After that time, market reactions would determine the future quantities to be put into production.

The Immediate Situation.   Since 20 of the previous year's 40 goods had remained unsold or were returned by clients and 90 more were becoming available from current production, the department involved had a real problem: How can we sell 110 this year when we sold only 20 last year to clients who are saying that they had a lot of trouble moving the merchandise? Most of the defects had already been eliminated from the new production, but the problem was how to convince the clients that this year they would encounter none of the problems they had experienced the year before.

Definition of the Problem.   The first step was to define the problem. This was done in a problem-solving conference with the salesmen, technical personnel, advertising personnel and others involved. There it was decided that the problem was not merely to sell 110, since a simple solution to that problem would be to lower the price until sales increased. Since these were quality goods, and much money had been spent in creating an image, merely selling the year's supply was not enough—it was a matter of ensuring continuity. Eventually, the group decided that the real problem was: How can we sell these 110, while improving the image to such an extent that it will aid sales of the same goods in future years?

Diagnosis. Once the statement of the problem was agreed upon, a full diagnosis of the causes of the poor image was initiated. It was immediately seen that the causes could be divided into two general categories, and then each subdivided.

1. *Causes due to XYZ*
   - Defects that have been corrected.
   - Defects that have not been corrected but can be corrected by immediate action.
   - Defects that have not been corrected but can soon be corrected.
   - Defects that have not been corrected and for which no correction is expected.

2. *Causes outside of XYZ's control*
   With these classifications in mind, a list of 17 causes due to XYZ was compiled, and these were then classed in the established categories. Of the 17, 12 were in the first or second categories, and only 1 was placed in the last category. This was done as an honest appraisal of the situation in order to see what could be done technically. The data were posted on the blackboard and appropriately labeled. Next to each objection, an approved action was written. An example, with a short comment where necessary, is given in Table I.

   Table I was complemented by Table II which outlined in the same manner the causes *outside* XYZ's control.

The Persuasion Design Process. Once these lists were prepared, the general persuasion design was then determined. Since most clients were expected to come to the showroom in a rather negative (if not actually irate) mood, it was decided that the persuasion should start with a distraction (Festinger and Maccoby, 1964). This distraction would also serve as an element in persuasion by analogy. The main point here was to prove that a new line cannot be put on the market without any flaws and that it takes time to produce a high-quality product. It was also deemed necessary to stress that XYZ had the capacity to eventually market such a product. The other persuasions were delegated out to smaller teams of salesmen. Each would decide whether

TABLE I

Objections	Class	Comment and proposed solution
1. Competition with other depts. of XYZ (Salesmen of other depts. of XYZ were telling clients to buy their goods and not Jewel.)	B	Present persuasion when finished to salesmen of other depts.
2. Lot sales (This style of goods had to be sold by lots instead of by the yard. Lots varied in yardage and clients complained they did not know how much they were buying.)	B	Improve conversion from lots to yards. Standardize lots as much as possible.
3. Edges unmarked (Product was not identified as Jewel.)	B	Corrected in about 70% of new line, but work into the persuasion.
4. Failures not identified (Identified flaws entitle clients to receive rebates.)	A	All flaws now identified.
5. Great number of defects	A	Corrected 98%. Persuasion.
6. Poor appearance when put on sales racks	B	Train in how to place on racks and include in persuasion.
7. Difficulties in sewing	B	Train in how to sew. Persuasion.
8. Summer collection too heavy in weight	B	Has been lightened, but show in persuasion that weight is not definer of insulation.
9. Cloth shifts while cutting	B	Study original source and work into persuasion if possible.
10. Competition with other depts. on credit availability (Other Salesmen would rush to sell their wares and so tie up all the available client's credit.)	B	Work into persuasion with other salesmen.
11. Excessive shrinkage	B	Problem solved. Persuasion.
12. Buyers want to use Jewel trademark (It was impossible at this time to allow all buyers to use the "Jewel" trademark.)	C	Persuasion.
13. Very rough "touch" of last year's printed goods	B	Almost fully corrected. Compare new production with last year's. Persuasion.
14. Uneven edges	B	Greatly improved in most cases. Persuasion.
15. Print collection very limited compared to last year's, which although small was very varied	C	Persuasion.
16. Unbalanced collection (Too many designs and colors of one style, while others lacking.)	D	Persuasion.
17. Uninformative advertising (Advertising had merely stressed quality but did not contain essential technical data.)	C	Persuasion.

TABLE II

Cause	Action to be taken
1. Client's general ignorance of this type of goods	Instruction and persuasion
2. Client's unaccustomed to buying by lots	Persuasion
3. World-wide ignorance of the use of this material for men's wear	Persuasion
4. Confusion of this material with similar goods made with lower grade fibers	Persuasion

analogy, successive approximations, or combinations of these or others would be used.

Finally, when each team had developed its solution to a particular problem, a general meeting was called, and the different parts joined together with particular reference to the functions of reticular formation, i.e., everyone was alert to see that the persuasion as a whole did not become monotonous. However, considerable leeway was to be allowed each individual salesman in the order of presentation of the arguments, depending on the client's previous experience. Not all clients had been troubled with the 17 objections listed, and not everyone had found them equally important. It was expected that sometimes the buyer would broach a certain subject; if not, the salesman would, provided it was pertinent for that client. This meant that all props, slides and other persuasion aids, had to often be presented in quite different order. To illustrate one order: A salesman would work as an assistant to a colleague. Once he saw which course the persuasion was taking, he would place the corresponding slides in the projector, even before being asked to do so. This procedure worked beautifully after a few rehearsals.

The Final Persuasion.   The client was first invited to visit the showroom. In order for social pressure to be effectively employed, he was asked to bring along at least three other persons. Figure 5.1 shows a plan of the showroom as prepared for this persuasion. In this plan, C, J, I, and K are curtains that ran from floor to ceiling. The whole decor was deliberately done in a rather dull tan pastel. The only visible props were a 9 ft long table at E and 4 chairs with backs to the wall for the client, a chair in front for the salesman, and a raised platform at G.

The client and his guests were seated in the appropriate chairs. In the following dialogue, which was recorded as soon as possible from a real-life case, the clients will be called: Abe, the owner and usually the man to make the final decision (a man rather high in social approval); Bill, the buyer; Cab, the cutter; and Dan, the head of the piece-goods sales department. This client had a Department store with its own shops where garments are manufactured for in-house sales, as well as for others. The salesman will be called Sam. It

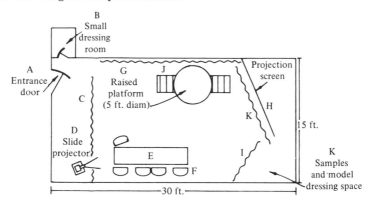

FIG. 5.1. Schematic representation of room prepared for application of persuasion design.

is quite evident from their looks that the clients are feeling uncomfortable. They have had tiffs with the company before, but nothing like what is being expected now. It is very probable that not only will they not buy but that they will wish to return what they have left of last year's goods. (This was the actual pre-announced position in the case of several clients).

SAM: (After the clients have taken their seats). Look, before we even start talking, I would like to ask you if you know what this is. (Slide showing a small group of sequoia seedlings just emerging in a flower pot held in a man's hand. Note that the screen was 10′ × 12′ and only 15 ft away from the clients. The plants look immense, but it is obvious that they are being held in a man's hand. Of course, curtain K had been runoff to the client's right field of view so the screen behind becomes visible, and all other lights were turned off immediately so that the image was sharp and bright.)

BILL: I've no idea. It looks like little plants.

ABE: What are they, weeds or flowers?

SAM: They are sequoias. You may have heard of the California Redwoods. They start out like this and eventually grow into this. (Slide of giant sequoia with three adults standing in front to give the correct size perspective.) These trees are among the oldest living things. It takes thousands of years to reach this stage, and there are some that are even older and larger.

ABE: I remember seeing a picture of one that has a tunnel cut in it so that a car can drive right through the trunk.

SAM: That one must be a lot older than this one. Well, do you know what this is? (Black and white slide of the Wright brothers' first flight. The previous slides were in brilliant color. This one is in black and white to provide variety in keeping with the functions of reticular formation. Even seeing many beautiful color slides wearies the mind, i.e., deactivates the reticular formation.)

ABE: That looks like one of the very earliest planes.

SAM: It is. As a matter of fact, it is the Wright brothers' first plane. Well now do you know what this is? (Black and white slide of lunar module.)

ABE: That's the thing that reached the moon.

SAM: Very good! Did you ever stop to think that it took only 60 years from the first flight at Kitty Hawk to Armstrong and Aldrin?

ABE: You know that's amazing. To think that my father is 70. All this has been done right in his own lifetime.

SAM: It really sounds incredible. It took man a lot less time to reach the moon than for a sequoia plant to grow into a great tree. Tell me, do you think that in general things appear full-blown or do they take time?

ABE: No, naturally, everything takes time.

SAM: How long have you been in business?

ABE: Fifteen years.

SAM: Was your place of business always as up-to-date in everything as it is today?

ABE: No, by no means. We were a little place when we opened. We didn't have too much credit with our suppliers, so we couldn't stock anywhere near the variety of goods we now have.

CAB: You didn't have any manufacturing then. It was only 8 years ago that you asked me to go to work for you, and remember it took quite a while to get that shop going.

DAN: Yes, and the Piece-Goods Department was off in a corner. When you bought the property next door, we were able to really expand.

ABE: That's right. And then we redecorated things very nicely. You know our place Sam! You know how much it's changed in several years. Even in the last four years we have grown a lot.

SAM: Yes, I certainly do, and I congratulate you. You've done a fine job. It's meant a lot of work for all of you. But tell me, do you think the quality of the yard goods we sold you 15 years ago was similar to what we have been delivering lately?

ABE: No! Not by any means! You have improved a lot. Some of that earlier stuff had more holes than cloth. We used to call some of if "swiss cheese cloth."

SAM: What do you think brought about this improvement in the quality of our products?

ABE: Well, I think you are a very responsible company. You have very good technical people. They keep up-to-date with what's going abroad all the time. Time and again I call for someone and find that he's off to Europe or the United States or somewhere. I suppose they have some fun when they are away, but you are always bringing in new things.

SAM: In our ability to change from something of doubtful quality to something of excellent quality, would you compare us to the sequoia or to the advance of flight to the moon?

ABE: No, you certainly aren't sequoias. You move very fast. I'd say you are more like these moon projects.

SAM: Do you believe then that we have the capacity and willingness to improve things if something goes wrong?

ABE: Of course! I've always had faith in you. (Cab, the cutter is frowning, while Dan, the Head of Sales is nodding approval.)

SAM: What about you Dan, do you think we are able to improve when we want to?

DAN: Definitely. There's no comparing some of the really high quality goods you have with some of the stuff you made even ten years ago.

SAM: What about you Bill?

BILL: Yes, you certainly are a company that keeps on their toes. I'd say that you are one of the fastest in improving when something goes wrong.

SAM: How do you feel about this Cab?

CAB: Well . . . I guess so. I guess you have fixed lots of things in the past.

SAM: Well let's talk about Jewel. Has Jewel been giving you trouble?
ABE: CAB, BILL, and DAN (in chorus)—Trouble! You don't know. Sure has! Oh my!
SAM: All right. Don't all jump on me at once. Suppose we take things one at a time. Can you mention one problem?

Time out: Sam has done several things so far. In the first place, he has created a distraction. This was not just "any" distraction, however, but one that could be directly linked with a persuasion by analogy.[3] In other words, by talking about sequoias, ancient planes, and lunar modules, he was leading directly to the notion that it takes time to produce anything and that the time required differs depending on the thing produced and who produces it.

Abe's state of dissonance can be characterized by two statements.

- I came here to complain very strongly about the trouble this merchandise has caused us and to refuse to buy any more, as well as to tell them what a poor outfit they are.
- I have publicly stated that it takes time to get things straight, that it took me some time before I achieved my present good status, and besides that XYZ has always made excellent goods.

Abe can now reduce his dissonance by changing his private cognition, that is, the first statement, thereby reducing his antagonism. Were we able to measure his latitude of rejection toward XYZ and toward Jewel, we would find that they had started to diminish. Furthermore, remember that Sam has obtained a further commitment, from *other* members of the group, to the effect that XYZ has improved a lot in its line of goods in general. This commitment prepares the ground for the general acceptance of the idea that XYZ may also be quite capable of improving Jewel. It should be noted that in obtaining the commitment to the notion that XYZ had actually improved, Sam resorted to the use of social pressure. The men who had faced the greatest difficulties with Jewel were those least apt to commit themselves in such a direction. Their thoughts were directed mainly towards their current problems. Abe, however, having more of an overall picture of his relations with XYZ, was quite willing to admit that the company had improved over the years. Dan was also nodding approval because he had piece goods sales to deal with, and other XYZ products meant much more to him in terms of volume of sales than Jewel did. Cab, the cutter, who was having the greatest trouble with Jewel but who also handled other XYZ lines, eventually assented.

A careful reading reveals that except for direct statements regarding

---

[3] In some cases a third analogy was introduced: the picture of a young colt was shown on the screen followed by that of several horses at the finish of a race. The client was asked how long it took for that little colt to grow into such a fine race horse. This was used particularly with racing fans. Everyone recognized that the colt had a hard time even standing on its legs at first and couldn't possibly win such a race. However, given adequate time and competent training, in two years a winner might result.

trees, planes, and a compliment to the client, the whole persuasion was done by means of questions leading to commitments. Had the salesman fallen into the trap of using direct persuasions, he would have caused reactance. Let us return now to Sam's request for just one specific complaint.

ABE:	I can mention one that's been giving us no end of trouble. One of the worst problems is the number of holes in the cloth. Besides, most of the holes are not identified by you, so that we can't take advantage of the discounts you give for such flaws.
SAM:	Am I to understand then that this has caused trouble with your clients?
BILL:	It sure has! You must remember that when a woman comes into the store and asks to see piece goods, the salesman usually unrolls about two or three yards. Imagine the customer's impression when she sees a huge hole right in the middle of the piece. She then asks to see another, and the same thing happens. Usually her reactions are so negative that she not only refuses to buy that material, which I think is quite natural, but she often just walks out of the store and we lose a sale and maybe even a customer.
CAB:	That's your problem Bill. Mine is different but just as bad. The client doesn't see the holes, but I do. I waste an awful lot of time trying to fit the useable parts. Sometimes it means salvaging bits and pieces. It's all very frustrating, and besides, it's expensive because more goes to waste than in any other cloth.
ABE:	Then by not marking these holes, you bill me as if they were first quality goods. You can certainly see that if this sort of thing continues, we will just not be able to carry Jewel any longer. (Sam has obtained a negative statement towards Jewel. However, this statement is considerably toned down from the vehemently scornful statements that had been heard up to then, even from this one client when he had been visited at his place of business.)
SAM:	I understand. Tell me, if it were possible for us to make a really important technical improvement introduction, to the extent of having the holes virtually disappear, do you think this would help you in your sales and in your garment manufacturing?
DAN:	No doubt about it. If you can fix that problem, we could sell better, but that doesn't mean that holes are the only problem we've had. There have been several others, and they are also really serious. (The persuasion is by no means finished, nor are the other problems forgotten.)
SAM:	Have you carried cloth of the same type as Jewel made by other manufacturers?
BILL:	Well, we have worked some, but not too much and mostly in other fibers. But we never had the problems with them that we have had with you! (Dan and Cab nod approval.)
SAM:	Do you think that in general there are apt to be more flaws in Jewel-type goods than in standard textiles? (Note the use of a negative subjective verb with the use of an abstract subject.)
ABE and CAB:	Well, that's true. Now that you mention it, they're not the same thing.
SAM:	Do you believe you do the right thing when you buy our Custom, Stream, Bytex and Striker lines. (Note the use of positive manifest verb with concrete object.)

ABE and CAB:	Well, yes. There's no trouble with those.
SAM:	Is the quality standard of those goods acceptable to you?
DAN:	Look! In the lines you mention the quality standards you have attained are really first class.
SAM:	How would you feel then if I were to tell you that the quality of Jewel has been brought up to the standard of these other goods? (There is a moment of absolute silence in which Sam merely bides his time.)
ABE:	(Doubting) Are you sure of that?
DAN:	(Positively) If that were true, then it would really be good news!
CAB and BILL:	(Slowly move their heads in a rather doubtful way but express nothing verbally.)
SAM:	What do you think, Bill?
BILL:	Well, if we keep in mind the last collection of Jewel that you sold us, that would be a really hard thing to believe. Of course, I know that you are a responsible outfit and that you were probably as aware of the problem as we were; so maybe you have been able to do something about it.
SAM:	It's precisely that responsibility, which all of you have acknowledged, that has led us in both the past and present to produce goods that you recognize as very good and that has made us look for the cause of the flaws we had. We wanted to find and apply solutions as rapidly as possible. We have done this by incorporating a new darning process which does away completely with the unsightly and costly holes. I therefore take pride in announcing that it has been possible to reduce the flaw you have mentioned by 98%. Besides, we have set up a rigorous inspection system which keeps very careful check on every piece that is approximately 40 yd in length. There will never be more than an occasional, maximum of three slight flaws in each of these, and they will be duly marked so that you can obtain the promised rebate. Should any goods come up with more than three flaws per 40 yd, they will automatically be considered second quality and be sold as such. How does that sound to you, Bill?
BILL:	Believe me, you not only impress me, but you let me regain the confidence I've had in you up to now.
SAM:	How do you feel, Abe?
ABE:	I'm entirely in agreement with Bill. If you've solved that, you've performed a feat.
SAM:	How about you Cab? How do you feel toward this proposal?
CAB:	As far as the holes are concerned, I'm satisfied too. It will completely solve my problems concerning that aspect, but there's something else I think is just as important. We've been having a lot of trouble on the cutting tables because the edges of Jewel are so uneven. It makes it extremely hard to get any sort of alignment when you cut several layers at once.
SAM:	You are absolutely right Cab! Bill has the same problem in the piece goods Sales Department. It makes the goods look sloppy. (Lights go out and a slide is projected showing a particularly terrible example of the flaw indicated by Cab. The edges of the sample photographed are really a disgrace.) Is this what you are referring to?

DAN and CAB: That's exactly it!
DAN: Although not all of them look as bad as that one.

Time out: Several commitments have been so skillfully obtained that the way is now open for Sam to make a positive communication regarding Jewel. Note, however, that Sam does *not* make a persuasive communication. He merely states a series of facts and resumes his questioning so that the clients will draw their own conclusions and commit themselves to these conclusions. Had Sam begun his persuasion by telling the good news that there was an entirely different manufacturing and inspection process, without having made the prior preparations, he would have provoked reactance. This would have created in his clients a desire to reestablish their freedom to think as they wished of Jewel. Since they were very angry, they would probably have simply not believed Sam's statement, particularly if he sounded as if he were making a persuasion attempt. (Such direct positive statements had been initially tried with a few clients, with precisely this negative result.)

Let us go on with our analysis: Before Sam had finished this part of the persuasion, that is, the one related to the holes, Dan had stated that even if that problem was remedied, there were still other problems to be considered. This reaction was to be expected; the holes merely happened to be the first problem mentioned. Thus, although the client had mentioned other flaws as well, Sam brought the discussion back to the matter of the holes and applied the prepared persuasion. Once the group was ready to hear a statement that sounded neutral and nonpersuading on the matter of the holes, they were ready to accept the conclusion that an improvement had been made. Then, as soon as that subject was successfully concluded, the matter of the rough edges came up. Sam was ready for this one, too, as we shall shortly see. The order in which the different topics were mentioned was determined entirely by the client. The salesman merely had to be ready to apply the persuasion already prepared for that particular topic.

This last point is related to a subject, the "order of presentation in persuasion," that has received much attention by researchers in social psychology. A book bearing that title was published in 1957 by Hovland and several colleagues. Such aspects as *primacy* and *recency, impact of first impressions, conditioning,* etc. were carefully studied. Unfortunately, no conclusive evidence about whether it is best to present the strongest arguments first or last can be drawn from these and later experiments. In the persuasion designs described here, other aspects are of much more importance than the order in which the arguments are presented. Since there are no direct, persuasive messages in the examples described in this book, compared to those in Hovland *et al.,* the reasoning and research concerning this point in the latter volume cannot really be applied to our work. It should also be recognized that the Hovland *et al.* study was principally concerned with mass media communications, whereas we are dealing with face-to-face persuasion. Nevertheless, several ideas have emerged in the course of designing face-to-face persuasions, which may possibly be applied for use in the mass media. If successful, they will result in persuasion designs that are far removed from the ones used normally in experimental designs or in the sales methods put forth on radio and TV, and in newspapers. At present, it is not possible to report such advances in the technology of persuasion, which is still in the design stage.

To return to the example: Sam has been confronted with a new objection for which he is now ready to present a persuasion.

SAM: (Slide changes and shows greatly magnified edge.) Have you ever stopped to notice these tiny little holes at the edges of the cloth?

CAB: No, I never saw that kind of flaw before.

SAM: Actually it isn't a flaw, and you'd have to have this high power magnification before you would be able to even notice it was there at all. Even here they are hard to see. These are the little holes made by the pincers of the tenter frame. Their object is to keep the cloth in shape while the machine establishes the correct width. You will note that in the slide I showed you first (goes back to poor edge slide) these little holes are spaced rather wide apart and at uneven intervals. This made the cloth go through the machine in uneven widths and that is why you got that poor end result. The reason for this is that we used the same tenter frame for this cloth that had been used for entirely different weaves. The bad part about it, and what also fooled us, was that it looked all right when it came off the machine. The defect showed up later in storage. We have therefore adapted new, special pincers for this new weave and can show this kind of edge as a result. (Slide showing little holes at perfectly regular spacing and a much straighter edge on the cloth. A second slide shows the cloth greatly magnified to intensify the effect of the eveness and proximity of the tenter frame holes.) From this slide you can appreciate that the tenter frame has more of a chance of giving a straighter edge to this new type of cloth. Do you think this may prove useful to you? (Lights go on.)

ABE: Decidedly. You've solved another very troublesome problem.

SAM: In what way is this useful to you?

ABE: Well, it makes the piece goods look a lot better, and it will help Cab a lot in laying his cloth out on the cutting tables.

SAM: Do you agree to that Cab?

CAB: Not only do I agree, but I think my personnel in the shop will see an end to a big, frustrating problem—and they will do their work with greater enthusiasm.

SAM: Gentlemen, would you care to see our new collection now?

ALL: Yes, Definitely! O.K., sure!

Until now, the persuasion design included only technical aspects. Two major weaknesses of Jewel had been attacked, and the clients had sufficiently committed themselves to a new, positive viewpoint. Sam noted this and therefore offered to show the collection. In other cases, when the clients voiced more major complaints, the salesman would merely use the designed procedure to obtain the appropriate result. The process in every case was continued until the salesman felt that the latitude of rejection had diminished significantly, although often only temporarily. In the present case, as we shall see later, Abe and his aides still have serious objections to Jewel. They have, however, temporarily forgotten them; and therefore Sam takes advantage of this lapse to continue the persuasion in other areas.

The lights are turned off again, and a series of very attractive slides is projected. These show models wearing dresses, slacks, bathing suits, blouses, etc., made of Jewel line A. Since there is to be a run of 12 or more slides, a whole photography technique has been created. It would take perhaps another chapter to describe what has been done in this area with photography, and an explanation would be out of place here because it is too specialized. (However, many pictures turn out to be remarkably effective in eliciting gasps of admiration from the small audience.)

More important than the photographic techniques, however, is the sequence in which the pictures are presented. A slide session can become very dull, but when presented in the right order, slides can make exciting viewing. We return to the device of activating the reticular formation: If two girls in blouses are shown, the third can be a girl in a bathing suit, followed by a girl in an evening gown, etc. If two or three outdoor scenes are shown in sequence, the following must be an indoor view. The sequence of colors is also carefully studied. Five slides of girls dressed in bright red become boring, however attractive they may be, even if the other elements are changed.

The salesman makes slight comments on the cloth in order to fix some aspect in the client's mind for future reference, when time comes to make out the order. He said: "This girl leaning against the boat is an xx—y denier weave with z finish. No remark whatever was made about the beauty of the garment, the girl, the pose, or the setting. This was left for each client to admire in his own way. Later, when the client was handling swatches for final selection, that particular piece of goods was often referred to as the "one of the girl leaning on the boat."

As soon as an adequate number of slides had been presented and long before the clients' interest had begun to wane, the slide projector was turned off. The room lighting, however, was now very different. Instead of using the fluorescent ceiling lights as before, a soft incandescent light fell on the clients while strong spot lights illuminated the area in front of them. At that precise moment, one of the models who had been shown photographed with a particular garment entered wearing that same garment. This was followed by a sequence of models each wearing the clothes that she had been seen wearing on the screen. The effect was impressive. More sequences of slides followed by model presentation were continued until the whole collection was shown. The number of slides and models in each of these sequences was made to vary in many details too numerous to mention.

At any moment, the client or one of his assistants might remember another one of the disadvantages of Jewel. Dan, for example, mentioned a problem that many women complained about. They said Jewel was very difficult to sew and that the seams never came out neatly. He mentioned several cases of puckering that customers had brought in. This objection had already been anticipated. It was mentioned by Dan as one of the models went by, because he noticed that the seams were perfect on the garment she was wearing. Sam immediately invited the group to a corner where a home sewing machine had been placed. He asked Dan, "Do you mean this"? and proceeded to sew a sample of Jewel, producing a badly wrinkled seam. The machine setting had been deliberately set to sew normal cloth—a setting that, used on Jewel, produced precisely this effect. When Dan assented, acknowledging that it was exactly the nature of the complaint, Sam pointed out the need of changing the machine setting when sewing Jewel. He did this and then sewed a perfect seam. Dan asked how he could pass on this information to his clients, at which point Sam gave him a printed leaflet with the adequate sewing instructions and offered to send Dan as many as he wished. (One could be included with each yard of Jewel sold.) After having obtained full commitment from Dan and the others to the effect that another problem had been effectively solved, Sam resumed his presentation of the collection.

The rest of the persuasion will not be given here because it would unduly lengthen the design description. One other point, however, merits careful consideration: immunity against counterpersuasion. McGuire (1964) conducted a series of very original studies on the possibility of inducing resistance to persuasion. He was able to show that under certain circumstances, it is possible after persuading a person to accept a certain viewpoint, to develop a strong resistance in this person against attempts to persuade him in a different direction (McGuire and Papageorgis, 1961; Papageorgis and McGuire, 1961). In a manner analogous to vaccination in medicine, McGuire gave his subjects toned-down arguments *in favor* of an *opposing* view. He also gave *strong* arguments in *favor* of the *initial stand.* In both cases he let some of his subjects take an active part. It was found that immunity was conferred in the case of subjects who were allowed to participate in weakened counter arguments. Interestingly, a generalization effect was found: If a person was immunized against counter-persuasion by the use of certain arguments against the position advocated and then exposed to a counter-persuasion using entirely different arguments, the person was equally resistant to these new counter arguments. This is important because it shows that immunization is not specialized or limited to the specific topics touched upon; rather, it becomes quite general (McGuire, 1961).

While McGuire's subjects, in all cases, participated in writing, we will combine his findings with those of Carlsmith *et al.* (1966), who showed that compliance produces considerably more opinion change when *spoken* to someone else than when written. Accordingly, designs for immunity against counter-persuasion have been made using verbal commitment. This is far simpler to achieve in the situations described here since the persons being persuaded are already in a face-to-face situation, where extensive dialogue is taking place. The spoken commitment for immunization can be obtained by direct questioning, analogy, successive approximations, social pressure, etc. Notwithstanding McGuire's generalization effect, our immunization designs included exposure to a large number of counter-arguments, i.e., as many as the client is likely to encounter, just to be safe.

In the particular case presented, there was a decided interest in having the client accept Jewel for men's wear—something that had been unheard of in the market. This application was feasible and would open new sales outlets. First, however, a persuasion had to be presented to induce the client to *try* Jewel for men's wear; then, a design for immunity against counter-persuasion had to be included. Otherwise, the client, after leaving quite convinced of the virtues of using Jewel for men's attire, would be faced with an environment of unbelievers who would dampen his enthusiasm with counter-arguments to which he himself might possibly subscribe.

The persuasion was initiated by having a male model accompany a female model at a certain stage of the presentation. Their garments were very differently made. All through the presentation, male models were included in increasing numbers, thus getting the client accustomed to the idea of having men's wear made of Jewel. It was then quite easy to obtain a commitment to the effect that men could wear this type of fabric as well as women. Once this commitment was obtained, the immunization procedure was started. The possible arguments that might be wielded against the use of Jewel for men's wear were:

- It has never been done here.
- It would be considered unmasculine.
- It does not adapt well to men's garments.

The dialogue related to this part of the immunization process continues:

SAM: (After having obtained full commitment to the effect that Jewel can and should be used for men's wear.) But tell me, is there a tendency for men's and women's wear, particularly in sports, to become differentiated, or are they actually drawing closer together?

ABE: They are growing closer and closer. Men are wearing bright-colored and printed shirts, printed bermudas, and many other things they would never have dared use a few years ago.

SAM: You're referring to the white-shirt period.

ABE: That's right. And even the women are now using men's white shirts.

SAM: Do you think that a man wearing printed shirts or bermudas looks less manly as a result?
ABE: No, not at all. You see many he-men in such outfits.
SAM: Do you think that having yielded their conservative attire has made them prone to attacks on their masculinity? (Note the step to a generalization and the use of a negative subjective verb with an abstract object, compared with the prior question, which was not only specific but also used a positive manifest verb with a concrete object.)
ABE: No, by no means!
SAM: (Obtaining a similar commitment from the rest of the group.) Would a man using a garment made of Jewel tend to be considered a sissy?
The GROUP: Never, why should he? What's wrong with it?

All concerned are now ready to repel any suggestion that using Jewel will make men look less masculine. As McGuire suggests, they have "rehearsed" the defense to counter-arguments. Similar immunizations were prepared for the other two arguments. The client and his aides could leave ready to face any outside opposition and to reply vehemently to anyone who dared suggest that their decision had been erroneous.

You should recall that one of the problems initially listed was that of competition with other departments within the company. Since the salesmen in other departments wanted to make as good a showing as Jewel, they emphasized Jewel's former problems when facing clients, in order to persuade the prospective client to buy more from them. The rivalry had reached such proportions that the head of the Jewel department was not on speaking terms with the head of at least one other department. This condition was effectively eliminated when, on the Sales Manager's initiative, the Jewel department showed the first sketch of its sales persuasion to the salesman of the other departments and asked for advice and criticism. Within a week, full-fledged cooperation was obtained to the extent that salesmen from other departments started passing tips to Jewel salesmen whenever they found interested clients or possibilities of placing orders.

The important result of this whole persuasion design is that Jewel sold all its stock and fully regained its reputation. The clients sold Jewel to their customers, and now the company is planning an expansion of Jewel's manufacturing facilities. All this has been achieved with no detriment to the other departments, who have also increased their sales and received support from Jewel salesmen. It is obvious that a good persuasion design can lead to healthy cooperation with mutual benefits to both parties.

It may now be pertinent to list some figures. Scheduling difficulties limited the above application to 45 clients. It was decided to bring in those considered most difficult, due to their negative stand. Of the 45, 43 bought in the anticipated quantities. A 44th client bought enthusiastically, but the salesman, in his elation, felt that inoculation was unnecessary. Two days later, this client called to cancel the whole order. Other clients were seen at their places of business in the customary manner. Of these, less than 50% bought Jewel on the first call. It took repeated calls to induce others to buy. Eventually many bought, but only after they saw that the first 43 were successful in selling to the public.

INTRODUCING A NEW PRODUCT IN A NEW MARKET

PQX is a very dynamic, rather small manufacturing company operating successfully in a South American country, A. It manufactures bedspreads, sheets, pillowcases and quilted bedcovers. Management decided that the operation was doing so well that it should consider establishing a similar operation in another South American country, B. An initial market survey in B showed that although that type of product was being widely sold by long-established reputable firms, there was reason for being optimistic about entering the market.

The General Situation.   Two reasons led to this optimism. The first was that due to competition in country B, both price and quality had been lowered. PQX is decidedly a quality-goods manufacturer and could therefore appeal to a large mass of clients who desired to have better goods than those available. The second reason was the PQX knew it could rely on the powerful, new persuasion design which had proved to be quite successful in country A. There was some doubt about whether the same principles would hold in society B (generally thought to be based on different values); however, ample evidence existed to suggest that the psychological and social psychological principles involved would indeed work well in B, whose differences from A had been rather exaggerated in relation to their similarities. Supporting the concept of cross-cultured cognitive similarity is some recent research by El-Abd (1969). He has shown that the intellectual structure of subjects belonging to at least 20 different tribes in Uganda representing four African races (Bantu, Nilotic, Milo-harnetic, and Sudanic) proved to be very similar to that of the white California subjects with whom Guilford had done research on his SI model, described in Chapter 2.

The Immediate Situation.   Based on these reasons and other financial, economic, and legal considerations, it was decided to start an operation in country B. Local salesmen were hired who possessed the requisite mental abilities, particularly in the semantic and behavioral areas. They were duly trained in social science technology, particularly with regard to persuasion. This proved to be an easy task. Persuasions were designed at meetings in which everyone freely gave his opinion, as described in our chapter on group problem solving.

Definition of the Problem.   One of the first obstacles encountered was that buyers in country B never went to their suppliers' places of business. They were used to having a salesman come to them with samples. This phenomenon, if not changed, would completely nullify any persuasion design that might be made in a showroom. Many in PQX thought it to be a virtually insurmountable obstacle: "If the buyers never visit the large, well-known reputable firms," they said, "how can we ever induce them to come to this completely unknown, rather out-of-the-way little outfit?" Clearly, a persuasion design that would induce the buyers to visit the company's premises was vital. This persuasion would have to take place at the client's place of business. Such a persuasion design had to be very brief, in order to minimize the probability of being interrupted.

The following is a verbatim report of one of those persuasions, written immediately after leaving a client's store.

SALES: Good afternoon, Mr. Lopez.

LOPEZ: Good afternoon. Pardon me sir, but how do you know my name? I don't believe I know you.

SALES: You are right Mr. Lopez. You don't know me, and I shall introduce myself— Juan Perez, and it's a pleasure meeting you. I am one of the representatives of PQX. The truth is I have heard a lot about you from some of your colleagues. When I called on them, many suggested I see you. You are supposed to be very experienced in these lines, and that's the reason for my visit.

LOPEZ: That's nice of them. Of what use can I be to you? What do you people make?

SALES: Well, we're new in the market. We are probably going to start out with beddings, although our major interest will be in home decoration and furnishing in general.

LOPEZ: What do you plan to do in the way of beddings?

SALES: Our outlook is rather broad. We'll probably go into sheets, pillows, and pillowcases, and even into quilted and other bedspreads.

LOPEZ: Sounds fine. Bring me some samples, and we'll see. If your prices are right, maybe we'll be able to make a deal.

SALES: Excuse me, Mr. Lopez, but perhaps I didn't make myself clear. I am not planning on selling you anything. Although before too long we will be manufacturing, what I would like from you, if it's at all possible, is to obtain some technical and commercial advice—something that can be of use to my firm. I ask for this based on the experience and reputation you have in this field.

LOPEZ: All right. Go ahead and ask anything you want.

SALES: Tell me, Mr. Lopez, is it true that quilted bedspreads give you a large profit margin?

LOPEZ: Why? Are you thinking of going into that first?

SALES: Well, it's one of the lines we are considering, but the reason I ask is that you seem to be carrying a very profitable line of these.

LOPEZ: No! I have to carry these because clients ask for them, but the mark-up is very low. It's often below 10%, and there are some in which there is no profit at all. They're no good commercially, and the competition has all but wrecked the prices and profits.

SALES: I suppose you make up for the low margin by having a high turnover due to massive sales.

LOPEZ: Not on your life! Everyone has them. Take the case of Kase: They cost 5.3 and they are selling them all over the place for 5.5. Do you think that's good business?

SALES: I suppose that looked at from that angle, you are right, but I bet you don't have any problems in deliveries. You probably order today and have the goods delivered in a day or two.

LOPEZ: What? Never! You don't seem to be too knowledgeable about these things. I have an urgent order placed a month-and-a-half ago, and here we are right in the middle of the season with no signs yet of delivery! How does that sound to you?

SALES: Gee, I appreciate these facts. I certainly see you are right, we do need advice.

LOPEZ: Yes, one has to have been in the market for sometime to know things, and if you wish to get ahead you had better have more information.

SALES: Well, you see now Mr. Lopez why I came to see you. Any advice you give me will certainly be useful to my firm. Tell me, Mr. Lopez, in your estimation what are the conditions that a quilted bedspread must fulfill in order to fulfill usefulness and still be easy for you to sell?

LOPEZ: To begin with, it must be competitively priced. It should be neatly made, should come in exclusive colors, have lots of filling, and especially not be sold to just anyone.

SALES: Do you think that a new firm could be successful if it did things well, that is, if it acted in the way you suggest?

LOPEZ: I can assure you. Besides, I'd be one of the first to buy.

SALES: Well Mr. Lopez, you can be sure that I'll make your comments known to our management, and I would like to invite you in the future to see our plant so that you can tell us if we have followed your advice. May I count on your paying us a call when we are ready to start production?

LOPEZ: You sure can, Mr. Perez. That's what we're all here for, to help one another to do more and work better.

SALES: Thank you very much, Mr. Lopez, for the time you've afforded me. As soon as things take shape, I'll be glad to call on you so we can set a date for your visit to us.

LOPEZ: All right. Thank you very much, Mr. Perez, I'll be very glad to pay you a call.

The above persuasion needs little comment. With variations according to different clients, it was successful in over 90% of the cases, compared with less than a 5% success with previous straight persuasion attempts. The salesman, of course, already knew of the drawbacks that Mr. Lopez mentioned. By making reactance-provoking statements, he got the client to find fault with his present goods. This incidentally was also the beginning of an immunity against counter-persuasion, a topic discussed in our previous persuasion example. Afterward, the conversation led naturally to a request for a definition of what the distinguishing traits should be for an acceptable product. The prior reactance led Mr. Lopez to make a definition of exactly the characteristics that PQX was going to incorporate into its product. This constituted a tremendous commitment on the client's part. If he defined so clearly what the product should be, it would be hard for him not to buy when offered with goods having exactly those qualifications.

More importantly, the whole persuasion was really a distraction, which led directly to the client's acceptance of the invitation. Again, we have here persuasion without reactance, or rather *with* reactance used at the appropriate places to produce a desired result. The salesman deliberately told the client that he was not there to sell, which was true since at the time no goods were available (the machinery had not even been installed). It is also important to note that the salesman's position in every case was so honest in wanting to be taught, that in many of these invitation persuasions, considerable data were obtained that eventually proved very helpful.

One final point is that most of the people in this field (buyers) seem to have a high need for approval. They want to be considered experts—something which they often are not. Byrne (1969), commenting on attitudes and attraction, cites Aristotle's "The Rhetoric": "We like those who praise our good qualities and especially if we are afraid that we do not possess them." This point has already been mentioned by Jones (1964): ". . . it is a person's *doubts* about an attribute in which he wishes to excel which render him open to flattery." Knowing all this enabled the persuader to increase his effectiveness with the client by feeding his approval motive.

Persuasion in the Showroom.   When eventually the client visited PQX, he was received by the salesman who had invited him and ushered into the showrooms. These are the first showrooms designed for persuasions of this type. There are hidden projection screens that can be immediately displayed, outside slides and movies that project through double-glass windows to eliminate noise, and hooks for spotlights that can be placed in different positions and pointed in any direction. The rooms are bare so that furniture, stands, and any other apparatus can be placed in varying positions to insure maximum flexibility for the design of future persuasions.

In this particular case, the buyer was urged to extend his invitation to others as well. This is, of course, meant to facilitate the use of social pressure at different points. When the client entered with three others from the same firm, all that could be seen in the room was a table with 5 chairs and an easel in front and to one side with white cardboard on it. The room was painted a dark green and heavily carpeted in a matching color. The ceiling was sound absorbent, and the whole room effectively soundproofed to avoid outside distractions.

The clients were asked to sit in the appropriate chairs. Besides Lopez, there was Mendez, Mario and Olmos. (The dialogue was reconstructed by the salesman and an assistant immediately after it had taken place. It has been edited omitting small talk, untranslated puns, jokes, etc.)

SALES: Mr. Lopez, as you may remember, the object of this invitation is to ask for advice regarding the type of product we intend to produce. I repeat that we know of your competence in this field and would like to take the greatest advantage of this visit.

LOPEZ: Well, Mr. Perez, I'm quite ready and willing to tell you anything I can, but I honestly think you are exaggerating when you speak about me that way. (This was said with false modesty.) I am interested in knowing what it's all about.

SALES: You're right, Mr. Lopez, and the first thing I'd like to ask you is regarding textile problems, since our goods are to be made of textiles as the principal raw materials.

LOPEZ: O.K., start asking.

SALES: Well, there's one thing I'm sure you know a lot about. What's your opinion as to bedding washability?

LOPEZ: (Hesitantly). You mean . . . technically, how they should be processed in manufacturing?

SALES: No, I mean concerning end use.

LOPEZ: (Reassured) Oh, well, I'd say that a very important point is that textile-made goods should not lose their shape on washing.

SALES: Do you think that *is* very important?

LOPEZ: Of course! If they deform on washing they can't be called "washable."

SALES: Excuse me, I'd like to take note of this and other comments of yours if you don't mind.

LOPEZ: Go right ahead. I don't mind at all. (Salesman writes down "Keep shape on washing" in his notebook.) Of course, that's not the only thing people want nowadays. Women are looking for an easy way to run a house, and one thing they want is to avoid using the iron. They want things that are washable and ready to use when dry. Another thing that is important is that the goods should be presentable.

SALES: Are you referring to the packaging? Do you think that is important?

LOPEZ: It sure is! An attractive wrapping helps sales and gives the goods an impression of quality.

SALES: But rather fancy wrapping might increase the cost of the product. Do you think this is justified?

LOPEZ: Well, with a little ingenuity you can design a good-looking wrapping that should not necessarily increase the price too much, but even so, the extra expense can add a lot to the general appearance and make any article look more attractive and salable.

SALES: That's very interesting. Let me take that down. (Writes in his notebook.) Can you think of anything else?

LOPEZ: No, I guess that about does it.

The salesman has obtained commitments to the effect that all these factors are important. Indeed, they are (the most obvious ones), and they have all of course been incorporated in the goods that PQX is going to present. This commitment on the part of the client prior to seeing the actual goods is extremely important. When he sees them, he will feel as if he had designed them himself. When the moment comes he will feel that he must buy; otherwise, he will experience cognitive dissonance. He could, however, reduce the dissonance in several ways. For example, he could say that he had initially exaggerated the importance of the features mentioned; but doing so would again produce dissonance. The client's easiest way out is simply to buy.

At this point in the persuasion, the salesman is aware of other features that are included in PQX's product that the client has not mentioned. By means of adequate questioning, the salesman must mention these features in such a way that the client, without constraint, feels *he* was the one discussing them in the first place and will therefore make a firm commitment regarding them. Take the subject of color fastness. The client knows very well that this is important. Since he has forgotten to mention it, the salesman himself must. This was done as follows:

SALES: Tell me Mr. Lopez, do you deal only in solid colors?

LOPEZ: No, certainly not. Most of the goods I have are in prints. That's what the buying public wants most these days.

SALES: In that case, is there anything in being washable that should not affect these prints?

LOPEZ: Oh yes! That's another point for you to take down. Colors should be fast. They should not run.

SALES: Have you ever run into trouble on account of this?

LOPEZ: Yes, we sure have. You must know that there are prints *and* prints. I always try to make sure not to get stuck with prints that will backfire on me. Yes, that is something that's very important for me.

SALES: That's very important. (Jots down in notebook.) This, in fact, confirms something we too had thought was important. I'm glad of your opinion on this because it shows we were steering in the right direction. You see, we feel that in order to achieve the best possible technology, we must lean on well-founded principles that are fundamental to such important areas as chemistry, metallurgy, plastics, and even textiles. If you'll allow me, I'll make myself more clear. I mean specifically that it is most important, in order to achieve an adequate and efficient end use, that we be able to exercise absolute control on the materials we are to use. Let's look into space technology, which is so closely related to metallurgy, plastics and others. (The lights go out, and a color slide of the spectacular launching of a rocket is projected on a large screen.) You see here the launching of a capsule destined to reach the moon. Generally, this stage of the process usually receives the greatest publicity. However, (slide showing another spectacular color drawing in which the capsule falls as a fire ball through the upper atmosphere) the correct use of materials is essential at this stage. The titanium shield (slide showing cross section of space capsule on reentry) has to withstand the terrific heat caused by the friction of the air, whereas the plastic backing gives total protection from this searing heat to the astronauts inside. Don't you think it remarkable that the outside temperature should be several thousand degrees while the inside should remain at a comfortable temperature?

LOPEZ: Say you know, that *is* remarkable. One is so impressed with the fact that it is possible to witness these events occurring as far away as the moon, that there is a tendency to overlook something like this.

The salesman has achieved three important things here: In the first place, he changed lighting, projected slides, and emphasized an entirely different point. At a point when Mr. Lopez was in danger of losing interest after a long period of answering questions, his attention is suddenly reactivated by several simultaneous changes in stimuli (visual, semantic, and auditory). Furthermore, the salesman altered his style and his voice to shift from *seeking* information to *giving* information. The new role serves to increase the client's level of arousal even more. In the third place, the salesman is creating a distraction which will make the client quite receptive to the material that follows. This is going to be presented in the form of persuasion by analogy, as we shall see.

SALES: We've been able to find out that this almost unbelievable insulation is obtained through the use of a special plastic material backing the white-hot titanium. Although the plastic is only a few inches thick, it blocks the heat effectively because it is really a mass of millions of little air cells, each of which is heat insulating. Such insulation is impossible to achieve in any other known way. (Since most clients knew very little about this, they generally show great interest.)

LOPEZ: You mean it's not the material that insulates, but the little air spaces? What about cork, which has so often been used as an insulator?

SALES: Well, cork is a natural material, actually the bark of a tree, and it too is composed of a great number of air cells—but nothing compared to what has been achieved with special plastics that have millions of more air cells per cubic inch. That's why cork could never have worked here, apart from the fact that it would be scorched. (Projects slide showing the cross-section of a house-hold refrigerator.) Here you can see something that's more familiar to most of us. This refrigerator is not insulated with the special, very expensive plastic used in the space capsule but with glass wool. You see, glass wool consists of a great number of extremely thin glass fibers all tangled together to form lots of little air spaces between them. (Slide projector is turned off and lights go on.) The salesman hands a piece of glass 6 in. $\times$ 6 in. $\times$ $\frac{1}{2}$ in. thick to the client together with a wad of glass wool. Here you see two different forms of glass. One is solid, and the other is hairlike fibers. Which seems to you to be the better insulator?

LOPEZ: Why the glass wool, of course. Ordinary glass isn't much of an insulator. I can see that when I sit in my car after the sun has been shining through the windshield.

Another activation of the reticular formation has taken place. Too many slides shown one after another make people feel drowsy, as anyone knows who has had to watch slides of a friend's trip. The salesman stops the slides and turns the lights on long before the client becomes drowsy. But before going back to the initial question and answer sessions, he now gives the client something to manipulate. Besides, he is now drawing nearer to persuasion on his first point.

SALES: Here I have a piece of iron wire about 12 in. long. I'm going to ask you please to push both ends against each other.

LOPEZ: (Takes the wire, pushes the ends, the wire buckles, and remains bent.)

SALES: As you see, the straight wire lost its initial shape. This happened because it was straight. Can you think of a shape we could give a wire so that on pushing the ends it will return to its initial position when you let go?

LOPEZ: I suppose you could bend it into a spiral spring like those on the front-end suspension of my car. They always bounce back when the tire hits a bump. (In this case, Mr. Lopez immediately hit on the idea of coiling the wire into a spring.

In other cases, it was frequently necessary to formulate a series of graded questions until the client finally discovered that a spring shape would solve the problem.)

SALES: I see that you know a lot about physics. Now here I have a handful of straight wires (takes in his left hand 8 straight wires similar to the one shown before), and here I have the same number of wires coiled into springs (takes in his right hand 8 similar but coiled wires). Please take them. (Hands them to Lopez.)

LOPEZ: (He takes the wires.)

SALES: Which seem to you to hold more air space?

LOPEZ: This one (holding up the coiled fist-full).

SALES: If we had to use a material that usually comes straight from the manufacturer, would you suggest we attempt to coil it like this for better insulation?

LOPEZ: Yes, definitely.

SALES: Why do you think so?

LOPEZ: Well, if this could be done on a large scale, you would have more air pockets and therefore increased insulation.

SALES: Mr. Lopez, I don't want you to think that I am taking up your time by playing with these gadgets, but you mentioned to me that it was very important for an article to be washable and that (looking at his note) it should not lose its shape.

LOPEZ: Yes, that's true, I've been saying that all along.

SALES: Well, following your line of thought, and with the intention of looking into the possibility of applying chemical and physical principles, we have been experimenting to see if we couldn't do with synthetic fibers what you just saw with wires. Synthetic fibers usually are produced straight, like the straight wires you just held, but our technicians began to wonder if it were possible to change their shape in order to achieve the end results we desire. (Lights go out and a girl is seen curling her hair with a curling iron. The girl is very attractive, but she is dressed in old-fashioned clothes and is making up an old-fashioned hairdo).

LOPEZ: Say, that picture is kind of dated. It's a shame to make up such a pretty girl like that. (The salesman has gone back to darkness and slides to reactivate the reticular formation and at the same time create a distraction.)

SALES: You're right, but I wanted to emphasize the point that girls for sometime have used appliances to curl their hair. The trouble is that hair keeps growing and the curls disappear. However, we have been able to use this same principle with artificial fibers.

LOPEZ: How did you ever do that?

SALES: (Turns on lights and withdraws blank board from easel. This reveals a schematic diagram showing how fibers pass through very small heated rollers in which they end in the shape of spiral coils. The salesman gives a brief description of how the process works.)

LOPEZ: Say, that's very interesting, but don't the fibers lose their shape with time?

SALES: No, they don't. You see, in order to flatten them out, they'd have to be subjected to an inverse process, at the same high temperature that was used to shape them in the first place, and this is very unlikely to happen in daily life. (Projects slides of highly magnified straight and curled fibers. This is done without turning out all the lights so that the easel is still visible.) How does this strike you? Where would you say that there will be more insulation?

LOPEZ: The left one, of course, the curled one.

SALES: Well that is our *AAA* processed fiber. Does it look similar to the coiled wire springs you saw a little while ago?

LOPEZ: Yes, there's a great similarity between *AAA* and the coiled springs.

SALES: Do you think that if we were to make a small pillow and fill it with *AAA* and if you were to press it and then let it go, it would tend to regain its original shape?

LOPEZ: Seen in this light, it would certainly seem to.

SALES: And once you press it and then let go, what do you think happens to the air cells and the insulation?

LOPEZ: Well, it's obvious that the air cells would be restored and that it would become very insulating again.

SALES: How does this fiber strike you if we were to use it as a filling in our quilted bedspreads? Do you think they would be warm and at the same time always maintain their original shape?

LOPEZ: Yes, I think you people have come up with a grand idea that will do away with sagging quiltings. You know I'm pretty tired of hearing housewives complain of deformation and flattened quilting after the first washing. Generally, they come in and say that there's a world of difference between the goods when new and after the first washing. They put their recent purchases next to the stuff we have on sale, and they make me feel embarrassed because they are right.

SALES: Well I'm very glad that we have followed the advice you gave us the other day and decided to use the specially processed *AAA* fiber, although it's more expensive. Do you think we are justified in going into the extra expense?

LOPEZ: Yes, please don't spare any expense in that, because I certainly would like to get rid of that mess. I like my clients to buy and never come back except to buy more or to send their friends.

Time out: The reader will now note how the whole persuasion, beginning with the initial one at the client's place of business, is bound together. In the persuasion designed to have the client come into the showroom, the client was first simply asked for *opinions.* This conversation involved having the client point out desirable features for the product at hand. At this meeting, the client first mentioned price and then nondeformation. The subject of deformation was taken up by interested questioning on the salesman's part and then by adroit use of changes of stimuli to keep up the client's interest. At no point had the salesman even insinuated that the client *buy.* However, the latter had already made so many commitments that whatever dissonance was later aroused by going to see a supplier (a thing he had never done in the past) and buying from an unknown firm (something of which he was very wary) had been reduced in advance by making statements that in essence constitute a commitment to buy.

Post-decision Regret. There is, however, another point related to social science findings that has generally been overlooked by salesmen who have had an apparently enthusiastic buyer later fail to purchase his goods. This is the phenomenon of post-decision regret. In two very important experiments, Walster and Festinger (1964) and Walster (1964) have shown that there are circumstances under which, after having made a decision between two possible choices, subjects immediately reduced dissonance by finding the selected choice more attractive and the rejected choice less attractive. However, with the passage of time, there tended to be a reduction in the process, such that the alternative *not* selected generally became more attractive in relation to the chosen one. The Walster experiment allowed a maximum of 90 minutes for this pehnomenon to take place, with subjects left in isolation and no outside influences to affect them.

In real life, clients leave the showroom and are affected by all kinds of stimuli. Among these are comments of partners, employees, rival salesmen, spouses, and others. Since these others have not been subjected to the type of persuasion described here, it is highly unlikely that they will share the buyer's enthusiasms and may well increase his post-decision regret. This is the probable reason for the phenomenon observed by many salesmen and other persuaders, who have been baffled by an about-face on the part of the person they had believed to be thoroughly persuaded.

There are two answers to this problem: One of them is to *over*-persuade. In other words, instead of being content with the buyer's virtual commitment to buy at this point, the salesman continues to get more commitments in as many areas as possible. This alternative also involves innoculation against counter-persuasion, as we saw in the previous persuasion example. Another method is to visit the client at his place of business within a reasonable period of time (at present this seems to be between 24 and 48 hours) and get him to recommit himself to his decision. This combination has been found very useful in reducing order cancellations, at a point when the client hasn't even seen the finished article.

Our experience in this latter method is supported by a number of social science findings. Cook and Insko (1968) studied the persistence of opinion change following a persuasive communication. In their experiment, they exposed subjects to persuasive communications and measured their attitudes both before and immediately after the communication. Following a certain elapsed time period, subjects were exposed to an abbreviated reexposure. It was shown that reexposure to the desired point of view contributed materially to the persistence of attitude change. The authors suggest that this "reexposure stimulates rehearsal and retention of the supporting arguments or rehearsal and retention of the communication point of view." Noted that in the Cook and Insko experiment, the subjects merely listened passively to persuasive communications. This method differs materially from the type of persuasion advocated in our designs, in which the active participation of the person being persuaded constitutes an essential ingredient. It is felt, however, that Cook and Insko did increase the subject's active participation by dissonance, i.e., changing privately held beliefs, and thereby increased the persistence stimulating them to reduce the attitude change.[4]

[4] We are preparing a theoretical model binding these phenomena together which is not essential to the matters expounded in this book and will therefore be published separately.

A third technique devised by some salesman has been to wait at the place of business until a customer comes in and do a similar persuasion on the customer (without all the gadgets and other equipment used in the showroom persuasion), thereby selling the article. This procedure constitutes positive reinforcement for the buyer, who will see that his decision was fully justified. Now let us return to the persuasion example.

SALES: Well, Mr. Lopez, I am very glad that we have been able to satisfy your requirements in that respect. You also mentioned that we should have fast colors.

From here on, it would be repetitious to show how, using different media, the salesman made demonstrations of color fastners, nonwrinkling of cloth, resistance to moth and other vermin, fast drying, and a special device that keeps the quilt from sliding off the bed when it's used. He also displayed a wide range of colors and styles, as well as some very modern, practical and useful packages. Finally, spot lights went on, brilliantly lighting up a corner of the room where a bed was laid with one of the quilted covers. The client was invited to go to the corner and see it (another change in stimulus). Assistants came in with other styles and rapidly changed the quilts. The salesman obtained further commitments, using mostly social pressure by observing and eliciting. After the showing of the collection and with the client fully committed even to specific quantities, it was a simple matter to return to the table and fill in the order. It is interesting to note that initial attempts at selling the articles at the client's place of business, using the customary persuasions, resulted in success only 5% of the time. In contrast, under the circumstances just described, *not a single client left without making a purchase.*

Another interesting point is that the clients invariably made gross under-estimations of the time they had spent in the showroom. Although the actual periods ranged from 1 to $2\frac{1}{2}$ hours, depending on the client's talkativeness, most thought they had spent about a half-hour. Many showed great surprise at the amount of the time that had elapsed. Clearly, the salesmen had been successful in keeping the clients' reticular formations activated at all times at just the optimal level in order to create and maintain the greatest possible interest.

COMMENT ON THE DESIGN OF COMPLEX PERSUASIONS

An important point that must be considered is one of an ethical nature. To what extent are we allowed to use such powerful tools to produce changes in the attitudes and behaviors of others? Does this constitute an invasion of privacy? Is it a dangerous tool to place in the hands of would-be dictators, authoritarians, and unscrupulous persons? We have given this matter con-considerable thought and offer several partial answers.

- Whenever there has been technological progress in any direction, there are always those who are ready to decry the use of the new methods by using the argument that it may fall into the wrong hands. While this has happened, in general it cannot be denied that humanity has gained more than it has lost through this progress. It is very probable that when Gutenberg invented the printing press, some people were worried that improper things would eventually be published and made available to the public. Many will say that this prediction has proved true, and the debate still continues about what is or is not proper to print. But it cannot be denied that printing, as one of the most powerful means of disseminating and recording information, has enormously benefited humanity. Besides, why assume that the new technology will be used exclusively by authoritarians to dominate others? We certainly hope that our readers will not be limited to high F scorers, but that well-intentioned, emotionally healthy persons will also use the material in a manner which will improve human welfare. Hopefully, those outnumber the ones who deliberately seek to destroy and enslave. To the contention that such men, albeit a minority, generally tend to be in positions of power, the reply is that *these techniques give more power to those who feel they do not belong to powerful elites.*

Another encouraging point is that in our experience, *high authoritarians, although they are at times intellectually able to grasp the principles of our persuasion designs, are totally incapable of applying them.* The same holds true for persons high in the Crowne-Marlowe social approval scale. Apparently, they are so concerned about making a good impression, and thus think so much about themselves, that they tend to overlook and disregard entirely the other person's processes, points of view, etc. In this connection, it might be well to cite an important comment in Skinner's "Walden II": "And what a strange discovery for a would-be tyrant, that the only effective technique of control is unselfish." Skinner was, of course, referring to positive reinforcement. Nevertheless, the sentiment can be extended to all the other principles used in this book.

- Persons who have used these persuasions have learned to be very careful with them, precisely because they are so powerful. More than once, an over-enthused group of salesmen has designed persuasions that sold more goods than the client could carry, or goods they were not able to move off their own shelves, with disastrous results for the organization making the sale. What occurred was a backfire effect that negatively affected the goods the organization had to offer. A warning is therefore voiced to those who would use these tools: *Size up your client, decide what is best for him, make a survey of his needs and possi-*

bilities, and then design a persuasion to sell him those requirements. If he buys this amount and finds that he can sell it, then he will feel very grateful, because at all times he will have the correct sensation that it was he himself who made the decision to buy.

- *One positive aspect of using these techniques is that they make us forget ourselves and think much more of others*—a very healthy mental attitude. Perhaps this is a hard thing to do in our modern complex societies, but it is precisely there where such an attitude is most needed. Writing on living conditions in the desert, Cloudsley-Thompson (1968) says: "When I first came to the Sudan, I felt saddened by the austerity of the lives of its inhabitants, both human and animal. With the passing years, however, I have come to realize that this assessment was superficial. As I became acclimatized to the heat and learned to ignore physical discomfort, I realized how much more important are good-natured hospitality, kindness and a sense of humor than the possession of the so-called luxuries of Western civilizations."

One of the goals of social science technology is to place in the hands of the greatest number of people the means whereby the virtues that Cloudsley-Thompson so praises and which seem to him to be absent from luxurious Western civilization can be regained. It is hoped that recovery of these values can be attained not only without losing these comforts but while making them universally available.

We are constantly trying to persuade others whether to go to a show, "to do things anyway" at home, at work, and in other settings. These persuasions often lead to bitter time and energy consuming controversy. The type of persuasion described above takes the unpleasant controversial aspect out of persuasion. It might perhaps be considered evil if this were put into the hands of a powerful elite, but this is not the case. The reader, who may perhaps resent this, has this material literally in his own hands to use as he sees fit. One of the primary purposes of this book is to disseminate this knowledge as widely as possible so that the material will not fall into the hands of an elite.

These comments, however, are not sufficient to blind social technology to the awareness of the responsibility it assumes for its own proper use. One of its prime tasks, therefore, is to devise methods that will insure that at long last man will create a technology that will not merely afford positive benefits of average quality, but will also eliminate the usual nefarious consequences that have accompanied many new technologies in the past. Restrictive legislation is obviously not the answer. This will be one corollary to that expounded in this book's final chapter. Whatever social technology devises for its own safeguards must arise from the clever use of the material derived from its own resources. This phase of the problem has been dealt with in our work by constant emphasis on integrity, but we are still devising other safeguards as well. Yet, one should not be too apprehensive. Modern biology and medicine, without the knowledge we have today, have been able to create a technology which while having potentially frightful consequences if used destructively, has nevertheless been of overwhelming benefit for humanity.

A very important aspect related to the design of these persuasions is that they require the use of considerable knowledge of the product and the market, as well as ingenuity, memory, etc. The models are therefore extremely difficult for only one individual to design, as he would have to be expert in all the areas mentioned. Besides, any persuasion designed by such a genius would be difficult to teach to ordinary salesmen, who are frequently enthusiastic about the method but reluctant to apply it. Accordingly, in order to design effective persuasions, such as those described in this chapter, the group problem-solving method has been employed. This technique will now be described in Chapter 6.

6

It is hereby declared that of all the differences of opinion that have divided the Uruguayans, there shall be neither victors nor vanquished.[1]

Peace Treaty of October 8, 1851

group problem

solving

An imposing body of literature exists that details both research results and theories concerning how people behave when they gather in groups either to work or to play. Very important findings have been reported on the way groups function. These studies are generally of two types. Some have investigated how a group operates, as well as what events occur when a small group of people gets together principally to discuss a subject or to solve a problem. A good deal of information on this topic can be obtained from texts on social psychology, such as those by Sargent and Williamson (1966), Newcomb *et al.* (1965), Secord and Backman (1964), McDavid and Harari (1968), Jones and Gerard (1967), and others.[2] By the time this book appears, even more infor-

[1] Part of Article 6 of the peace treaty that ended the 9-year Uruguayan civil war.

[2] More detailed data are available in books specializing in group functioning, such as "Group Achievement" by Stogdill (1959); also relevant are volumes by Hare *et al.* (1955), Cartwright and Zander (1960), Bass (1960), Golembiewski (1962), and Sherif (1962). In addition, there are excellent books that contain articles by leading researchers, such as Hollander and Hunt (1963), Backman and Secord (1966), Vinacke *et al.* (1964), Maccoby *et al.* (1958), and many others. A very good account of research findings related to group decision-making processes is found in Collins and Gueztkow (1964).

mation will doubtless have become available. However, the majority of the findings given in these volumes (also see footnote 2), although providing very good information as to *why* things happen when groups get together, particularly why they don't seem to agree, give little data on *what* to do when groups simply do not get along.

Another topic that has been investigated is how to conduct groups. The vast majority of these books are written by people who have had a lot of practical experience and who, in some way, have stumbled on methods that are more or less effective in conducting group discussion. Some good pointers can be obtained from these, but we are faced here with the canopener type of solution which was mentioned in Chapter 3. There is seldom a shred of theoretical evidence given about *why* a certain method works better than others.

There is also a third line of research, of which we know only one or two cases. This is the type that gives results of experiments in which actual groups employ different methods. One of these is by Blake *et al.* (1964), which is limited only to solving conflict. The other is by Maier (1963). Maier has performed a great number of experiments—sometimes with the collaboration of others, among whom R. Richard Hoffman can be considered outstanding. Hoffman (1965) decries the lack of coordination among the different types of research conducted in the area of group problem solving. He states: "With rare exceptions there has been a notable lack of a continued, consistent and additive effort in this area. The typical experimenter does one or two studies on a single facet of the topic, with a problem (described in too general and vague terms) which nobody else has ever used. He produces suggestive but inconclusive results, and is never heard from again. This practice has left the literature on group problem solving a large conglomeration of unrelated experiments, with only the faintest suggestion of commonality. Also, most of the experiments to date have concentrated in identifying the barriers to effective problem solving, rather than on discovering the means to stimulate group creativity. Admittedly, the barriers discovered so far occur so ubiquitously, that unless they are overcome, the chance of promoting creative problem solving is rather small. Nevertheless, effort directed to inventing and testing new ways of encouraging creative group problem solving should advance our knowledge of the problem-solving process and, when successful, would have practical value for the society as well." Hoffman hopes that the lack of unity, which he deplores, will eventually disappear so that there will be a better understanding of the group process, with a consequent practical value for society. Organizational psychology (Bass, 1965; Leavitt, 1964; Bennis *et al.*, 1964; Argyris, 1970), which is based on empirical research, while often sharing my goals, uses such different methodology that integration with this work becomes difficult. But hopefully, ingenuity will eventually unite these different though effective approaches.

PROBLEM SOLVING BASED ON INTEGRATED THEORIES

Our approach starts where Hoffman's ends, with the question: How can all this immense amount of apparently unrelated material be useful in creating the conditions that will lead to successful problem solving? This chapter will explain and illustrate how findings, often from quite unrelated areas, have been used to conduct effective problem solving meetings. The author is indebted to Maier and Hayes (1962) and Maier (1963) for the backbone of his approach. However, he differs fundamentally in the way the problem has been faced. Whereas Maier shows that *developmental discussion* produces a higher quality decision in 39.7% of the cases studied, instead of the 18.9% obtained with free discussion, he does not give the underlying reason *why* such a difference comes about. His work, although very valuable, is entirely empirical. In our design for group problem solving, a theoretical principle will often be used to explain the action of a conference leader. (This practice often coincides with what is recommended by Maier.) Nevertheless, it may make the reader feel that he is treading on firmer ground because he will know the underlying mental processes of the individual group members. After knowing these processes and how they work, he will be able to design solutions to new and unusual situations whenever these occur and not feel bound by formulae that do not apply in the new case. He will not merely be following a set of rules. Besides, if he diagnoses his group well, he will often skip parts of the process because he realizes that these are unnecessary. Going through certain steps merely because they are prescribed by someone else might even slow down the meeting or ruin it altogether.

Many of the social science findings that are used in the solution of problems in groups have already been given in earlier chapters in devising solutions for other problems. At this stage, however, some additional data must be introduced if we wish to advance further.

BASIC CONCEPTS

Some of the most important experiments of our century have been performed in the area of social science. It is quite possible that as a result of these experiments, the 20th century will be remembered more for these findings than for its achievements in what now seem to us to be the more spectacular fields of electronics, rocketry, space travel, etc. One of these crucial social experiments was performed by Sherif *et al.* (1961). For the first time, conflict between human groups was investigated experimentally and possible solutions to artificially created conflicts were attempted. Also for the first time, it was possible to affirm, as the result of an experiment, that certain forms of solutions proposed by well-intentioned persons for the solution to social strife would never achieve the desired results; whereas, another solution proposed by other equally well-intentioned persons would. This achievement opened the way for the further study of conflict that has been followed by Blake and Mouton (1962), and others.

WIN-LOSE CONFLICT

A win-lose conflict may be defined as a tension-filled situation in which two or more groups are each competing to gain precedence over the other(s). Sherif's experiments provide a good example of such conflict.

Sherif formed two groups of young boys at summer camps, both of which were matched for age, education, etc. He kept the groups apart for some time and then started competitions between them. In these competitions, which involved different skills, he managed to have group A always win. This state of affairs eventually caused such frustration for the members of group B that they became antagonistic toward group A. Eventually, this led to open conflict in which severe damage was inflicted by each group upon the members and property of the other. It is interesting to note that the boys had been perfect strangers to each other before this event, had traveled in buses together to reach camping sites, and had even sometimes developed friendships; yet they became bitter enemies when the right conditions were created for conflict to occur. Significantly, when conflict can be so easily created, it seems quite probable that most other conflicts between human groups may also be due to artificial causes and might therefore be avoidable. We shall concentrate on this aspect later.

Solving Win-Lose Conflicts.   Once Sherif had his two groups in severe conflict against one another, he attempted two different types of solutions. One of these was based on the theory that *all you have to do to get people to stop fighting is to get them together, get them to talk and to know one another*. This thesis was maintained by Andrew Carnegie (1933), an earnest campaigner for peace, when he stated: "It is mainly the ignorance of contending parties of each other's virtues that breeds quarrels everywhere throughout the world, between individuals, between corporations and their men—and between nations. 'We only hate those we do not know' is a sound maxim which we do well ever to bear in mind."

Sherif set out to test the validity of this type of suggestion. He got the two conflicting groups to engage in pleasurable activities together. The result was disaster. The contending groups, taking advantage of the pleasurable activities in which presumably they would have a chance to know one another better and so to create more favorable relations, raised the conflict to an even higher pitch. The result is important because a scientifically conducted experiment did away with the hope that strife can be resolved by merely getting people together. One is reminded of Galileo's experiments of dropping a heavy and a light stone to the ground from the Tower of Pisa to prove whether the heavier one fell faster, which everyone believed since Aristotle's definite pronouncement on the subject. Several centuries of philosophizing on this topic had to be discarded on the basis of one simple experiment. Sherif's experiment was not quite so simple, but it has produced comparable effects. It is quite unfortunate that those who proposed merely integrating universities as a solution to the problem of racial inequalities did not look carefully into the implications of Sherif's experiment. If they had, they would probably have decided to think further before taking such steps, or they might have done other things that, as a result of additional experiments, we now see clearly must be done.

The second theory tested by Sherif was the hypothesis that *establishing a superordinate goal would help solve the conflict problem.* A superordinate goal is defined as one that is considered essential by both groups but that cannot be attained by one group alone. It can only be reached if both groups work cooperatively toward its attainment. To test this theory, Sherif arranged to cut off the water supply to both camps. This caused a severe crisis. Without water for drinking, washing, cooking, and sanitation, it was necessary to leave the premises at once. But the supply could be restored if the damage could be repaired. This was a task so devised that it could not be done by either group working alone; cooperation was an essential ingredient. The task was indeed performed, and conflict subsided to a lower level. Other similar superordinate goals were established, and eventually, the conflict subsided still further, although the situation never returned to its original peaceful level.

Sherif therefore proved that one way in which conflict can be reduced in intensity is by finding superordinate goals and inducing groups to engage in the activities required to attain them. However, two objections can be found to this technique: One is that often it is very difficult to find a suitable superordinate goal. Furthermore, the parties may be so angry with one another that it is impossible to get them to engage in cooperative activity even if such a goal were available and even if each side may suffer heavily as a consequence of this mutual stubbornness. The second objection is that the superordinate goal more often than not may be: "Let's all get together to beat up the other big group." In other words, fiercely competing groups may band together for an even bigger conflict with a larger group. Small conflicts are therefore ignored because there is an even bigger conflict to be dealt with. This phenomenon occurs in time of war when the differences between political parties are generally forgotten in order to join in the common goal of beating the enemy. This seems to be a horrible prescription to recommend for ending strife between parties. We believe that other solutions must be sought.

Effects of Win-Lose Conflicts.   Let us turn to some more research findings. Blake and Mouton (1962) conducted a series of experiments dealing with conflict between groups of supervisors in order to study what happens when groups come into conflict with one another. It is most important to study these findings, since, when combined with results of other investigations, they will give us the insight necessary to do something much more important than merely solve conflict. Chapter 7 will present our ideas on conflict resolution when such conflict exists, but the present chapter will give the findings and technology necessary to conduct a meeting in which conflict cannot even begin.

One of Blake and Mouton's experiments shows that *when groups are openly competing in a win-lose situation in which the possibility of resolving differences by compromises is entirely ruled out, then each group will strangely tend to overvalue its own position and undervalue that of the opponent.* This is a frequently observed phenomenon in elections, whether they are national or primaries or whether they are held in clubs, associations, unions, etc. Each person believes that his own group has the best position, while the other group's is all wrong. The sharper the issue and the more acute the struggle, the greater the tendency for this to happen.

Another set of findings concerns group cohesion in the context of win-lose conflicts. Grossack (1954) found that *groups which are given a common fate show significantly more cohesive behavior than those which are not.* In other words, when a group is threatened, the members tend to feel closer to one another. This feeling may have several simultaneous causes. One of these is derived from Asch's (1952) and Crutchfield's (1955) findings on social pressure: In such situations, the members of a group who do not think like the others are virtually compelled to go along with the majority. There is, however, another important factor involved. Schacter (1959), through a series of very ingenious experiments, showed that people in a state of anxiety want to band together with other people. In particular, they wish to be with people who are in the same predicament. (An incidental but very important finding was that this principle holds more for the first-born member of the family (or only child) than for those born later.) Similarly, Deutsch (1949) found that groups with a common fate demonstrated high mutual influence, i.e., the individuals tended to go along with the ideas of other group members.

Blake and Mouton (1964) have also described some of the other effects of win-lose conflict. They noted the *consolidation of the leader's position in each group as the conflict develops.* An interesting corollary is that the leader of the opposing group seems to exercise an almost mystical power over the members of his group and derives this power not so much from his innate ability as from the opposition that we are creating to his group. Our group is, of course, seen by our opponents in the same light. The menace they feel binds them strongly together behind their leader. This is a most important finding that must be kept in mind while leading problem-solving conferences or while designing conflict resolutions.

Another consequence is that there are *distortions of perception*. This phenomenon explains why two groups in conflict see the same events in entirely different ways. Perceptions of the people involved are also distorted. The opponents appear to lack any redeeming features. Moreover, there is a great tendency to emphasize the differences of opinion between the two groups, while forgetting the many points they may have in common. Such behavior is common in political parties. Another example is how the differences between two groups of Christians regarding how humanity might be saved caused the dreadful Thirty Years War. Since both warring factions shared similar faiths, their differences appear actually to have been quite small compared to their similarities (also compared to differences between peoples of entirely different faiths).

Blake and Mouton also mention the *hero-traitor dynamics*. A member of a group who even dares suggest that there might be something of value in the other's position will be considered a traitor by the rest; whereas, anyone who can demolish the opponents becomes a hero. Unfortunately, what the hero does is exactly the opposite of what is required to solve the conflict. This loyalty of representatives to the ingroup position was shown to exist in an experiment performed by Blake and Mouton (1961).

It is easy to see from these examples and from other literature—particularly Blake and Mouton (1964) and Collins and Guetzkow (1964)—that although it may eventually be possible to design solutions to conflicts, *it is far easier to avoid the conflict in the first place*. This statement should be kept in mind by the leader of any problem-solving group. At no time must he allow win-lose conflict to emerge. Methods whereby this goal may be attained will be given later.

COMMUNICATION NETWORKS

Leavitt (1958), following the work of Bavelas (1948), has developed techniques for measuring the efficiency and satisfaction of persons working together at solving a given task. Basing his work on the principle that adequate communications are a necessary pre-condition for successful group problem solving, he tested how groups and individuals reacted when the communications among the members were restricted in several ways. Thus, instead of allowing each member to communicate with every other member, he managed to create several different conditions, using an ingenious experimental setup. Shaw (1964) summarizes the research generated by Leavitt's earlier work, describing 23 different types of networks involving 3 to 5 persons. Some of these are shown in Fig. 6.1, where the small circles represent persons and the

| Chain | Circle | Wheel | Y | Comcon |

FIG. 6.1. Types of communication networks. [Adapted from Shaw (1964) by permission.]

lines joining them represent the allowed channels of communication. It can be seen, for example, that in the wheel, one person centralizes communications; whereas, in the comcon, each member can communicate with all the others.

Shaw (1964) states: "The free flow of information among various members of a group determines to a large extent the efficiency of the group and the satisfaction of its members." The Leavitt experiments consisted of a rather simple task. Each member was given a series of symbols—there being only one symbol common to all members. By exchanging written messages, the members had to identify a certain symbol. Leavitt found that groups in a circle arrangement made the greatest number of errors and those in the Y, the smallest number. On measuring satisfaction in the first four setups, it was found that *circle* members reported the *greatest* satisfaction. The members of the *wheel* were the *least* satisfied, except the member at the center, who had the highest satisfaction score of any subject regardless of the communication network involved. (The wheel can also be represented graphically, as shown in Fig. 6.2.) A very close second in terms of satisfaction was the member at the junction of the three lines of Y.

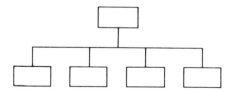

FIG. 6.2. Alternative diagram of wheel network.

This scheme will be recognized as the usual arrangement in an organization in which a supervisor has four subordinates. Assuming that communication exists only between each subordinate and the supervisor (not among the subordinates), the person who most enjoys solving a problem that involves all four subordinates will probably be the supervisor. The other four members will be at least satisfied. If at a meeting the same pattern of communication holds, that is, if the supervisor asks for information from each subordinate and then, after hearing them all, decides everything himself, the supervisor will feel quite pleased, leaving his subordinates frustrated because they had only a small share in the whole solution. The greatest satisfaction will be felt by those in the comcon, where each member feels as if he were at the center of a wheel.

Interaction.   One immediate application of this finding is that the supervisor, group leader, teacher, etc., should make *the greatest effort to create as much communication as possible among members of the group.* Satisfaction will be highest when everyone is interacting with everyone else, as in the comcon. As a matter of fact, the supervisor himself will achieve the greatest possible satisfaction if he is not even included in the group but simply acts as if he were in a third dimension overseeing the maximum interaction among all the persons concerned.

The reader may perhaps wonder at this point why so much fuss is being made over interaction. As a partial reply, let us consider some of Kurt Lewin's contributions to this area. Lewin (1953) reported on attempts to persuade housewives during World War II to try using animal organ meats instead of the usual cuts, which were unavailable. Some groups of housewives were merely told how important it was to use these foods, not only to aid the war effort but also to obtain needed calories, vitamins, etc. Other groups heard the same arguments but were allowed to discuss them. The lectured group subsequently used these strange foods in only 3% of the cases, compared with 32% of the groups that were allowed discussion. Apparently, greater success was achieved, at least in part, through greater participation and involvement, which together stimulated a more active orientation among the discussion groups. This and other experiments have led Abelson (1959) to state: "No normal person is happy in a situation that he cannot control to some extent." Maier (1963) agrees that the way a decision is made is an important part of the total group process: "Two different dimensions seem to be relevant in appraising a decision's potential effectiveness. One of these is the objective or impersonal *quality* of the decision; the other has to do with its *acceptance* or the way the persons who must execute the decision *feel* about it. Failure to differentiate leads to complications in discussion because one person may be using the term 'good' to describe the quality of the decision, another to describe its acceptability, and a third may be thinking in terms of the outcome, which depends on both."

Maier represents these concepts schematically (see Fig. 6.3) as a guideline for the leader of problem-solving groups. According to Maier, aiming at both quality and acceptance, as shown at A, achieves neither. The

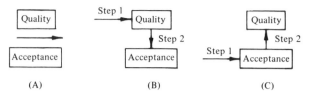

Fɪɢ. 6.3. Quality and acceptance as goals for problem solving. [Adapted from Maier (1963) by permission.]

traditional approach is shown in B, where one strives to achieve quality and then by means of persuasion, cajolery or merely issuing an order, tries to gain acceptance for putting the solution into operation. Maier goes on to state that when the primary objective is acceptance, as in C, then acceptance is assured, and the leader can concentrate on improving the quality. Maier concludes from his experiments with groups that this type of discussion leads to solutions of much higher quality than do either of the other two initial methods.

In actual applications and in training leaders in these techniques, we pose a problem to the leader, ask him to take his time and try to think of the best solution, write it down, and then lay it aside. He is then asked to lead a group of his subordinates concerned with the problem, forgetting his own solution but using the techniques to be described later. In every case in which the leader has used these techniques, he later avowed that the group solution was far superior to his own. Some have gone so far as to say they did not believe that they could ever have reached such a high quality solution by themselves.

Physical Arrangement.   There are many ways whereby the greatest exchange of communications among members of a group can be assured. Heise and Miller (1951), in experiments similar to Leavitt's but using verbal communications and word and sentence construction problems (with considerable interfering noise) showed that the most centrally located member of a group is likely to emerge as the leader. Howells and Becker (1962) confirm this relationship between the emergence of leadership and seating arrangement. Festinger *et al.* (1950) showed that communication between individuals tends to be greatest when they are opposite one another, and least when they are next to each other. Therefore, *the perfect physical arrangement for getting maximum communication among all individuals,* and to minimize the emergence of one who will attempt to become a leader, *is to seat the members at as round a table as possible.*[3]

---

[3] King Arthur had the right idea. If he eventually failed, the reason was that he did not use some of the other techniques derived from social science findings which are being presented here.

INDIVIDUAL DIFFERENCES AMONG GROUP MEMBERS

This is a book on social science technology, and, as such, it cannot be content to find solutions by using *some* findings, or even many findings, from just one area. We will now add some data from an entirely different area, which, when combined with the rest of the material on group problem solving, has made it possible to create impressive solutions. The two persuasions presented in Chapter 5 were developed by using this newly integrated technique. For more background material, we must define some relevant personal characteristics and their effect in groups.

Shaw (1964) considers the effects of individual differences among group members as possible variables in their behavior. He cites the experimental work of Berkowitz (1956) on ascendance and Shaw (1959) on authoritarianism and leadership style, which was important in the work of Lewin *et al.* (1939). Schutz (1958) has developed a group problem-solving theory based on these personal characteristics, i.e., the degree of being part of the group, determination of the activities of others, and warmth of interpersonal responsiveness. We shall go much deeper than Schutz.

DIFFERENTIATION OF FUNCTION
IN GROUP PROBLEM SOLVING

Guilford (1967) offers an operational model for problem solving in general, which is a direct derivation of his SI model and refers to the internal process by which a person solves a given problem. Figure 6.4 is a simplified representation of the original. Guilford's model reflects his belief that "problem solving is as about as broad as behavior itself." According to the said model, a person receives a given input and filters this input while his attention is aroused. He also draws on his memory storage for relevant information, evaluates the material, and may produce a solution. However, upon receiving a further input or information from memory storage, a cognition may result, that is, the person senses and structures the problem, whereupon he uses his divergent production to generate answers. These are then evaluated, returned to memory storage, etc., until a final solution is given to the problem. Of course, the whole process will be limited by the level of the subject's skill in his weakest area. For example, if the subject has a poor memory, he may simply fail to recall information that might prove useful to the solution. If he is low in divergent production, many ideas will be bypassed merely because they never occur to him. Or, he may have thousands of ideas and not be able to decide which is the best because he ranks low in the evaluation of implications. Since the SI model (which was devised when less than 30 abilities had been discovered) proposes that there are now a total of 120 abilities—

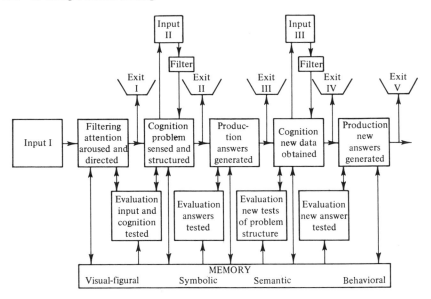

Fig. 6.4. Operational model for problem solving. [Adapted from Guilford (1967) by permission.]

99 having already been studied (personal communication from Dr. Guilford) —it is highly unlikely that any one individual will score in the 90th percentile in all of them. This point has already been discussed in Chapter 2; however, when persons get together to discuss in a group, there will quite likely be a variety of abilities represented. Therefore, a skillful group leader, knowing the makeup of the members of his group, can take full advantage of these differences and channel the discussion at appropriate points to the persons who have the abilities required for that phase of the solution of the problem.

This recommendation is in direct opposition to Osborn's (1953) *brainstorming* technique. Let us look at the findings of Besse *et al.* (1958), who cite the case of a failure of a brainstorming session: A French industrialist wanted to find an adequate translation for the English word "survey." He therefore held a brainstorming meeting with 9 participants that lasted 30 minutes and produced 154 suggestions, none of which was usable. Had he instead called in only one or two persons who were high in the divergent production of semantic units, he probably would have solved the problem in a few minutes.

An even more impressive case, which incidentally shows the lack of communication between researchers in different areas of the social sciences is given by Swingle (1968). Recognizing that there is a greater probability of obtaining an appropriate combination of abilities in groups than in single individuals, a paper by Dunnette, Campbell, and Jaastad (1963) is reprinted in full. In this study, the authors conclude that group participation inhibits the output of ideas whereas individual action does not. Two types of problems were posed. The first kind is typified by examples like, "What benefits or difficulties would result from people having an extra thumb?" and, "What would be the consequences of a stabilization in the average height of Americans at 80 inches?" These are, however, exactly the type of problem that constitutes the test formulated by Christensen, Merrifield, and Guilford (1958). These workers have found such questions to be highly loaded on divergent production of behavioral transformations. Therefore, problems of this type are used to measure this ability. The other kind of problem is typified by, for example, "In view of the fact that 50% of all those leaving college will have to enter teaching, what steps would have to be taken to ensure the continuation of a high teaching standard?" or, "What could be done to increase tourism?" Again, this reflects an isolated ability: cognition of behavioral implications as developed by Berger and Guilford (1960). Dunnette et al., obviously unaware of the work of Guilford et al., were giving groups presumably complex problems. The problems cited by the authors of the tests had actually been identified as simple problems involving the use of only one ability. Small wonder then that those who scored high in these abilities were more productive when working alone than when interfered with by workers who scored low in the same test. The Dunnette et al. study corroborates the writer's contention that when a single ability is involved, those highest in that ability should be consulted individually. This is more effective than calling for a group solution involving individuals normally distributed along that dimension. It is evident that Dunnette and his co-workers were doing their research unaware of the fact that in an entirely different area Guilford and his co-workers were providing an explanation for the negative results obtained by Dunnette.

In order to train supervisors in the value of the proposed method, we gathered together a group of persons in an Uruguayan company, including the President, several Managers, and some Department Heads. They were asked which of them were versed in soccer—the Uruguayan national sport. Four out of the 12 members present claimed to have quite a good knowledge not only of the intricacies of the game but also of the different clubs, players, etc. The large group was therefore divided into four smaller groups of three members each. Since these persons had already been tested on divergent production of semantic systems and implications and on divergent production of figural implications, one person high on the former and another high on the latter was placed in each group. One soccer expert was also included in each group. Then the following problem was posed: "Mr. Smith, President of the River Soccer Club, has asked us to design an insignia for its club. The insignia must incorporate a design which is related to the history or present status of the club and which includes a five-word sentence or slogan in which the beginning letters of the words are, successively, r, i, v, e, and r. Let's see how good at this sort of thing each one of these four groups is. You will have 15 minutes."

It was most interesting to watch this performance. Each group had to hear the story of the club first from the member who knew more about soccer. (Here is the operation of memory skills.) As this happened, each began to think in terms of the area in which he was strongest, although no one was aware of this, since no one had been informed of the test results. Thus, the Head of Social Relations (who knew football) had to instruct the President, who knew nothing, as well as the Head of the Typing Pool. Then the President, who was extremely high in divergent production of semantic systems but low in the figural area, began to write the different possible slogans. At the same time, Head of the Typing Pool, who was good in the figural skills, began to draw different designs. There were immediate consultations with the man who knew football in order to evaluate the products. When the 15 minutes had elapsed, each group had created a variety of extremely ingenious solutions. One of the groups had designed flags; the other designed shields; while the remaining two had devised lapel buttons. The signs of win-lose conflict on a grand scale immediately emerged. As each group presented their solutions, the others derided them. Since the writer had deliberately omitted writing the instructions on the blackboard, the subject of the discussion turned to what kind of design had originally been requested. Some remembered that insignia had been asked for; others recalled instructions for an emblem or device. The discussion rapidly took the form of "looking into the past." (We shall see how unconstructive this type of behavior can be.) After it had continued for a little while, the members of all four groups were made to see how easily one can fall into win-lose conflict and how much easier it would have been either to use just one sub-group or else to use the whole group of 12.

But what became most apparent to all was that abilities should indeed be combined if a successful product is to be produced. Everyone freely admitted that he could never have turned out anything as good as the final designs created, even allotted a much longer time. Even the President saw that he needed two other people in order to be able to contribute to a good product. Since that first meeting, all concerned have learned solving a problem with their groups is not simply a matter of creating a comcon network in which everyone faces and talks with everyone else; rather, to be effective, the discussion must be properly channeled. There are phases like the one of divergent production (when the group is looking for possible solutions) in which some people have great ability and enjoy using it. Others who do not possess this skill feel quite uncomfortable and out of place if asked to contribute a new idea. However, during the evaluation phase, those who had remained silent may be called upon. Everyone feels good because he has participated in the area where he feels strongest.

THE AREA OF FREEDOM

This concept is taken directly from Maier (1963), who states: "Problem solving is successful only if the solution reached is one that can be put into practice." He also notes that attempts to fix blame and/or correct past mistakes are impracticable and therefore serve only to hinder the problem-solving process:

"Ideas for improvement are frequently expressed in the form of actions that others should take. Workers tend to blame their superiors or higher management when things go wrong, and higher management tends to blame the attitude of workers for production difficulties. Thus the problem solver tends to overlook himself as an object of change. This tendency to formulate solutions that others should execute is unproductive because it requires action from an outsider, and the problem solver finds himself rather helpless while he waits for other persons to make the changes he recommends . . . Furthermore, groups are best informed on matters that concern their own activity. Thus the solutions recommended tend to be based upon factual considerations, and this knowledge operates to improve the quality of decisions. However, this does not mean that the group that takes the problem under consideration is morally obliged to make the improvements. Justice would demand that the persons at fault should change. However, at this point we are not considering the matter of justice; rather our concern is with how to improve matters and make the best of a given situation. The questions of justice and how best to improve a situation are independent objectives and should not be confused . . . The tendency to blame others is a backwards-looking approach. The past is beyond control and cannot be altered. Only the present and the future are subject to change, and hence only they can be controlled through decisions. The problem-solving approach, therefore, must incorporate an attitude that accepts the past and takes up the problem of what to do to reach present objectives . . . This problem-solving attitude is not present during frustration. Frustrated persons are most inclined to blame others. Solutions designed to fix blame are in conflict with a problem-solving attitude because they represent attempts to correct the past rather than to control the future . . . Since it is human to be subject to frustration and hence to become handicapped in problem solving, it follows that group decisions made by persons who are angry or on the defensive will lack quality. True problem solving can only begin after this adverse condition has been corrected."

It would be impossible to overemphasize *the importance of not fixing blame.* In our first attempts to lead problem-solving groups according to findings integrated from several areas, this was the only point on which we had to firmly intervene. After starting a meeting and carefully explaining the necessity to avoid blaming, invariably someone would do so anyway, placing the guilt on someone from outside. We, as group leader, would then stop the discussion and say: "I ask you if you believe if this lies within our area of freedom?" Many would recognize that it was not. Then the next question would be: "Under whose area would that be?" Frequently, the answer would be: "That belongs to X Department." At this, the leader would ask the group: "Would you prefer that we continue within the area of freedom of this group, or else call in the Head of X Department?" At first, this had to be done repeatedly. Now, in experienced groups, as soon as there is the slightest hint that someone else is being talked about, there will be at least two or three participants who will say: "Let's stop right here and call in Joe."

With regard to the past, the same situation holds true. Experienced groups now meet to solve a problem caused by a mistake on the part of an easily identifiable individual, and not a word is mentioned to him about his mistake. The identifiable individual sits with the rest and works just as hard as anyone to see how they can extricate themselves from the mess that his error has caused.[4]

INITIAL PROCEDURES FOR GROUP PROBLEM SOLVING

LIMITING TIME FOR SOLVING A PROBLEM

It quite often happens that groups meet in order to solve a problem and then leave the meeting in a state of rather bitter frustration because a lot was discussed, most of it quite interesting, but no conclusion was reached. Sometimes this failure may result from the generation of win-lose conflict which divides the participants into those in favor of idea A, those in favor of idea B, and the neutrals who don't seem to lean either way (in spite of the determined efforts of both sides to win them over). On other occasions, the failure may have been caused by the fact that too much time was devoted to trivial matters. Often a meeting may be called for a given time, but the length of the meeting is not determined in advance. It therefore drags on and on, until someone says he has an appointment, or the meeting is otherwise disbanded.

In our first experience with group problem solving in well-organized companies, the practice was always to set a starting time and a closing time

[4] Although this discussion varies somewhat from what Maier suggests, principally in the reasons for which certain things are done, the reader is urged to read Maier (1963) for a great number of useful tips, only some of which will be mentioned here.

for the meeting. For example, a meeting might be called from 9:00 A.M.–9:55 A.M. The five-minute reduction from the full hour was made to give people time to get back to their offices for 10:00 A.M. appointments. Nevertheless, it seemed that no matter how important or trivial the problem, it always took one hour to find a solution. Our experience was supported by Aronson and Gerard (1966), who tested Parkinson's (1957) whimsical law that "work expands to fill the time available." They gave subjects very easy tasks to do. Then, by means of a trick, they allowed some only 5 minutes to complete it, while giving 15 minutes to others to perform the same task. The subjects then had to perform a second task—this time with no time limitation. It was found that the subjects who had had only 5 minutes in which to do the first easy task spent a median time of 3.6 minutes in performing the second easy task. In contrast, the median time on task number 2, for those who were initially allowed 15 minutes, was 7.8 minutes. In other words, persons who had initially had more time available to do a certain task, now *needed* more time to finish a similar task later on. Obviously, a certain set is formed by the original instructions which carries over to other situations.

We mentioned this finding to the very next group which was being trained in group problem solving. The group was asked to apply this finding to more efficient solutions of its own problems. Eventually, it was decided that at the start of every problem-solving session the leader would state which problems needed solutions and ask the group how much time each problem deserved. Because of the knowledge and experience of the participants, it was quite easy to get estimates from them as to the time it would be necessary and desirable to spend on any one problem. (This pre-estimation has now become standard procedure.) After the group has decided how much time should be spent, the individual members will experience cognitive dissonance if they take up more than the allotted time. They will reduce the dissonance by hurrying up the discussion and leaving trifles aside in order to get to the best solution within the prescribed, reasonable period of time. We have seen some remarkably ingenious solutions arise out of very short meetings—some of them attempts to seek an emergency way out of an uncomfortable situation.

DEFINING THE PROBLEM

The first prerequisite for good group problem solving is knowing *which problem one wants to solve*. Mackworth (1965) makes a clear distinction between problem solving and problem finding. His thesis is that in this age of computers, there are far more facilities for problem solving than for finding problems for the computers to solve. Gagne (1966), although recognizing that there may be a valid distinction between the two processes, adds that

Mackworth's distinction "does not add much to our understanding of problem solving." This statement may be true at the theoretical level where, as usual, scientists are engaged in finding the profound truth of why certain processes occur. Nevertheless, faced with the search for adequate technology to solve practical, day-to-day difficulties, we have found that distinguishing between problem finding and problem solving with a group is of the utmost importance.

Sometime ago, one of the leading social psychologists in the United States informed us that a group, each member of which represented one of several conflicting views on a major topic related to social psychology, would spend a year at a study center discussing their various and often violently conflicting viewpoints. After this scientist mentioned the name of each representative, we remarked that there would be one person missing in the group. Quite surprised at having forgotten one viewpoint, the scientist asked "What tendency have I missed? Who else should be there?" The writer's answer was: "Dr. Norman R. F. Maier, the man that could make you all reach an agreement. Otherwise, you will run the risk of leaving the sessions in greater antagonism than existed before starting the discussions." This advice was not followed, and the result was a book that further obscures the controversies.

Maier (1963) makes the point that locating the problem is essential to achieving a solution. Very often a group meets to solve a problem, arrives at a solution, and later learns, to the chagrin of all, that the problem did not lie where they had thought. A perhaps trivial, though interesting case, occurred when a group in a company got together to decide how to keep outsiders from going into the company washrooms, thereby keeping them neat. A solution was finally adopted: The washrooms would be locked and every employee given a key. In this way, no outsider could have access to the washrooms, and they would therefore remain clean. The locks were duly put in place, and keys carefully issued to all with the admonition that they were for personal use only. Later inspections showed that the washrooms continued to be just as messy as before. Obviously, the problem had not been solved. The elimination of outsiders had been thoroughly accomplished, to the discomfiture of clients, friends and other visitors who found they could no longer make use of these facilities. When eventually a meeting was called to solve the problem of "what can be done to assure that our washrooms are tidy at all times?" an extremely simple solution involving brief training sessions was found. The washrooms are now perfectly tidy; they are open to the general public; and most of the employees have misplaced or lost their keys, which had proved to be an utterly useless expense.

The problem described above was a minor one in which a minor expense and some discomfort to others was involved. Nevertheless, solving the wrong problem quite often proves to be very costly and embarrassing to many, and it can create conflict as well. Therefore, although there has been little theoretical work done in this area, as Gagne states, we will certainly rely on whatever empirical research is available.

It is here that Maier (1963) comes to our aid. Maier gives a person the following problem: From the ceiling of a room hang two strings that reach the floor. A little bit of the lower ends lie on the floor. The strings are rather far apart. The subject is asked to tie the two strings into a knot. It is obvious that this is an impossible task, because when the subject takes one end of the strings and tries to reach the other, he fails because the two are still too far away. Maier has shown how different persons react to this situation by locating the problem in different areas. These reactions are given in Table I. In each case, the person's action is linked to his particular location of where the problem lies. In spite of the fact that four different approaches are attempted, none is successful.

TABLE I*

Case	Person's action	Location of the problem
1.	Grabs string A with left hand and reaches as far as he can with right arm, trying to stretch the latter in an attempt to reach string B.	My right arm is too short.
2.	Grabs A with left hand, reaches for B. Since this cannot be accomplished, plays out as much as he can of A until holding just its very tip with fingers' ends.	String A is too short.
3.	Grabs A, stretches it as far as possible, and then makes a fast run to catch string B before string A falls back.	String A won't stay put.
4.	Grabs string A, goes as near as possible to string B and waves air from string B towards him with his hand.	String B won't come to me.

* Adapted from Maier (1963) by permission.

However, at the moment that the person is attempting to solve the problem using any of the listed approaches, Maier enters and offers the subject a pair of pliers to see whether this won't help solve the problem. It is interesting to note how each reacts. Case 1, who located the problem in the shortness of his arms, uses the pliers to extend them in order to reach farther. He is not successful. Case 2, who concluded that string A was too short, tries to solve the problem by opening the pliers, tying the end of one handle to the string, and obtaining an appreciable lengthening of it when they open the pliers. The problem is not solved by this means either. Case 3, who found that A did not stay put, pulls A as close as possible to B, and tries to hold A in place by using the pliers as a weight. Case 4, who at first might have seemed the most absurd, actually solved the problem by tying the pliers to B as a pendulum. Then he set B swinging and waited for it to come to him, while at the same time holding string A.

As can be seen from this simple but clear example, the location of the problem made all the difference in subjects' ability to reach a solution when new tools became available. This situation is something that occurs to us in daily life. Our first reaction is frequently to jump to an immediate conclusion about where the problem lies and then to make every effort to solve *that* problem. Maier warns us to spend considerable time "exploring, choosing and isolating a starting point. In order to develop these skills, it is necessary to suppress an interest in *solutions* and develop a greater interest in exploring the *problem*."

Some people may object to Maier's recommendations on the grounds that a person who wants to find a solution will find it very hard to devote his time instead to locating the problem so that others may find the solution. As a matter of fact, at least two objections to Maier's position have been formally stated, one by Maier himself (1962). One problem he poses is how to determine where a project such as the training of managers should begin. He objects to sending managers one by one to outside courses from which they return to their respective companies to find themselves in a minority. We heartily concur with this objection.

However, Maier also adds that it is best to start at the departmental level: "Beginning at the top seems to be a logical approach, but in practice the executive group is not available or is more concerned with financial rather than human relations considerations." We do not accept this statement. It has been our policy to start with the top group and get them enthusiastically engaged in the program—with everyone considering it to be as important as the financial and other considerations—or we will not start at all. If top management does not get fully involved and give top priority to personnel matters, realizing that all other troubles arise from personnel considerations, it is useless to begin at all.

Sherif (1962) is even more explicit. In his preface to the Blake and Mouton article, he recommends future research into factors that cause a change in top policy authority, in order to accept what Blake and Mouton call *behavioral science intervention*. He adds: "It is well known that policy makers in any organization are inclined to be rather jealous of these prerogatives." Sherif's point is well taken. It is difficult to have these top policy makers relinquish their prerogatives, not only to a behavioral scientist, but even worse to their own subordinates. Nevertheless, this apparently insoluble problem has been solved. It would require more space than can be given in an introductory book on social science technology to show how this solution can be accomplished, although a part of the answer may be found in the chapters on simple and complex persuasion. Eventually, perhaps, this most important and fascinating topic will be handled in full detail elsewhere.

Here, however, we will assume that *we* are not going to try to persuade someone else to do this but rather that the reader himself will apply the technology described. A possible immediate objection might be: "How can I apply this technology when I am not the officially designated group leader?" An example of how this was done by a person who was familiar with the technology, yet was not the officially designated leader, is given in Chapter 9.

Blame.   Returning, therefore, to the question of locating the problem, one of the most useful concepts that Maier provides is the possibility of classifying the location or source of a problem as:

- The situation
- An individual
- A group of individuals

Maier states that "when a supervisor (we might add: any other person) is emotionally involved, the most obvious thing for him to do is to locate the problem in some individual. This occurs because frustration makes people seek someone to blame." This is stated by Maier as a result of observation, but there is experimental evidence to prove that this actually does occur with almost monotonous regularity. For example, Dollard *et al.* (1939) have stated: "The strongest instigation aroused by frustration is to acts of aggression directed against the agent *perceived* to be the source of the frustration" (italics added). It is in perception and not in the true facts that this misdirected aggression lies. Therefore, the danger lies in that the aggression, or any other corrective action to a problem, may be directed at where the cause is *perceived* to be, when the actual cause may lie in an entirely different area. Berkowitz and Green (1962) were able to show that the direction of the aggression is directed towards a disliked person—even though this dislike had been experimentally induced only a few moments before! More recently, Freedman and Doob (1968) have shown that there is a strong tendency for a frustrated person to be aggressive toward a person who is perceived as deviant. Although there may be some disparities between this and other studies, such as Stricker's (1963), they all indicate that when persons are frustrated, they tend to be more aggressive toward someone else. This aggression has been measured objectively by seeing how much electric shock a subject is willing to give another, or whether he chose the latter at all for such shocks.

However, there are other ways in which persons can express their aggression. Buss (1961), in a classification of aggression that has proved useful in our work, lists the following forms aggression may take.

- Resentment: A feeling of anger over real or fancied mistreatment, verbalized in annoyance, whining, complaining, and demanding.
- Suspicion: An attitude of distrust in which hostility or aggressiveness is projected onto others.
- Verbal: A style of verbalization; included are yelling, cursing, being caustic, ironic, teasing. (We add: finding fault with work performed or manners, etc.)
- Assault: Acts of violence.
- Indirect: Aggression expressed in a roundabout or passive fashion; included are negativism, recalcitrance, spiteful silence, destruction of another's property.

The most common form of aggression, and the one that will most concern us here, is the *verbal* one. The frustrated supervisor, or a person in any position, will immediately say something that shows he is directing his aggression against the person he perceives as frustrating him. Maier adds: "The least likely location of a problem under such circumstances is the situation." In other words, we tend to blame *a person* and not just to accept the notion that the cause lies in a given situation and not necessarily another person. Besides, Maier adds that since the supervisor (or any person in that particular situation) blames someone else and overlooks the possibility that it is the situation that must change, he forgets that he himself is part of the situation and that he may therefore be partly to blame for his frustration. This discussion may sound complex; so let us present a recent example that ties in beautifully with the example that Maier (1963) gives about how to locate a problem and how to present the problem to a group.

In the offices of a large South American company, the telephone lines were often busy, and clients were having a difficult time reaching the different offices of the company. This situation became very frustrating to one of the top managers, particularly when he himself couldn't get through to some offices or could not get his calls to outside offices fast enough. It must be added that throughout most of South America, it is very difficult to get extra telephone lines installed. Capacity simply has not kept up with the tremendously increased demand. The solution of getting extra lines was therefore outside the area of freedom. This frustrating situation called forth a virtually inexorable rule of human behavior, i.e., to blame someone else. Accordingly, it was concluded that someone in the organization was to blame. Now it is a matter of pure observation, since nothing in the scientific literature has been found to justify it, that on such occasions, the women in the company are seen to be the guilty parties. It is felt that they tend to make many more and much longer personal calls than men do. Perhaps women are seen as deviant in a company, as Freedman and Doob (1968) have shown, or perhaps because they constitute a minority, they are thus susceptible as objects of aggression. The fact is that time and again, when this problem arises, some manager blames the women.

In this particular case, the manager involved was probably one of the most gentlemanly and agreeable persons in the organization. His frustration therefore did not take the form of physical aggression, shouting, sarcasm, etc.; rather, it took a verbal form. He called all the women in the company together to a meeting and very kindly explained the problem they were having, asking them to please cooperate in keeping their private calls to a minimum and in making them as short as possible. Since his approach was so respectful and amiable, there were no comments at the meeting, but quite by chance, we had the opportunity to hear some of the remarks made after the meeting: "I never make any calls (defensive); I only make calls when they are urgent (defensive); How about my boss and all the calls he makes to his girl friends? (ironic, caustic); How about all the private calls I have to make for my boss? (aggressive, caustic)." It can be seen from the above reactions that the probability of getting voluntary improvement from all concerned would be rather low. Besides, it was immediately revealed that many of the *men* were making and receiving long private calls and that there were probably many other reasons for the phone tie-up. One was the habit many people had of holding a client on the line with nonessential talk for as much as 10 minutes, while an employee was getting information the client had requested.

Clearly, the frustrated manager involved had done the natural thing. He had placed the blame on someone else, had gone directly to those involved, and in the women's estimation, been aggressive to them. But the problem was not: "How can I best tell these women to stop using the phones?" The *real* problem was: "How can we all expedite the use of the phone?" Had the latter been seen as the location of the problem, good cooperation could probably have been obtained.

Let us look at the problem from the *reactance* viewpoint. Brehm (1966) has shown that when a person's freedom is threatened in a certain way, he tends to restore this freedom either by engaging in the forbidden activity or else by engaging in some other, even more obnoxious behavior. It is interesting to note that as soon as the meeting described was over, more than half the women present went to their desks to make extended outside calls to explain to their relatives, friends, etc., what had happened and that it would be harder to talk in the future. In other words, the meeting had an immediate adverse effect on the very problem the manager was trying to solve! It is obvious, therefore, that if we wish to ensure a group's cooperation in reaching a good quality solution to a problem, we must not cause reactance. Any location of the problem that fixes the blame on someone, no matter how well presented, is likely to cause reactance. Two things must be done: The first is to cool off, so that we will not blame a scapegoat for our frustration and thereby cause many more frustrations. The second rule, which requires a little practice and use of divergent ability in semantic transformations, is to change our original "blaming so-and-so" location of the problem to a non-reactance provoking location and communication of the problem to the group. Maier's example (1963) is a good one that can be readily analyzed in terms of the social science concepts that have been presented in this book. The statement of the problem is quoted in full by permission.

"Jim Telfer is the supervisor in a general office of an insurance company. The group he supervises is made up of five girls who work at desks. A good deal of the work involves telephone contacts with company people who require information which various girls have in their files. Since all of the phones are on one line, the person who answers uses a buzzer signal, and in this way the person requested, or the person who has the needed information, can take over the call. Mr. Telfer never answers the phone unless one of the girls informs him by buzzer that the call is for him. Ordinarily the girl with the least service answers the phone and then buzzes the girl who can handle the call.

A relief period of fifteen minutes both morning and afternoon is given to the girls, and this is regarded as adequate for the usual personal needs. Mr. Telfer has asked them to take their relief one at a time so as to keep coverage of the office. When the work is heavy, the girls frequently skip their relief.

Mr. Telfer's boss complained that Telfer was hard to reach by phone because the line was always busy. He said that he could reach other units which do the same type of work as Telfer's, and he expressed the opinion that Telfer's group was making too many personal calls. Telfer knows that the girls make outside calls rather freely and that they receive quite a number of personal calls because, on several occasions, he picked up his phone and found that the conversation had nothing to do with business. For example, twice during the past week he found Irene Wilson talking with her boyfriend. Telfer told his boss that he would do something about it and has decided to talk the problem over with the girls."

Table II shows some of the different possible locations, the psychological processes involved, and the possible reactions.

PRESENTING THE PROBLEM TO THE GROUP

The example given refers in part to the location of the problem, but the way in which the problem should be presented to the group has also been

TABLE II*

Problem location	Behavioral	Situational
Group abuse	"How can we best deal with the matter of unnecessary use of the company phone for personal purposes?" (Provokes reactance)	"What would be a fair goal to set for personal calls?" (Reactance-provoking from whole group, although less than statement at left)
Individual's abuse	"Some of us use the phone for personal purposes more than others. To what extent and how should we control this?" (Provokes more reactance from some and tends to divide group)	"Should we keep records of personal calls by individuals or by the whole unit?" (Provokes reactance from some, although less than statement at left)
Attitude of Telfer's superior	"My boss has complained about the use of the phone for personal purposes. What can we do to make ourselves less subject to his criticism?" (Reactance-provoking and tends to place Telfer and group in win-lose conflict)	"My boss has difficulty in reaching this office. Is there any way we can plan our work so as to make this unit more available to him?" (Slightly reactance provoking)
Efficient use of phones	"How can we use our phones more efficiently?" (Dissonance-provoking since they felt they used phones efficiently and it is now suggested they do not)	"How can the present work be organized to get the most service out of our single line?" (No dissonance nor reactance here, although there may be a tendency to limit the area of discussion to the phone)
Better service	"How can we do a better job in giving service to the persons requesting information?" (Dissonance-provoking since they were giving the best service)	"What kind of service index might we establish for our unit?" (No dissonance, no reactance, no conflict. Leaves problem wide open for improvement in many areas. Perhaps the problem did not even lie in the phone service at all)

* Adapted from Maier (1963) by permission.

touched upon. In a certain sense, these two points are inseparable. Maier states several guiding principles that are useful in assuring the best possible participation, as well as the best possible, positive thinking toward high quality solutions. These principles are listed, along with a comment on each one.

Use Situational Rather than Behavioral Statements of Problem!   [A behavioral statement causes reactance, which in turn may cause such resentment among those present that activity will be directed toward creating a defensive attitude rather than solving the problem. In other words, it is likely that references to bad or undesirable behavior, or even the hint of blaming someone (however mildly worded), will tend to agitate the individual to the point where he can no longer freely apply his mental abilities.]

State the Problem in Such a Way That It Encourages Freedom of Thought.   [One way in which this can be done is to state the problem in nonreactance-provoking terms, as shown above. Another is to avoid even hinting at solutions or suggestions. Giving solutions may be dissonance- or reactance-provoking: If the solution differs from what the participants had in mind, there will be cognitive dissonance, which will probably be reduced by finding fault with the proposed solution. If the solution given is restrictive or perceived as such, then it will be reactance-provoking.]

Statement of the Problem Should Incorporate Mutual Interests.   [Very often, a supervisor, harassed by a certain problem, assumes that his subordinates feel the same frustration. For example, a manager troubled with rising costs will often assume that his foreman should also be as interested in the subject as he is. However, the foreman may be more interested in seeing that production gets through, or ensuring plant safety. A problem presented in such a way as not to interest the participants will elicit little participation. If, on the other hand, a little ingenuity is used to present the problem in terms that affect the participants, there will be much more interest in seeking a solution. It is wise to recall Abelson's (1959) statement: "No normal person is happy in a situation that he cannot control to some extent." There will be further reference to participation in Chapter 9.]

Statement of the Problem Should Specify One Objective.   [This is an extremely practical and valuable suggestion, with nothing but common sense and experience to support it. If more than one problem is presented, different members will embark on different problems and chaos will result. Maier probably makes this recommendation because it is very common for group leaders to start out by stating two or three problems. The meeting then results in general confusion.]

The Statement of the Problem Should Be Brief.   [This would seem to be a corollary of the preceding statement. Once the problem is presented to the group, the leader must remember that although he has been giving the matter a lot of thought, the group has not. (In most polite society, silences are the exception rather than the rule. Reasons, like "it must be 20 minutes to" or "an angel passed" as superstitious explanations for the silence, are given as explanations for silences at parties and other gatherings.) However, when silence greets the leader's announcement of the problem to the group, this is normal. Different people need more or less time to start thinking in a new direction. The leader, however, often feels a terrible urge to fill in this silence, frequently by adding data, which are usually dissonance- or reactance-provoking, or by presenting yet another problem. In any case, continuing to talk interferes with the earliest stage of the problem-solving process of the group, that is, getting the others to start thinking and expressing their views. A leader must therefore learn how to pose a problem and wait with absolute unconcern for minutes (that may seem like centuries), until *someone else* speaks. This may be very difficult for some people, but it is an essential requisite for success.]

Sharing Essential Information. [Very often this objection is raised to group-oriented problem solving: The leader knows more of the overall picture than does the group; and he has, besides, data that the group does not have that is essential to reach an adequate solution. Both statements may be true. As a reply to the first, it must be stated that although the leader may have a better overall picture, he lacks many day-to-day details that his subordinates may know. As a reply to the second part of the objection, we follow Maier's admonition—share this information with the group. But Maier warns us again that this sharing must be done in an absolutely neutral and nondirective way. In other words, the information imparted should be given in such a way as to provoke neither reactance nor dissonance that will be reduced by derogating the authority. Instead of saying, "Here's a comparison of waste during last month and this month, note how much more waste we had this month," the leader can tell the group, "I have here figures which you may find of interest; they are the waste figures for the past two months—April x and May y." Maier notes that this sharing of information can take place at any moment in the discussion. At many of our own meetings, it is usual for a leader to stop the discussion for a moment and say, "I have some information bearing on this point that I would like to share with you."]

Give Assurance. [Although this point is stated later in Maier's book and not with the main principles governing the start of a discussion, we feel that it is so important that it should be incorporated into the discussion of how to state the problem.

Fear, anxiety, instability, are all states of mind that are not conducive to good problem solving. It is therefore imperative that the very statement of the problem, as well as its location, be made in such a manner as to avoid all possibility of creating fear or anxiety among group members. Very often the installation of computers in organizations has caused great reactance because workers fear the computer is going to limit freedom and displace people. Everyone therefore feels threatened, and no one is in a proper frame of mind to think of the best utilization of the computer. The same reasoning applies when a "methods" department is installed in an organization. Usually the reason for installing this type of department is that supervisors are too busy to think of new ideas on how to improve the operation. Therefore, an outsider is called in to study the matter and devise a better way to run the department. The supervisor, on hearing of this, immediately feels threatened and consequently invents all sorts of reasons why the newly proposed methods are not acceptable. The supervisor feels a loss of freedom regarding how he may do his job, with reactance the inevitable result. In this way, Methods Departments frequently cause reactance and dissonance among employees.

The group leader should therefore start out by reassuring the group and eliminating the perceived threat. An excellent way to do so is to tell the members that no decision will be taken concerning the subject that is not unanimously adopted by the group. If said in good faith and later carried out, this promise can work wonders.]

PROMOTING CONSTRUCTIVE PROBLEM SOLVING

TWO TYPES OF DISCUSSION

Maier makes a clear distinction between two types of discussions that may occur at any time—the feeling or *emotional* and the intellectual or *rational*. The emotional discussion is quite common and is, in general, irrational (observe arguments between extreme partisans of politics, philosophies, religions, sports, etc.). Each side is violent and unswerving in his ideas. The individual listens to the other side only to counter whatever the opponent has said. This type of discussion often leads to destructive conflict, war, revolution, or other forms of bloodshed, or to bitter destructive antagonisms in organizations. The rational type of discussion, on the other hand, is one in which the individuals involved are all genuinely concerned with finding the solution to a given problem.

However, appearances must not mislead us. It is quite possible for the irrational type of discussion to seem very polite when seen from outside the group. The individuals may be aggressive in very polite or subtle ways. Resentment, suspicion, silence, sarcastic remarks, may all be expressed in apparently courteous terms and thus not easily observed by others. On the other hand, a rational type of discussion may be very vehement. There may be a lot of excitement involved—shouting or intense and ardent arguing —which nevertheless lacks the hostile feeling content to which Maier refers.

If a leader wishes to achieve a good solution with maximum acceptance, he must keep in mind that his conduct will vary widely depending on the type of discussion that he sees occurring. It is therefore necessary for him to be able to diagnose the discussion so that he may act accordingly. People who are very hostile or fearful or who are experiencing approach-avoidance conflict or reactance are not very constructive group members and will tend to oppose all the suggestions presented. The leader must therefore be constantly on the alert to prevent rational discussion from suddenly or gradually turning into an emotional one. This change is, unfortunately, quite a common occurrence.

The Irrational Discussion. This type of discussion, as just stated, is one in which the participants let their feelings control their thinking. In such a situation, the overwrought members are in no condition to contribute constructively toward a satisfactory solution. On a physiological level, their higher mental processes are apparently blocked by excessive reticular activation. As a result, they are of no practical use in terms of problem solving.

In such cases, one of the major tasks of the group leader is to reduce the emotional level so that the individuals can fully utilize their mental abilities. One of the greatest social discoveries of the 18th century was that men need not be subjected to the whims and wills of hereditary authorities, so one of the greatest discoveries of the 20th century is probably that men are often subjected to the tyranny of their own passions, which cause considerable misery both to themselves and to others. Perhaps an even greater discovery is the fact that ways have been found whereby men can *help one another* regain the intellectual freedom that each has lost and could not regain by himself. In this treatment of the irrational type of discussion, we will see that there is much that each one of us can do to help others regain this priceless freedom—the freedom to have full use of the different abilities with which each happens to be endowed.

Diagnosis. The first thing a group leader (or any person who wishes to help another regain his intellectual freedom) must do is to diagnose whether a state of emotionality exists. As usual, we cannot prescribe action until we have diagnosed the problem. One important reason for this diagnosis is that normally we are used to countering such emotional states with facts and reasons. This is all right if the person involved is freed from his emotions and can think rationally by using his mental abilities to understand what is being said. However, if the person is in an emotional state, say, he is fearful of losing his job because of a new system, process or machine being installed, he will be quite impervious to all the arguments we can marshal to prove to him that the change will actually be beneficial to him. To him, facts and reasons mean nothing if he perceives the proposed change as threatening his security.

Fortunately, there are many ways we can diagnose the existence of intellect-blocking emotionality, all of which involve identifying the symptoms that different individuals exhibit. An alert leader is constantly on guard to detect these symptoms; if he finds them, he proceeds immediately to eliminate their source. If not, he will run the risk of creating an emotionally charged, destructive meeting, or a meeting in which some members are unjustly deprived of their full intellectual capacity while something important, which could eventually affect them, is being discussed.

Symptoms of irrationality. We shall now give some symptoms of an irrational meeting and then detail several types of action the leader may take in order to reduce the noxious emotionality.

Aggression. We have already referred to the different forms aggression may take. Aggression here does not only refer to physical assault (one member of a group grabs the other by his tie and starts punching him). We also recognize the many subtle and socially approved ways in which aggression can be shown, such as sarcasm, hostility projected toward others, ironic comments, and caustic remarks. For example, someone may state in the middle of a meeting: "One solution would be for the maintenance men to take along a small supply of the most used spare parts." Another member replies: "Of course, with the splendid service we get from The Spare Parts Department, this will always work fine." If we know that the second member has been having trouble procuring spare parts, such a statement is a symptom of aggression and therefore of emotionality, however well hidden by his outwardly polite appearance. The same thing may happen in the home if someone says: "Ah! You can always count on Aunt Jane." If we know that Aunt Jane is unreliable, we realize this statement was made sarcastically and therefore constitutes aggression.

Regression. This has already been discussed as a reaction to approach-avoidance conflict in Chapter 3. It is defined as acting in a childish manner. For example, when someone is asked what he thinks of a certain idea he may reply: "I don't want to be bothered with all this. I want to be left alone and out of it."

Fixation. This has also been mentioned as a symptom in approach-avoidance situations investigated by Maier (1949). At meetings it is evidenced by a person who continues to insist on a suggestion he made long after the group has progressed to other ideas. It's the man who keeps saying: "I still think a pressure washer is the solution to the vibration problem." He knows all kinds of pressure washers have been tried but that there are still many complaints from product users about parts working loose. Yet, he seems incapable of abandoning his fixed solution.

Rationalization. The same explanation of this process given in connection with approach-avoidance conflict also applies here.

Projection. This was also discussed in Chapter 3, and its definition applies here as well, with the slight difference that in meetings, projection takes an aggressive form and is therefore easier to detect.

Action to promote rationality. Once a symptom of emotionality has been detected, the underlying cause should be dealt with immediately. This section presents some forms of action that can be taken to reduce emotionality.

Giving assurance. This is suggested by Maier (1963). For example, if the meeting is called to discuss the introduction of a new machine or process —something that will immediately create symptoms of emotionality—full assurance should be given to the group that the new element will in no way impair the present or future standing of those present. Of course, this must be the true intention. If the change is going to adversely affect those present, then holding a meeting about how to obtain the best results from the change would be a leadership blunder.

As previously stated, we have often seen the reactions in organizations when it is mentioned that a computer will be installed. When those promoting such an installation point to the saving in manpower as the main advantage, they often create such opposition that the effectiveness of the computer is virtually nullified. On the other hand, when the computer is introduced as a tool that will make it possible to accomplish more work and that it may necessitate hiring extra personnel (as often happens), all signs of fear vanish. The participants lay their negative feelings aside and contribute with great interest and enthusiasm to thinking of ways in which to use the computer.

One way we have found effective in reducing fear is for the leader to begin to offer an opinion but then stop. When one of the participants asks him: "What is your solution to this?" he replies: "My solution to this problem is the one that you as a group will arrive at unanimously. It would be folly for me to give a solution when all those present, because they are much closer to the work situation, know so much more than I do." This is said in all honesty, even concerning personnel matters in which we are considered to be an authoritative consultant. A solution imposed or sold by the group leader is useless if there is fear on the part of some of the participants, because the solution will not be accepted.

Catharsis. This term refers to what happens when a person is allowed to "talk out" his gripe. Instead of telling him to be reasonable and to please calm down, the leader very interestedly asks him to expand on the subject. We have seen at least one group leader use this method very effectively. After letting the man rant and rave and asking him questions until the leader felt the cathartic effect had run its course, he then asked: "Look, this seems so important, but at the same time so complex, that I would like to hear a summary of it so we can post it on the blackboard and analyze it." The participant, completely calmed down, merely said: "Maybe things aren't that bad. It's just that sometimes they look like that to me." Other reactions were similar.

The reader may perhaps feel shocked and consider it unethical to deal in such a manner with a human being. In many parts of this book, similar treatments are advocated which may also provoke negative reactions from some readers. It sounds like "manipulating" people, which has always been considered incorrect—if not completely immoral. There are several replies to this objection: Although this kind of manipulation may be repudiated by many, it is often necessary to avoid even worse consequences. To consider an analogy: Would the reader deliberately cut deeply with a blunt penknife into a person's leg, making two deep crosses $\frac{1}{2}$ in. long $\times$ $\frac{1}{4}$ in. deep, in order to create two wounds that bleed profusely? Such a suggestion would probably be met with a horrified look. However, if it is explained that the cuts are to be made at the two points where a rattlesnake has just buried its fangs and we are far from any aid, the same apparently barbarous act would be considered a deed of mercy because it would save a man's life. A similar situation occurs in the case cited earlier. Such a deliberate manipulation done for no reason at all is indeed reprehensible, but if it is done in order to restore the person's freedom to think, it is analogous to cutting a person to save his life from poisoning. The dangers of snake poison are easy to visualize. We must become equally accustomed to recognizing the dangers of "mind poisoning," particularly in the very common cases of self-poisoning. We must therefore be willing to use certain types of manipulation.

There is another aspect involved. Persons not trained in the use of these techniques may be afraid to try them because they may be shy or perhaps rank somewhat low in behavioral skills. The same thing probably happens to the young medical student faced with making his first incision. Eventually, however, he gets quite used to making frightful cuts, sawing bones, tying arteries, etc., and can do all this almost automatically. Similarly, if we wish to be therapeutic in social affairs, we must be just as willing to use tools and methods that may at first strike us as revolting.

Silence.   On some occasions, a prolonged silence will contribute greatly to reducing tensions. This is not an easy thing to do. As mentioned before, we are used to filling in silences in general conversation. However, if the meeting has gotten out of hand, the leader might kindly say: "Wait a minute. I would like the group to remain silent for a moment while I ponder over this." No matter how antagonistic two or more persons have been, or how heated the discussion, a silence of 5 to 8 minutes' duration will make it very difficult for a group to restore the discussion with the same intensity, particularly if the silence is eventually broken by the leader asking a rather innocuous question on a noncontroversial side topic. The silence device, however, should be used only in extreme instances. If the rational discussion has been well conducted, the group will never reach the stage in which this expedient becomes necessary.

Reflecting.   This method, originally devised by Rogers (1942) has been extended by Maier to use in problem-solving discussions (1963). It is particularly effective in reducing emotionality expressed in the form of aggression and rationalization. Specifically, it consists of repeating the speaker's emotional feeling in different words. However, this restatement must be expressed in a nonevaluative way, in wording as well as tone of voice, i.e., the leader must give no hint of approval or disapproval.

For example, a group member may say: "That would be impossible because the way the Cost Department delays in giving the figures, we would never be able to supply the information, so we would never be able to keep up with the rest." The leader recognizes this statement as aggressive and therefore emotionally laden. He might reflect by looking interestedly at the speaker and saying: "You mean that if the Cost Department were to provide you with better service, you would find it easier to perform your share?" He says this almost as an interested question. It is not a full question but rather a musing remark. Note that the wording is different. Thus, to use this technique, the leader should be good at divergent production of semantic transformation, or lacking this skill, he must repeatedly practice the device.

It is worthwhile here to delve more deeply into the psychology of reflecting. In general, whenever we make a strong, aggressive statement, we can expect to receive one of two responses: either support, asserting that what we said is correct, or a strong rebuttal. Both of these responses serve to make us even more aggressive—the first because it constitutes positive reinforcement toward our stand, and the second because it is either dissonance or reactance provoking. Dissonance, in this case, would be reduced by strongly denying the refutation or belittling the source. If reactance is provoked, we will assert our position even more strongly in order to regain our threatened freedom to think as we please. What we are totally unprepared for is a sympathetic listener who not only looks as if he is listening but who also shows so much understanding that he is able to repeat our feeling in entirely different words. This is so unusual that it is completely disarming.

It's interesting to note that even in practice sessions in which a subject is asked to express an aggressive statement so that someone else can try his hand at reflecting, there is a marked change of tone. The aggressor, replying to the reflector, tones down his conversation. Perhaps the mild tone of voice used by the leader helps also in lowering aggressiveness. Whatever the reason, reflecting (without evaluation, of course) is one of the most powerful tools a group leader can use for keeping his meeting rational. Incidentally, many who have become very proficient at reflecting state that the tool is useful not only when conducting a problem-solving group but also at a party or a club, and most particularly at home.

Other tools designed to cope with emotionality mentioned by Maier are (a) letting someone speak his piece (akin to catharsis), (b) asking other, uncommitted persons to repeat the content of the expressed sentiment to see whether the meaning is correct, and (c) asking for concrete examples. When a person who feels aggressive toward another is asked to specify the actual incidents that justify his stand, he will tend to withdraw when he sees that they were only rare instances in an otherwise normal relationship.

The Rational Discussion.   Having noted the different ways in which emotionality and irrational feelings can be handled in a discussion, we can now proceed to the rational discussion itself. One of our main concerns will be to try to keep a rational discussion from reverting into an irrational one. This can happen very easily if we allow the group to fall into a win-lose conflict over different aspects of the discussion. A method has been designed to avert this. The original idea stemmed from Maier (1963) in which he defines the two-column method of discussion. This idea has been further developed and integrated with findings from other areas. The result is a design that has proved effective in keeping discussions rational and in greatly increasing interested participation, as well as in improving the quality of the solution.

In order to present this design as clearly as possible, an actual, recent case will be given, consisting of an almost verbatim transcript of a meeting that took place to solve a particular problem. As the dialogue unfolds, specific points will be mentioned to explain the principles involved. In general, the presence of a tape recorder can be unsettling; however, in this particular case, the group was so used to working together that a recorder was used. A recorder is *never* used unless all parties are aware of its existence and accept its use.

The general situation.   PQR is a commercial company employing 380 persons. It is located in a country in which wages have been frozen for some time. As a result, there has been considerable labor unrest, because in spite of a simultaneous price freeze, price increases have been authorized. Management is aware that their personnel are having trouble making ends meet. The company is now in a position in which it can raise all salaries by $x\%$. The lawyers have found a procedure to do this, which is quite legal within the existing situation. Few people in the company know anything about this.

The General Manager therefore decides to call a meeting with his top staff to study the best way of communicating the good news to all personnel. The participants are:

GENERAL MANAGER   ADMINISTRATIVE MANAGER
FINANCIAL MANAGER   PERSONNEL MANAGER
SALES MANAGER   ASSISTANT to the PRESIDENT

In order to keep the roles clear, these people will be designated by their positions instead of by arbitrary names.

The immediate situation. Some facts about each participant are necessary to understand the operation of the meeting. The General Manager is exceedingly high in Cognition, Divergent Production, and Evaluation in the semantic areas. He is also high in Cognition and Evaluation of Behavioral areas but not too high in Divergent Production. He ranks rather low on the Figural but very high in several of the Symbolic areas. His score on the F scale is very low, while he falls at the mean on the MC scale.

The Administrative Manager is exceedingly high in the Symbolic areas and quite high in the Behavioral and Semantic areas. At the same time, he stands low on both the F and MC scales.

The Sales Manager is very high in Cognition of Semantic areas, except for Implications. Like the General Manager, he ranks very high in the Cognition and Evaluation of Behavioral units but low in their Divergent Production. He is low on the F scale, very high on the MC scale, and in general is an ingratiator, using virtually all the processes described by Jones (1964).

The Financial Manager is extraordinarily high in the Symbolic and Semantic areas but low in the Behavioral areas, particularly Cognition, Divergent Production, and Evaluation of Implications. He is also low in Semantic Divergent Production but probably above average in F and MC scales.

The Personnel Manager is extremely high in the Semantic and Behavioral areas and medium in the Symbolic. He is low on the F and MC scales.

The Assistant to the General Manager is high in the Semantic and Behavioral areas. He is low in the F scale and medium on the MC scale.

Once the meeting was called, the dialogue was as follows:

MANG.:   I have called you because I have some good news. It seems that we can raise everybody's salaries by $x\%$. Before doing so, however, I would like to get your opinions on how to communicate this to all our personnel. Who is willing to act as leader?

PERS.:   I'd rather not because there's probably a lot that I would like to say about such a topic.

SALES: Me, too.

MANG.:   (To assistant.) Will you lead us then? You see, I have a lot of ideas on this score, too.

ASST.:   O.K. Well, the first thing to do is to define how much time we should spend on this. Any suggestions?

FINAN.:   This shouldn't take over 10 to 15 minutes.

PERS.:   I'm not so sure about that; it looks like 30 minutes to me.

ASST.:   What do you think, Sales?

SALES: I think 30 minutes is a good period. This is a rather ticklish subject, and I've had lots of complaints about salaries from my Department.

ASST.:   How about you, Administrative?

ADM.:   Well some of my Departments are rather quiet, but there has been a little rumbling in costs and in invoicing, I'd like 30 minutes.

ASST.:   How about you, Manager?

MANG.:   I'll settle for 30 minutes, too. I think there's a lot to talk about to make sure we make a good decision.

ASST.:   What do you say to that, Financial?

FINAN.:   All right, but I wouldn't be surprised if we got an answer sooner. (Social pressure here, but it has caused reactance. It seems he has a ready solution and so feels there's no need for more discussion. The leader notes this and keeps it in the back of his mind for further use. There may be some irrationality here.)

ASST.:   All right, it is now 10:05. We will have until 10:35. We must now define the problem. We can raise $x\%$, and the Manager wants to know how to communicate. Do you think this defines the problem completely?

SALES: No. If we are going to discuss how to communicate this, it is because we want to get the best results.

ASST.:   Shall we define the problem as "how can we communicate this in order to get the best results?"

PERS.:   I don't think that's enough, because it doesn't define what we mean by "results."

FINAN.:   Results to me, means getting the people to be more efficient.

ASST.:   Is that satisfactory to you, Personnel?

PERS.:   No. Efficiency is the result of a lot of other things. It's a whole system of dealing with personnel, and we certainly haven't achieved our present high levels by means of high salaries alone. Besides, efficiency isn't our only goal. There's a social side to this. I would suggest that the problem be defined as to "how to communicate the raise so as to create the best possible relations between all levels of our personnel." (The difference between Personnel and Financial in Cognition of Behavioral Implications is clearly seen here. The leader was clever in steering the question to Personnel so as to take advantage of his skill in Divergent Production of Behavioral and Semantic units.)

ASST.:   How does this sound?

ALL: Very good. Fine. Good definition.

ASST.:   O.K. I'll post this on the blackboard. (Writes problem definition at top of blackboard.)

ASST.:   Well, now that we have defined the problem, have we any ideas?

FINAN.:   I'd say the best way is to post a notice on the bulletin boards on Monday morning to the effect that there will be a general raise of $x\%$ as of this month.

ASST.:   (Turns to the blackboard and writes to one side "Post notice." Turns to rest of group.) Any other suggestions?

MANG.:   I think it would be better if we called a general meeting of all supervisors. At such a meeting I could communicate this personally to all of them at once. I could tell them the reasons for this raise, why it is limited to $x\%$, get their reactions, and so be able to see the effect it makes. I'd like to see a lot of sur-prised and happy faces.

ASST.:   (Turns to blackboard and writes next to "Post notice," "Meeting.") I put abbreviated in order to not waste time and space, but we all know what they stand for.

Time out: In the first place, it was easy to get agreement on a time limit, although now we see why Financial didn't see why more than 10 minutes should be spent on deciding to put up a notice on the bulletin board. With his poor Divergent Production of Behavioral units, he was unable to have any other ideas. After this, the leader quickly got the group to define the problem and then asked for suggestions. We must now analyze what goes on in the minds of the participants who have given suggestions so far.

FINANCIAL: He had the idea to start with that a notice should be put on the board. When the group was asked for suggestions, he immediately blurted his out. The leader, without making any value judgment about this suggestion, posted it on the blackboard. This constituted recognition or posi-tive reinforcement and made Financial feel quite pleased with his contribu-tion. He then turned to the group to see how they took it. He was rudely shocked to see that the leader also turned to the group and, as if disregarding his idea, asked whether anyone had any other suggestions. "As if there could ever be any other solution!" was his probable private reaction. His disap-pointment was quite visible in his facial expression. Then Manager delivered his little speech on how he would like to hold a large meeting with all the supervisors. Financial is now in a state of dissonance. He had given a sug-gestion that he thought was good and turned to look for approval. He was then faced with the dissonant cognition that another entirely different idea from his own was presented. He will probably reduce this dissonance by finding fault with the new idea, and he now mentally lists all the possible flaws in it.

MANAGER: We must remember he is medium on the MC scale. Therefore, it is quite possible that he suggested the general meeting so that he could be the 'hero of the day,' since he would be announcing the good news. When Financial suggested posting a notice on the bulletin board, as had been done in the past, Manager sees his speech, which he was probably starting to mentally prepare, run the danger of being undelivered. He is therefore ready to find all sorts of faults with Financial's idea. The roots of win-lose conflict are here. The rest of the group either have their own differ-ent ideas or are aligning themselves with the two presented. There is a great risk that this will turn into a free-for-all, ending when Manager, exerting his greater authority, heatedly states that he *orders* the general meeting to take place. This would leave everybody with the impression that these meetings to discuss problems are useless, since the boss always does what he wants anyway. The leader must do something. He gauged that Financial was probably experiencing greater dissonance than Manager, because he had given his idea first and then seen it apparently swept aside by Manager. Based on this, the dialogue continued:

ASST.:   Manager, can you please give me a pro for posting the announcement on the bulletin board?

MANG.:   But I said we should hold a meeting.

ASST.:   (In a pleasant tone.) I know, but just the same, I'm asking you to give me a pro for this other idea.

MANG.:   I can't think of any.

ASST.:   Please. There must be *some* merit to it. Think a bit, please.

ADM.:   One advantage . . .

ASST.:   (Very kindly cutting him off before he gets a chance.) Please Administrative, I'll get your opinion in a second. Let's wait until Manager gives a pro himself. Have you thought of one, Manager?

MANG.:   Well, I suppose one advantage is that we wouldn't leave the company without any supervision if we posted the notice while a meeting was being held.

ASST.:   (Turns to blackboard and under "Post Notice" writes "Saves time" in the pro column. This act completely disarmed Financial. He was getting ready to fight for his idea by pointing to all its advantages, when suddenly his apparent enemy cites one of the very advantages he was ready to point out himself. By not letting Administrative intervene with a pro, he deprived Financial of a possible ally, who would have bolstered his antagonistic position, as Asch has shown. Besides, he gets Manager to commit himself publicly to an advantage of the "Post Notice" idea. Manager must reduce the dissonance thus caused by persuading himself that maybe posting a notice isn't as bad an idea as he had thought and, what is more important, that there may be alternatives to the idea he presented.)

(Turning to Financial.) Can you please give me a pro for holding a general meeting?

FINAN.:   Well, I suppose we will be more sure that everyone will get the message at the same time.

ASST.:   (Writes in the pro column under "meeting," "simultaneous.") Manager, can you give me a disadvantage to holding a meeting? (Note that the leader was careful not to identify any proposal with the original proponent, contrary to what is advised by Robert's Rules of Order. Such identification ties a man to an idea, and dissonance makes it very hard for him to ever abandon it. Moreover, any criticisms of *his* idea will provoke reactance, leading him to restore his freedom by reasserting his suggestion in increasingly vehement and irrational terms. Since the leader already knew that original ideas always undergo modification, he avoided crystallization by referring only to "holding meeting," with no reference to authorship. As a result, virtually everyone forgot who had contributed which idea. Another important point to note with respect to Robert's Rules of Order is that within the framework of these new principles, there can —one might almost say, there must—be several motions on the floor at once. By allowing only one motion at a time and then voting on it, Robert's Rules ensure that there will always be win-lose conflict with consequent dissonance and reactance on the part of the loser. The latter then searches for ways to "get back at the others, eventually.")

MANG.: One I can think of is that the gathering might be very large and that there would not be too much opportunity for interaction with everyone.

ASST.: (Writes on blackboard "low interaction.") It might be a good idea to know how many people would be involved. Can anyone here tell us how many persons we have supervising others?

PERS.: If we count those present here, Department and Section Heads and those in charge of small groups, we have a total of 43.

ASST.: (To Manager.) Is 43 too large for you?

MANG.: Yes, a meeting with 43 people would virtually be limited to my speech, with some interaction from the boldest persons. (Note that the leader was getting further commitments in order to reduce the dissonance which Manager would experience should his idea eventually be modified or even eliminated.)

ASST.: Financial, can you give me an objection to posting on the bulletin board?

ADM.: Well, I suppose there will be less feedback than at the meeting.

ASST.: (Writes in the con column, under "Post Notice," "Less feedback.") Does this group feel that feedback is necessary? I ask the question because I see that it is an issue with both suggestions.

GROUP: Yes, definitely. (Head nods from others).

ASST.: Well, then our problem seems to have turned to how to get the maximum amount of feedback from the participants. Are there any suggestions? (At this point the blackboard looks like Fig. 6.5)

PROBLEM: How can we communicate raise to help create best possible relations at all levels?

Post Notice		Meeting	
Pro	Con	Pro	Con
Saves time	Less feedback	Simultaneous	Low interaction

FIG. 6.5. Diagramatic representation of constructive problem solving designed to avoid win-lose conflict.

PERS.: Well, neither of those two suggestions assures a maximum communication and feedback with the supervisors. I suppose it will be even worse when the supervisors communicate this to their people.

SALES: I personally would like to give the good news to my own people. I know them well. And since they are a smaller number, I feel that I can guess their reactions a lot better.

ADM.: Me, too. I only have seven to deal with. I'd much rather have small groups.

ASST.: Are you proposing that each one of those present should communicate the news to his subordinate?

ADM.: Yes, I guess that's my idea.

ASST.: Sales, you seem to have a similar idea. Would you discuss it directly with Administrative?

ADM.: Well, that depends. If I talk to all my supervisors and their subordinates who are also supervisors, it looks like I'd have about 13. How many do you have?

SALES: Counting everyone who supervises, I have 11. How about you, Financial?

FINAN.: I have 12.
PERS.: I'm the one who has least. I have only 2. But there are other supervisors that are not under any of us.
MANG.: Who?
PERS.: Well, there's the man working on the new project—he generally works with you.
MANG.: That's right, and there's the head of the Executive secretaries. I guess I have . . . wait a minute, I guess I have 5 in all directly under me. But a meeting with those five would look kind of silly because they belong to such different levels.
ASST.: Shall I post this as another possible suggestion?
GROUP: Yes, let's see what the advantages and disadvantages are.
ASST.: (Posts "Separate meetings" on blackboard alongside "Meeting.")

Time out: Let us see what the leader has done. He succeeded in getting considerable interaction among the members. The meeting was beginning to take the form of a wheel type of network (with himself as the center). However, by getting the members to discuss among themselves, seizing the first opportunity to steer the meeting in this direction, he turned the meeting into a comcon network. He thereby virtually put himself out of the discussion except in the sense of possibly acting as a recording secretary. The group also saw that there was a possible third alternative, something which was extremely important in destroying the win-lose mentality. With a third possibility available, the group was no longer blind to the possibility of still other alternatives. The alternative presented seemed to have the approval of all except the Manager, who felt his group was too heterogeneous to be called together in one meeting. The leader quickly realized that this was a rationalization, since the same unevenness would also exist in the large group, which Manager had initially proposed. He therefore saw he had to deal with this incipient emotionality on the part of the General Manager.

ASST.: Manager, you feel that telling the news to a group composed of different levels detracts from the value of the communication (reflecting).
MANG.: Well, yes. You see, the man on the new project is a very important technician, and he might not like to be included in a group with secretaries.
ASST.: You feel that this technician might react adversely if he were in the company of people of lesser rank (again reflecting).
MANG.: Well, I don't think he would act adversely. He is a very stable man. It's just I thought that maybe he wouldn't like it.
ASST.: You fear that his not liking this will hurt your relations with him (again reflecting).
MANG.: No, I wouldn't go that far. Look, actually it's not that important. (The emotionality was brought down to manageable proportions.)
ASST.: Could you then give me a pro for holding these separate meetings, apart from the better feedback that was originally given?
MANG.: Well . . . I suppose one advantage would be that we wouldn't be taking all the supervisors off the job at once. These meetings could be scheduled so as not to coincide.
ASST.: (Writes under pro for "Separate Meetings," "not simult.")

PERS.:   But that would be a disadvantage, because some supervisors would get to know the news before the others, and the good effect would be lost when the ones to be called last already know what the meeting is about.

ASST.:   What do you say to that Manager?

MANG.:   We might swear them into secrecy.

ADM.:   I think it's almost impossible to ask that. The news is too good to be kept secret. I don't think you can expect that much of 43 persons.

ASST.:   Well, Manager, can you give me another pro for separate meetings?

SALES: I can think of one.

ASST.:   What is it?

SALES: It doesn't weaken our authority with our personnel. I think that if we each communicate this to his own group, the General Manager will not necessarily lose authority, but if he does the communicating, and . . . well if we are in the meeting, it will make us all look a little bit silly.

ASST.:   (Posts as con to separate meetings "authority.")
          What is your opinion with regard to this objection, Manager?

MANG.:   I think it's very valid, but I would add something else. If you feel that you would lose authority because I give the news virtually over your heads and deprive you of the privilege of giving the news to your subordinate supervisors, won't you be doing the same if you bring in your Section Heads together with *their* subordinate supervisors? Won't the section heads also feel silly and left out while they hear others tell the good news? (Strong commitment from Manager against his original general meeting idea.)

ADM.:   That's a very good point. I would put that as an objection both to the general meeting and to the individual meetings.

ASST.:   (Posts this objection in the con column under "Meetings" and under "Separate meetings.")

SALES: I have another idea then. Let's each of us hold a meeting with his own immediate subordinates and then let each one of those hold a similar meeting with their subordinate supervisors so that the supervisors can hold meetings with personnel.

ASST.:   (Posts "Meetings Im. Sub.") Can anyone give me some disadvantages? What about you, Financial? (The leader has seen from the expressions of approval that the meeting is moving towards more individualized and personal attention toward the persons who are to receive the news. Therefore, he asks for objections before the group gets too enthusiastic over the new solution evolved, which now everyone believes to be of better quality but which perhaps can be further improved upon if the group notes possible disadvantages. At this stage, only 15 minutes had passed; so there was still plenty of time left in which to continue seeking improvement. Of course, the leader does not have the slightest idea of what the final solution will be. As Maier (1963) advises (p. 57), he is more concerned with the problem-solving process than with contributing towards finding a solution.)

FINAN.:   Look, I only have 4 immediate subordinates. I think I can do a better job if I take them one by one rather than holding a meeting. After all, it's something I can communicate to each in just a few minutes.

ASST.:   (Posts "One by one" on the blackboard.)

Time out: Since the blackboard had begun to get pretty full, and more space might be needed, it was necessary to erase some of the ideas already posted.

However, the leader should never erase a posted idea without the consent of the man who originally suggested it. Although never referring to the authorship of the individual ideas, the leader must always remember who it was that made the several suggestions. If not, reactance will later occur when the author of the idea restores his freedom in a quite unexpected form. The leader should therefore say rather unconcernedly to the group: "This is getting a little crowded here, I wonder if I can erase one of these." He will get a reply from the group telling him to erase, say, "Post Notice" or "Meeting." The suggestion will, in general, come from someone other than the originator, although often the very originator will make the erasure suggestion. If someone else suggests it, he should turn to the rest of the group and ask, "May I erase?" The group will, in general, consent. At that, the leader looks straight at the originator and asks him, "O.K. with you?" But the question must not appear especially significant. The author of the idea in question usually complies. If he doesn't, the leader doesn't erase. It means that there is fixation here, and he had better put his emotion-reducing tools to work.

ASST.:   Can you give me pros and cons for "One by one"?
PERS.:   They will all certainly be more pleased. Besides, you can get a very good impression of their individual reactions without social pressure from the rest.
ASST.:   (Posts under pro, "Ind. React." "No Press.") Any more?
FINAN.:   Tell me, do these people get the raise, too?
MANG.:   Yes, I said it would include everyone.
FINAN.:   Well, then, I think we can start by telling them that they get the raise and then tell them to communicate this to their subordinate supervisors, so that they can in turn tell this to their personnel.
SALES: That's a very good idea. It's about how I was beginning to feel. I would do it that way.
ADM.:   Yes, that should be very effective.
PERS.:   There's a question I'd like to ask. Do you all feel that it is better to tell them that they got $x\%$ raise, or do you think it's better to tell them what their new salaries will be?
ASST.:   Shall I post that as suggestions?
MANG.:   Yes, I think that can be posted as two different ways of doing it, and we can discuss the pros and cons of each.
ASST.:   (Needing more space, gets approval for erasing other suggestions which obviously no longer hold. One advantage of erasing is that no one considers these old and evidently inferior solutions any longer, and they concentrate on the new ones. Conducting these meetings with a blackboard is superior to using paper pads and dry pens because even if you cross out with dry pens, the message is still there to remind the original author that he was passed over. Assistant posts "$\%$" and "New salary.") Will you give me pros and cons for each?
FINAN.:   Giving percentages is much easier.
ASST.:   (Posts "Easier" under "pro" in "$\%$.")
PERS.:   Giving the actual salaries is more effective. It's more meaningful to the individuals involved.

ASST.: (Posts "Effective" under pro in "New salary.")

FINAN.: Yes, that's all right, but you can do that for your own immediate subordinates. They would have to give the full salaries to their subordinate supervisors, and they in turn would have to calculate all this for their personnel. The calculations aren't easy. You have to take percentages on actual salaries and round out the figures, as we have done in the past. It sounds too complicated to me.

ASST.: (Posts "complicated" under the con column in "New Salary.")

MANG.: Telling each one their salary would allow us to tell everyone what his actual take-home pay would be, and we would avoid the Galanter effect.

ASST.: (Posts "Galanter" under "con" of "%.")

FINAN.: What's the Galanter effect?

MANG.: That's right, you weren't here when this was explained. I know how it works. Personnel can do a better job of explaining what it is. Won't you tell Financial what the Galanter effect is? Besides, it will act as a refresher for me.

PERS.: Dr. Eugene Galanter investigated the value people place on money and found that it was not necessarily proportional to the amount of money received. For example, he would ask people to imagine he was giving them, say, $100, which came out of a very large foundation fund. He would ask them to think how much pleasure this caused them. He then asked them to think of how much money he would now have to give them in order to produce twice as much as the initial pleasure. He found that his subjects in general needed much more than another $100 (sometimes as much as $200) to duplicate the pleasure. He devised a method whereby he could thus measure the subjective value of money. He then tried another experiment. He would ask different people to do a certain task in order to gain a monetary reward. I think the task was a certain amount of proofreading. He paid some 2 cents, others $1.00, others $5.00, and others $7.00 for doing exactly the same job. But then to those who had been offered the initial $7.00, when the moment came to pay, he gave a plausible excuse as to why he couldn't pay the promised $7.00 but that he could give the subjects $5.00 instead. The amazing thing was that the amount of satisfaction of these subjects on receiving the $5.00 was not equal to those who had been initially promised and eventually got $5.00. The amount of satisfaction fell to the level of those who got only 2 cents. That's why we are now announcing take-home pay instead of gross pay in our advertisements looking for personnel. Haven't you had the experience of feeling let down when you collected less because of welfare and other discounts?

ADM.: Yes, I have often griped about that.

SALES: Me, too.

FINAN.: It's something I've always thought unfair.

MANG.: I never liked it either. It's an awful letdown, and besides there's always the problem of explaining it to my wife. She was counting on the actual figure.

ASST.: Then do you think we should communicate take-home pay instead of the pay raise?

FINAN.: The idea is good, but look how complicated all this has become. How in the world are we to make all those calculations and keep the thing secret?

ASST.: Wait a minute. I believe the problem has shifted. Does everyone here agree that the Galanter effect is important enough to concern us?

GROUP: Yes.

ASST.: Then we can shift the problem to how can we make best use of the Galanter effect?

MANG.:	Yes, I think that's our problem now. If we solve that, the rest seems feasible.
ADM.:	I think that's an easy job for the computer.
FINAN.:	But how are you going to do it without letting the people in Data Processing know about it?
PERS.:	We can encode, as we did before when we made estimates on possible salary changes and didn't want anyone to even know what we were considering. It was lucky that we did it that way because we never were able to make the salary changes.
MANG.:	Can you use the same codes?
ADM.:	Yes. I have them, and I think Personnel does too.
PERS.:	Yes, I have them.
MANG.:	How long would it take you to encode, prepare a program, and process the data?
ADM.:	The programs are already made for any salary changes. All we have to do is to give the necessary instructions as to what percentages will be applied. I think all this can be done in one day if Personnel works with me and the Assistant to the Manager, together with one of the trusted Personnel Assistants.
MANG.:	All right, that means that by tomorrow, or let's say Friday morning, you can have all the information.
ADM.:	Yes, I'm sure we can do this.
ASST.:	Let's see how we stand now. Administrative, Personnel, with an assistant, and myself will work on encoding and preparing the material for the computer. What's to be done with the material once it comes off the computer?
PERS.:	I would suggest that we place the names of the persons involved next to the present and new take-home pay on the computer sheets. Since this will be done by sections, each one of those present can give his subordinate supervisors the sheets so that they will have the information handy to inform every employee.
ASST.:	How does that sound? Does it seem feasible?
GROUP:	Yes.
ASST.:	(To Financial.) Does that answer your doubts as to the possibility of doing this?
FINAN.:	Yes. I see that it can be done.
ASST.:	Do you think Friday will be a good day to announce this?
PERS.:	Yes, everyone will spend a happier weekend.
ASST.:	Then all we have to do is to see how this will be carried out.

Time out: Maier states that it is important to summarize the decision because there must not be any doubt in anyone's mind. This must include the time allotted for the decision to be put into effect, the duties each member is to assume, steps or conditions that must be included to implement the decision, and plans for follow-up that will test the effectiveness of the decision. Maier further states that this is the leader's responsibility. We have made a modification. In order to get the greatest commitment from the group for immediate action, the group itself is asked to state what steps are needed, who is to carry them out, and who is to do the follow-up. In this case, the decisions were made as follows:

| ASST.: | I shall write the final decision on the blackboard. (Writes "Communication to be made individually by every supervisor to his subordinates, telling him that |

his take-home pay instead of being his present x will be z, as of this month.")
Is that correct?

GROUP: O.K. Yes. Right.

ASST.: What steps are to be taken and by whom and when?

ADM.: Well, we already decided that you and Personnel, with his assistant, will work on encoding.

ASST.: (Posts this on board.) When will that start?

ADM.: I'd say right now.

PERS.: Could we do it in half an hour? I have a few things to get off, and then I can concentrate on this.

ADM.: O.K. with me.

ASST.: Who will alert Data Processing to have available computer time?

ADM.: I will.

ASST.: When will you do it?

ADM.: As soon as we leave this meeting.

ASST.: (Posts the above on board.) Who will write the names after we get the sheets from the computer?

FINAN.: I say that each one should write the part that belongs to him.

ASST.: When will this be done?

ADM.: The computer will deliver the sheets tomorrow about four o'clock.

MANG.: I can write in my five names immediately.

ADM.: I have a bigger job; could you help me, Personnel?

PERS.: Of course. I have a few names to write; so I can see you, say, tomorrow at 4:00.

ADM.: That's fine.

ASST.: How about you, Finance?

FINAN.: I think I can handle it myself. If I don't finish in time, I'll take it home and do it tomorrow night.

ASST.: When will you start communicating?

MANG.: I suggest we start at 8:30 Friday morning.

GROUP: O.K.

ASST.: (Posts all this on blackboard.)
How will you keep the news from spreading unduly?

ADM.: I can start with Departments that are distant from one another, and as soon as the supervisor leaves, he will start communicating to his subordinates. I think we can instruct the supervisors to tell their personnel about the raise and, at the same time, either get them to make a phone call or give them something urgent to do. If the supervisors are clever enough to keep their subordinates busy immediately after they've received the news, this whole process can be done without spreading the news through the wrong channels.

FINAN.: What will happen when everyone finds out that everyone else got a raise? Won't they feel depressed?

SALES: Do you think they would feel more depressed than if a notice had been put on the board?

FINAN.: You have a point.

PERS.: I can assure you that everyone will be so happy that they'll be glad to share the joy with others. Besides, everyone will feel positive towards his supervisor, who gave him the good news.

ASST.: Who will do the follow-up to see that all this is being carried out and also be alert in case of snags so that corrective measures can be taken in time?

PERS.: I'll be glad to do that.

ASST.:   When shall we have another meeting to exchange impressions on how this worked out?

FINAN.:   I suggest Monday at 8:30.

SALES: Sorry, but I won't have had time to get any feedback. The boys will be talking to me about this all day Monday.

ADM.:   Yes, I think I need at least a day to judge the effects.

PERS.:   I'd say we need more than a day. We'll know at once who is pleased. What worries me is the man who will be disgruntled because he expected more. They take longer to speak out. If we have many of these, we will have to devise something else. I suggest we meet early Wednesday morning.

MANG.:   I can't. I have an appointment until 10:00.

ASST.:   10:00 o'clock Wednesday all right for everyone?

GROUP: Yes.

ASST.:   Well, let's get going.

A CONCLUDING COMMENT

The communication was a smashing success. No reports of dissatisfied people materialized, and everyone was extremely pleased with their supervisors, the company, and particularly with top management. It is interesting to note that although the General Manager seemed to be losing control, since he delegated so much of it, actually he gained a lot. Tannenbaum (1968) has theorized that as authority in organizations is spread over more people, there is a tendency toward more overall authority, instead of each individual having a lesser share. In other words, by spreading the responsibility for control, the increase in overall responsibility is so great that the persons who initially relinquished it actually gain more in the long run.

The problem solved in our description may sound trivial to many. How can one put so much time and effort into communicating a general pay raise? It's never been done before; usually it's done after there has been considerable pressure from the union. In this case, many supervisors were able to establish even closer bonds than they already had with their subordinates. There were reciprocal questions of "what are you going to do with the extra money?" etc. It is the sum of many such meetings, designed to solve many such apparently trivial problems, that creates a good climate in an organization (added to all the other processes described in this book). Moreover, the same basic problem-solving approach used in this example to stifle a win-lose conflict between two initial solutions, which, in the light of the final solution, now looks naive, can be and has been used to solve very important and apparently difficult problems. If this procedure appears overly complex to some readers, let them reflect on the degree to which water treatment plants, hospitals, and other complex operations have helped improve general health. The same attention to detail, however complicated it may seem, can be very useful in avoiding conflict. By taking such careful action when faced with problems, conflicts are prevented and good solutions are found—all of which justify the effort expended.

THE IMPORTANCE OF THE LEADER

We should conclude with a few comments about the qualifications needed for group leaders because it is obvious that individual differences exist among leaders in terms of effectiveness. From observing the results obtained, some conclusions can be drawn. First and foremost, the leader must be convinced that the method he is using *works*. One very good way to achieve this conviction is to explain the different principles to an experienced leader and then have him lead the group in a ticklish problem and see how the desired result is obtained. The experienced leader must allow the group to think that his contribution to the solution, as far as giving or judging ideas, was nil. This vicarious reinforcement, as studied by Bandura and Walters (1963), is very effective.

At first, the neophyte leader should not be given full control of a meeting. Maximum success has been achieved by having people play different parts at meetings, say, try to deal with emotionality, try to use the two-column method, attempt to summarize, etc. If he tries to conduct a full meeting, the new leader will probably fail and become discouraged.

Turning now to other qualifications: Excellent leaders are generally low on the F and MC scales, high in Semantic abilities (particularly Cognitions and Divergent Production of Transformations), high on the Mach IV scale (Christie and Geis, 1970), and high in the Behavioral Cognitive abilities.

Our next chapter will now deal with what to do when, through neglect or any other cause, conflict has been allowed to erupt.

Note added in proof: Social science technology moves fast, and since this chapter was written great strides have been made in problem solving, particularly by using the Guilford SI model in locating the problem. The new approach, although partly incorporating some of Maier's empirical work (which I have already cited), has become much more systematic in a scientific sense.

Locating a problem constitutes a cognition. It may be correctly cognized or incorrectly cognized, and hence guide the problem-solver or lead him astray. Table III, giving all possible cognitions as proposed in the SI model, has proved to be of inestimable aid. The twenty-four possible cognitions given in Table III have been numbered for ease of reference.

Maier's dictum that frustrated persons tend to place as well as to present problems in behavioral and therefore improductive terms means that the parties tend to place the problem in location 4 (CBU). In win-lose conflict,

TABLE III

POSSIBLE COGNITIONS BASED ON GUILFORD'S SI MODEL

	Figural	Symbolic	Semantic	Behavioral
Units	1	2	3	4
Classes	5	6	7	8
Relations	9	10	11	12
Systems	13	14	15	16
Transformations	17	18	19	20
Implications	21	22	23	24

there is the same tendency to locate the problem in someone else's behavior. However, as supervisors have gained familiarity with the SI model concepts, it has been a relatively simple matter for the group leader to ask for locations in other possible cognitions. This has been possible even in cases in which considerable emotionality has been involved, which made those involved automatically place the problem in position 4.

A typical case was that of external auditors, who on finding their work inordinately delayed, asked their internal auditor colleagues if they always faced the same type of difficulty in obtaining data. The initial tendency was to locate in position 4; that is, "the behavior of the organization's personnel is uncooperative." This made the persons, who felt they were being attacked, also place the problem in position 4; that is "the external auditors are inept at asking for data." This of course would lead to no constructive action. A higher authority tended to place the problem in position 12; that is "there is friction between the auditors and our personnel." This would have led to efforts at reducing the friction. When the group, however, looked for other locations, the problem was placed in positions 14 and 15 as one of incompatibility of symbolic and semantic systems. The external auditors' methods did not match the highly computerized data processing methods that had been introduced by the organization. A problem that had started in the behavioral area was soon moved to the symbolic and semantic areas and immediately many excellent solutions emerged. Another recent case which involved a change of codes used to identify certain raw materials suggested by the methods department met with instant opposition from the plant supervisors. The problem was initially placed in position 4. However, a rather short meeting clearly showed that a number of other areas were involved such as 14 (symbolic systems), 20 (behavioral transformation, i.e., retraining plant personnel in the use of the new codes), and 15 (semantic systems, i.e., reprogramming at the computer). Solutions were devised for each of these.

If the title of this book attracted the reader's attention, it may perhaps interest him to know that it was determined using these concepts.

7

Wagner

conflict resolution

Science, it is often said, has produced fantastic technological achievements but has contributed almost nothing toward eliminating two of man's major social problems—destructive conflict and social strife. Man can reach the moon, yet he cannot maintain the peace in a city block.

This chapter describes the phase of technology, based on social-science findings, that *has* led to effective designs for the solution of conflicts. These conflict resolution designs, like the persuasion designs, are completely prepared before being put into practice; the completeness of this preparation even includes a time table with a set deadline for the final solution. In several of the specific cases in which this method has been tried, the conflict has been solved exactly on the previously set deadline. It is therefore possible to design solutions to apparently insoluble conflicts with a high degree of precision. This accomplishment shows that social-science technology has come of age.

CONFLICT RESOLUTION DEFINED

A definition of *conflict resolution* is now in order. The term is defined as a solution agreed upon by two parties, each of whom feels it serves his own best interest. Conflict resolution is not a *compromise*, as defined by Henry Clay in his famous speech on the Compromise of 1850. What he described was "a work of compromise in which, for the sake of peace and concord, one party abates his extreme demands in consideration of an abatement of the extreme demands by the other party; it is a measure of mutual concession—a measure of mutual sacrifice" (Clay, 1958). The goal of his solution was peace and concord, but this may mean only a temporary truce. The Compromise of 1850 was no more than that; it merely delayed the Civil War for a few years. By not solving the basic problem, it probably made that conflict more bitter because it allowed additional time for resentment to accumulate on both sides. Conflict resolution, as we define it, means making the parties reach an agreement on the *fundamental* issues that led to the conflict. It also means that by cooperating together, both sides will find their own solutions to the problems that first caused the conflict to become critical. Very often these issues may look trivial to outsiders, but they become crucial and highly emotional for all those involved.

A MUSICAL EXAMPLE

This musical score at the beginning of this chapter is one of the most remarkable expressions of conflict resolution that has ever been written. For nonmusicians, the background story is quite simple. The Mastersingers of Nuremberg were a corporation devoted to musical composition. They were bound by certain rules of composition that had become rigid and that were strongly enforced by obdurate individuals. This inflexibility made it impossible for innovating young men to become members and thus revitalize the corporation. When Walter, a young man, entered a competition with an entirely new kind of song, his violations of the rules were unrelentingly noted by one of the most ridiculously unbending of the corporation's members. Conflict naturally arose between the old and the new. Wagner sketches the story in the Overture. After musically describing the conflict between the two opposing tendencies, he shows in the magnificent passage we have quoted how they could be reconciled without giving up either position. Theme 1 is Walter's prize song, which has been toned down from its initial, youthful impetuousness but which is now even more beautiful. Theme 2 is the symbol of the Mastersingers, which by being enlivened by the influence of the new youthful ideas and which, when later repeated alone, gains in grandeur.

Theme 3 is the Mastersingers, which stands unchanged as a symbol of the fundamental value saved by the solution of a senseless conflict that had threatened to destroy the institution. The fusion of the past art with the new innovation creates a harmony that saves the basic values involved.

We shall describe in detail an actual design for conflict resolution that was successfully carried out. It should be regarded only as an example and not as a pattern for the solution of all conflicts because other conflicts must each be dealt with in entirely different ways. Nevertheless, the basic principles used here have been used in all other conflict-resolution designs. The would-be conflict solver must design his own solutions for each case in the same way that an engineer designs every new structure for a particular purpose. After learning how structures are generally designed (by studying the basic principles and applying them to specific cases), the new engineer proceeds to design simple structures and then more complex ones. Eventually, with time, experience, increased knowledge, and a good dose of divergent thinking abilities, he will be able to design the truly remarkable works of engineering that we often admire.

The same principle of design holds true for conflict resolution. The would-be social-science technologist should, after some exercise in simple persuasions, proceed to the more complex types. He can then try his hand at solving simple conflicts, and as he acquires experience and knowledge, he can tackle the really complex problems. It must be stressed that he needs to know a good deal about social science if he wants to solve truly difficult conflicts because he must have at his disposal a vast array of findings that could be used in very diverse situations. To continue the engineering parallel, a thorough knowledge of such fundamentals as stress design and materials is often what makes the difference between a good and a mediocre engineer. Similarly, the good practitioner of social problem solving is often characterized by his familiarity with social-science findings.

CONFLICT RESOLUTION DESIGN

What follows is the description of a design for the solution of a very specific conflict. Facts on the background and the persons involved will first be given in order to clearly establish the nature of the conflict. The identities of the real participants, who must necessarily be very frankly described, have been so disguised as to make them unrecognizable to even those persons actually involved. The two persons who do know the participants were themselves actors in this conflict. They helped prepare this report shortly after the events took place, and I am very grateful for their assistance. Many of the principles employed in conflict resolution have already been described; so it will not be necessary to repeat definitions or other basic material.

THE COMPANY

XYZ is an organization in a South American country that provides a necessary service to the general public. Some aspects of this service are of a technical nature. The central organization employs about 600 persons. These include the five-man Board of Directors, who supervise a General Manager. The latter in turn supervises the four managers of the Technical, Administrative, Financial, and Sales Departments. The Technical Department, which will concern us here, is composed of three Divisions. These in turn are concerned with Design, Production, and Service. There are many highly trained technicians in all three of these divisions.

THE PERSONS INVOLVED

It is impossible to design a good solution to a conflict without knowing quite a bit about the persons involved, particularly concerning those traits that will be crucial to the execution of an adequate design. Accordingly, a sort of *dramatis personae* will be given, together with a description of the individuals' abilities, personality traits, political leanings, and other data relevant to the problem, the conflict, the design, and the final solution.

The type of judgment used may seem unscientific because it is subjective and not based on instruments that are normally used to appraise such characteristics. Nevertheless, it is the type of judgment used by an engineer, for example, in the design of foundations. It is quite probable that the reader is sitting in a house built on ground whose bearing capacity was estimated in a subjective manner, analogous to that suggested here, in spite of the fact that there are many scientific ways of analyzing the bearing capacity of soil. The foundations of the reader's house are nevertheless safe enough for him to go on reading without being terribly worried. With sufficient house-building experience, the builder acquires the ability to estimate the bearing capacity of soil without scientific methods. In the same way, the social science technologist with sufficient experience is able to judge accurately certain personal characteristics. Naturally, there is always a certain element of risk involved in making this type of judgment. The problem-solver, as well as the builder, must always be ready to change his design should it appear, during the application phase, that he made an incorrect estimate concerning an important element. With these remarks in mind, the participants to the conflict under consideration will now be introduced.

The Board of Directors.   *Alvin* (President of the Board of the Directors) is a hyperactive individual, probably high in cognition, convergent production and evaluation of symbolic and semantic units, classes, relations, systems and transformations. In other words, he is proficient in the handling of symbols and language. He is also very high in authoritarianism and in the need for social approval. He is poor at handling social situations and can be described politically as very far right.

Baker (an old-time technician and member of the Board of Directors) has not been too successful lately. He was appointed to the Board by some influential people more as a means of providing him with an income than as a measure of his true worth. These circumstances have created in him a high need for approval, which probably reflects his need to recover his old prestige. He had at one time been very active but now probably lacks Alvin's mental capacities in most areas. However, he ranks rather high in the figural area. Politically, he had been a liberal in his earlier years and would probably score low in the F scale even now; at present he might better be placed at the middle of the left-right dimension.

Corby (another old-time technician and member of the Board of Directors) had once been very rich and successful. He had actually retired until he was appointed to this post. He would probably rank high in the figural and semantic abilities but has poor behavioral skills. Aristocratic and strongly desirous of approval, he is politically very conservative and has been far to the right since his high-school days.

Dalton (member of the Board of Directors) is a very amiable man, who probably lacks ability in most of the implication and transformation functions. He does not care very much about the organization and always goes along with the majority. Very acquiescent and difficult to define for this reason, he had been put on the Board of Directors for reasons totally unrelated to his abilities.

Ewart (an ex-auditor, finance man and member of the Board of Directors) is a very spry and active person, always concerned with minor details and obviously disturbed when the discussion turns to complex or major issues. Intellectually, he would probably score low in terms of implications and transformations but very high in the evaluation of symbolic units and classes. He could be classed as middle-of-the-road politically, although he was never much concerned with the subject. Rather, his main concern is detail, whatever the topic. He once held up an important meeting for over an hour on a procedural trifle that at most might have saved the organization $500 a year.

The Board in general is a rather heterogeneous group under the highly authoritarian and active President Alvin. They go along with Alvin's desires in most financial, administrative and legal affairs (with the exception of Ewart's incursions on minor points of order). When matters turn technical,

Baker and Corby always give their opinions. Since Alvin knows nothing of the technical aspects, this is their only chance to excel. It is interesting to note that although Baker and Corby were totally different and had been antagonists when young, they generally coincide on technical matters. It is as if a tacit agreement has been reached whereby each bolsters the other's ego before the rest of the Board, and particularly before Alvin. This behavior allows them to show how competent they are in technical matters about which the others are totally ignorant. The two technicians can, therefore, occasionally tell even the very authoritarian Alvin what to do. Alvin always bowed to them on technical matters, thereby characteristically yielding part of his power to a higher authority in a particular area.

This sort of situation is not too different from that which exists in some degree in numerous organizations. A certain modus vivendi had been reached, and the members gave an appearance of getting along fairly well. They had worked together for five years.

The Supervisors.   *Manger* (General Manager) has been with the organization for many years. A mediocre technician, he shows the sole uncanny ability of having maintained his position through several, major Board changes, although these successive Boards had held widely divergent viewpoints and policies. Manger has thus become a mere relayer of orders from the Board to the members of the organization or vice versa. This information is always supplied without any hint or recommendation for action. A perfect ingratiator, the few suggestions he makes are those he thinks would be agreeable to the President on general affairs or to Corby and Baker on technical matters. Very able to detect and carry out anything that would enhance the prestige of Alvin, Baker, and Corby, Manger has always been described by these three as "a very able administrator."

Tinker (Manager of the Technical Department under Manger) is a brilliant technician, very well-organized, and competent in the handling of his subordinates. He manages to make them work as a team and appears to have highly developed interpersonal skills. Very liberal politically and flexible, as well as independent of social approval needs, he is quite patient in accepting conflicting orders from above. He is fully aware of Manger's tendency to avoid responsibility, but this does not damage the relationship between them. Tactful and diplomatic in handling situations, he is liked and respected by all.

Prentice (Head of the Products Division) is a rather conservative, middle-aged technician, much more concerned with the technical aspects of his work than in handling subordinates. He is probably below the median on the F and MC scales and high in the semantic and figural abilities. He is generally rather quiet in his ways and usually conciliatory in his attitudes toward others.

Heder (Head of the Design Section) is a hard-working, competent technician, able to get along with his work group. Somewhat conservative in his ideas, he neverthelesss allows considerable latitude to his subordinates in matters of design. Some of these subordinates rank very high in divergent production abilities, as well as in evaluation, and are therefore quite capable of generating high quality, ingenious solutions.

Personnel.   Apart from some administrative personnel, who will not concern us, Heder has under him eight designers—most of them products of a rather new training institution noted for high quality instruction and the liberal views of its director, instructors, and students. Most of the eight can be described as moderate to very liberal. They all respect Heder. Two of them played key roles in the conflict we are considering.

Witkin is the most conservative man of the group, quite noted for his stubbornness.

Weston is one of the most brilliant and dynamic of the technicians in the group and very high in the divergent production abilities required for the job. Rather left-wing, he is a brilliant conversationalist with a high degree of culture.

THE SITUATION

Having given a thumbnail sketch of each of the chief actors, it is now possible to describe the situation that existed prior to the final conflict.

There had been considerable tension between the Board and most of the personnel in all departments. A series of arbitrary measures had been introduced in order to obtain a higher degree of so-called "efficiency." It is true that XYZ was a rather inefficient outfit, but the measures taken had created considerable resentment and failed to produce tangible results. The failure of these methods led the Board to attribute the lack of efficiency in the company to the deliberate activity of infiltrated, left-wing agitators. Most of the measures that had been taken were in the form of direct orders about how to perform tasks in the several departments. These orders had often been given directly by the Board members to the personnel involved, thereby passing over the heads of the corresponding supervisors. Other measures taken to improve efficiency were severe penalties for breaking rules or not following orders from the Board. Penalties were commonly applied inequitably and ranged from very severe suspensions to mild reprimands for what was generally considered to be virtually the same offense. In other cases, there was a tendency to treat all offenders alike. An example was the ruling related to vacations. The existing general rule was that vacations could not be split into two periods; they had to be taken all at once. In a later directive and in order to contemplate special cases, the Board allowed some individuals to split their vacations into two equal periods. Sometime after this, the organization became lax in the matter of split vacations, and many people started taking them in a manner contrary to the ruling. When, at a later date, several problems cropped up in different departments, the Board attributed the trouble to the fact that some key people were away on vacation and that these vacations had been illegally split. Those persons were accordingly suspended for having taken vacations irregularly. There had been nothing said in the original directive to the effect that split vacations would make the person subject to sanctions. Besides, among those suspended was at least one person whom the Board had specially authorized to split his vacation. (Many other instances could be cited. Perhaps the reader, on perusing this account, may conclude that XYZ is a poorly run organization. It certainly is not the best, but the situation is far from unique.)

In the Technical Department, the reaction to the crackdown had taken the form of exercising considerable independence on technical affairs. This is a clear case of psychological reactance by implication in which severe limitation of freedom in the administrative aspects of the job was compensated for by engaging in freedom-restoring acts that Alvin was not in a position to judge. (See the explanation or reestablishment of freedom by implication—Brehm, 1966, p. 10.) This reaction went so far that the technicians began to make designs quite out of line with the organization's primary objective. As a result, Baker and Corby could stand up at Board meetings and point to these deviations, delighting in the rare opportunity to dominate Alvin. Corby particularly emphasized the political aspect, attributing the whole difficulty to leftist infiltration and thereby adding considerably to the already existing friction between the Board and the personnel. The left-leaning technicians, of course, blamed the whole situation on a "fascist" plot of the Board to try to get rid of those who did not hold their own political views. The exaggerations and distortions in perception are clearly seen on both sides.

All this friction, increasing in intensity over a period of years, led to a strong reaction on the part of most of the personnel. The supervisors, prodded by personnel at all levels, asked to meet with the Board of Directors in order to air a long list of grievances. It was at this precise stage that the writer was approached by one of President Alvin's assistants, who had heard that social-science techniques might be applied, to help alleviate the situation.

INITIAL ACTION

After two extended interviews with Alvin, in which he described his perception of the situation and several current problems, it became evident that a major cause of the state of tension between the Board and its personnel was a lack of adequate communications, which lead to a considerable misunderstanding among all concerned parties.

It was decided to start holding a series of meetings, twice weekly, within office hours and on the organization's premises. The participants included Alvin, Manger, and the Heads and Assistant Heads of all the departments. At these meetings several social-science principles were expounded and freely discussed in relation to their current problems. The main principles discussed were: positive reinforcement, approach-avoidance conflict, cognitive dissonance, win-lose conflict, individual differences in ability, and social pressure. Some 12 meetings took place. The series culminated with an exposition of the principles and techniques of group problem solving, as explained in Chapter 9. Several meetings were devoted to role-playing. At each of these members took turns leading the group in solving specific problems of the organization. In several of these the new leaders were quite successful in getting the group to reach good, unanimous conclusions. Problems that had been considered difficult were solved. The general unanimity constituted positive reinforcement to continue in this vein, and most participants were becoming optimistic.

An interesting and important by-product of the meetings was that Alvin accepted the author's role as leader in the first practice sessions in various procedural matters. Alvin was willing to follow the rules of order, to remain silent while others were making proposals, to be on time, and to allow the meetings to end when the leader so ordered. This does not mean that Alvin changed in any way. Rather, like most authoritarians, he was willing to submit to another authority and to reduce dissonance easily by submitting to social pressure (Adorno *et al.*, 1950; Crowne and Marlowe, 1964). The author's initial role as group leader was then easily passed on to other members of the group, and Alvin would accept this transference even though this new leader was, in real life, his subordinate. Alvin occasionally led the group himself and freely asked for opinions. He was not the best of group leaders. Lacking interpersonal skills, he was never very much aware of the meaning of facial expressions of approval or disapproval and so could not capitalize on them. Neither was he ever able to master the use of social pressure to achieve unanimity on minor points. At least, however, he refrained from dogmatically giving his opinions as gospel, as he had been used to doing. These changes in Alvin, however, lasted only during the meetings and for a short time later, after which he resumed his habitual attitudes.

A CRISIS ARISES

Although only a few initial steps had been taken at the meetings mentioned and only limited results obtained, Alvin and the Department Heads, together with their assistants, had become very enthusiastic over the progress that was being made. The author was asked to conduct a similar series of meetings with lower level supervisors, which would have included Heder and the others.

However, unknown to the author, a crisis was developing in the Design Section, directed by Heder. A significant product expansion was under consideration, and the design of an important component had been entrusted to Witkin, the rather stubborn and more conservative technician. But since Baker and Corby, the two technical members of the Board, felt they knew a lot about this project, they contacted Witkin directly in order to check his approach to the problem. This was merely another gesture performed to impress Alvin, who, it will be recalled, was ignorant in technical matters. Witkin gave Baker and Corby an outline of how he intended to tackle the problem, and they rather pompously accepted his plan. It must be added that this contact was made over the heads of everyone else in the organization. This is a common occurrence that has been mentioned before and that is highly dissonance-provoking to all supervisors.

Witkin, who although stubborn was consciencious and painstaking, went ahead with the design. However, either because he changed it somewhat from his original idea or because Baker and Corby again found it necessary to impress Alvin, a crisis arose. Corby, once more passing over all the supervisors, managed to see the almost finished design. He claimed that it had been changed from the original idea, sought Baker's aid, which was immediately forthcoming, and brought the matter up at the next Board meeting. This part of the meeting did not last long, but it is interesting enough to describe in some detail:

Corby stated that Witkin's virtually finished design had a major flaw in it, which was a flagrant violation of what had originally been agreed upon among Baker, Corby and Witkin. The essential difference was that one element that should have been placed facing right had instead been placed facing left. It is important to note that neutral technicians consulted on the subject stated that the difference between the two proposed designs did not seem to be important. However, the change on which Corby insisted meant that the component had to be completely redesigned. Besides, Corby presented the case in such a manner as to indicate that Witkin had disobeyed his and Baker's directive. Alvin, being an authoritarian and therefore prone to giving priority to power, status and discipline, took this as another expression of insubordination provoked by the left-wingers and immediately went along with his two technical colleagues. Dalton, the very amiable and acquiescent fourth member, concurred, and Ewart, eager to get rid of what to him was a noxiously complex issue, also gave his assent. Accordingly, a directive was unanimously approved ordering Witkin to change his design to make it conform to Corby's instructions, i.e., to make the element in question face left. Manger, the ever-compliant General Manager who was present at the meeting, failed to warn that this would have an explosive effect on the technicians as well as on the rest of the organization's personnel because the situation was already quite sensitive. He merely passed this order on to Tinker, thereby avoiding his own involvement.

Tinker, of course, immediately reacted because he was sure Witkin would refuse to make a change in something that he felt had been approved in principle some time ago by those who were now finding fault with his work. Besides, he knew very well that all the other technicians would rally around Witkin because this kind of order would be considered damaging to their self-esteem as technicians. Tinker tried to get Manger to have the order withdrawn. Manger, as usual, washed his hands of the whole affair and told Tinker that if he wished, he could see Alvin directly. Tinker talked to Alvin and found him adamant. "Discipline must be enforced," was Alvin's reply, and he added that if Witkin did not do exactly as he was told, he himself would propose that he be subjected to a severe penalty. Tinker then talked to Heder, Witkin's supervisor, and Heder agreed that the attempt to execute such an order would lead to disaster. Nevertheless, they felt there was little they could do since Corby, feeling well-buttressed by Alvin and the rest of the Board, continually asked whether the new design was being made as ordered. They therefore felt there was nothing they could do but communicate the Board's decision to Witkin.

At this point, the reader may run the risk of perceiving the whole crisis as being created by Corby. Such a judgment would be unfair. It must be remembered that there had been a whole history of acts on both sides in which the technicians had shown their independence in technical affairs, as a reactance to threats from administrative areas, in open defiance of the stated objectives of the organization. When an attempt is made to solve a problem, there is no point whatever in trying to fix the blame on someone. As in most cases of conflict, there is not just one cause but an extremely complex situation in which each party sees his position as just, while maintaining that the position of the other party is untenable. In a situation like this, trying to fix blame or to find out who is right is about the most useless and often most damaging thing one could do. This point has also been discussed with respect to win-lose conflict and the area of freedom in Chapter 6, "Group Problem Solving."

As expected, the reaction of the technicians was very strong. To a man, they sided with Witkin. Work virtually stopped. Nothing else was talked about, and the technicians seriously began considering the possibility of going on strike. Weston was the most outspoken and became the leader of the group. Since he was the one who initiated numerous interactions, many were also directed toward him (Collins and Guetzkow, 1964, prop. 9.2, p. 170). The grapevine brought the news almost immediately to Baker and Corby, who also reacted. Both sides became even more adamant. The Board members insisted that there was no way out except to impose final authority by having the new design made exactly as ordered by them. The technicians, on the other hand, insisted on maintaining the old design because it embodied their right to design things as they technically saw fit. It became a clear case of win-lose conflict in which both parties clung tenaciously to their positions. Each one decided that either one or the other design had to be accepted, with neither side willing to make the slightest concession (Blake and Mouton, 1962). Corby felt fully supported by the authority of the Board. Witkin felt equally justified by the unanimous support of his colleagues. Besides, each side saw the conflict as a test case between the political conservatives and liberals.

Just before one of the regular social-science meetings with Alvin and his top staff, Tinker approached the author and said: "I have here a bombshell. It is a design that I am sending up to the Board from the technicians. All hell will break loose. I've done all I can, but I think this time we've run up against something that's insoluble." After being asked what it was all about, Tinker gave a brief description of the conflict, adding that in spite of the fact that conflict resolution had been discussed at our meetings, this was an impossible case. It was, he said, a smoldering conflict that had gradually built up to a critical and irreversible point and was now erupting over a minor issue.

Tinker was asked whether he could not somehow delay submitting the design for two or three days. He said that he might but that this would only make matters worse because Witkin had submitted the design without making the slightest adjustment in accordance with the Board's dictates. He compared the situation to medieval times, when knights were ready to "do battle" if the design were modified in the slightest degree. The Board, on the other hand, was in the position of the opposing knights who expected the gauntlet and were ready with all the power their position commanded to take up the dare and to retaliate with the sternest measures in order to "make an example" of this case. The Board felt this retaliation would permanently eradicate insubordination. (It is quite possible that the reader may have found himself in one of these opposing positions with respect to work, family, political, national or international issues, or at least he has certainly seen others in such quandaries.)

Tinker nevertheless agreed to withhold the design and meet with the author in order to study the possibility of constructing a design for the solution of this conflict.

THE DESIGN

A list was prepared that included the names of those considered to be involved in the conflict. These names were then separated into three degrees of involvement:

Most involved and indignant
Witkin   —   the designer
Weston   —   his chief supporter and group leader
Corby   —   the technical Member of the Board most involved in the incident

Second in degree of involvement and emotionality
Alvin   —   who felt that the whole principle of authority was at stake, but had other matters to think about
Heder   —   who felt that the Board had gone too far and was in conflict about whether to support the Board or his technicial subordinates

The six other technicians supporting Witkin in what they felt was a struggle for technical liberty
Baker   —   who was very much committed to supporting Corby and who also felt that his own prestige was at stake

Least involved
Dalton   —   who could be counted on to go along with the Board whether it kept on the same course or completely reversed itself
Ewart   —   who, as usual, would be glad to rid himself of the whole affair
Prentice   —   who had been far from the Board, the technicians and others since he had been very busy on unrelated projects at the time
Manger   —   who, as expected, didn't care too much what happened, provided it did not damage his position
Tinker   —   who was very upset but also very willing to help find a solution, although he was skeptical about the possibility of achieving success

Once this list had been prepared, it was decided that action had to be taken to persuade the parties involved to change their attitudes on several points. First, the Board had to recognize that it must delegate authority and not get bogged down in detail. Secondly, the technicians had to admit that although they should have a certain freedom in their designs, this should be within the general objectives of the organization as defined by the Board. These aims can be stated more formally.

Final objectives

    (A) To obtain full and hearty cooperation among the technicians, Corby, and Baker on the design of the component;

    (B) To have the technicians recognize that it is necessary for them to keep designs within the principal objectives of the organization, as well as the general directives to be dictated by the Board;

    (C) To have the technical members of the Board recognize that they must limit their action to giving broad technical directives, thereby leaving considerable leeway in the actual implementation of these directive to the different technicians in the different departments. In other words, the technical Members of the Board must not go into detail, nor should they make direct contact with subordinates.

Since it was felt that these aims would be impossible to obtain in one step, due to the high degree of polarization and intensity of feeling on both sides, it was decided to first adopt more limited objectives. Objective (A) was established as the initial step toward the much more important objectives (B) and (C). These were considered most important for setting the stage for a better working pattern for the future. However, it was felt that even objective (A) would be unattainable under the given circumstances. Each side understood cooperation to mean that the other side would give in completely. For the technicians, therefore, a more limited initial objective was established. This was:

    (D) To have the technicians admit that the initial design (Witkin's or Witkin's modified by Corby's) could be improved upon. The improvement need not necessarily be in the direction indicated by the opposing party.

It was decided to present this limited objective to the different actors in the following order:

- Prentice with Tinker present.
- Heder with Tinker and Prentice present.
- Witkin with Heder, Prentice, and Tinker present.
- Witkin, Weston, and the six other technicians all together in a group with Heder and Tinker present.

This limited objective was not presented to the Board Members. They had not been so involved in the actual details of the project, and it was felt that it might be worthwhile to try objective (C) with Baker first. If this succeeded, then it would be tried with Alvin, with Baker present. If successful, it would finally be tried with Corby, with Baker and Alvin present.

It was estimated that at least a day should separate the several meetings in order to encourage a "sleeper effect" and to allow time for the persons involved to reduce the dissonance caused by changes in attitudes; i.e., by discussing the matter with friends and family and finding social support for the new opinion. Each subsequent meeting was scheduled with others who had already committed themselves to the new attitude in order to maximize social pressure upon the not yet committed individuals.

Before continuing our description of the conflict resolution design, a comment is in order. It might seem that this was not a case of conflict resolution but that it was merely a case of multiple persuasion. In a sense, it is a mixture of both. One of these is the principle of delegation of authority. With respect to convincing the Board to delegate authority, for example, the conflict-resolver's role was merely one of straight persuasion. Delegation of authority is recognized, theoretically, by almost everyone in a management position, but it seems to be perversely difficult to put into practice. However, with respect to the design of the component, the conflict solver did not have the slightest idea of what final shape the component would take; he simply did not care. The important point was to evolve a design acceptable to all; one that would not necessarily be either of those being discussed. (In other cases in which conflict has been successfully solved, the actual division of duties between different persons in an organization was the crucial problem. It was successfully solved by the use of techniques described here, combined with group problem solving.) It would be an error for the conflict solver to think up a solution and then sell it to the participants. This type of persuasion can only be practiced with something as obvious as the principle of delegation of authority. The rest must be left to the participants. The most interesting part of the conflict-resolution design described here, therefore, is that part related to the design of the component because this involved true problem solving. Nevertheless, the entire series of events will be described.

The deadline for the solution was set at 12 working days. At the end of that time, a meeting including Alvin, Baker, Corby, Manger, Tinker, Prentice, Heder, Witkin, Weston, and as many of the other six technicians as cared to participate would be held. At this meeting all parties present would heartily and unreservedly agree to cooperate in the design of the component that would best serve the interests of the organization. In addition, commitments would be obtained to objectives (B) and (C) from all present. At the time, such an ambitious goal seemed impossible to neutral observers.

APPLICATION OF THE DESIGN

According to schedule, Prentice was called in by Tinker and the author to discuss the situation. After being asked for his opinion, Prentice said he found it hopeless because it was obvious that neither side would yield at all.

The conflict-solver will, from now on, be designated as X. The following dialogue ensued:

X: In your experience, when designs are prepared, do you believe they are final or is there always a chance for making some improvement?

PRENTICE: Well, in general there is a limit on how far you can go on improving things. If you work over something too much, you reach a point of diminishing returns. The improvement obtained may not warrant the effort expended.

X: Do you think the projects made here in general always reach that stage?

PRENTICE: By no means. Due to the general discontent that has occurred over the last year or two, I'd say that a good portion of the work is well below an acceptable standard.

X: You feel that if there were not so many distracting circumstances due to all these conflicts the work could come out better and that everyone would be less disturbed? (Note the use of negative subjective verb with abstract object.)

PRENTICE: I've no doubt about it. Of course, I don't refer to all the work, but I've seen too much time wasted here in thinking about the conflict and trying to find solutions to that, than to think of better ways to do things. Of course, you must realize that I've been away from the present conflict, but in the area that I've been engaged in it's also affected the work.

X: Have you seen Witkin's design?

PRENTICE: Yes. After learning about all this, I went over to see him and he showed it to me.

X: Do you feel that it is the best possible?

PRENTICE: (Immediately on guard) I don't know. I really can't tell. But the Board should certainly not try to get in on details.

X: No, I don't mean that. Forgetting the Board's suggestion, do you think it would be absolutely impossible to improve on Witkin's design in any way?

PRENTICE: Well, I haven't seen it much in detail. I think he did a good job.

X: But again, from your past experience, if it were worked over by Witkin himself, forgetting the Board's directive, and under calmer circumstances, do you think he might make some improvement?

PRENTICE: Well, probably. Witkin has not been his normal self working on this. Who would be? If he didn't have to work under this kind of pressure, he probably could improve on it.

X: Do you think Heder thinks as you do?

PRENTICE: I don't know. We might ask him. But I'll tell you. He sure is standing by his boys.

X: Why don't we call him in and ask him. Remember—we don't want to ask him if he is willing to accept the Board's ruling, but whether he thinks that under calmer circumstances Witkin or maybe somebody else couldn't improve on some aspect or other of the design.

PRENTICE: There's no harm in trying. I don't think he'll have objections to going along with that. (It is important to note that by a method of successive approximations a commitment has been obtained from Prentice that it may be possible to make improvements on the design. He will now reduce the dissonance this admission causes by trying to persuade Heder that Witkin could, under more favorable circumstances, turn out a better design. He will seek social support from Heder. This will be in a direction completely unexpected by Heder.)

X: Call him in. Don't tell him what it's all about. Let's all three talk to him together. (If Prentice gives Heder the final conclusion before coming to the meeting, the latter will surely experience reactance. The same process of persuasion that was successful with the less highly involved Prentice must also work now with the more involved Heder. Therefore, it is imperative that it begin without reactance on Heder's part.)

The above conversation lasted about 20 minutes and was repeated in almost the same way with Heder. When Heder was seen to be doubtful about a point in this sequence, opinions would be obtained from Prentice and Tinker. Since both were already prepared to agree (Prentice now more heartily than during the period in which he was being persuaded), this social pressure was always sufficient to sway Heder. After all, he was not being asked to betray his technicians—all that was being requested was an opinion about whether it was possible or impossible to improve on the component. After 30 minutes it was Heder himself who suggested that Witkin be called in and hear the suggestion.

There were now three persons to apply social pressure upon Witkin. It will be remembered that Witkin was originally considered very stubborn and therefore unlikely to give in. Nevertheless, Tinker, now fully aware of how to conduct the persuasion, did it masterfully himself. He merely asked questions about the possibility for improvement, very gradually, and continually insisted that the proposed modification had nothing to do with the Board's ruling. When Witkin saw that Heder, whom he felt to be a loyal supporter, also agreed that perhaps Witkin himself might be able to come up with an even better design, he also committed himself to that position. Moreover, by means of more adroit questioning, he agreed that others might contribute ideas, adding that he would not object if someone else designed the component. He said he would be willing to do it himself or cooperate with whomever was designated or whomever would volunteer. Of course, the subject of the Board's ruling came up time and again, but Witkin was always pacified by the reassurance that the modifications under consideration had nothing to do with the Board's ruling.

The meeting with Witkin had been deliberately scheduled for a Friday afternoon because he was leaving town until Monday and would therefore have no chance to discuss the matter with the other technicians, who had not yet been persuaded. However, because Witkin said that he would eventually have to talk to the other technicians, a meeting with these men was scheduled for early Monday, as an added precaution. Witkin agreed not to discuss the situation with anyone else in the organization nor to later help persuade the others to adopt his new viewpoint.

It will be noted that throughout all these persuasions the persuader limits his role to that of asking questions and getting commitments to a new point of view. Once the latitude of rejection is reduced slightly, a new situation results. A new question, now one step nearer to the right direction, will again bring acceptance, commitment, and another reduction in the latitude of rejection. This follows exactly the method explained under persuasion by approximations (Chapter 4). At no point was a direct attempt made to give positive arguments, which would have merely caused reactance. In a conflict situation, where the emotional pitch is very high, such reactance is much more serious than it is in straight persuasion. The person being persuaded must be given maximum freedom to express and then commit himself to a position. He must also feel completely free from coersion.

The Monday meeting with the technicians was very interesting, although by now the routine had become almost monotonous. Witkin had been asked to contribute only when specifically requested to do so. A series of questions similar to the ones above was posed to the group. The principal difference was that the persuasion, instead of being directed to one person, was now directed to a group. The group was initially very hostile when the subject of the design was brought up. The hostility was so marked that progress seemed almost impossible. Nevertheless, after a little time, the dialogue went as follows (omitting side comments, long anecdotes, and jokes):

X: Has it ever happened to any of you that a long time after you designed some-
            thing, suddenly an idea hits you, and you feel that if you'd had the idea at the
            right time you could have improved the design? (X scans all the faces to see
            if anyone shows signs of agreeing. Most are so irate that they simply cannot
            recall cases. Yet, technician number three seems to assent. We will call him T3.)
T3:   Well . . . yes . . . I recall a design I did 3 years ago. I was very
            proud of it. Yet just a few days ago it occurred to me that if I had made a
            change it would have meant quite an improvement. I was telling the boys
            about it the other day. Remember T5?
T5:   You mean the ABC project. Your new idea would have made a world of
            difference and would have avoided a lot of complaints. But we can't somehow
            always think of all the right ideas the right time. I had a similar experience
            myself on the HKL project. I could have changed a component and we would
            have saved a lot of trouble later in assemblies. (X scans the group and sees
            that T4 and T6 still look adamant. He decides to let T5 continue.)
X: That's very interesting, T5. Tell us more about it, that is, if you don't mind
            owning up to having made a mistake. (T5 goes into detail about his past
            experience. X sees that T4 and T6 are still unbending, although they have said
            nothing for some time.)
X: Tell me Witkin. Have you ever had a similar experience?
WITKIN: Yes, I have them all the time. I actually believe that in technical jobs such as
            ours success comes to the man who makes the fewest mistakes. The man who
            never makes mistakes just doesn't exist.
X: How about you, Heder?
HEDER: Well, I have to admit that I often make mistakes. The boys here tell me about
            them but I agree with Witkin. The people who don't make mistakes either
            don't exist or else they are the ones that never do anything. Only last week,
            T4 here told me just in time when I was about to err on a recommendation

on MNO project. (This obviously tells on T4. The incident had not been pre-planned. It came very naturally in the course of the conversation. Such incidents are very common. The problem-solver must be very alert to catch and utilize their significance to see which reactions are forthcoming from the different individuals.)

X: That's interesting. Do you remember the case, T4?

T4:   Yes, I do. But Heder makes too much out of a little thing.

X: Has it ever happened to you?

T4:   Yes, I guess it has. I'm not immune.

X: Do you remember any one particular case? (T4 launches into a vivid description of a case in which he got an idea just in time and another in which he thought of it too late. T6 begins to change. This is the effect described by Asch that occurs when the subject loses an accomplice. He tends to go along with the majority, particularly if he is as rigid as T6 seemed to be, at least temporarily. Whatever the cause, the effect of the overwhelming social pressure is too much for him and the problem solver notices a change in attitude. Of course, the latter should be watching carefully for this to happen.)

X: (After T4 has finished.) How about you, T6?

T6:   (T6 pitches in heartily, and now it is agreed in a general discussion that every design, even if completed, is subject to change.)

X: How about you, Witkin? Do you think this much debated component in which you are involved can be improved upon? I don't mean in the direction suggested by the Board, but in any other way that might suddenly occur to you or to anyone else? (There are immediate signs of tension and possible return to hostility from the rest of the group.)

WITKIN: I'm *sure* it can be improved upon. I'd be a fool if I didn't admit that. (The group tension immediately reduces when they see that Witkin himself is not inflexible.)

X: What are the chances of redesigning it, then?

WITKIN: I'd much rather let someone else take a crack at it. I guess my mind is in too much of a rut on the subject.

T2:   But what sense would there be to redesigning? Wouldn't we just be giving the Board the pleasure of a victory won over us?

X: By no means. The new design would not necessarily be in line with the Board's ruling.

T2:   Then, they'll never O.K. it. All they want is to see that we are well crushed.

X: Tell me. Do you think that any new design would benefit if everyone were to pitch in and give ideas?

T4:   Well, in general we all consult among ourselves on all projects. We're continually interchanging ideas and impressions.

X: Forgetting all this that has happened up to now, what do you think of Baker technically? I know he is of the old school compared to you, but do you think he could contribute something to a discussion, one in which he could not be in a position to impose his ideas?

WITKIN: Yes, I think he could. He was quite active in his day, although he is a little dated now. I'd be willing to listen to his ideas, provided he doesn't think he has to tell me what I have to do. (This statement coming from Witkin makes a great impression on the group.)

X: What would you think if it were possible to hold a meeting with all of you and with Baker, but with a Baker that wouldn't try to impose his ideas?

WITKIN: I see no objection.

X: How about you, T4?

T4:   All right by me, provided he doesn't impose his ideas.

X: Let's assume that he wouldn't. Would that be satisfactory?

T6:   I guess it's all right. But how about Corby? He would want to come, too.

X: Would you object to his being there, provided he too were only to give suggestions and no orders?

T3:   I see no objection. But it sounds impossible. Knowing them, I know it'll never work.

X: If it can be arranged with a formal commitment on their part not to impose their ideas, would you all be willing to accept such a meeting? (X scans their faces for approval. Starting with those showing the most approval, he asks each to state what possible advantages would be obtained from such a meeting not only for himself but also for the Design Section and the whole institution. Eventually, by again using social pressure, all agree. Someone noted, and others agreed, that if such a meeting was attempted and failed, things wouldn't be any worse than they already were.)

This excerpt gives a sketch of the way the meeting was conducted. The whole meeting actually took one hour and 20 minutes, but the above account gives the core of the persuasions. An amusing incident was provoked by Weston, the man who had originally backed Witkin so strongly and had become leader of the technician group. It will be noted that no mention was made of him; indeed, he arrived quite late at the meeting. When he found that the whole group, including Witkin, had accepted the plan to revise the component and was even contemplating meeting with the Board to discuss the design with them, he became furious. The dissonance is easy to observe. Weston had two cognitions:

- He had come prepared with all sorts of arguments to support his adamant friend in a crisis.
- His friend and other supporters had changed their positions completely.

When he gradually sized up the new situation, he just couldn't reconcile himself to it. He virtually called Witkin a traitor for having betrayed him. The others laughed heartily at this, saying that he sounded as if he had been the designer and that Witkin, his supporter, had abandoned him. From then on, they did the persuading. He eventually went along with the rest, although reluctantly. Considering his position at this moment and at earlier stages, Weston's positions at the end of the conflict stands in a curious light, as we shall shortly see.

Once this result with the technicians was achieved, it was time to act with the Board, according to the schedule initially laid out. The first meeting took place with Baker alone, and an initial goal was defined: Since widely publicized conflict with the technicians would be damaging to Baker's image, the conflict-solver felt that he might be persuaded to admit that the Board should give only general directives. The author began by setting up a scale of Baker's expected attitudes toward the maintenance of rigid discipline versus freedom for the technicians. Knowledge of Baker's early history of radical politics allowed him to approximate which statement would be relatively more and less acceptable, thereby defining a structure for persuasion by successive approximation. These statements were made to range from $+3$ (maximum acceptance) to -3 (maximum rejection). In general, after talking to someone for a while about the subject of his conflict, it is relatively easy to construct such a scale. Of course, the scale is not administered. It merely expresses, to the best of the conflict-solver's knowledge, the reactions that the subject *would* have to such items had they been presented to him by a neutral researcher in random order and interspersed with other items. Thus the instrument is similar to those described in the chapter on persuasion. The items here can be presented in Table I.

TABLE I

Item	Expected attitude	Statement
I	$+3$	Discipline must be rigidly maintained.
II	$+2$	Good, loyal technicians should be given some leeway.
III	$+1$	When I was young, I was quite a rebel.
IV	-1	Those nearer to the work being performed are more up to matters of detail than those in the upper echelons.
V	-2	The young technicians have a right to design things the best way they see fit in matters of detail.
VI	-3	The Board should give only general directives.

Back of all this in addition, was Baker's wish to enhance his self-esteem, which would be aided by positive recognition among the young technicians. Such recognition would probably be forthcoming if Baker supported the technicians, and it might very well make him less concerned with impressing Alvin. In contrast, the present crisis had focused all of Baker's attention upon wanting to appear in a good light before Alvin.

Armed with this memorized list of statements, the conflict solver now approached Baker. The following is a partial reconstruction of the conversation, with amenities, anecdotes, and side comments omitted.

X: I see you are having trouble with the technicians. I'm sorry to see that.
BAKER: Yes, but we must be firm. We can't let these upstarts have their way every time.

X: You believe then that firm, iron discipline is what the young technicians need. (This statement was reactance-provoking. In his younger years, Baker had been quite liberal and had prided himself upon fighting against iron discipline.)

BAKER: I wouldn't go as far as to say that iron discipline is what we need. That would be going too far, but we are facing a rebellion and a minimum of respect for authority is what I ask for.

X: I see. You mean that the sign of a good loyal technician is one who does exactly as he is told and no more. (This is again reactance-provoking because of Baker's liberal background. Indeed, one of the items of the F scale, endorsed by high authoritarians, refers precisely to obedience and respect for authority. Thus, we again see the need for predesign diagnosis of the individuals involved.)

BAKER: No. A good loyal technician is one who is able to carry out orders but who also uses his imagination in order to create something. Otherwise, we wouldn't need technicians.

X: In your past career, did you ever face someone who insisted on telling you exactly what to do at every step?

BAKER: I should say so! When I was with . . . (Here Baker launched into a long story about the time he worked under an authoritarian who wouldn't allow him any leeway. He mentioned some of the bright ideas he had had that because of his supervisor's vetoes, had never been put into practice. In fact, Baker said, some of his ideas had only been instituted after he had left, as if they were the supervisor's own.)

X: In the eyes of the rest of the organization, who do you think came out best in terms of prestige?

BAKER: I did, of course! Everyone laughed and made sarcastic remarks about my boss —not to his face, of course—and I felt that they respected me for the ideas I had. Several came to me for advice, but I never saw them going to the boss. (Note how Baker has been moved through persuasion by analogy on this item. By getting him to admit the validity of a reasoning that was once favorable to him, he must now maintain cognitive consistency by changing his present attitude.)

X: Do you think that the fact you were closer to the work situation put you in a better condition to think up new ideas than your boss. In other words, was he as close to the work as you were?

BAKER: Of course not. He was busy with many other things, and I was quite close to the work. He couldn't possibly know all the details I knew, yet somehow he insisted on giving opinion on the slightest detail. He hadn't been in detail work for quite some time. (Again, Baker is committing himself to a principle on an unrelated issue, which nevertheless applies to the case at hand. He must therefore change his belief in the present crisis in order to reduce the dissonance that this causes. However, it is possible for Baker to rationalize by saying that the two situations are not comparable; it is therefore necessary to get a commitment to the general principle, not only to the special case under consideration, as we explained in Chapter 5 under persuasion by analogy.)

X: Do you think then that in general people who are close to the work can apply information about details better than, say, a General Manager?

BAKER: Of course. As people rise in organizations, they have to keep a more general view of the whole domain that comes under them; and they can't keep up to date on every detail.

X: Even if he had the capacity to keep up to date on every detail, do you think that is the role of the person higher up?

BAKER: By no means. He can't abandon detail altogether, but there is a great danger that if he gets into too much detail, he will lose sight of the general picture.

We now have a full commitment regarding the general principle of delegation. It must be remembered that the conversation was much longer than reported here and that by the time these principles were expounded and a commitment obtained, Baker had been talking for such a long time about his past problems that the present crisis had been completely ignored. Baker, however, is now in a state of dissonance and must therefore change his belief about the handling of the present crisis. At this point, if someone were to give him the initial attitude scale, the results would probably be like the ones shown in Table II.

TABLE II

Statement number	Attitude before persuasion attempt	Attitude at this stage of persuasion	Statement
I	+3	+1	Discipline must be rigidly maintained.
II	+2	+3	Good loyal technicians should be given some leeway.
III	+1	+3	When I was young, I was quite a rebel.
IV	−1	+2	Those nearer to the work performed are more up on matters of detail than those in the upper echelons.
V	−2	−1	The young technicians have a right to design things the best way they see fit in matters of detail.
VI	−3	−2	The Board should give only general directives.

Thus, the latitude of rejection has been reduced to 2, and the items that were at first barely accepted are now fully accepted—except item I, which was merely used as a starter and which will eventually be rejected. At this stage in the persuasion, two courses were open. One was to continue as planned. The other was to let the sleeper effect work so that Baker would reach the conclusion on his own, i.e., reaching a +3 on item VI. Since the persuasion was going well, the conflict-solver decided to continue in a manner designed to consolidate the attitude change.

X: (After some more conversation on the topic.) Tell me, do you think it is important for the general public and the organization's personnel to have a good image of the Board?

BAKER: Definitely. Every Board of a corporation must be careful of its public and private image.

X: Does this apply to the Board as a whole, or to the individual members?

BAKER: To both. You can't have prestige in a corporation unless every member contributes to it with his own share.

X: Would you feel then that you personally would be seen in a better light by everyone by giving detailed instructions or rather by giving broad directives?

BAKER: I think it is much more effective to give broad directives, provided the personnel is able and willing to carry them out.

X: Do you think the technicians of this corporation are able to carry the broad directives out?

BAKER: Yes, they are able. They don't seem to be willing.

X: But is the matter under discussion a matter of broad policies or of detail?

BAKER: Well, actually it's a matter of detail.

X: Is it in some way similar to the experiences you had?

BAKER: Well, I suppose it is, except that now they aren't even willing to talk.

X: But assuming the hypothetical case of their being willing to talk and to recognize the Board's authority, would you admit to them that it's the Board's duty to give broad directives only?

BAKER: Yes, but I don't think that's possible.

X: And if I were to tell you that I have spoken to Witkin and the other technicians and that they are not only willing but also eager to talk to you and Corby?

BAKER: I don't believe it! How could such a thing have happened?

X: Well, Witkin isn't as bad as you may think he is; and he definitely said he would be glad to talk to you and the rest of the Board.

BAKER: Well, that certainly would change things.

X: Under the circumstances then, in view of their willingness to talk and reach some sort of agreement, would you admit to them that the Board's job is to give broad directives?

BAKER: Yes, I personally would, but I don't know what Corby would say. You know, after all, this was his idea, not mine. I went along because I felt we had to pull together.

X: Do you think that there is a possibility that the technicians have been feeling that the Board was interfering with them as professionals when the order was given on that detail?

BAKER: Yes, it's quite possible.

X: Could it have been similar to what you felt when you went through the bad experiences you were telling me a while ago?

BAKER: Yes, it's probable.

X: Then how about talking to Alvin about this?

BAKER: All right, but you will have to tell him about Witkin. He will never believe it if I tell him.

X: Sure, I don't mind; let's see if he is in.

It was not possible to see Alvin immediately because he was busy with visitors from abroad; the interview had to be scheduled for three days later. (Alvin's support would be needed later to convince Corby.) In the interim, Baker was briefly contacted every day to ensure that there would be no post-decision regret. The technicians were also contacted to be sure that they did not revert to their former antagonism.

Alvin turned out to be much easier to persuade than expected. Since he was now busy with other matters, he was glad to see that there might be an opportunity to solve the problem without disrupting his other activities. He suggested that Corby be contacted and volunteered to go along. In Alvin's persuasion to this new course, prestige played a part: There had been some labor unrest in other organizations, which had been quite clearly ascribed to management errors, and Alvin did not want to be thought of as another President who did not know how to handle personnel problems.

With Alvin's support, the persuasion of Corby proceeded smoothly. An interview similar to the one held with Baker took place; now, however, Alvin and Corby were present. A small portion of the key part of the interview is transcribed.

X: Do you think this problem may cause conflict?

CORBY: It may, but discipline must be enforced, and these young radicals put in their place.

X: Do you think there is a chance that they will go on strike?

CORBY: Maybe, but let them; we'll hire others.

X: Is there a possibility that their colleagues will support them?

CORBY: Probably many will, mostly the leftists; but others will be willing to come to work.

X: What do you think will be the effect of all this on the public image of the organization?

CORBY: We may be criticized by some, but I'm sure we will be backed by others.

ALVIN: Don't be so sure. See how much they've criticized RST for the trouble they're having.

X: That's true, but Corby has a point because the conditions are different. [Alvin had overreached, and X found it necessary to agree with Corby's position. Other research has shown that the effectiveness of a communication is enhanced if the persuader expresses some view already held by the person he is trying to influence (Ewing, 1942).]

CORBY: That's right, our case is entirely different.

X: How would it strike you if the technicians were willing to redesign the component?

CORBY: They'll never do that. All this is just another excuse that the leftists use to disrupt everything.

X: And if I told you that they have already agreed to redesign?

CORBY: What? Impossible!

X: Not so impossible. They had a meeting and decided it would be in the interest of the organization to give the whole thing a new try. They said they'd be very willing to meet with you and Baker to see if the design can be improved on.

CORBY: You mean they've given in? See Alvin. I knew what we had to do was to be tough and they'd back down. Are they accepting our directives?

BAKER: Look, I think if they're willing to sit in with us and talk things over, we've accomplished a lot. After all, what we want is to have some order here, not necessarily to humiliate them. (Note that Baker, who had previously committed himself to this position, is now seeking social support by trying to persuade Corby. Corby is now under considerable social pressure from Baker and Alvin, and since he strongly desires approval from others, is prone to go along with the majority—even a majority of only 2. As Asch has shown, majorities of 3 or more are most effective. Someone less dependent upon the approval of others would likely have required the consensus of at least four persons to change his mind. In this case, the other two Board members, Dalton and Ewart, would have been persuaded first. Corby would have been faced at a meeting with a majority of 4, who believed it was better to try a meeting than to go into certain conflict. This would almost certainly persuade even a less approval-motive-minded person than Corby.)

X: (Note that as far as social pressure is concerned, X's opinion does not count because X has not given opinions but simply asked questions. Also, he has communicated only factual information; the technicians are willing to review the design in cooperation with the Board members, for example.)

Once Corby was persuaded and committed, it was an easy matter to arrange for a general meeting including Alvin, Baker, Corby, Manger, Tinker, Heder, Prentice, Witkin, Weston, and two more technicians. The other technicians were also invited, but by now they had lost interest in the case.

The meeting was cordial. Each one agreed that it would be a very good idea to work cooperatively, and the subject of delegating authority was raised. Baker stated that he believed the Board should limit its action to matters of major policy, leaving details in the hands of the technicians. The technicians expressed their great appreciation and said they would abide by the Board's rulings more than they had in the past. Witkin said, however, that he believed that as the Board members were more experienced than he, he would occasionally consult them if they would make themselves available.

It was finally decided to completely redesign the component. One person would be chiefly responsible for the design but would consult the others. Witkin declined, saying he had become too committed to the older design. Then, quite unexpectedly, Weston offered to do the design himself. Remember that Weston had been Witkin's chief ally and group leader in the conflict against the Board. He had also been infuriated, when he had arrived late at the general technicians' meeting, to find that the group's attitude had changed.

Eventually, a new design for the component was made that was totally different from the initial one and that incorporated neither Witkin's nor Corby's original ideas. Nevertheless, it was judged by all—including Witkin and Corby—to be far superior in every respect to the two original proposals. Moreover, as a consequence of this successful conflict resolution, relations between the technicians and the Board showed a marked improvement.

THE ROLE OF REINFORCEMENT

An important point should be noted concerning negative reinforcement. In technical literature we often see the term negative reinforcement equated with punishment. For example, a child that is spanked every time he tries to topple a small table is said to be negatively reinforced. We prefer to use the term "punishment" for that kind of act rather than the term *negative reinforcement*, as defined by B. F. Skinner in *Science and Human Behavior* (1953):

> Events which are found to be reinforcing are of two sorts. Some reinforcements consist of *presenting* stimuli, of adding something—for example food, water or sexual contact—to the situation. These we call *positive* reinforcers. Others consist of *removing* something—for example, a loud noise, a very bright light, extreme cold or heat, or electric shock from the situation. These we call *negative* reinforcers. In both cases the effect of reinforcement is the same—the probability of response is increased. We cannot avoid this distinction by arguing that what is reinforcing in the negative case is the *absence* of the bright light, loud noise, and so on; for it is absence after presence which is effective, and this is only another way of saying that the stimulus is removed. The difference between the two cases will be clearer when we consider the *presentation* of a *negative* reinforcer or the *removal* of a *positive*. These are the consequences which we call punishment.

In general, when groups of persons are in conflict, the persons are in a state of tension. At first, this does not seem too disturbing, but after some time the state of tension becomes uncomfortable. Tension eventually reaches a very high level and becomes so unbearable to those involved that they seem almost to prefer an open conflict as a means of releasing that tension. This has been noted in the burst of patriotism and initial rush to take up arms that occur when nations go to war after prolonged, international stress.

With conflict resolution following a design such as the one we have just described, however, every step leads the participants to tension reduction—no matter how slight. This procedure constitutes negative reinforcement. At first, the effect is small, and the persons involved are frequently unaware that negative reinforcement is even taking place. The conflict reducer may increase the effect by calling attention to the operation of such reinforcement and making the individuals more aware of it.

In another recent conflict that was also successfully solved, an employee named Smith was suffering from insomnia as a result of problems at work. He also said that everything he ate disagreed with him, that he was losing weight, and that the whole affair was having an adverse effect on his relationships with his family and friends.

After the conflict resolution had advanced to a stage similar to that in which the technicians all agreed to give the component design a new try, it was evident that there had been a reduction in tension. The following dialogue took place:

X: How did you sleep last night?
SMITH: Fine, why do you ask?
X: Just wanted to know. What did you have for lunch yesterday? (Smith describes a hearty meal.)
X: Did it agree with you?
SMITH: Yes, of course, why shouldn't it?
X: Well, this sounds very different from the way you felt ten days ago.
SMITH: (Rather amazed) Say, that's right! I hadn't noticed it. I guess things are improving a lot. (He was made to elaborate on this and later asked to repeat the difference he now felt to another one of the parties in conflict. This brought a reply from the other to the effect that he too felt more at ease and enjoyed movies or television more.)

Note how the conflict-solver obtains commitments from the parties recognizing that negative reinforcement is actually operating. This gives us a combination of several effects:

(1) The subjects become aware of the existence of negative reinforcement.

(2) They commit themselves to the fact that as a consequence they feel better and that therefore there is hope to be found in this new course of action.

(3) They reduce the dissonance created between this new commitment and the prior attitude that the conflict was insoluble by changing their private beliefs in the direction of the newly expressed hope for a solution. Moreover, in their need to reduce this dissonance, they seek social support by trying to persuade the other parties in the conflict that everyone must pull together to try to solve the problem. It is most interesting, at a certain stage, to watch how everyone is talking to everyone else about how well matters are proceeding.

CONCLUSION

The example in this chapter describes one of several conflicts that have been successfully solved. The design in every case varies depending upon the persons involved, the situations, and other factors. The same general principles, however, are always followed: dissonance reduction after verbal commitment to a new attitude; social support; social pressure and its interaction with the approval motive and authoritarianism; psychological reactance; and the diagnosis and purposeful use of mental abilities, attitudes, and so forth.

Note that not once did the conflict solvers allow the parties to maneuver them into the role of *arbitrators*. This would have completely destroyed their effectiveness. Sometimes the conflict solver is asked, "But what is your opinion on this issue?" There is only one standard answer: "I do not know enough about it to dare judge. My best solution for this will be the one that all of you will arrive at cooperatively." The conflict solver should at no time show even the slightest hint of his preferences, however temporary. In order to be fully effective, he must show concern for the solution of the problem and avoid taking sides, even on minor issues.

Since arbitration has so often been proposed as a panacea for the solution of conflict, further elaboration seems necessary. Opinions in favor of arbitration as a means of settling disputes are innumerable. They are also well-intentioned. Andrew Carnegie, in referring to the Pan-American Conference in which 16 nations of the hemisphere decided to adopt arbitration as a principle of American International Law for the settlement of all disputes that might arise among them, remarked that this was "a mighty step forward in the march of human progress" (Carnegie, 1933). More recently, the American Management Association published *Management Report No. 85* (1965) in which the merits of commercial arbitration are extolled. Although this report defends arbitration, several statements made within it point to the inherent weakness of the method. For example, the qualifications of the arbitrator are defined in a purely negative way: It states that no person can become an arbitrator if he has an interest in the result of the arbitration (p. 77). Later, in an attempt to be more specific, the report says that it is virtually impossible to evaluate the degree to which an individual possesses the characteristics required to be a good arbitrator; It does not state what these characteristics are. It also adds that formal training of arbitrators, while not impossible, is so difficult as to be virtually impracticable.

All these statements and many more point to one important conclusion: Although those who believe in arbitration as a cure for conflict are well-intentioned, they have failed to take into account the findings about conflict resolution derived from experimental social psychology. Perhaps those empirical findings are best expressed by Blake and Mouton (1962):

> Since the winner is difficult to determine through representatives, for reasons given above, an impartial judge is called on to make the decision in circumstances paralleling arbitration. Not being vested with membership interests, he is able to do so, usually without too much hesitation or hedging. He renders his verdict. One group wins, the other loses.
>
> How is the impartial judge perceived? Prior to this verdict, both groups agree he is intelligent, fair, honest, thoughtful, unprejudiced, unbiased, tactful and capable. After the verdict, the picture shifts dramatically. Those awarded victory are reinforced in their positive perceptions of him. His verdict "proves" that he was a "good" judge. This is not so in the defeated group. The judge's ability to render a competent verdict is now questioned. He is still seen as intelligent and basically honest; but he is now perceived by members of the losing group as unfair, thoughtless, biased, and tactless. The reaction in the

> defeated group is, "It was not we who had the inferior position and were
> wrong. It was the judge who failed to comprehend. "

In reality, the pathology lies in the inability to accept neutral judgment as valid judgment. The losing side erects rationalizations which protect their position in spite of defeat. A third and equally negative consideration is that arbitration too frequently results in warring factions absolving themselves of responsibility to work together, and thus "throwing away" the privilege of acting with reason.

The excellent explanation for the failure of arbitration given by Blake and Mouton may be further reinforced by reasoning from the theory of cognitive dissonance. Before the arbitrator acts, he is perceived to be intelligent, fair, etc.—not because he really is but because dissonance reduction requires that he be viewed this way. The position of the person giving the opinion can be expressed as follows: I am in the right. My position is flawless. If there is to be an arbitrator, he will obviously recognize this fully. However, dissonance reduction requires that this arbitrator must not be just "anyone." He must be intelligent, fair, and judicious. A "bum" on my side would be worthless for dissonance reduction purposes. His approval of my position might even be embarrassing to me. Therefore, I must see him as a really valuable person. It is very probable that he will be overvalued. However, as soon as he starts to render a verdict that is not in total agreement with my position, I am in a state of dissonance. In other words, my perception of my position is infallible; it is inconsistent with the fact that a person whose judgment I respect does not agree. This must be reduced by disparaging the source of my dissonance (Schachter, 1951). Therefore, the arbitrator is now seen by me to be unfair and biased. Arbitration, therefore, has its own built-in cognitive dissonance and will never be able to take the place of efficient, well-designed conflict resolution.

The conflict-resolution design we have described will probably be improved upon by social-science technicians using these and other principles in increasingly imaginative ways. Gradually, as in the design of physical structures, new methods will be created—each superseding the old ones in scope, ingenuity, and the use of principles yet to be discovered. In time, the conflict design described here will seem as dated as the Wright Brothers' plane, Ford's Model T, and Bell's telephone. But it will have shared with these inventions the merit that it was among the first successful, scientifically designed conflict resolution. And, as today's technicians are giving us more and better planes to fly, more and better means of universal communication, and more and better cars with which to move about, so the future social-science technicians will gradually be able to solve increasingly difficult conflicts, until the moment when humanity will solve its social problems by using intelligence rather than by using force, threats, or violence.

8

some problems and

some solutions

In Chapter 3 we stressed the need to diagnose problems before taking action. By now, the reader should agree that taking action without making an adequate, prior diagnosis is as foolhardy in dealing with social matters as it would be in treating medical cases. It is also quite clear, however, that there is a great difference between knowing what causes a certain state of affairs and knowing what to do about it. For example, it is one thing to know that a person has hydrophobia, but it is quite another matter to try to save him. In medicine there are two general approaches to health problems: One is to wait until the person falls ill and then cure him. This is what usually happens with such diseases as pneumonia. The other is to prevent people from getting sick. A typical example is the case of typhoid, in which filtering and otherwise treating drinking water has been found to be an expedient way of preventing people from catching the disease.

THE TREATMENT OF SOCIAL PROBLEMS

We may apply the same methods—prevention and cure—to the social sphere. We saw in Chapter 1 how a potential problem was avoided by preventing dissonance from occurring in the first place. In fact our technique even used dissonance to avoid the after effects that usually occur when someone is promoted. There are cases, however, in which problems arise that necessitate some kind of action. This is where the real social-science technology is needed—in the design of solutions for such situations. It should be obvious that due to the immense range of possible problems and combinations of problems, combined with the many individual differences that exist among peoples, there cannot possibly be one formula that is applicable to all. Even similar problems will require an individual diagnosis and an unique solution design. To a certain degree, therefore, everyone who is willing to tackle problems and really solve them should become a social-science technologist.

PUNISHMENT

One of the oldest methods of treating social problems has been to establish laws and rules that apply equally to all members of a particular society. These regulations are usually announced together with the appropriate punishment that will be administered for noncompliance. In other words, the general solution to most social misbehavior has been punishment or the threat of punishment. However, much experimentation in the social sciences has created strong doubts about the usefulness of punishment for either solving or preventing problems. In order to proceed to the design of better solutions, therefore, we should first introduce some of the concepts and results derived from the social-science experimentation.

CONDITIONED RESPONSE

Toward the beginning of this century, two scientists, one in Russia and the other in the United States, were simultaneously investigating the learning process of animals. Unknown to each other, they could not guess that they were starting a great rivalry between scientists over the mechanisms whereby we and other animals learn and that eventually both of their findings would be combined to create solutions to practical problems.

Ivan Pavlov, the Russian, discovered the *conditioned reflex*. Although the term may be very familiar to most people, it would still be useful to give a brief description of it. Pavlov, experimenting with dogs, tried to measure the output of their saliva when they were presented with diverse types of food. He perforated the dog's cheeks, collected the saliva drops, and then counted the number of drops that came out during any given period. He was able to determine that hungry dogs, when presented with food, have a tendency to greatly increase their flow of saliva. This is similar to the feeling we all experience when our mouths "water" at the sight of tempting food. But Pavlov was also able to show that if he rang a bell a short time before presenting food to the dog and if he repeated this procedure several times, the dog would eventually "learn" to increase its output of saliva merely upon hearing the sound of the bell. The unconditioned reflex was salivation at the actual sight of food; the conditioned reflex was the salivation upon hearing the bell. It is called a *conditioned response* because ringing a bell does not normally call forth salivation; a response can be conditioned to a particular stimulus only by employing the proper techniques.

It is impossible to discuss here the many fascinating derivations that have resulted from this famous experiment. One, however, merits special mention because of its social implications. In many experiments, dogs were conditioned to discriminate, i.e., to try to differentiate between one type of *sound* and another. They would have to salivate at the sound of a bell but not at the sound of a buzzer. In *visual* discrimination experiments, the dog had to distinguish between a circle and a rather elongated ellipse, before he was rewarded. This was a task the dogs learned rather quickly. Then, instead of presenting a very elongated ellipse, a less elongated one was shown. This gradual alteration was continued until the ellipse was very similar in shape to the circle. The dogs that were well-behaved and cooperative until then suddenly exhibited a dramatic change. Instead of salivating or continuing in their discrimination efforts, they started to snarl, bite at their harnesses, etc. They had been placed in what we can now describe as an approach-avoidance situation. Instead of solving the problem, they became aggressive and showed no desire for food, although they were still hungry. This was the animals' response to a task that involved using an ability to an extent they simply did not possess

While Pavlov was busy watching how his different experiments made his dog's mouth water, Thorndyke, in the United States, was trying to see how different animals reacted to a rather unusual situation. He placed them inside cages while they were hungry. Tempting food was available outside the cage, but to reach it the animal had to pull a ring or do some similar act. Normally, an animal would never be able to reason his way to such a complicated solution. However, since most hungry animals are quite active physically, it was only a question of time before it accidentally pulled on the ring, thus opening the cage door.

Skinner was able to devise much more sophisticated equipment. Today, the "Skinner box," designed to operate with rats, pigeons, cats or other animals, is standard equipment that can be obtained from appropriate supply companies. A Skinner box for rats, for example, is a compartment that is totally bare except for a lever at one end and a receptacle in which a food pellet is dropped every time the lever is pressed. Of course, a hungry rat placed inside such a contraption knows nothing about the connection between food and the lever. Since hungry rats are very active and exploratory in their behavior, however, they will run hither and yon, stand on their hind legs, and scratch at everything—including the bar. The food pellet will probably drop when the rat isn't even looking in that direction. Eventually, however, the rat finds the pellet and continues with its scratching and excursions until it again depresses the bar. After doing this a few times, the rat begins to press the bar at a faster and faster rate until it has had enough to eat. Thus, the animal appears to have discovered the connection between lever-pressing and food.

In both the Pavlov and Skinner experiments, the animals learn something, but there is a distinct difference between these two kinds of learning. In the Pavlov experiment, the animals are merely passive and learn to respond to some stimulus in a way that would not normally have occurred. In the Skinner box, the animal, through its active exploration of the environment, learns to do something as a consequence of having received a reward each time he does it. Peculiar behavior (if electric current is connected to the food-supplying bar, for example) can also be produced in the Skinner box situation, as it was in the Pavlovian context. Masserman made his cats alcoholics in a similar experiment.

POSITIVE REINFORCEMENT

Skinner has called the food that the animals receive *positive reinforcement*. Any reward that tends to make an organism repeat an act is called positive reinforcement. There have been a great number of experiments performed to study different types of reinforcement. One of the experiments that yielded quite unexpected results is related to what is called *partial reinforcement*. Partial reinforcement means that instead of giving the rats a bit of food *every time* they pull the bar, the reward will be given only at certain times; at other times the rat will receive no reward at all for performing the same act. The fascinating discovery was that when it was eventually decided to cut off *all* reinforcement in an effort to make the rat "forget" the whole affair and lose the habit of lowering the bar, there was a marked difference in the rate of forgetting or of *extinguishing* the response compared with the program of total reinforcement. The more the rat had been rewarded while learning, the faster he would discontinue pulling at the bar once the food supply was cut off. Conversely, the fewer the rewarded bar-pullings while learning, the longer the rat would persist in pulling the bar after the reward had been granted. Skinner (1957) cites the extreme case of a pigeon who after receiving only one reinforcement per 900 peckings during the learning period, continued to peck for another 73,000 times (without resting) after the reward was cut off.

Many explanations have been offered for this unexpected behavior. The first one that comes to mind is that the pigeon or rat that was taught with partial reinforcement does not "expect" a reward immediately and thus continues to respond—hoping that the reward will soon be forthcoming. Apparently the animal continues to respond for a long, long, time until he is finally convinced that there will never again be any reward. As social-science technologists, we are very interested in the fact that many experiments have confirmed this finding. If we were dealing with pure science, we would be interested simply in knowing why this occurs. (Perhaps we would even be content with the "expectation" theory, mentioned to groups who are being trained in social-science technology.) However, further experimentation has proven that such an explanation is totally inadequate because it does not fit many other experimental results, too numerous to mention.

What is impressive is the discovery by Lawrence and Festinger (1962) that the lack of extinction after training with partial reinforcement can be explained as a consequence of the theory of cognitive dissonance. The reasoning behind the experiments that were brilliantly devised and executed is too complex to be adequately explained here, but so far no refutation of their explanation has been presented. It is important to note that the theory of dissonance reduction is indeed very general and powerful if it explains such different phenomena as the effect of partial reinforcement, persuasion by expressing an idea opposed to a privately held belief, and many others mentioned in this book.

Another extremely important finding that has evolved from experimentation with the learning process concerns the effectiveness of punishment. Punishment, as we have said, has been the traditional method used to control the behavior of men and animals. Skinner (1938) performed an experiment designed to test the effectiveness of punishment in extinguishing undesirable behavior. After training rats to pull on a bar in order to get food, he tried to obtain extinction through two different ways. One was the standard method of merely cutting off the food supply. The second method not only cuts off the food supply but, in addition, it administered punishment for pulling down the bar. The punishment consisted of slapping the rat everytime it pulled on the bar. The slapped rats diminished their bar pulling drastically for a certain period. However, by the end of four hours, they had accumulated as many bar pulls as the unpunished rats. This means that although the rat showed an initial reaction to the punishment, it did not extinguish the undesired response any faster than in the other animals.

This finding should probably rank among the most important discoveries of the 20th century. For many centuries society has used punishment to enforce laws and to otherwise curb what is considered to be obnoxious behavior. The fact that punishment has an immediate effect but then a later reversal is something that is not known or understood by those who propose punishment as the means of controlling behavior. The prototype experiment we described has been repeated many times, using different kinds of punishment in different ways, but the results are virtually always the same. If we add to this the fact that punishment always creates a negative attitude in the punished person and that in the approach-avoidance situation it will increase the avoidance effects, we should not be surprised that punishment, in the long run, only makes matters worse. Hence, social-science technology should not employ punishment as a tool until someone proves that it really is a useful problem-solving technique.

Some attempts have been made to show that punishment does work under certain circumstances, but these experiments will not be thoroughly discussed here, primarily because the results are not very convincing. Furthermore, even if punishment could be shown to be a possible means of behavior modification, the deleterious side effects would still preclude its use. Finally, society's desire to use punishment as a tool is so strong, even when it has been understood that positive reinforcement is the best way of obtaining results, that the social scientist is obligated to re-emphasize the need for positive reinforcement and the abolition of punishment.

Another important experimental finding related to positive reinforcement is the ability to mold behavior. Originally, experiments were constructed so that it was essential for the organism to perform a fully integrated act before receiving the reward. Skinner (1958) describes how, by judiciously using positive reinforcement with imperfect responses, it is possible to train pigeons to bowl! The story can best be told in Skinner's own words.

> The pigeon was to send a wooden ball down a miniature alley toward a set of toy pins by swiping the ball with a sharp sideward movement of the beak. To condition the response we put the ball on the floor of an experimental box and prepared to operate the food-magazine as soon as the first swipe occurred. But nothing happened. Though we had all the time in the world, we grew tired of waiting. We decided to reinforce any response which had the slightest resemblance to a swipe—perhaps, at first, merely the behavior of looking at the ball—and then to select responses which more closely approximated the final form. The result amazed us. In a few minutes, the ball was caroming off the walls of the box as if the pigeon had been a champion squash player.

This "molding of behavior" eventually led to the development of the presently popular teaching machines and other methods of programmed instruction. However, by combining this method with techniques and findings from other areas, we have been able to solve many kinds of social problems in ways that differ considerably from the standard teaching machine or programmed texts.

SPECIFIC SOLUTIONS BASED ON GENERAL PRINCIPLES

In the chapter on group problem solving, we described solutions that mainly utilized the devices of positive and negative reinforcement. Now we shall present solutions based on the whole gamut of social-science findings, which we have subsequently described. Four specific problems have been selected as examples, each of which requires a unique solution. The different processes whereby each solution is developed from our general principles will be explicitly described. Hopefully, the reader will now be equipped to recognize all the different principles involved in both the problems and their solutions. For example, the reader should be able to follow the intellectual exercise whereby a person from an Accounting Department was able to solve a problem at home by using the problem-solving techniques learned in his job.

HOW TO GIVE AN ORDER

One very common problem in many organizations is knowing how to give orders to subordinates, and there are innumerable books and pamphlets that offer good advice on how to correctly give an order. Quite often, in fact, when it becomes obvious to everyone that certain supervisors handle their subordinates poorly, managers or personnel men make these supervisors read the books or pamphlets, convinced that by merely "reasoning" their way into better behavior, the supervisors will automatically change. One such publication, written by the Director of Training of an important corporation, gives several bits of advice, including the admonition to give orders clearly, concisely, and distinctly and to study the men well in order to recognize individual differences. The author has seen such pamphlets distributed to foremen of a plant, without any noticeable success. The only satisfied person seemed to be the man who initiated the distribution of these pamphlets. He generally felt proud of his idea.

It is very possible that the reason for the lack of change may be that it is one thing to be told theoretically what should be done and quite another to be able to go out and do it. A common example of this type of approach is the so-called "sensitivity training" laboratory, in which supervisors undergo the disagreeable experience of seeing people being overly frank with one another. Presumably, that week's experience will cause an individual to completely change his method of handling his people.

As we have stated repeatedly, when something anomalous happens, there is always a cause. We gain nothing by treating the symptoms if we don't reach the *causes* of these symptoms. Therefore, if we find several supervisors handling their subordinates roughly, we had better carefully scrutinize top management in our search for the cause of this mishandling. One situation in which mishandling is likely to occur is when a supervisor has to tell a subordinate that something must be done. Generally unless there has been intensive training about how to do this or unless the supervisor has somehow acquired the knack, this communication is poorly made. The fact that the people who receive these orders do not seem to complain does not justify the supervisors' approach. Reactions to problems, as we saw in the chapter on "Judging People We Know," may seem most unlikely and apparently unrelated to the problem itself.

Two causes for giving poor instructions can exist: One may be the fact that the supervisor is in an approach-avoidance or dissonance situation. The other reason may be that he simply was never trained in how to give the proper instructions. Quite often both of these causes exist simultaneously, with rough treatment as the symptom. We shall now describe an actual case for which a successful solution was found.

Dave was the supervisor of about 20 persons, doing diverse jobs, in an industrial plant. His manner with his subordinates was described as horrible. Specifically, he was very curt in giving orders. There had been many complaints to the Personnel Department, and the Manager of Dave's section had often heard him give orders to his men in terms that were very irritating. It was decided to make an appraisal. From this, it became apparent that Dave was very good at all the technical aspects of the operation but that he was poor in interpersonal contacts. Besides, there was a particular cause that made him conspicuously different from everyone else. (Although the cause itself will not be cited here, it was neither religious, racial, nor ideological.) It was recalled that his favorite jokes were always related to his particular deviance. Had Freedman and Doob (1968) published their work earlier, this deviancy might have been handled by utilizing some of their results and experimental designs. At the time, however, it was decided that there was very little that could be done about Dave's difference. Nevertheless, it was recognized that although he was intelligent and socially well-behaved, he had never received training about how to give an order. A special design was created that has subsequently been useful in many other cases. It is interesting to note that the design has worked even in cases where there is another cause behind the aggressive order-giving. In other words, a symptom is being treated by itself. This is acceptable provided it is not the only action being taken, that is, the cause itself must also be attacked.

In this particular situation, it was felt that Dave could be taught how to give instructions to his subordinates by using positive reinforcement. Being very interested in technical solutions, Dave liked to go to the Personnel Department because he saw that there were technical ways of dealing with people. It was suspected that in a way he felt he was receiving some support for his deviance. The Personnel Department is, of course, trained to treat deviants as though they were average people, and he probably felt comfortable there. He would often ask for advice about how to handle certain problems. It was decided, therefore, that at one of these interviews, a qualified person would seize the opportunity to train him in order-giving by using positive reinforcement. What follows is a reconstruction of the interview. (Note that for this and other purposes there are always portable tape recorders available, although nothing is ever recorded without the full knowledge and consent of all those concerned.)

Dave started to talk about general topics and the problems he was facing when, at a certain point, the Personnel man, labeled X in the ensuing dialogue, asked a question:

X: What would you say, looking at the overall picture, is your worst problem now?
DAVE: Well, . . . probably our biggest problem is the supply of phosphates. This need to change suppliers from different countries when there is a scarcity of foreign exchange never lets us set up the equipment so things will run smoothly. Somebody ought to set up a plant in this country.
X: Do you think such a plant would be perfectly reliable as to quality?
DAVE: Well, I guess not. They'd have problems too with *their* suppliers. Besides, I understand it takes quite a while for that kind of plant to get adjusted to where there are no problems and quality becomes absolutely uniform.
X: What would you say your second worst problem is?
DAVE: That's easy. It's the one that keeps me coming into this office—personnel.
X: Yes, personnel is really a problem. What would you say is the worst problem you have with personnel?
DAVE·   I just think the worst thing about them is that they don't want to work. So often you tell them to do things and they just don't do them. Sometimes I have to say things three or four times before I can get someone to do it. Besides, when they finally get around to doing it, they grumble and look as if I'd ordered the impossible. They don't seem to realize that that's what they get paid for.
X: Why do you think it's necessary to repeat orders so often?
DAVE: Well, I just think they're incompetent and don't feel like working.
X: You think, for example, that Joe is incompetent?
DAVE: No! There's a good example. He's no fool, but he's sure antagonistic.
X: In what way does he show his ill will?
DAVE: Well, I've told him several times to put tools back in place after he's used them,

and he not only never does so, but he's actually sneered at me when I look at him, wondering what he's going to do about the tools that are lying around. (X asked questions about other cases. It became apparent that the subordinates were all very different people. There did not seem to be any one visible cause for their misbehavior, nor any one way in which this misbehavior was uniform. Dave recognized this and found it curious that no one cause could be found. Here, use was being made of dissonance theory. Dave was expressing an opinion contrary to his earlier belief that it was a uniform fault of the workers that caused all the trouble. His prior belief changed consequently and became harmonious with the newly expressed idea: although he had attributed everything to the ill will of his subordinates, Dave now found that this was an insufficient explanation.)

X: Tell me . . .   When a person gives an order to another, in general, how many people are involved? Say, for example, when Ed, your Manager, gives you an order, how many are concerned?

DAVE: There may be many eventually concerned, but at that moment there are only two.

X: When Ed gives you an order, is it always perfectly clear and intelligible.

DAVE: No, by no means, but I try to interpret it, and the order gets carried out.

X: Do you think your workers interpret your orders well?

DAVE: They should. That's part of their job.

X: Have you ever heard yourself giving an order?

DAVE: No, never. How could I?

X: If it were possible for you to hear yourself giving an order, do you think it would be worthwhile?

DAVE: Well, I guess it would be an experience. I suppose that it would be good to listen to oneself, but how could I ever do that? I'd have to carry a tape recorder around with me all day.

X: In what way do you think that hearing yourself give an order could be useful to you?

DAVE: Well . . .   I think one can always improve. Honest, I know I do lots of things that maybe could be done better. At least I think I do things well. Maybe I could even improve the way I give orders. (X has obtained quite a commitment to the possibility that: (a) the way Dave gives the orders may have something to do with the problem; and (b) there may be a chance for improvement.)

X: I'll tell you one way we can do it. There's a tape recorder here. Let's suppose I'm one of your workers. You have to give an order. Just give it to me, we'll record it, you hear how it sounds, and then we can erase it. Want to try?

DAVE: All right, no harm done.

X: Well, what's a typical order you'd have to go out and give now?

DAVE: (After reflecting a bit.) Well there's a shipment of parts coming in, and there are empty salt barrels on the loading platform. I have to order those barrels taken out.

X: Who would you give this order to?

DAVE: Either Bill or Dan.

X: O.K. Suppose I'm Dan. Go ahead as if I were Dan and tell me what to do. (Starts tape recorder.)

DAVE: Hey Dan! get those barrels back there. (In spite of his effort to make this sound as good as possible, Dave said this in his usual gruff tone of voice.)

X: All right. Let's play it back now and see how it sounds. (The tape was replayed. Dave was obviously shocked. Most people are when they hear their voices recorded for the first time, particularly if it refers to something related to the work situation. There is a great difference between the perception they have of themselves and the unsettling reality they suddenly face. X maintained a straight face, as if all this were perfectly normal.)

X: (With no hint of criticism.) How does it sound to you?

DAVE: Awful! Terrible! . . . I never thought I sounded like that.

X: It doesn't sound too bad to me. What do you find wrong with it?

DAVE: Don't know . . . it's harsh . . . what can I say . . . if anyone talked to me like that, I wouldn't like it. (It is to be noted that X never pointed out the errors. This would have created dissonance, since Dave originally thought he was good at his job. He let Dave point out his own flaws. As a result, he is in a dissonant condition: He believed he was good but has now expressed an opinion contrary to this belief. He is therefore open to change, since no reactance is involved.)

X: If you think it's so bad, why don't you try it again? (The recorder has been turned off.)

DAVE: All right . . . let's see, Dan, Won't you take those barrels down to the back, please?

X: That sounds very well. Try it again. (X let Dave try it several times until a very decided improvement over the first time was noted. This was all done *without recording.*)

X: (As soon as he heard one that was a decided improvement over the initial order.) Let's try and record that one and see how it sounds. (This is recorded next to the initial order.)

DAVE: Please, Dan. Won't you stack those empty barrels in back so we'll have enough room for the spare parts that are coming in this afternoon?

X: (Plays back both the first recording and this improvement. Upon hearing them sequentially, Dave noted a great improvement, which constituted strong positive reinforcement. X offered no praise; he merely let Dave discover that he did indeed improve a great deal and that this improvement came about in a matter of minutes.)

X: How do they sound to you?

DAVE: No comparison. The second one is a lot better than the first one. Still, I think it could be improved.

X: How?

DAVE: Well . . . the tone of voice . . . something . . .

X: Want to try again?

DAVE: Sure. (Again, several nonrecorded trials were made. As soon as X noted a decided improvement, which would also be recognized as an improvement by Dave, he asked the latter to repeat the order so that it could be recorded.)

X: Now, let's hear all three together. (The recorder was made to play back the first, second, and third versions. Dave winced when he heard the first one. He was pleased with the second but even more satisfied with his last effort.)

X: You seem happy over this last one. Why don't you go out right now and give Dan this order just as you did to me just now and see what happens.

DAVE: O.K. I'll see if it works. (Dave went out and gave the order and in a few minutes was back in the Personnel Department smiling broadly.)

DAVE: Say, you know that worked! Dan went right out and did it. He even smiled. I don't know if he was laughing at me because, honest, I never talked to anyone like that before in my life.

X: How do you feel now that you've done it?

DAVE: Fine. The trouble is, can I remember to keep it up?

X: Well, anytime you want to try out before you give an order, just drop in and we'll rehearse it like you did just then. Only don't let anyone know you're doing this here. It's worth a lot more to the men and they'll respect you more if they think you worked it out alone, which in fact is the truth. Maybe a few will start joking about your change of tone toward them, but don't you mind. Eventually, everyone will like it more. Wouldn't you like it more if everyone always talked to you kindly? (Note that X has obtained a number of things. Without causing reactance, he has had Dave admit that there might be a problem in how he gave orders. Secondly, he got Dave to try the recorder. Thirdly, he gave Dave a strong positive reinforcement—initially by seeing how he could improve results with the recorder and later by getting results in practice. Furthermore, all this was accomplished in 20 minutes.)

Naturally, this particular case did not end with this brief dialogue. For days the supervisor was interviewed briefly to see how things were progressing. Several more sessions were held with the recorder. At first, there was a lot of covert snickering among his subordinate's about Dave's change of tone. After about two weeks, however, the men became accustomed to it, and there was a noticeable improvement in the general atmosphere of the department—at least this was what Dave's manager saw. Of course, Dave's manager was made aware of the whole process. It was then decided that Dave's manager would ask to see Dave on or about the 15th day (following a day on which things had gone exceptionally well in the department) and congratulate Dave on the great improvement in his Department and on Dave's remarkable adeptness in handling people. This was, of course, more positive reinforcement for Dave, which brought him back for more sessions with the recorder.

Eventually, one of his subordinates told Dave that he was very pleased because he had noticed a great change in the way he was being treated. He said that about a month ago he had been ready to quit but that now he would never think of leaving. This was further positive reinforcement for Dave who was soon in the Personnel Department telling X what had happened.

Today, Dave has been promoted for his ability to handle people. (Of course, this was not the only thing that brought about the change.) He was trained in social-science technology, and now uses this kind of method to help solve the problems of his subordinates.

An important aspect of this example should be stressed. Since Dave ranks rather high in behavioral abilities, he readily detected the change in his subordinates' attitudes toward him. It was possible, therefore, to rely on the feedback, which we knew would be forthcoming, as an additional means of positive reinforcement in continuing the new behavior. However, when this method has been tried with persons who are *low* in cognition of behavioral units, systems, and transformations, they are unable to detect the attitude changes. The reinforcement in these cases has to be made by using outside sources. For example, the manager could say he overheard some of his subordinates state how pleased they were with Dave's change, or he could even get another manager, who is further removed from the situation, to make the same remark. In each case, adequate positive reinforcement has to be found. However, if the man is so low in behavioral abilities as not to recognize the changes in others' attitudes and behaviors, then it would be best to place him in a position where he does not have to handle people.

LATENESS

There are few things that make a supervisor angrier than to see one or several people come in late day after day. It is interesting to note that this occurs even among supervisors who are often late themselves. Their most common reactions are to look sternly at the late arrival, to call him in and bawl him out, to "explain and reason" with the latecomer about the need for punctuality, and to apply "sanctions" in the form of fines, suspensions, etc. Rarely is this lateness regarded as a symptom of a deeper problem. In Chapter 3 we saw how it was possible to properly diagnose symptoms in order to avoid the foolish trap of treating them instead of the causes. In fact, one of the symptoms we discussed was absenteeism, including tardiness. But, as we have constantly repeated, there is a world of difference between knowing what the cause of a certain phenomenon is and knowing what to do about it. We shall therefore present a case in which late arrival was the noticeable symptom, and a description of the behavioral principles employed to create a solution for the cause of this symptom.

Again, we should warn the reader that this is not necessarily a standard procedure or formula to be used in all cases in which lateness is a problem. To do so would be making the mistake of treating all human beings and all situations alike. Therefore, this case is presented merely as a guide to show that this sort of thing can be done and that results can be obtained. It takes careful diagnosis, followed by adequate planning in which considerable ingenuity is required, before a good design that will really solve the problem can be constructed. Of course, firing the person appears simpler, but it has been shown that the feeling of instability thus caused among the remaining personnel will create resentment. Besides, if the basic cause is not corrected, there is no assurance that the new employee will be perfectly satisfied and that there will be no approach-avoidance conflict with attendant symptoms. To the claim that this procedure is too long and cumbersome, we reply that if doctors had taken the same attitude toward certain types of illness, many of our readers would probably not be alive today. If we wish to cure social illness, we must attack it rationally, not in a way that will create even more social illness.

To proceed with our case: Gloria is a young lady who has been with an organization for several years and for whom the approval motive is important. It was noticed that at a certain period she began to come in late—occasionally as much as an hour or more. Otherwise, she was the perfect worker. She was competent, had very good ideas about how to organize her work, and was extremely neat. There was never any waste in her work, in either time or materials. One could always count on her having things ready when she promised—*but* . . . she came in late!

Her supervisor was quite annoyed at this tardiness, but since many social-science techniques had been introduced in the new company, he knew that he should not directly mention her late arrival. He had learned that lateness was a symptom. Moreover, because Gloria was a good worker in other respects, she had to be saved; it was up to him to find the cause of the problem. Appraisal was made in which it was found that Gloria was coming in late not only because she lived far away but also because she had recently lost her roommate with whom she shared the daily chores. She found that although these chores were now lessened, she had to do them all herself. Indeed, Gloria had mentioned that she should move closer to work so that she would have more time to do her housekeeping.

Gloria's supervisor asked the Personnel Assistant in the Personnel Manager's Office to verify this diagnosis through a well-conducted interview. This was done, and by exploring which areas of work she liked best and which she liked least, it was discovered that there had been changes in work assignments in the department sometime before Gloria had started to come in late. As part of Gloria's new assignment, she had been given tasks that were considered to be of very low status by everyone in her department. Almost from the beginning, they had kidded her about this; consequently, a certain distance between her and the rest of the group had arisen. This was very significant because feeling that she was part of the group meant a lot to Gloria. The new task also required considerable use of memory of symbolic units and systems (skills in which she ranked low); as a result, the new work was very difficult for her. Her strengths lay in the semantic area. The interview with the Personnel Assistant ended with no reference whatever to the late arrivals.

It was therefore seen that the initial diagnosis had been only partially correct, since there were other elements besides the roommate incident involved. Because she lived so far away and had to do all the work herself, Gloria could easily rationalize to herself and others the reason for her tardiness, if the subject were mentioned, but neither the Personnel Assistant nor the Supervisor mentioned it. Instead, they designed the following solution to the problem.

To begin with, the Supervisor recognized that he had erred in assigning work without matching the mental abilities and other qualifications required by the task to the specific employee. He also saw that there were several other employees who possessed the necessary skills for that part of Gloria's work that she disliked and who were not being used. The final plan they adopted included four sequential steps.

(1) Gradually transfer the duties in question to those capable of handling them.

(2) Raise the status of such duties to avoid creating dissonance for the employees about to be assigned those duties.

(3) Treat Gloria's symptom of lateness because it may have become a habit.

The reader may be surprised to see that step (3) suggests that the symptom itself be treated. Such advice would seem to be in direct contradiction to what has been stated so far. However, symptom treatment often occurs in medicine, and there is no reason why the analogy should not also apply to social-science pathology. A doctor often prescribes medicine to relieve pain (a symptom), while he is at the same time doing other things to cure the patient of the cause of the pain. Thus, as mentioned earlier, it is permissible to treat a symptom if at the same time something is also being done about its cause.

Gradual Transfer.   This was not too hard to do, particularly since it was decided to take step (2) first. Once this had been accomplished, there was no trouble in making the transfer.

Raising the Status.   It was felt that merely stating that the work was important would not be enough. It would be necessary to resort to another type of persuasion. In this case, it was decided to combine findings by Walster and Festinger (1962) and by Weick (1964). According to the former, persuasions counter to an attitude held by a person were more effective when "overheard" than when the same persuasion was made directly to the subjects. In the Weick experiment, subjects were made to like tasks more by *making* them volunteer for them and by then having them go to extra efforts to do a good job. As stated by Weick, ". . . changes in cognitions about beliefs and about behavior operate as complementary or mutually reinforcing tactics of dissonance reduction."

This was done by the Supervisor in the following manner: He first persuaded the group that the task was important by stressing the fact in a telephone conversation with someone else, which was overheard by the group; they then became convinced that the task was really important and worthwhile. Thus, the employees did not believe that the persuasion was directed at them but rather that their Supervisor had discussed the subject with someone of importance. Later, the Supervisor asked which of two individuals, high in the required abilities, would be willing to do a rush job on this recently classified low-status work. He, of course, made no reference to the status of the task. Both persons volunteered. He allowed them to spend quite a bit of time on the job and as soon as it was completed, telephoned the person who was most interested in this particular work. The two volunteers now "overheard" the Supervisor say that the task had been completed in a short time. This was, of course, positively reinforcing for the volunteers. We see here a very neat case of applying social-science technology, based on findings from three entirely different areas, to solving the work-status problem. Incidentally, it was gradually noted that the heretofore neglected task began to gain in status.

Gloria's Symptom.   By this time, Gloria had become accustomed to coming in late, regardless of the amelioration of the underlying problem. It was decided to treat this symptom by using positive reinforcement to mold her behavior. For several days, the schedule of arrivals was closely observed. Although the official starting time was 8:30 A.M., her arrivals were usually 8:47, 8:50, 8:52, 8:46, 8:49, and 8:37 A.M. There seemed to be considerable variations, thereby making it possible to provide positive reinforcement every time there was an improvement in the time of arrival. For example, in the above schedule, positive reinforcement could be administered on the sixth day, since this was a decided improvement over the previous days. Careful thought was given to the question of what would constitute positive reinforcement for Gloria (what is rewarding for one person may not be for another). Because Gloria was known to have a strong need for approval, it was felt that any praise related to her work or her dress would be satisfactory. Since she also ranked high in semantic skills, agreeing with an opinion of her's should also work.

The next time a marked improvement was noticed in Gloria's punctuality, her supervisor told her immediately upon her arrival: "There was a call a little while ago from X Department, thanking us for the job we did for them yesterday. Since you had a big share of this, I thought you'd like to know—so congratulations and thanks." (Note that the supervisor said this the moment she came in.) Skinner has shown that for the reinforcement to be effective, it must be immediately contingent on the performance of the act. Thus, if one wishes to train pigeons to peck hard but does not reinforce them until they lift their heads after pecking, the reinforcement will have been given for an act different from the one to be conditioned, that is, for lifting the head instead of for pecking hard.

A week went by with little improvement. Then one day Gloria arrived at 8:35 A.M. The supervisor, very alert to this change and noting that Gloria was wearing a dress he had not seen before, immediately said, "That's a nice dress you're wearing," and told her of an urgent job that had to be done as fast as possible. Several days passed, during which the tardiness continued, but finally there was an 8:32 arrival. The supervisor then remarked that he had changed his opinion on the subject they had discussed sometime ago, and now thought that she was right. This particular discussion concerned a change that Gloria had suggested in the way her desk should be placed, which the supervisor had resisted. The supervisor now agreed with her and said the desk should be changed at once. This tactic constitutes positive reinforcement by concurring with an expressed attitude.

The work required lots of patience and alertness, but the supervisor eventually reached his objective. Gloria is now very happy and is very seldom late—never more than 6 or 7 minutes.

It might surprise the reader to see that here the supervisor is treating a symptom. A lot has been said before in this book (and more will be said) about the folly of curing symptoms and not attacking the real causes. Isn't this a colossal contradiction? There are two replies. One is again based on the medical analogy. A doctor uses a symptom such as pain in order to diagnose, but while he is attacking the cause, he may simultaneously give the patient a sedative in order to relieve the pain. The error would be if he only relieved the pain. This has been referred to earlier.

A second more tangible evidence is given by La Fave and Teely (1967) in which they showed that habits acquired under certain circumstances often tend to contrive or to acquire what Allport termed "functional autonomy" long after the cause that generated the habit has disappeared. It is therefore necessary to do something about the acquired, and no longer justifiable, habit. It is interesting to note that the principle of functional autonomy initially postulated by Allport and which fell into disrepute (Hall and Lindzey, 1970) is now revived with tangible experimental evidence to substantiate it.

JOB STABILITY

There is no question that one thing most workers want is stability. Herzberg et al. (1959) found that the absence of certain factors in the work situation can make people very unhappy—although the existence of any one factor does not insure happiness nor high productivity. Among these, job stability was cited as one of the principal factors causing job dissatisfaction.

Stability or instability in a job, however, cannot be determined objectively; it is something that is *perceived* by the individuals involved. Such perception is not induced by *statements* made by the organization for which the individual works but rather by the employee's interpretation of what the organization *does*.

Cognitive dissonance plays an important part in this perception. A person may experience two dissonant cognitions:

- He has been working for years in an organization in a position in which he feels secure.
- He comes to work one day and finds that two of his fellow workers have been fired.

These two dissonant cognitions provoke in the subject a desire to reduce the dissonance. An excellent way is to say to himself: "I'm going to find another job and quit before they fire me." The author, who has had the opportunity to interview thousands of job-seekers in several countries, can safely say fear of dismissal is a very powerful motive that has been mentioned by many persons, particularly by those who do not appear to have much divergent ability in the behavioral and semantic areas and who are therefore not imaginative at finding new jobs. Besides, the fear of dismissal can have devastating effects upon someone's efficiency on the job. In a recent case a person who feared dismissal finally quit, although it later turned out that his organization considered him to be their most valued employee. In actual fact, he would have been the last to be fired. Nevertheless, he felt his dismissal was imminent, and for almost a month, before making the decision to quit, he had become virtually useless to the company.

The decision to quit when a person fears that he may be fired might be prompted by a desire for security or perhaps for prestige (since no one has ever fired him before). It may also be motivated by a need to have a clean record as far as future job references are concerned. But again, as we saw in Chapter 1, the decision to quit is dissonance-provoking. The two dissonant cognitions are:

- I have been working in this organization for many years and thought it was good.
- I have now decided to leave this organization.

Such dissonance has to be reduced. Since the person does not yet know where he is going, he will probably create a mythical company in his mind that must naturally be better in some way than the one he is working for now. One obvious advantage the subject can attribute to the hypothetical company is a higher salary. Accordingly, the individual will conclude that his present salary is too low. This rationalization requires social support, thereby leading the worker to seek others who will support him in his contention that salaries here are low. This will not be too difficult if he finds others who are in the same state of anxiety because of job insecurity (Schachter, 1959). Grove and Kerr (1951) have shown that a feeling of insecurity caused employees "to express discontent with their actually superior pay and working conditions." This result can now be easily predicted utilizing the theory of cognitive dissonance.

Organizations must therefore be very careful about how they go about terminating employees. If this is done as a final act of "justice" brought about by misbehavior, after compiling a full dossier of the person's "misdemeanors," it will certainly not instill confidence in other employees who have made the same type of errors. Contrary to popular belief, this method has a devastating effect on the other workers rather than making an "example" of the fired man for the rest to observe. Perhaps the reader who has used the "making an example of him" or "justice" approach may resent this conclusion as illogical. The reply is that although this may not sound logical, it *is* the way human beings act. We are therefore faced with the problem of how to fire a man and yet not create the feeling of instability that follows every such separation.

All this closely parallels the reasoning, based on social-science findings, concerning the promotion example in Chapter 1. There, it was seen how a solution could be found to an apparently inevitable discontent, following the announcement of an appointment. In some respects, the solution devised for separation is similar to the one for a promotion. One conclusion we can draw from both cases is that there must be a clear distinction between the *decision* to separate the person and the actual *act* of firing him. The latter need not follow immediately after the first, although this practice is quite common.

Actually, there are many things we have to think about before executing the separation. If the person does not do his job well and if we find, from an appraisal of the type described in Chapter 3, that the problem lies in something intrinsic (the person's lack of essential mental abilities, required interests, or personality traits—things that cannot be remedied), we must recognize that the fault is ours and not his; we placed him in the position he presently holds. Although we have already stated that no time will be wasted in trying to place the blame, we do know that the fault is not the worker's. Therefore, we would be performing the gravest injustice if we fire him for incompetence. If we wish to do justice and set "this man up as an example," we should really do exactly the opposite of what we had originally planned. The problem now is not to find who is at fault but rather how to separate the worker without unjustly firing him for incompetence, thereby producing a trauma of insecurity in a man against whom we have nothing. Furthermore, he must be fired without leaving among the remaining co-workers the dissonant impression that "this is an insecure place to work for." At first, the solution to the problem seems difficult, but the use of social-science findings allows us to design an acceptable solution. Before explaining an actual case, however, a word of warning is in order. Telling a man "You're fired!" is quick, efficient, and does not leave time for feeling qualms. Doing what was done in the case we are about to relate is much more time-consuming and requires ingenuity. In the end, however, it pays greater dividends.

George worked in the Invoice Department of a certain company. His task was to take the monthly delivery notices and make out the monthly invoices. It was an easy task, but he was terrible at it. Not only did he make many errors, but he often left papers hidden in and behind drawers. Once, when he was sick for several days, another employee who knew the job was asked to take over because the work had been delayed. He found several important papers that should have been converted to invoices sometime before. This meant loss of income to the company, interest on the money due, etc. The Head of the Department was furious and wanted to fire George at once. The company, however, had established the policy that no mention whatever was to be made of firing someone without first discussing the problem with the Personnel Department.

After listening to all the evidence, it was clear that George should never have been hired in the first place. But he *had* been hired and even given raises on the strength of which he had married and now had two small children. Also, besides being sloppy and inadequate, George was well-liked by everyone. The Personnel Manager emphasized to the Department Head what a bad effect summary dismissal would have on the others. The Department Head replied that everyone knew George was incompetent. This remark was countered by the fact that the company would promote an image of heartlessness by firing George, even if he were given severance pay, at a moment when jobs were hard to obtain. Besides, with his poor skills, everyone would pity George because where would he find a job that would pay him as much as he was making?

The Department Head, Art, insisted that George must go. The Personnel Manager, Ben, said that he understood the situation, but that the firing had to be done in a way that would not ruin the general morale, which was fortunately quite high at the time. Accordingly, a problem-solving meeting was called for Art, Ben, Case (Art's supervisor), and Martha, one of the girls in Personnel. At this meeting Ben explained that in general when a supervisor is dissatisfied with a subordinate, the subordinate is also dissatisfied with the supervisor. As a corollary to this, if the subordinate is dissatisfied with the supervisor, it is quite likely that he himself may have thought of leaving more than once. One way would be to ask for a transfer to another department. It was learned that George had never asked to be transferred, but it was still likely that he had, even halfheartedly, looked for work opportunities elsewhere. It was decided to find out whether George had had such thoughts and if so, what direction they were taking.

It was obvious that since there had already been tension between Art and George, Art could not conduct such an interview. Instead, Martha, who had been trained in social-science technology and was a skillful interviewer, would do this part of the fact-finding. A complete plan was devised.

(1)   Martha would interview George at the earliest possible opportunity and find out whether he was dissatisfied with his job and with Art. If so, she would also find out whether George had thought of any solutions to the situation.

(2)   The results of the interview would, of course, be communicated to the rest of the group. Two days after the interview, assuming it were successful, Martha would go back to George and tell him that she had been thinking about his problem, that she was very upset about it, and that she thought that George should talk about the matter to Ben, who was very understanding and would surely be helpful.

(3)   George would go to Ben, who would encourage him to pursue one of the solutions that he had mentioned to Martha.

(4)   Martha would contact George to get an impression of the interview with Ben.

(5)   The "sleeper effect" would work, and eventually George would resign.

(6)   Art would tell George that he was very sorry to see him leave and give him full severance pay, plus a small, extra bonus.

The process worked exactly as described. Martha saw George, who described how badly he felt in his work because Art was very hard on him. Martha asked what plans he had. George admitted that he had answered a newspaper advertisement for another job, but he had had no reply. Also, he and a friend might possibly go into the duplicating business together. George liked the duplicating idea best of all, but he needed a little capital and had none available. Martha showed great interest in all this, and they parted.

Three days later, Martha returned. At a meeting of the four who were discussing the problem, it was noted that the severance pay George would normally receive if fired would be just a little above what he said he needed for starting his own duplicating business; therefore, Martha could easily tell George to speak to Ben. She did this so well that an hour later, George was talking to Ben about all his troubles and possible plans. Of course, Ben acted as if he knew nothing of the whole affair. After hearing the whole story, Ben seemed to ruminate and then told George that he thought he was wasting his time in the company if he had such a good opportunity. This was done in a manner similar to persuasion by successive approximations described in Chapter 4. During all this, Ben acted as if he had had no contact with Art. However, there was the serious problem of the required capital. In other words, if George resigned, he would not be entitled to the severance pay that he would get if he were fired. Ben told George that although he couldn't speak for Art, he was sure Art liked George and would be sorry to see him go but that he certainly wouldn't let him go empty-handed. "If severance pay is given to a person who is fired," he said, "I am sure that he will give as much to someone like yourself who has devoted all his time to this organization." Ben did not offer to mediate between Art and George; he merely acted as a counselor.

The next morning Martha arranged to meet George in the lobby, while they were leaving, and asked him whether he had talked to Ben. George said he had, and her impression was that George, although looking somewhat troubled, felt generally relieved. He said that he had discussed the subject with his wife and that his wife was very much in favor of his leaving the company.

We should digress a moment to describe the *sleeper effect*. This effect was found in some of the experiments reported by Hovland *et al.* (1953) in which the effect of a persuasive communication appeared to affect opinion change more as time elapsed. It was expected that this sleeper effect would work on George, especially since his wife would also be contributing to it.

Several weeks passed, and Art could stand it no longer. One day he stormed into the Personnel Department and said that he was going to fire George immediately, showing new evidence for his decision. Nevertheless, Ben stuck by the original decision and was supported by Case, Art's supervisor. Art simply had to be patient until the thing worked itself out as planned. Finally, two months after the original meeting, George called Case and said he wanted to see him at his home. (George had worked for Case when Case had been Head of the Invoice Department before being promoted and replaced by Art). George came in and said, in a very regretful tone of voice, that he had news—he had decided to leave the company to go into the duplicating business. Case, who had been in on the whole plan from the beginning, told George he was very sorry to hear this and asked him whether he had spoken to Art. George replied that he hadn't; so Case then suggested he tell Art the next morning.

Art, forewarned of these events, received George the next morning and heard the latter state his intention of withdrawing from the company. Art played his part well. He told George how sorry he was to see him go, that he liked George a lot although at times he might have been rough on him, and that he certainly did not want him to leave with only the pay that was due him. He and George figured what the severance pay would amount to, and then he added some additional money. He ordered the paymaster to make out a check for this total, plus George's salary to that date. George was delighted and thanked Art effusively. He went out and told the rest of his fellow workers how he was going to set himself up in a small business. They all threw a little party for him, and he left in the highest of spirits. Morale in the department continued to be high; George is now doing quite well in his own business; and to this day, no one except the author and the four persons concerned know that George had really been fired.

GROUP COOPERATION

An actual solution will now be presented for a problem that had become so serious that it was about to turn into open conflict. One of the supervisors, who works in a company in which social-science techniques were frequently applied, found himself in the newer position of having to apply these techniques to his home environment. The following account is a transcription of a tape recording, made with his consent,[1] describing how he solved the problem. This solution (the facts of which were later checked independently) also demonstrates how a supervisor, who uses social-science technology in the work situation, is able to apply the same principles to social problems in other areas. The habit of dealing with problems in this way becomes so ingrained that it constitutes a way of life for him.

The characters in the dialogue will be the Interviewer (I) and the Supervisor (S).

I: You say you solved a problem about a Porter. Well, tell me how you handled it.

S: Well, you know that any apartment house in which each dweller is the owner of his apartment, and which is well run, has a regular proprietor's meeting. I moved in three months ago, maybe a little more than that, and the first problem that came up concerned the Porter.

I: Just a moment, how many owners are there in all?

S: There are 22 apartments.

I: Each with its independent owner?

S: Yes, each with its owner, although they don't all come to these meetings. Only 14 or 15 come, generally with their wives.

I: With their wives and maybe a son or daughter?

S: No, only the owners, some of them with their wives.

I: Was the Porter always present at these meetings, or wasn't there any Porter yet?

S: No, that's just it. There was a Porter; and the most serious problem, aside from others we had, was that the majority wanted a change of Porter. I was kind of new at this sort of thing, never having owned an apartment before.

[1] It has been the author's policy to record nothing without the consent and full knowledge of those involved. Many problem solving meetings have been thus recorded, but since they have always been part of a larger problem, they have seemed unsuitable to include here. Moreover, to do so would require a great amount of additional explanatory material in order to make the discussion relevant to the reader.

I: Had the others been there longer?

S: Yes, I was the last one to occupy an apartment.

I: And the one who had been there longest, how long was that?

S: Two years.

I: Is that when the building was inaugurated?

S: Yes, but the trouble was that the building hadn't been finished yet, but there were some people who just didn't have anywhere else to go to live, so they had moved into the unfinished building.

I: How long had the Porter been there?

S: From the beginning.

I: I see. Had the Porter worked in the construction of the building?

S: Yes, that's just it and that was one of problems that came up. He had never been a porter in his life.

I: Had he been a bricklayer?

S: No, has was one of the watchmen of the building during its construction, and this is something that came up during the discussion. Well, in general, the Porter is present at these general meetings because questions come up regarding the building and the only one that knows quite a bit about the building is the Porter. This particular meeting was being conducted by the Building Manager.

I: Is he one of the owners?

S: No, we have contracted the services of a man who manages several buildings. He takes care of collections and other general matters.

I: Has he been engaged by the proprietors?

S: He has been engaged by a Committee of proprietors. There are 13 on this committee. The Building Manager had been contracted precisely in order to avoid problems.

I: What are the duties of the Building Manager?

S: Well, besides collecting the monthly contributions from all of us, he has to take care of the general problems that arise which do not belong directly to the Porter; for example, getting electric power connections to the new apartments, buy fuel in winter as needed for the central heating, buy hallway equipment, finish the entrance hall, see to it that the elevators operate normally and are in good state of repair   .   .   .

I: If a pump breaks down   .   .   .

S: .   .   .   he calls the appropriate service companies   .   .   .

I: .   .   .   and then figures the share of the cost of this repair to each owner?

S: Yes. We all pay fixed sums, and he keeps control of this and of expenses. It's much easier if we pay a fixed sum and he then makes monthly calculations of expenses.

I: Does he then make the yearly adjustments for any differences?

S: At the end of the fiscal year, a fund is set up with the surplus. Since the expenses have been less than our contribution, there is a neat surplus and we are now using this in order to make the garden surrounding the building. But in the meeting I'm telling you about, the real problem was the Porter. As soon as the meeting was called to order, everyone started laying it on him real hard.

I: Was this unanimous?

S: Well, let's say there was no one to support him outright. There were some who just didn't seem to care too much about the problem. I admit I was one of these. I had been living in the building only for a fortnight, and I had other things than the Porter to worry about. That's when I decided to see if this problem couldn't be tackled the way we tackle the problems here in the company, that is, first listen and then try to diagnose when everyone has had their say. Well, I soon saw that the problems didn't seem to be that important. For example, one lady had dropped a bottle of milk in the hallway and the Porter had told her, "Well, this is one mess you'll have to clean up yourself." It seems the Porter never said "good morning" or "hello" to anyone as they went in and out of the building. The building was not as clean as it should be. There was some disagreement on this. Some saw it as O.K., while others saw it as a mess. It's true that there are so many small children that it's hard to keep it ideally clean, but it seemed to me that those who were attacking him most were finding the building very dirty. This is the type of thing we've seen so often here in the company—how perceptions change when the attitudes do. But no one mentioned his defects—things that to me would have been important. No one said he was dishonest or nosey.

I: No one criticized him on those points?

S: No, no one claimed to have had things stolen or lost.

I: And as to his duties, his hours of work?

S: Precisely. One of the criticisms was that he was too strict about hours. Well, when I saw that everyone had talked and talked themselves out; in other words, when I felt that the cathartic effect had operated and therefore everyone had quieted down, I tried to see the problem from its very beginning. I asked the group had anyone told the Porter what his duties were, and what was expected of him. It was obvious that no one had told him a thing.

I: How did the group react when you asked that question?

S: Well, they seemed quite surprised at first. I think their main surprise was to see that one of the group simply was not as worked up over the problem as the rest. I believe that if I had taken this attitude at the beginning, they would have reacted strongly against me. They were also surprised that someone was asking such a concrete question.

I: At that moment, did you give them the impression that you were taking sides?

S: Decidedly not! At a certain moment I even confessed to this. I presented this from another angle. I said that we had no light or water meters in the building. I asked the group if they didn't think that this might be a more important problem than the Porter. They agreed; so I asked them how much time they thought we ought to devote to the meter and the Porter problems. Apparently, all that had been done so far was to criticize the Porter, and I asked if they did not think that we ought to now settle down and look for solutions to these and other problems. They fully agreed. Therefore, I asked them if they didn't think if we should decide first whether we could do something about the present Porter or go out and find a new one. In this case, we had to decide whether we could find another Porter with the same virtues this one had but without his other defects. When I asked this, then everyone started to describe the ideal Porter.

I: In other words, you started defining the Porter's job.

S: Yes, we started to define how a Porter should be. Several opinions were given, and there a new point came up. This was that 22 of us couldn't keep telling him from 8 AM to 8 PM what he should or should not be doing but that we must tell him what his principal duties were, what was expected of him, and how far his authority went. We had the case of a lady that took her dog down the main elevator and he told her "Look lady, that dog has to use the service elevator." The lady got quite mad over this. The rest of the members at the meeting tried to reason with her that after all the Porter had been trying to keep the main elevator as clean as possible and that obviously people with animals should use the service elevator.

I: I see that by using the technique of asking questions you became the leader of the group.

S: Well, . . . I'd say that at one point I was virtually leading the group.

I: You were the leader in the sense we use here?

S: Yes. We understand the leader to be not the person presiding over the meeting but the person who knows how to lead a discussion. Well, the group slowly, by means of questions I asked, reached the conclusion that the Porter had never been told precisely what he should do. Some said that they had told him to do one thing or another and that he had proved quite willing. There seemed to be a problem—this may sound a bit subjective—of telling the Porter in very clear terms what was expected of him and making sure that he would understand. Another problem was concerned with the time of putting the trash and garbage out. There were problems I knew nothing about when I lived in my former home, and they seemed pretty important to me now. There were some owners who complained that some people made a lot of noise in the early morning putting the refuse out, while others complained that the refuse cans were out at night. On being left overnight in the hall, there was often disagreeable stench in the hallways. To this some retorted they couldn't get up every day at 6 AM just to please the garbage collectors.

I: What was the usual hour of the public garbage collection?

S: 6 AM. But it is true that many people just left a pail full of garbage at night, and next morning you could smell this throughout the building. Well, I'm not going to give you all the details, but from this you can get an idea of what the situation was. It was finally unanimously decided that a committee of three should be charged with giving the Porter instructions. It was decided that the committee included the Building Manager, one of the owners who had been there the longest, and they all asked me to serve on that committee. Next morning, we three sat very informally with the Porter and one of the group said something very appropriate. "We want you to feel as if you were another one of the owners of these apartments. (He lived in a small apartment in the same building.) We believe that these are your principal duties. Look this over and tell us if you think this is right. You do not have 22 bosses because it's almost impossible to work under 22 bosses and keep them all happy. If you have any problems or doubts, you can come to any one of us, and we'll try to straighten it out." It seemed to us that there was probably a personality problem. He (the Porter) was rather harsh and withdrawing. We tried to explain to him that saying "Hello" to people may seem a bit repetitive but that it makes people feel better and causes a good impression; that when someone comes in, it makes people uncomfortable if he just stares at them instead of saying "Good afternoon." All this happened some 2 months ago. I won't say that all our troubles are over, nor do I . . .

I: But let's see. For example, does he say "Hello" to the tenants and visitors now?

S: Oh yes.

I: To everyone, or just to some?

S: To everyone.

I: Does the dog use the main or the service elevator?

S: The service elevator.

I: And does the lady complain?

S: No, she is quite satisfied.

I: How was the garbage problem solved?

S: Very well. We found an entirely new solution, quite different from what anyone had expected, which is very satisfactory to all. At 9 PM all trash and garbage has to be outside. You see, he (the Porter) has to be in uniform from 5 to 9 PM every afternoon. At 9 he goes to his apartment, takes off his uniform, dons overalls, and at 9:05 he collects all the garbage.

I: Have you done away with the hallway stench?

S: Decidedly. The most the trash is out is 15 minutes, because he dumps it all in a large can which is put outside the building for the municipal garbage collectors. Well, the

Porter used to complain that the people didn't put out their garbage in time, but now he no longer complains.

I: And does this work well now?

S: To perfection.

I: Have you had incidents such as that one of the lady that dropped the milk   . . .

S: No more of those. He still is not too courteous. If a lady comes in loaded with packages, he is not a man . . .

I: . . . to say "May I help you?" but do you think there has been an improvement?

S: A great improvement, 90%.

I: And is he happy?

S: Very happy. He even refused to take his vacation. This was in part because we paid him for it, but he really wants it that way. We find him very often taking the initiative, whereas before he never took initiative on anything. He never gave any ideas. At first, this irked even me, when he used to tell me: "Look, if you see anything wrong, just tell me and I'll do it." Well, this may seem very small to you, but we had no mat at the door, and everytime it rained the hall became a mess, particularly because the gardeners had dirt all over the place outside. Well, one day he came to me and said: "Don't you think it might be a good idea if we bought a floor mat so people can wipe their feet when they come in?" This may sound obvious and trifling to you, but it was the first suggestion he ever made. It seemed to me that he was starting to take an interest in the building. The suggestion was immediately accepted as a step which constituted positive reinforcement toward molding more cooperative behavior.

But let me tell you about the hours of work. He has been told that he has to clean up from 5 AM to 9 AM and to stand at the door from 5 PM to 9 PM in uniform as Porter. You see, he is a mixture of Porter-Janitor. But he takes this to extremes. He is at the door exactly at 5 PM even on Christmas and New Year's day. He could have said that he would have liked to go out with his family or go visiting. He never once asked, could I leave a little early tonight? Well, now he is very happy. He is a great supporter of "XXX" football club, and we talk about it. He'll tell me, "Look, I'd like to go to the Stadium tonight if possible. Do you think I might get off an hour early?" Since it's not something that is considered vital that he should be there at that hour, I've told him to go ahead. There's been a great difference. His attitude is now much milder.

I: Might I say that a more human contact has been established with this man?

S: Yes, there were no communications prior to this. Communications were very poor.

I: And now you've established a system.

S: Yes, we have a system. But better yet, the proprietors' meetings have changed greatly. We deal with real problems, and no longer with mere trifles that result from misunderstandings and wrong perceptions. We no longer even talk about whether the Porter cleans here or there. We scarcely mention him now.

I: Do the other owners continue to give the Porter orders?

S: Not directly. That is, they may occasionally ask him, "Could you please help me with these packages?" If they have a problem, they talk to our committee, but he no longer has 22 bosses, which is one of the things that looked worse to me and that I later found out made him feel terrible.

I: What type of people are the owners of the other apartments?

S: Well, there's the manager of a warehouse, a professor, a food salesman, a man that owns a drug store, there are other salesmen, and several others . . . and their wives!

I: Are the wives variable too?

S: Almost none of them hold jobs. One works at the University, but the rest don't work.
I: How is the Professor's wife?
S: She's all right. Rather inconspicuous, the rest are younger.
I: Which?
S: There's the wife of a man that works in a bank, the wife of the warehouseman, the wife of the builder who put up the building. They live on the top floor.
I: And how is she?
S: She's very tough.
I: In what do you find her tough?
S: Well, she says she knows other Porters. She doubtless has experience. As her husband builds better and better buildings, they keep moving to the better one. At that first meeting she said she knew a Porter who was like this and another who was like that. She was the worst. But she was the one who eventually at that first meeting said that the Porter should be made to feel as if he were one of the owners of the building.
I: Did she finally recognize that you could keep your present Porter?
S: Yes.
I: And how long did you have to wait for the cathartic effect to work on her?
S: Oh, about 7 or 8 minutes in which she talked continuously against him.
I: And after she had let off all that pressure?
S: Then she started to recognize that there were good points to this man. You see I began to ask her, in view of her past experience, specific facts about other Porters she had known, and it turned out that they all had serious flaws. The level seemed to be quite similar in the different places at which she had lived.
I. I am very pleased to see that our system seems to have worked well in a place where people differ much from one another. We often hear the objection that group problem-solving is effective only when you have very homogenous groups, as we have here in the Company. Our personnel selection program has assured us of this. However, you have made it work in a place where there were people of very different make-ups, mental abilities, backgrounds, etc.
S: Yes, I must recognize that here in the company the people are much more homogeneous when we form our problem-solving groups.
I: But it would be too bad if it didn't work for heterogenous groups because we generally can't pick, and human beings are heterogenous. Effective group problem solving wouldn't be of much help to humanity if it were limited to very specially chosen groups.
S: It's true. You seldom find groups of people as brilliant as you do in our company.
I: Of course. You can't select the man that's going to move into the apartment next to yours. Well, congratulations, you conducted this very well. You have given me great hope that all this that we have developed may be used by a large number of people in all sorts of everyday situations to ease tensions, reduce conflict, and avoid misery to others. Think of the effect on that man if that Porter had been fired, as he certainly would have been except for your timely intervention. Thank you very much.

CONCLUSION

Some of the solutions constructed for the preceding examples may seem imperfect to the reader. The author, after seeing the results of his and others' social-science designs and their applications, has often been aware of this imperfection. Mackworth (1965), however, has noted that this gap between real and ideal is stimulating to the technologist. He states: "The inventor is also often stimulated to further efforts by no more than the differences between a strong mental image of the ideal version of his intended device and the actual miserable achievements to be seen in his prototype equipment." Mackworth is certainly right because the discrepancy between the actual results and the ideal have often spurred the author to attempt further improvements. This and the past seven chapters have given the reader a glimpse of some of the imperfect solutions that have actually been accomplished. The next chapter will present the author's mental image of the ideal social-science design.

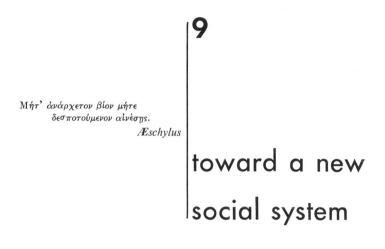

9

Μήτ’ ἀνάρχετον βίον μήτε
δεσποτούμενον αἰνέσῃς.

Æschylus

toward a new
social system

WHY THIS BOOK IS AN INTRODUCTION

There are several reasons why this book can be considered an "introduction." The case examples illustrating how social-science findings are used for the solution of social problems have presented only sufficient material to enable the reader to construct his own problem designs. In addition, this material, with regard to both design and application, has been presented in an increasing order of complexity. Furthermore, instead of giving *all* the principles *first*, which might seem more logical, and then presenting the applications, new social-science principles were introduced and explained as they were relevant to the subject matter. Hopefully, this procedure has made the material more interesting and easier to assimilate.

The major difficulty involved in writing this book was not to find enough examples and cases to illustrate the principles but to determine how much to *exclude*. The variety of solutions to numerous social problems that have been designed would alone fill several volumes. It was felt, however, that giving too many cases would clutter up the material to the point that the reader wouldn't be able to see the forest for the trees! The examples given should be useful to managers, teachers, supervisors, foremen, and anyone else who has to deal with people—which includes just about everybody except certified hermits and misanthropes. Our main purpose, however, has not been to present loosely connected, odd bits of information and solutions. Although the individual trees may each be shown to be particularly useful, our main object has been to present the forest. But before offering an overview of the goals we had hoped to achieve, we should cite the other reasons for calling this book an introduction.

Although many relevant cases in which problems were solved have been omitted, it must be recognized that some problems have only been partially solved and others have not been solved at all. This failure, or partial failure, may have been caused by several factors. Perhaps the diagnosis was wrong, or the design or its application was incorrectly executed. These three errors may, in turn, have resulted from lack of ability on the part of the persons conducting the diagnoses, designs, and applications, from insufficient knowledge of social-psychology findings, or merely from lack of the necessary skills and ingenuity needed to design a solution and then put it into practice.

The amount of reported research results is so immense that it is quite difficult for a would-be technologist to keep up-to-date with everything that may be applicable. It is highly likely that a finding that would have proven extremely useful in the design of a solution was completely overlooked. According to Mowrer (1960), a person who wants to keep up-to-date with the literature on learning alone would have to read four articles or monographs a day. If we add to this all that is published in every other relevant field of social science (plus what is published outside the United States), one can see that even keeping up-to-date with the *titles*, let alone the contents, is an imposing task. Besides, there is the added task of separating the wheat from the chaff—it must be honestly recognized that much "chaff" is printed and widely publicized. Therefore, it is quite probable that this book has omitted some very important finding, with which the reader may be familiar and which he feels could have been utilized much more profitably in certain case examples than the ones expounded by the author. If the reader is irked about this omission, the author can only say, "I accept your criticism heartily. If you feel, for example, that the work of Heider, or Osgood, or Helson; or all the work on game theory; the early work of Hovland, Janis, and Kelly, and the rest of the Yale group on persuasion; or many other studies could have been used to produce a better product—by all means get to work, design a better product, try it out, and let me hear about it. I would be delighted to use your design if it can give me better results than those we have obtained." In this kind of work, there is no room for the kind of prestige or need for approval that dictate only the use of one's own invention. This would constitute a self-defeating attitude. All technologies have succeeded because many people working in many fields have joined efforts and used each other's work to achieve results. If there has been progress in technology, it has been not because one giant stood on the shoulders of others but because many men of not-such-great stature have been willing to stand on the shoulders of those who, in turn, have stood on the shoulders of others, until a tall, all-encompassing pyramid attained far-reaching success.

Another reason for considering this book an introduction is purely technical. Although many solutions have been given and, in a great number of cases, the outcomes were what had been predicted before the design was applied, the element of *quantification* is missing from these predictions. To use the analogy described in the Preface, an engineer designs a refrigerator from his knowledge of thermodynamics, heat transfer, oils, insulation, metals, electricity, refrigerants, etc. Experiments are performed on each of these factors, and the designer therefore has essential figures at his command. He is thus able to calculate exactly what diameter piping he must use, how much refrigerant, how much compressor displacement, how much condenser area he must use, and so on. On the basis of numerical computations, he sees that each sector is adequate in order to create a harmonious refrigerator capable of performing a necessary service economically.

In *One Hoss Shay* Oliver Wendell Holmes describes how a deacon came to the conclusion that carriages broke down because one part failed before the others and that in order to make a carriage last forever, it was necessary "to make each part uz strong uz the rest." In technological design, whether it is a simple beam or an extremely complex solution to a social problem, the principle is similar—not to attain the eternal durability that the deacon sought but to achieve more rational aims. There is always the danger of underdesigning any one part because this will make the structure as weak as its weak point; overdesigning the rest would thus be a waste of money because the structure will never need so much strength at any one point. Besides, there is the grave danger that the structure will fail when the calculated load is placed on it. Suppose, for example, that we have to make a beam to carry a heavy load, and we design it accordingly for moment, shear, and tension stresses, with appropriate safety factors. But suppose, in addition, that we provide enough concrete to carry a 30-ton compression stress load. This extra concrete will be completely wasted material. A good design, therefore, achieves balance among the needs of the different parts, and this can only be accomplished by careful calculation that yields numerical results.

The author has already made an attempt to develop numerical predictions, using findings given by researchers in their own publications, but we admit that little headway has been made. There are probably several reasons for this failure. In the first place, most experimenters are content merely to prove that a result is significant at a certain level of confidence. This is not very helpful to a designer of solutions. To know that p was less than 0.05 and that the null hypothesis was rejected is fine, but the author knows of no way to incorporate this finding into another study, whose results are announced in similar fashion. It is as if the yield point of a certain steel were announced only as "above 30,000 lbs. per square inch." An engineer would immediately ask, "How much more? What is the exact yield strength of this material? Unless I know this figure, I am unable to make an economical design."

A second factor stands as a stumbling block in making numerical calculations based on combinations of social-science findings. We know that about 35% of the people yield to certain social pressure, that is, to opinions given by others (proven by Asch in his length-of-line judging experiments). We also know from Freedman and Fraser (1966) that persons yielding to a small request are more prone to yield to a larger request. In order to combine these two numerical results, that is, when we apply social pressure to persons who have already yielded to the small request, we would have to know whether the people who went along with the majority in the Asch experiment were also those who would have acceded to the large request in the Freedman and Fraser experiment. At present we do not know. Hopefully, future activity in social-science technology will continue to be of interest and will attract investigators who will begin to design their studies and announce their findings in ways that will be mathematically usable to the technologist.

An additional reason why social-science predictions have not been quantified may be that the writer simply does not possess the necessary mathematical equipment, or perhaps he does not have the necessary insight to be able to implement this crucial device. However, until this important step is taken, the whole area of applied social-science findings will have to be labeled merely as an "introduction" to social-science technology. The author does believe that eventually the essential quantification approach will be made and that in the not-too-distant future designs will incorporate expected predictions in numerical terms.

There is still another reason for considering this book an introduction. Although a tremendous amount of research has been conducted and although extremely important and unexpected principles have been discovered, research in the social sciences continues. Very probably some of the greatest discoveries about ourselves are still to be made. As in most technologies, there is a perpetual sense of wonder at how much has already been accomplished. Such was the state when the first locomotive was able to outrun a horse, when the steam engine was introduced in ships, when the first transcontinental airmail service was established, and when the first artificial satellites were launched. All of these, however, eventually became relics compared with what was later accomplished when new discoveries permitted still greater advances in technologies. Therefore, it is quite probable, and should certainly be encouraged, that before long the revolutionary-sounding material contained in this book will seem quaint compared with what will have been achieved.

AN OVERVIEW

In spite of all the shortcomings we have just cited, we still know enough to be able to see the forest, and it is important that we do so.

Perhaps as the reader went through the book, he experienced cognitive dissonance at seeing solutions to problems that differ considerably from what is today common practice. As each new principle was applied, it became apparent that often the solution to a problem meant doing almost the *opposite* of what we have been used to doing. For example, in trying to convince a friend that he must see a doctor, instead of trying to give him numerous reasons for doing so, we actually led him to make this conclusion on his own by telling him the *contrary* of what we felt he should favor. One supervisor, who has become very skillful at this social-science technique, was faced with a problem that his mother was ill and needed an operation but was terrified of the prospect. After designing an appropriate persuasion, he sat near her as she lay in the hospital bed and started the reactance-provoking series of statements needed in a persuasion by successive approximation. The man's sister, sitting next to him, knew nothing of this. As she heard him make all these apparently absurd remarks, she started to kick him under the bed. Here was this beloved son, whom his mother thought very clever, actually saying that the mother did not need an operation, that the doctors probably didn't know what they were doing, etc. The sister was horrified. However, she was completely taken aback when after 15 minutes the mother said, "You know what? I'm telling that doctor as soon as he comes in that I want him to operate on me tomorrow if he can possibly make it." The operation was performed; it was a complete success; and everyone is now very happy and satisfied. Moreover, the sister is a convert to this new method of persuasion. But at first she reacted just as the reader of this book may have reacted. At other times in this book, instead of reprimanding, warning, or otherwise disciplining (something that has been for centuries in all the rule books) we have actually offered praise! The reader may wonder whether all these outlandish proposed solutions are merely meant to scandalize, since they go against everything that common sense and custom have dictated. He is right in assuming, however, that there is a factor unifying all the case examples presented in this book. But this factor is not the desire to shock by presenting unusual solutions. Rather, it is *the search for scientific truths to aid us in eliminating social malfunctioning.* Perhaps an analogy with medicine would be fitting.

Eighty-six years ago an event took place that was to have far-reaching consequences for everyone. It is quite possible that many of our readers would not be alive and in good health today had this event not occurred. On July 6, 1885, Louis Pasteur injected attenuated hydrophobia virus into Josef Meister, a young boy who had been terribly bitten by a mad dog. The boy, who otherwise would have died a horrible death, was saved, and modern medicine was born. Humanity was no longer condemned to stand by help-lessly as people suffered and died. At last there was something positive that could be done. The great challenge was taken up by an increasing number of people in the biological and medical professions. The result has been such marvels of modern medicine as the development of sulfa, penicillin, and other drugs that Pasteur could never have dreamed of. We now have sani-tation, immunology, and other technologies that all resulted from that great event of 86 years ago.

Until that time medicine was devoted mainly to treating symptoms. The cures ranged from the cruel to the ridiculous. A favorite cure for the dreaded disease diphtheria in mid-Europe was to hitch two widows to a plow and have them make a furrow around the town at midnight. A few years later Roux discovered that the toxin generated by diphtheria bacilli was the cause of the disease. Here we have a clear case of a distinction between diagnosis and cure. Roux discovered the cause, and it took several years to do so, but this did not tell him what to do about it. It took Behring, with infinite patience and thousands of trials, to invent the antidiphtheria vaccine, and it was not until 1891 that its application saved the first children. Presumably, until then the widows kept plowing the outskirts of towns. Roux and Behring soon put a stop to all that nonsense, and it is now a rare child who dies of diphtheria in civilized countries.

When Mozart lay very ill on December 5, 1791, "Dr." Closset was asked to come. When he arrived and felt Mozart's extremely warm temples, he immediately ordered cold compresses placed on them to reduce the tempera-ture. This affected Mozart so severely that he lost consciousness almost immediately and died a few hours later. It is not yet clear what caused his death, although we can be sure that Dr. Closset's treatment hastened his end. Diagnosis was virtually nonexistent in 1791, but it is quite possible that modern medicine would have saved him.

These anecdotes give an indication of the state of medicine before Pasteur started his revolution. Pasteur himself was laughed at by his contemporaries when he suggested that different diseases are caused by specific microorganisms. The dissonance for the doctors of the day was too great for them to reduce by accepting the new theories. They preferred to reduce it by disparaging the source of the dissonant cognition (Pasteur). It took the incident of saving young Josef Meister's life to dramatize Pasteur's theories to the world. After that the skeptics diminished in number, as new vaccines such as Behring's were invented. Eventually, the world so fully accepted the concept of vaccination that it reached a state of almost hysterical impatience waiting for a vaccine for polio, before Salk and Sabin finally achieved their goal. It is interesting to note in how short a time the world's attitude had changed. But there is a tragic sequel to the story of the first human being saved by a scientifically designed vaccine.[1] In 1940, when the Germans invaded Paris and asked to see Pasteur's grave, Josef Meister, employed as a porter at the Pasteur Institute, elected to commit suicide rather than comply with their request. Koestler (1964) remarks that "Josef Meister was predestined to become a victim of one form of rabidness or another."

Modern medicine has changed greatly from the pre-Pasteur era of charlatanism, but unfortunately social pathology has not. We still insist on treating symptoms instead of curing the causes. We reprimand a color-blind person for making a mistake in mixing colors. We suspend a man who is aggressive toward fellow workers, when the man is in a severe approach-avoidance conflict perhaps caused by the very supervisor giving or recommending the reprimand. Until now we have had the same excuse Dr. Closset had; he just did not know any better because the discovery that a high temperature and other symptoms are generally caused by some microorganism had not yet been made. Even had he known, however, there was nothing he could have done because there were no sulfas, penicillin or other antibiotics available. Besides, the public was not ready for a new treatment. Public ignorance on health matters paralleled the medical profession's. In a long letter to his father giving details of his mother's death in 1778, Mozart tells his father of the dangers of drinking "pure water." He states that he always takes the precaution of putting a little wine in it so that it shall not be "pure." Obviously, humanity's ideas about health have changed quite a bit, and it might be stated that without this change in public attitudes, it would have been very difficult for the medical profession to achieve the amazing advances that it has.

Following the same reasoning in this analogy, we must state that for the new discoveries in the social sciences to be really effective in curing social ills, it is essential that all this knowledge be confined not to the minds of a privileged few but be instilled in the conscious and subconscious attitudes and

[1] Jenner's smallpox vaccination is excluded because, although it was developed earlier, it was more accidentally discovered than scientifically designed.

behavior of the entire population. Miller (1969) has admirably stated this belief:

> There is no possibility of legislating the changes I have in mind. Passing laws that people must change their conceptions of themselves and others is precisely the opposite of what we need. Education would seem to be our only possibility. I do not mean only education in the school room, although that is probably the best communication channel presently at our disposal. I have in mind a more ambitious program of educating the general public. It is critically important to shape this education to fit the perceived needs of the people who receive it. . . . In order to get a factory supervisor or a ghetto mother involved, we must give them something they can use. Abstract theories, however elegant, or sensitivity training, however insightful, are too remote from the specific troubles they face. In order to get started, we must begin with people where they are, not assume we know where they should be. If a supervisor is having trouble with his men, perhaps we should teach him how to write a job description and how to evaluate the abilities and personalities of those who fill the job; perhaps we should teach him the art of persuasion or the time and place for positive reinforcement. If a ghetto mother is not giving her children sufficient intellectual challenge, perhaps we should teach her how to encourage their motor, perceptual, and linguistic skills. The techniques involved are not some esoteric branch of witchcraft that must be reserved for those with Ph.D. degrees in psychology. . . .
>
> There are many obvious and useful suggestions that we could make and that nonpsychologists could exploit. If our suggestions actually work, people should be eager to learn more. But we should not try to give people something whose value they cannot recognize, then complain when they do not return for a second meeting.

A PRESCRIPTION FOR SOCIAL ILLS

A CHANGE OF PARADIGMS

In a thought-provoking book analyzing the scientific revolutions that have occurred as a result of discoveries made through experimentation or observation, Kuhn (1962) uses the word *paradigm* to represent the established pattern of ideas that guide people in the solution of problems they must face. We have such paradigms for many different kinds of daily activities but Kuhn analyzes them from the viewpoint of the history of science. His contention is that in general, in the sciences, crises have arisen when the existing paradigms or rules for solving problems are no longer useful, when they cannot solve new problems. Kuhn gives several examples, taken from the physical sciences, and shows how these crises brought a revolutionary change in paradigms. Referring to the new paradigms, Kuhn states, "Paradigms gain their status because they become more successful than their competitors in solving a few problems that the group of practitioners has come to recognize as acute."

This book has demonstrated a series of solutions based on discoveries that have been developed as a result of serious research in the social sciences. Enough examples have been given to show that it has been possible to solve certain problems that had become acute because they did not seem soluble through existing paradigms. Social strife, international conflict of all types, problems in universities throughout the world, racial problems, and many others that the reader sees in the daily press are simply not being solved. Many solutions have been proposed—most of them involving radical changes in existing structures. Often the Establishment is blamed as a cause, but it is interesting to note that even where there have been major social changes in the structure of major institutions, the social problems continue.

What seems to be universally as well as urgently needed is a change in the paradigm by which solutions to prevailing social problems are attempted. Based on this conviction and on the belief that such guidelines are necessary for present and future work, formulations of the prevailing paradigm, as well as the paradigm indicated by discoveries in the social sciences, have been prepared. These have been gradually modified in wording and in conception as time has passed, with the assistance of many persons, and may still undergo further modification and additions. The original and the ideal paradigms can be formulated in eleven distinct statements. These will be presented and then followed by individual comments on each one.

PREVAILING PARADIGM

This is the existing paradigm by means of which the solutions to social problems are presently being sought.

(1) All men are created equal.

(2) When something goes wrong, someone is to blame.

(3) The guilty should be punished.

(4) Time and effort should not be spared to establish guilt.

(5) The guilty are largely responsible for their own misbehavior and for their own improvement.

(6) Unreasonableness can be countered by facts and logic.

(7) One truth underlies all controversy.

(8) Conflict is generally inevitable.

(9) Most behavior is economically motivated.

(10) Capable supervisors should devise solutions and see that their subordinates carry them out.

(11) Supervisors are too busy and have no time to become experts in social-science technology.

All Men Are Created Equal. Many will deny that anyone seriously believes this assertion today. Nevertheless, the important point to consider is not whether people believe it but whether they act as if *they believe it*. For example, when we set up a ruling that anyone who comes in late shall be disciplined, and eventually fired if he continues to be late, we have set up a ruling that essentially tells everyone in the organization, be it large or small, "I think you are all alike; there's no difference between Jane's coming in late and Joe's not being on time." Yet, we have seen from our study of approach-avoidance conflict, dissonance, etc. that there are enormous differences in the causes for people's tardiness—differences not only in their make-up but also in how they react to different situations. A dogmatic ruling will get us nowhere if we really want to solve the tardiness problem. Our only chance for success is to make a detailed diagnosis of each different individual and to try to determine why each comes in late. The causes may vary greatly. Our duty is to correct the individual causes in each case.

When we set up piece-rates for work performed, give salesmen commissions, etc., we are assuming that all the individuals involved are equally motivated by financial incentive. When we find that certain individuals don't react to this type of incentive, we become infuriated because they do not conform to our notion that "money makes people go"—*all* people.

Unfortunately, Thomas Jefferson revised his first draft of the Declaration of Independence. Perhaps if he had left his original words, we would not have clung tenaciously to the belief of unreserved equality among all human beings. The original version (copies of which may be obtained from the Library of Congress) stated, in paragraph 2: "We hold these truths to be self-evident [here two words have been obliterated]: that all men are created equal *and independent;* that *from that equal creation they derive* certain *inherent and* inalienable rights   .   .   ." It is clearer from this version that what Jefferson meant was that certain *rights* were equally available for all, not that persons were actually equal. Cattell (1950) expounded this point when he stated, "belief in equality of opportunity does not require belief in biological equality, but rather an acceptance of individuality."

Nevertheless, we must not blame Jefferson for his change. The belief that all men are equal is quite ingrained in us; it dates from the Code of Hammurabi, or possibly earlier. The keynote of Hammurabi's and all subsequent codes is that they established punishments for misdemeanors, crimes, etc. that were independent of the individuals involved. It is true that mitigating or aggravating circumstances have been added and that insanity has been recognized, thus allowing a distinction between the mentally ill and the "conscious" criminal, but laws are still being made as if all persons were equal. The man who speeds in his automobile is fined the same amount whether he is a millionaire playboy out on a romp or an unemployed man who has just landed a job, received an advance, and is trying to go to the bank to pay off part of a loan to prevent repossession of his home.

In industrial, commercial, or other organizations the same principles hold true. Rules are set and applied with unconditional uniformity to everyone. Legal thinking is so ingrained that it has been transferred from the society of which we form a part to the small sub-societies in which most of us work. The fact that these rules and regulations, uniformly applied, have not improved conditions has not yet awakened us to the full realization that a system based on such gross error will simply never work. So far, there is only a growing resentment among people, but they do not know against whom. Before the American and French Revolutions, it was easy to point to the King and nobility as the causes of the trouble. They were considered to be unfair and authoritarian; besides, what was most irritating, this authority was hereditary. Hereditary rule was abolished, and it was decided that the people would have their own voice by choosing rulers through elections. (It was not known then that elections would eventually bring with them destructive win-lose conflicts, with all their undesirable consequences.)

At this point, the reader might believe that a case is being made for anarchy and lawlessness, but our thesis is quite the contrary. We are now surrounded by anarchy and lawlessness. Few countries (some extreme dictatorships are exceptions) are free from these evils, but very few human beings, except the highly frustrated and the highly authoritarians, want to change to a truly dictatorial form of government.

The point here is that what we call "man-made law" and what we call the "laws of nature" are two quite different concepts, although we tend to treat them alike. We know that all bodies attract one another with a force that is proportional to the square of the distance between them. That is Newton's Law of Gravitation, and all physical bodies can be considered equal with respect to it. But a law passed forbidding all humans to perform certain acts, which implies that all people are alike, is not set down by nature. There are two excellent elaborations on the difference between scientific and legal law. One of these, by the Columbia Associates in Philosophy (1923), emphasizes the difference between the two. The other, by Lawrence Cranberg (1968), deals more with the similarities. Both are worth reading in connection with this discussion. The Columbia Associates point out that man-made laws are made by legislators, while the actual implementation is carried out by the lawyers and the courts. They add that reflective thinking in law might be more efficient if the process were not so rudely interrupted by a change of hands. (There is probably a lot of truth to this). Later, the authors explain how the law is first made and then tested in practice. This trial-and-error method has produced some benefits. For example, penalties have been reduced. Whereas less than 200 years ago horrible tortures were inflicted for trifling offences, these have disappeared and been replaced by prison terms, although Menninger and others have shown us how horrible these still are. On the other hand, Cranberg states that ". . . science drained of moral passions is likely to be as sterile as law divorced from experience." Instead of making a trial-and-error experience, we can begin by receiving the experience derived from research in the social sciences. We then come to the conclusion that we simply cannot construct *rules* for tardiness, for work spoilage, or for any other reprehensible behavior. We do so merely because of our ingrained belief that all men are created equal and will therefore react in the same way to our laws or rules.

When Something Goes Wrong, Someone Is to Blame. This has been the basis of all legal procedure, and it has been carried over into organization structure as well. Therefore, when we find that something has gone wrong— a client returned goods because they were not shipped as ordered; there was a mistake in the bank balance in the account and a check bounced; a client was promised a delivery that couldn't possibly be met—the first thing we do is to blow up and say, "Who is responsible for this?" There may even be a court of inquiry established to find the culprit. At other times, speedier processes prevail. Toland (1959) relates a critical moment in the Battle of the Bulge, December 22, 1944, when Major Donald Boyer, Jr., was taken prisoner and kept in custody by two extremely tired German soldiers. Suddenly, Marshall von Runstedt, Supreme Commander for that operation, came up. It is best to quote Toland from here on: "Rundstedt turned sharply on the young colonel. 'Where did you get these slovenly guards?' 'They've been fighting all night, sir.' 'This place is a disgrace. Look at it!' Rundstedt wheeled about and strode out of the room. The colonel reprimanded a major, then left. The major shouted at a lieutenant. A few minutes later a corporal was swearing at the filthy guards. Boyer smiled for the first time in five days. They pass the buck in every army." Rundstedt had expected to see the same neat and trim guards in the midst of a terrible battle as he expected to see in a peacetime barracks. Here, the common desire to place the blame on someone else is very apparent.

We all tend to feel a sort of moral sense of responsibility that leads us to find out who was responsible for what we believe are reprehensible deeds. We believe we would be shirking our duty if we failed to do so. This leads naturally to the third statement.

The Guilty Should Be Punished. Once we have followed the above procedure and found the culprit, we would look silly if we just stood around and did nothing. We feel that punishment must be administered and that the punishment must be made "to fit the crime." We justify this behavior in many ways. Originally, punishment was justified mainly in terms of a concept of vengeance, at least that is the spirit of the Code of Hammurabi. Later, when vengeance assumed a bad connotation, it was more fashionable to say that "we must make an example of him." Another alternative is to say that punishment must be administered as a deterrent. Although there have been recent findings to the effect that in some cases punishment does seem to deter undesired behavior, we must keep in mind Skinner's contrary conclusion, mentioned in Chapter 8. We must also remember the principles of approach-avoidance conflicts, from which we learn that even were we able to create a deterrent to obnoxious behavior, it might produce even worse effects than if it were eliminated. By using punishment, we fail to eliminate the basic cause and add more complications, including an element of danger. Sooner or later an explosion is bound to occur, as many tyrants who have used punishment as a deterrent have discovered. It would seem that punishment as a means of eliminating misbehavior is effective only if it is total. When Rome completely destroyed Carthage, tore down the buildings, plowed the fields, strewed them with salt, killed most of its citizens, and sold the rest into slavery, misbehavior in Carthage was eliminated. Today no one would suggest or carry out such ruthless solutions. Nevertheless, we always insist that the guilty should be punished and draw up all sorts of scales of degrees of punishment, depending on the misbehavior. This happens not only in society as a whole but also in organizations, where people work and play (members can be reprimanded, suspended, or expelled from clubs), in school, in the family, and so on. Then, when we apply a large number of corrective measures and deterrents, and things still get worse, we wonder why people are so "ornery" and why they refuse to change when we are obviously performing our duties for their own welfare. The trouble lies in the fact that people *are* as they *are* and not as we *wish they were*. Among other things, this book has tried to explain how people *are* and how we should act toward them, according to what social science has taught us.

Concerning this distinction, Sachar (1963) refers to a possible clash between behavioral science and criminal law. He states that criminal law has been based on the concept of moral condemnation and deterrence by punishment, which in turn depends on man's having a "free will."

> The law in its moral aspect rules out consideration of the possible role of social forces in the making of a criminal because such would be inconsistent with the postulate of free will. The behavioral sciences proceed from premises diametrically opposed to the moral premises of the law as they are stated here. The goals of the behavioral sciences are the understanding and the manipulation of behavior. For these ends the concept of free will, whatever its value in constructing systems of morality (or, for that matter, its value in everyday personal decisions), is of no use. On the contrary, it is necessary to postulate that the behavior and the thought of men are determined in accordance with discoverable laws. Only with this working premise can the determinants—social psychological, psychological and cultural—be identified and their workings analyzed.
> It may be that in many areas men have a largely free and "undetermined"

choice, but the scientific exploration of behavior cannot begin unless that notion is excluded, just as in physics the notion of the "miraculous" is excluded. Knowledge of certain aspects of behavior may be "indeterminable," that is, unascertainable. The laws of behavior become then, like all scientific law, statements of probability. The ideal of order and lawfulness remains, however, the guiding faith of behavioral science.

Devised for quite different purposes and resting on different premises, the legal and the scientific views of behavior are able to exist in conceptual independence of each other. They do not come into conflict until they are brought into the ostensibly desirable collaboration that is urged by professionals on both sides.

This clash has not been so apparent in the parallel situation within organizations. As we have seen, the legal view has been accepted by all. Nevertheless, we have been able to show that it is possible to run an organization *without* the necessity of wedding the two tendencies. The legal viewpoint has largely disappeared, having been replaced by other forms of action based on social-science findings. If this limited success can be further extended, predictions about what may eventually happen in the larger society may tentatively be made. (These will be reserved for the end of this chapter.)

Time and Effort Should Not Be Spared to Establish Guilt.   If the culprit is not found at once, we insist that every effort be made to locate him. Of course, this effort depends on the gravity of the crime. If someone threw a cigarette butt in the hallway, an act forbidden by the rules, probably little effort would be made to try to find out who tossed the cigarette. If the problem caused considerable embarrassment to the higher authorities or damage to the organization, however, a full-fledged manhunt might be expected. What happens in these industrial cases is consistent with the more prevailing paradigm in our society. If a person steals a car and later abandons it undamaged a few blocks away, an overworked police force may make only a half-hearted attempt at trying to discover the culprit. But if some robbers break into a bank and get away with several hundred thousand dollars, then there will be an unlimited effort to try to find the actual thieves, as well as those who aided and abetted the crime.

The Guilty Are Largely Responsible for Their Own Misbehavior and for Their Own Improvement.   This belief is reflected in the "advice" a foreman gives a worker. It may be harsh, fatherly, or even friendly. The same may happen with a professor in connection with a student. Nevertheless, the principle is the same. "I'm telling you what's wrong with you so that you may, on your own, take the necessary steps to improve." The fact that this has sometimes proved successful, or apparently successful (since we sometimes like to pride ourselves that the talking-to actually worked, we actually perceive a change for the better regardless of the facts), makes us believe that the method should work in all cases. This conclusion, as we have seen, is absurd. If the person merely has a bad habit, is willing to improve, and respects the person giving the advice, he may make a conscious effort to change the habit. But if the man is color-blind or has strong avoidance feelings about his job because he cannot fully utilize his abilities, or if he is in an unsettling setting, a talking-to will merely aggravate the situation. Nevertheless, because we *believe* that people can change by merely talking to them, we continue to do so, in organizations, in the family, in the club, and so forth —disregarding the obvious observation that this method is simply not producing results. As Macaulay once said: "Few of the wise apothegms which have been uttered have prevented a single foolish action."

Unreasonableness Can Be Countered by Facts and Logic.   *Be reasonable* is an admonition we often give to a person who is tense, nervous, or undergoing some great stress. We try to reason with a mother who is terrified that her baby is being taken away from her, although it may be for a good cause (a health examination) and it is only temporary. If she has not been trained to see things that way, reasoning will be useless. We try to reason with workers concerning the advantages for all by a cutback on production, thereby reducing personnel, because this will give the organization a sounder financial basis. Since everyone feels that his job is threatened, reasoning will do no earthly good. Robespierre, absolute master of France in the last days of the Revolution, made a speech at the convention in which he tried to reason with the members to the effect that there were traitors around, some of whom were in their midst right there in the convention. He named no one, making so many of them feel unsafe that they quickly reacted; Robespierre was sent to the guillotine by the same convention with which he had tried to reason. What may seem logical to me today, may be entirely useless to another person who is in a state of panic. If I am in a state of panic today, the reasons and logic that were perfectly valid to me yesterday will be useless now.

In spite of all this, however, we never cease to try to reason with the other fellow. The fact that we so often fail in peace negotiations and in strike situations does not deter us. Someone else will say: "It's this incompetent negotiator who tried reasoning with them who just didn't know how. Just give me a chance, and I'll show you." This is a common occurrence, but whoever expresses this feeling, soon finds that he can't get these people to be reasonable either—so he calls them stubborn, blockheads, etc. He prefers the name-calling rather than recognize that it is simply impossible to counter an emotional state with facts and logic.

One Truth Underlies All Controversy.   This conviction again comes from our legal heritage. Courts have been established in order to determine who was right and who was guilty in specific cases. Not too long ago, by civilization's time standards, the method of determining the truth was trial by combat. The two contenders merely fought it out. The one who killed the other was declared free, and the dead man was of course pronounced guilty. Some time later it began to dawn on people that who was right was totally unrelated to who was more skillful at handling a sword. The basic idea, however, that someone *had* to be right still remained. People believed that one truth lay behind the whole affair, and sounder methods were devised for determining what that truth was. Once this truth was proved conclusively, a verdict could be rendered. Successive laws and jurisprudence have made matters much more complex, until now it becomes a really major proposition to try to find out who was really right. After looking over the extremely tangled state of affairs at many trials, some wit has defined a lawyer as a man charged with affairs that wouldn't exist if there weren't any lawyers.

We see this attitude when someone asks, "Why did Joe and Mary break up?" or "Why did John quit his job?" As we commented in Chapter 3, there is a great tendency to search for one and only one reason. If we hear a lot of gossip about the break-up between Mary and Joe and make our own resumé of what we have heard and proceed to decide what the real reason was, then we blandly go out and defend that viewpoint, satisfied that we have discovered the *one truth* behind the whole affair.

Conflict Is Generally Inevitable. Many people, including those who form peace movements, may deny that they believe this statement. Those who believe in peace do not think conflict is inevitable. Yet, these very people are quite willing to fight it out with those who do not hold the same beliefs. Similarly, the author is a great admirer of Handel's Messiah, but he cannot help feeling uncomfortable with his changed perception of the music that precedes the renowned Hallelujah Chorus. The music has a different meaning for him now than it did years ago when he first heard it. The message of peace and hope that the whole oratorio expresses is spoiled by the eternal human reaction to frustrations when well-laid plans go awry. The written text in this part says that the nations that rage furiously, together with the people who imagine vain things, shall be held in derision and eventually broken with a rod of iron and dashed to pieces like a potter's vessel. Handel's music, which is sublime in the rest of the work where peace and hope are promised, becomes harsh and disagreeable by comparison in the section where wrong-doers, who have not been converted, must be punished in an inevitable conflict.

We cannot assume such an aggressive attitude if we wish to be good social-science technologists. If we believe conflict is inevitable, we are probably playing into a self-fulfilling prophecy: "Since conflict is inevitable," we say, "there is nothing I can do about it. Or, if I try to do something and my methods fail, then it's not my fault but theirs. Then all that's left for me to do is to take a rod of iron and break them like a potter's vessel for not going along with my methods or with my peace proposals." In other words, we resort to force and threats.

There was a time in medicine when virtually every disease was considered untreatable. Even with today's great advances, there are still some conditions that doctors feel are incurable. But they do not shrug their shoulders and say, "There is nothing I can do about this." The immense amount of cancer research that has and is being conducted is testimony to the faith of modern medicine that this dreaded disease will eventually be eliminated. Our attitude toward social conflict must be the same. Instead of saying, "It's useless. It will never be possible for East and West or blacks and whites to reconcile," we should make every effort to try to solve these conflicts. During the dreadful religious wars of the 18th Century, it was considered impossible for Catholics and Protestants to work, play, or cohabit together. Today, relatively few people care very much about religious differences, and it is actually quite difficult to reconstruct the ferocity of attitudes and acts that arose over those differences of opinion. To the people who lived through those wars, the conflict was inevitable. We pity those who suffered so much, and some even scorn them for having wasted such a tremendous amount of time and caused such human suffering for such a trifle. Perhaps future generations will look at our present apparently "inevitable conflicts" and feel either pity or scorn toward us for having allowed ourselves to fall into the many win-lose traps in which we are now engaged.

Most Behavior Is Economically Motivated.   Here, again, is a belief that will probably be stoutly disavowed. To prove the falseness of this assertion, the disbelievers cite their own cases as examples. Nevertheless, when it comes to judging others, they say, "I don't understand the workers at XYZ plant. They make the highest salaries in town, and they still are going on strike for higher wages." Salesmen are hired and paid commissions. All sorts of wage-incentive plans are concocted. We offer monetary rewards for the return of lost goods. Everytime we are faced with getting others to do something, we tend to use as the prime incentive money or material goods (cash or valuable prizes, such as home appliances). Thus, in spite of the many contrary declarations, the great majority of people act toward others as if material things were all that mattered or, at least, as if they were much more important than any other considerations.

In discussing this point in Chapter 1, it was shown how people often reduce dissonance on the job by deciding to quit and then justifying that decision by stating that their present salaries are too low. Very often, when we do not wish to buy something because avoidance outweighs attraction, we rationalize to the salesman by saying that the price is too high. This rationalization leads the salesman to believe that price is virtually the only thing clients consider. Constant repetition of these situations in our daily lives has naturally led us to believe that money is what matters most to other people.

Some years ago, in order to introduce supervisors to the subject of motivation, the author asked them to rank ten possible motives in the order in which they thought these were important to the average worker. This was done first by the top-level supervisors, who were asked to rate the motivations of their immediate subordinates. Salary was rated highest, while safety invariably was placed last. Then they were asked to rate several different job offers for *themselves*. Each position offered a certain monetary increase over what the individual was then making, but it also contained a drawback. For example, one offer was "30% more than you are now making but with a boss that continually bawls you out in front of coworkers." Another job promised "60% more than you are making now but with risk of serious injury." One alternative always included was simply to "remain as I am now with the present salary." Very few took the tempting offers that entailed a disagreeable element; most preferred to remain where they were. Yet, each felt that their *subordinates* were thinking of money first and foremost. The experiment was conducted again, this time by asking the *subordinates* to rate similar job offers for *themselves* and also to rate their *own* subordinates on the motivational preferences. The findings were the same as in the first case. As one supervisor said, "I see now how we are. When it comes to me, I want a lot of other things that are more important than money to me; but when I think of others, they always look to me as if money were the most important thing to them."

Capable Supervisors Should Devise Solutions and See to It That Their Subordinates Carry Them Out. This is a very common belief not necessarily confined to industry. We believe that if only so-and-so were to be named head of X Department, everything would be all right because he would immediately know how to organize things, decide what should be done, tell each one what to do, and then follow-up to see that all orders are carried out. (Punishment would, of course, be applied if orders were not carried out.) But even outside industry, we often hear comments such as: "If only they could get a real good man to direct the men's ward at X hospital," or "If only they got a really strong man as police commissioner, the crime wave would stop." In other words, we are always thinking of the providential man, the redeemer, who will come and somehow straighten out the mess. Most democracies put a tremendous faith in "our next President" or "our next

Mayor," who will surely put things in order. Some want a strong man, others an efficient man, others an experienced man, but it's always the providential man. We read stories in the newspapers and in history about providential men who solved problems, situations, or crises. We believe that all this is so, and because it may occasionally have happened, we are always waiting for *the man* who will solve the problems in the different areas of an organization or of a nation. In war the commanding general is regarded as the cause of success or failure.

It has been stated that historians are divided on the subject of the result of the battle of Waterloo. Some are concerned about why Napoleon lost the battle, while the rest are concerned about what it was that made Wellington win. The present author—who has read some material on the history of war, as well as detailed accounts of battles of all ages, in an intense desire to know more about conflict—has tentatively reached the conclusion that except for those cases in which the numerical and material superiority was overwhelming, most battles have not been won by the brilliance of the commanding general but rather by the stupidity of the losing one.

We can eventually hope that humanity, through the good use of social-science technology, will have no further use for battles and that win-lose conflict will tend to diminish. While win-lose conflict continues to prevail, however, the leader who will experience the most success will not be the providential man but the skillful leader who, by withdrawing into the background himself, will make the best use of the talents of those surrounding him through well-conducted, problem-solving conferences like those described in Chapter 6.

Supervisors Are Too Busy and Have No Time to Become Experts in Social Science Techniques. This is a strongly held belief, in spite of what some practitioners may contend. The supervisor is always "too busy with the complex daily affairs" to be bothered with personnel problems. Usually, he wants the Personnel Department to do it all. During the last few decades, there has been increased interest and activity in what has been termed "human relations," and courses and seminars have been established so that supervisors will gain greater insight into the handling of personnel problems. Sensitivity training, T-group training, seminars prepared by technical associations, and other similar methods have proliferated.

Unfortunately, books are generally written for supervisors in terminology "that they will be able to understand." In other words, they are treated as morons who have to have things very simply presented to them so that they will be able to understand them. Sensitivity training makes the subjects live through certain experiences, presumably to allow them to gain insight into how disagreeable these experiences can be. From this insight, they should conclude that they must not subject their subordinates to that type of treatment. Since the subordinates are also human beings, they will presumably have similar, negative reactions to those supervisors who went through such a "laboratory group training."

All this might be cited as evidence that our opening statement has ceased to be true. Nevertheless, this is not what the author has in mind. His contention is that these seminars, simplified books, etc., provide only a smattering of something that concerns the relations among human beings. There is very little technology behind all this, and certainly very little theoretical social research. (This matter will be further elaborated in the parallel statement found in the new paradigm that is based on actual social-science findings.)

Thus, we see that society is constantly attempting to solve its problems with this paradigm. The fact that it is getting nowhere, that social problems are increasing, and that conflict is as difficult to solve as ever does not seem to alter our belief in the efficacy of this paradigm. Although we may not admit that we believe any of the 11 prevailing statements, when faced with a crisis, we invariably act as if they were true. It is what we *do* and not what we *believe* that counts to the people who are suffering the consequences of social malfunction and who are expecting reform. They see that when we have trouble in the universities, we use force and punishment to deter "misbehavior" and to bring about improvement. These threats are addressed to all alike. When workers go on strike, we enjoin them to come back to work at the risk of losing their jobs. We try to reason with people who are highly emotional and become infuriated when they do not immediately see "our side of the question." The list goes on and on. Let the reader look at today's newspapers in any country, and he will see signs everywhere of the paradigm we have just described. Let him look around where he works, whether it is publicly or privately owned, and the same situation prevails. Let him look at his own family and see how often he and the other members have acted as if those statements were true.

The author recalls an incident that although ludicrous, was quite unsettling. At a renowned institute in the United States, where positive reinforcement was being used to attempt to improve retarded children, the Director was a competent Skinnerian who was usually a bit rough with his staff. At one moment, able to bear it no longer, a subordinate faced him squarely and asked, "You who are so competent in the field of reinforcement! How about some positive reinforcement for us?" The reply was immediate and curt: "Do you think that with all I have to do thinking up ways to use reinforcement on these children, I have a minute's time to think of giving positive reinforcement to you?" He turned and left. It has been possible to train many supervisors in Uruguay to a point where they have perhaps a fraction of the theoretical knowledge possessed by this competent Director, but the difference is that they understood what they have learned and have made it a part of their life pattern. They use it virtually unconsciously in normal situations and are able to design solutions using reinforcement in more complex cases.

A historical analogy already cited may be useful in helping to distinguish between the two paradigms presented here. For a long time, over two centuries ago, there existed a paradigm concerning the existing social structure, i.e., kings had absolute power over their subjects by "divine right." In some countries they were the owners of the country and of its human and natural resources. A hereditary nobility with powerful rights constituted the government. Gradually, starting with the Encyclopedists, Rousseau and others in France, and with Jefferson and the American independence movement, these beliefs were questioned. It was eventually proved that a nation, or any nation, could successfully endure without a hereditary monarchy. People could run a country counter to beliefs that had been cherished for centuries. The fundamental aspect was that men became aware of a sense of injustice. It was easy then to point to the cause: The administrators of nations were authoritarian, unjust, and—what was worse—privileged to rule by heredity. It was equally easy to identify the culprits: George VI, Louis XVI, and the lesser nobles. The reasoning was simple: If we can get rid of those guilty and let the people run their own affairs, everything will be all right. Eventually, in a greater number of countries, this goal was achieved. But there were several problems that arose when democracy was established: How were the people to run their own countries? The answer was easy: Just let them choose their own rulers. The latter will derive their just powers from the consent of the governed.

For some time, the new system was the delight of liberal-minded people, but then trouble arose. The fact that the people had to choose their rulers necessitated elections, and elections have the win-lose conflict built into them. Besides, the losers, who at first had been sure they were going to win, naturally experienced considerable cognitive dissonance, which was reduced in nonconstructive ways. Of course, the enthusiasm over the "democratic" system meant that it had to be carried over to all other activities where men gathered in large enough numbers to need someone to act as a leader. Elections are now held within parties, in clubs, in unions, in professional organizations—the list is endless.

Stagner (1956) has shown the enormous differences in attitudes, perceptions, etc. that pertain to different leadership positions. When a prominent social scientist who was elected to the presidency of the American Psychological Association is replaced by someone else, he loses little prestige. He still continues to be a prominent social scientist. But when Joe Jones, who is president of the Union Local and therefore has contacts with big shots and exercises a certain power and influence among the rank and file, gets ousted and returns to his job as floorsweeper, a tremendous loss of prestige is involved. The democratic process of elections that we had championed failed to recognize that not only are all men *not* created equal but that there are great differences in the structures of clubs, unions, corporations, professional societies, and other groups that require some one person to act as chief.

Today, we find an almost universal element of revolt against the existing social structure. But there is a serious problem because the charges are similar to those existing before the American and French Revolutions. There is injustice and authoritarianism as before, but there is no George III to blame or Louis XVI to guillotine. Some people tend to blame the current administration, but a new one comes into office and the evils still continue. The same holds true for corporations and professional associations. Many say, "If only my man could be given the opportunity to lead." Often that man does get the opportunity; yet no improvement is seen. This predicament was discussed in connection with the "providential" man. In this situation, dissonance increases but we don't know whom to blame. Then we propose changing the whole system. Still, as we have pointed out, countries that have radically changed their political systems remain plagued by the same problems of general and rising discontent.

There is a reason for this. When democracy was first, firmly established, the constitutions of free nations were made up without adequate knowledge of how people act. It should not surprise us, therefore, that we have run into trouble. If we design a bridge, such as the Tacoma Narrows bridge, with an insufficient knowledge of wind stresses, we should not be too surprised later when a peculiar wind of a certain force tears the structure down. Engineers were shocked, but not surprised, when this actually occurred. This sort of thing has happened before. When it does, instead of getting furious at the wind, engineers do research on wind stresses. Structures designed after these studies were made have incorporated this knowledge and, as a result, are safer. The failure of the great Quebec cantilever bridge was the result of insufficient knowledge about lacing on large structural members. Engineers immediately started to conduct research on lacing, and it is likely that many of today's large structures have successfully stood as a result of such research.

With respect to social problems, what we must do is simply cease to act as if the prevailing paradigm were true and replace it with a new paradigm that has evolved from the application of newly discovered knowledge about ourselves. Before describing this new paradigm, a warning is in order.

Reference has already been made to Kuhn's analysis of the structure of scientific revolutions. Long before Kuhn wrote his book, Albert Einstein made a similar comment, which seems relevant to the present discussion (Einstein and Infeld, 1938).

> There are no eternal theories in science. It always happens that some of the facts predicted by a theory are disproved by experiment. Every theory has its period of gradual development and triumph, after which it may experience a rapid decline. . . . Nearly every great advance in science arises in a crisis in the old theory, through an endeavour to find a way out of the difficulties created.

It is quite possible that the new paradigm about to be presented will prove useful in solving problems that have seemed insoluble with the prevailing paradigm. This has certainly been true, at least in the cases described in the earlier chapters of this book. Perhaps if (and when) it is universally applied, it will yield good initial and even long-range results. However, even this new paradigm may eventually fail because of the appearance of new problems—the nature of which we cannot even begin to imagine. Could Henry VIII have even guessed what the consequences would be of a prolonged newspaper strike? But we must not be pessimistic. If men had always been afraid to attempt something new simply because events might later occur that would invalidate the innovation, we would be still in the stone age. Thus, we should not hesitate to apply the new paradigm and build a new social-science technology around it.

PROPOSED PROBLEM-SOLVING PARADIGMS

Again, the statements describing the problem-solving paradigm, which is based on the application of social-science data, will be followed with individual, explanatory comments.

(1)   There are great individual differences among humans.

(2)   Positive incitement is a better modifier of behavior than punishment or threat.

(3)   Social problems are solved by correcting causes not symptoms.

(4)   Human conflict is no more inevitable than disease and can be solved or, even better, prevented.

(5)   Irrational feelings must be reduced before people can reason.

(6)   Human motivation is complex; no one does or fails to do something for only one reason.

(7)   Problems are solved more effectively in groups than individually.

(8)   Perceptions are more relevant to social problems than are "true facts."

(9)   Time and effort are not available in infinite amounts for problem solving.

(10) Responsibility for individual improvement of subordinates, students, and others should shift largely from them to higher authorities.
(11) Supervisors and teachers should receive intensive training in social science technology.

There Are Great Individual Differences among Humans. If we not only believe this assertion but also practice it, it will lead us to cease treating all persons as if they were equal. This means that we cannot set up "rules" for behavior with corresponding sanctions for their violation. We must study each case individually, diagnosing the causes of what we believe to be misbehavior. This will make us aware of the enormous complexity of the human mind, with its 120 mental abilities, and of the physical traits, interests, personality, etc., as expounded in Chapter 2. It may be objected that such attention to detail will make life very complicated. There are two replies to this. One is that life is already complicated, partly because we have made it so by overlooking just such important things as correct diagnosis and treatment of individual cases. The other is that such techniques are necessary, in view of the complexity of human beings. The fact that the human *body* is complicated has not deterred medicine from advancing. Advances in medicine, including our increasing freedom from disease, have come about *precisely because* the medical, biological, and related disciplines—as well as the general public—have recognized that the human body is extremely complex and requires complex treatment. Miller has stated (1969):

> The most urgent problems of our world today are the problems we have made for ourselves. They have not been caused by some heedless or malicious inanimate Nature, nor have they been imposed on us as punishment by the will of God. They are human problems whose solutions will require us to change our behavior and our social institutions.

In accordance with this first statement, one behavior we must change is the tendency to stereotype. "All workers want more money." "All managers are ambitious." "All labor leaders are left-wingers." "All leftists are destructive." "All capitalists are greedy." All these are corollaries to the notion that "All men are created equal." Many people will not admit that we stereotype, but most of us do. What we must train ourselves to do is study persons as *individuals*. Imagine a doctor saying, "All persons with pneumonia must receive 100,000 units of penicillin," without seeing a single pneumonia patient in order to know his past history, to find out whether he is allergic to penicillin, what stage of pneumonia he is in, etc. Our procedure in treating social problems must similarly be based on study and experience. This principle holds not only in dealings with our subordinates but also with members of the family, friends, and many others. Not that we must suspend family relationships or friendliness and become psychological analysts! This would be almost as absurd as setting up rules that presumably apply to everyone equally. There is an intermediate position. For example, we are not continuously measuring our friends to see how tall or heavy they are. But if we see a rather short person always trying to reach books on a very high shelf, we will provide him with a ladder or stool to ease his work. This same recognition of physical individuality must be adopted for psychological individuality.

Positive Incitement Is a Better Modifier of Behavior than Punishment or Threat. We have seen how positive reinforcement can be used to modify behavior; there is also an added advantage when this course of action is adopted. In the same way that aggressiveness can be contagious, thinking of others, praising their work, and saying pleasant things makes life more agreeable not only to the receiver but also to the giver. It is extraordinary to see what a tremendous change in climate can come about in an organization that changes from punitive methods to the rational and ingenious use of positive reinforcement. Skinner (1948), in *Walden II*, describes a society in which all aspects of life are guided by positive reinforcement. Although his account exaggerates the potential of positive reinforcement to the extent of discarding everything else that has been discovered in social science, at certain points its use is definitely uplifting. In particular, one remark already cited in Chapter 5 must be repeated: "And what a strange discovery for a would-be tyrant, that the only effective technique of control is unselfish." Skinner was thinking only of positive reinforcement, but the same remark would hold for the type of persuasion presented in this book, as well as for our brand of conflict resolution, group problem-solving, and other social-science techniques. No would-be authoritarian tyrant, as we have noted, could possibly make use of all this, and if he did, he would merely be doing what others want done, thereby eliminating his authoritarianism.

A pertinent question might now be asked: "Why is it that humanity has virtually always resorted to punishment?" The answer lies in the very curve with which Skinner proved the futility of punishment. It will be remembered that when the rats were punished, there was an immediate decrement in the rate of responses, although later the total number of responses recovered (as if punishment had never been applied). To the punisher, this *immediate diminution* in rate of response constitutes positive reinforcement. It shows him very clearly that punishment works. He sees the immediate results and therefore concludes that his method is the proper way to go about correcting people. The other, more subtle aftereffects are harder to notice and much harder to tie in with the original punishment.

It is therefore possible that we have simply "learned" that punishment works. If we add to this a desire for revenge when we are frustrated, it is not too hard to see why humanity has used punishment as a means of control for countless centuries. The sun will really rise over a new world when we all use positive reinforcement in its many forms. This book has covered an introductory phase to this subject. A more advanced text would give many more subtle ways in which reinforcement can be administered. Doubtless, willing and ingenious readers can design many more.

Social Problems Are Solved by Correcting Causes Not Symptoms. Lenin once stated: "It would be absurd, nay even immoral for someone without a medicine to try to cure the sick. How much more absurd and immoral is it for a person to try to cure social ills without knowing their causes." But knowing causes implies diagnosis, and it is only in recent times that we have learned how to diagnose social causes. We probably still have a lot to learn, but with present knowledge we at least end the absurdity of penalizing a worker because he has made a mistake. The mistake is the symptom, and it is our duty to find the cause. Similarly, we are prone to say that the cause of a strike is demands for higher pay. Ample evidence has been given throughout this book to the effect that people may "talk money" when the issue is really something else. Stagner (1956) quotes a union organizer on the real problem in a strike in a small Illinois factory: "The real issue wasn't the 15¢ an hour we asked for or the 5¢ we got. The real cause of the strike was that we had to convince that guy he couldn't be a little dictator any longer." Perhaps not all persons who are in a conflict situation can see their motives so clearly, nor are the motives usually as simple. It is imperative, however, for those of us who wish to serve humanity by helping to solve conflict to take such a searching attitude. We must look beyond what is seen and discussed to find the real causes. This takes knowing a bit of psychology—the more the better. As our knowledge of psychology increases, we will be able to perform better diagnoses and avoid taking action that, in the light of these new findings, is stupid simply because it does not solve the difficulty but merely makes matters worse.

The need for diagnosis cannot be stressed too strongly. The natural desire to oversimplify has led men to dreadfully incorrect behaviors throughout history. The witch-hunters, who burned thousands of persons to death, make us shudder today. We shudder at the ignorance that led to such excesses. The flogging of the insane is another case in point. At the same time that we feel shocked upon reading about these past practices, we are committing similar errors because of faulty diagnosis. Fortunately, however, there's a difference between the past and the present. The people of past ages just did not know any better. We have noted Dr. Closset's ignorance when he treated the dying Mozart. Today, we *do* know better, and it is therefore inexcusable for us to continue to be social-science charlatans by misjudging causes and performing foolish diagnoses. This is especially true when the information is available that allows us to determine *correctly* what factors underlie our present problems. We would consider a modern doctor to be an irresponsible quack if he put cold compresses on the temples of a person with a high temperature. However, we are acting like social-science technology quacks when we bawl out a man who is caught in a serious approach-avoidance conflict for being aggressive toward others.

In order to achieve this new approach and put it into practice, social science must not remain in the ivory tower of the research laboratories and technical journals, which are difficult for the general public to both read and understand. In his splendid address, part of which has already been quoted, Miller (1969) recognizes that there may be difficulty in passing the results of psychological research to the general public. Yet, he states:

> On the other hand, difficulty is no excuse for surrender. There is a sense in which the unattainable is the best goal to pursue. So let us continue our struggle to advance psychology as a means of promoting human welfare, each in our own way. For myself, however, I can imagine nothing we could do that would be more relevant to human welfare, and nothing that could pose a greater challenge to the next generation of psychologists, than to discover how best to give psychology away.

Miller's goal of explaining social psychology to others has been the main preoccupation of the author during the past years.

Human Conflict Is No More Inevitable than Disease and Can Be Solved or, Even Better, Prevented. The chapter on conflict resolution shows how a specific conflict was solved by using an appropriate design based on social-science findings. When the author has talked about these solutions to groups, there is invariably someone who asks: "But what would you do in the case of a conflict in which there have been violent deeds done on both parts, in which neither is willing to give way, and in which on both sides everything depends on the will of an authoritarian?" There is a reply to this. To begin with, the question is unfair, because one cannot prescribe or design a solution without knowing a good deal more. It is like asking a doctor who is expounding the principles of medicine, "What would you do with a patient that has double pneumonia, three broken ribs, hepatitis, diabetes, and heart failure from a coronary?" The doctor would reply that this extremely complicated case would have to be seen and studied before he could even venture to give an opinion, let alone prescribe treatment. But there is another answer. Why refer to the most complex and refractory, as well as the rarest, cases? Why not consider some simpler and much more abundant pathologies, whether they be physical or social? We must try our hand at the simpler cases before we proceed to the more complex ones. The conflict solved in Chapter 8, for example, must be recognized as a minor conflict compared to a major war or cold war. But what is important is that a cure *has been found* for the little conflict. To pass from that to the larger one is now a matter of elaboration. When Bell invented the telephone, the first message was transmitted over a distance of a few yards. Perhaps someone could have objected that complicated gadgets like that were not necessary for such short distances, when shouting would do. The objection might also have been raised that the then prevailing obstacles to long-distance communications would make the latter impossible. Yet, now men reach the moon and talk unconcernedly back and forth with men on the earth—something Bell probably never envisaged. Many similar cases can be cited, but in every one of these, the important fact is that even on a small scale the solution *was* successful.

Even more important than attaining the ability to *solve* conflict, is the possibility to avoid it. Different examples have been given to show how this can be done in a group setting. In these cases, what might have degenerated into serious conflict was solved to everyone's satisfaction. Attention to diagnosis and treatment by means of appraisals may keep an organization free of the factors that generate conflict. The same may apply to an institution of higher learning, to a nation, or to all the nations of the world. It is simply "giving psychology away," as Miller states, that will eventually give not only the leaders but also the masses the means whereby the causes of destructive conflict can be dissipated long before the storm clouds begin to gather.

Another medical analogy may be useful here. Making a successful heart transplant is a spectacular feat. Avoiding typhoid fever by treating city water is not. But prevention of illness, although not so glamorous, is much more useful to the general welfare than difficult cures. Seeing firemen fight a great blaze may also be spectacular, but the work of architects, builders, and building inspectors in assuring fireproof structures, while appearing much less dramatic, saves many more lives and property. In the same way, solving a conflict may leave a person with a great sense of accomplishment. (Actually, conflict solving is really not so glamorous because, if well-conducted and effective, the parties involved must receive the impression that they, and not the leader, solved the difficulty.) In contrast, the day-to-day task of avoiding friction, diagnosing, applying, reinforcement, persuading, etc. may not give the doer such a sense of accomplishment, although in the long run this kind of work will prove to be much more effective. If properly carried out, the work of prevention will obviate the need to solve conflicts. If social-science technologists take this attitude and make it work, destructive conflict will be as much a thing of the past as smallpox epidemics.

Irrational Feelings Must Be Reduced before People Can Reason. This point has already been discussed to some extent in the sixth statement of the prevailing paradigm. We now know that if someone is upset about something, we have to quiet him down before he will be able to reason. His agitated condition serves to block the functioning of the cerebral cortex where rational thinking takes place. Therefore, we must acquire the habit of being as alert to signs of emotionality in others as we are to signs of physical illness, and under no circumstances, must we attempt to use logic or reasoning, until we have found the cause of this irrationality and have found ways to make it disappear.

Similarly, we must present problems to people in a way that interests them, does not cause reactance, or generate cognitive dissonance. To do so, may seem difficult at first, but eventually it will become second nature. Physical hygiene must have been difficult to introduce initially, but it has now become a way of life for great numbers of people. It is common practice to use bandaids for a cut finger. If an injury or illness gets worse and goes beyond what the individual can do for himself, he knows he must consult a doctor. The same attitude must eventually prevail with respect to social-science technology. Laymen must first do all they can with the knowledge they have available to diagnose and see whether the correction of the cause is within their abilities. If not or if the diagnosis is too difficult, we must send for a specialist. Part of the wisdom a population gains when science is introduced for its welfare, whether it is medicine or social-science technology, is the ability to decide when the nature of the case is such that the individual can handle it himself or when the case should be referred to a specialist. Our experience so far has been that the general population can learn a good deal of social science; enough, at least, to enable most people to solve an enormous number of cases that occur daily, thereby enriching their lives to an invaluable degree.

Human Motivation Is Complex; No One Does or Fails to Do Anything for Only One Reason.   The author credits Dr. George A. Miller with author-ship of the second part of this statement. Our analysis of the approach-avoidance conflict has illustrated how we often have reasons for doing things that make us reject a proposed course of action. This was discussed, in part, in the sixth statement of the prevailing paradigm, which states that most behavior is economically motivated. Here we assert that not only is money *not* the principal motivation for people but that there are always many other motives, often in conflict with one another. It is this complex interaction that we must take into account when we diagnose. Since social problems are solved by correcting causes, not symptoms, we must carefully analyze con-flicting motivations before we can even dream of designing action.

Unfortunately, the intention of limiting this book to an introduction has precluded all analysis of conflicting social norms; that is, of situations in which a person who belongs to two groups finds that his allegiances are endangered because the two groups are in conflict. This is the conflict Blanche finds herself in Shakespeare's *King John*, Act III Scene I, when she exclaims: "Whoever wins, on that side I shall lose." One of our duties, if we apply social-science technology correctly, is to avoid placing human beings in such impossible dilemmas.

Problems Are Solved More Effectively in Groups than Individually. In our chapter on group problem solving, theoretical and practical evidence was presented to show how persons can solve problems better when working together. However, this result is achieved only if certain conditions are obtained. In general, the literature on the subject contains mostly the results of experiments that show why groups do *not* work well together; for example, studies that emphasize the barriers to understanding that normally occur when people gather to discuss a topic. Win-lose conflict is one of the worst such barriers. We are confident, however, that skillful leadership, which is available to almost anyone—except perhaps extreme authoritarians—can lead to full understanding, harmony, and unanimity in the development of high quality solutions by groups.

We should also note that far from coercing, the methods presented here are designated to liberate men's minds from their passions, which prevent their normal exercise of reason. The importance of this freedom to think is probably one of the greatest gifts we have received from the social sciences. The early proponents of democracy could not have realized that often the worst coercions come not from outside but from within ourselves. Circumstances, contact with others, win-lose conflicts—all lead to emotional states that often deprive us of the use of our reason. We are then frustrated and begin looking for the "enemy" that is restricting us, not realizing that this enemy may be inside us. A good group leader will thus be a person who, instead of imposing his ideas, will liberate the minds of others so that they can give their utmost. This must be done with the skills we have described and with careful attention to the mental abilities of each of the individuals involved. Under such circumstances, it will be difficult for any one individual to produce a product that is better than that of a group conducted in this manner.[2]

Perceptions Are More Relevant to Social Problems than Are True Facts. Stagner (1956) has admirably stated this:

> The tendency to blame "bad" union leaders or "bad" capitalists is easily evoked. If we assume that these conflicting issues derive from "true facts" we shall inevitably wind up blaming some villain for industrial conflict. But if we keep in mind that each person behaves in terms of the facts *as he sees them*, we can concentrate on the fundamental problem: why do the facts look that way to him; and is there another way of looking at the situation which will be equally satisfactory without leading to conflict?

[2] Recent research by Tajfel (1970) suggests valuable ideas whereby analogous preferences may be turned into even more powerful tools for conflict resolution than the material used here.

Since this is an introductory book, very little has been said about the complexities of perception. Stagner sums this up well. Very often, following the implications of the prevailing paradigm, committees or courts of inquiry are appointed to determine the "facts" and thereby determine the culprit. This process can be endless. If, on the other hand, we start to study the perceptions of the different persons involved, analyze what cause them, and perhaps design adequate persuasions, we may solve social problems in new different ways and perhaps even ameliorate them long before they become acute enough to warrant a court trial. However, if we insist on finding out who was right or where the "truth" lies, we will end up with greater problems than we had in the beginning.

Time and Effort Are Not Available in Infinite Amounts for Problem Solving. The author owes this statement to an anonymous member of a group who was discussing this matter and to Maier (1963). The desire to find the culprit is so ingrained in us that even after hearing all the evidence in favor of them and after acknowledging the truth of all these propositions, there are still people who insist that the past should be investigated in order to serve as a guide for the future. This means, of course, that the guilty party should always be found. In one of these discussions, one of the participants (who has preferred to remain unknown) countered such an argument with, "But don't you see that if we want to be practical, we haven't got all the time in the world? Why, we could spend weeks exploring the past, probably getting nowhere, and in the meantime leave aside urgent things to be done." Maier's contribution to this statement comes from his discussion of the Area of Freedom.

> Problem solving is successful only when the solution reached is one that can be put into practice. . . . Ideas for improvement are frequently expressed in the form of actions that others should take . . . Justice would demand that the persons at fault should change. However, at this point we are not considering the matter of justice; rather, our concern is how to improve matters and make the best of a given situation. The question of justice and how best to improve a situation are independent objectives and should not be confused.
>
> The tendency to blame others is a backward-looking approach. The past is beyond control and cannot be altered. Only the present and the future are subject to change, and hence only they can be controlled through decisions. The problem-solving approach, therefore, must incorporate an attitude that accepts the past and takes up the problems of what to do to reach present objectives.

How can this be prevented from happening again?

These concepts agree with the contention that it is useless to fix the blame on someone when something goes wrong and even more useless to administer punishment. If the reader will stop and think about the statements of the old paradigm, which operate conjunctively, he will probably realize the extreme absurdity of our usual methods of solving problems.

The wisdom of the new approach can probably be easily seen and understood. However, we must remember that in order to carry out the techniques recommended here, good intentions are not enough. We must find ways to apply these principles to the real, practical problems people face daily. Otherwise, we will probably eventually turn them into a kind of religion, which, lacking such practical applicability, will fail. This failure will frustrate us and make us wish for the "rod of iron" to break, as we broke the potter's vessel, those whom we consider stubborn because they do not think and act as we want them to.

Responsibility for Individual Improvement of Subordinates, Students, and Others Should Shift Largely from Them to Higher Authorities.   This is almost a corollary of all that we have said before; it will create the greatest changes. Instead of saying to someone, "You must improve!" we ask ourselves, "What can I do to help this person improve?" Some of the things that can be done have been set forth in several chapters of this book. Probably many others will appear as more people develop this new attitude. Without a doubt, however, we must cease telling the other person that he must change. As Mark Twain remarked, "To be good is noble, but to teach others how to be good is nobler—and less trouble."

The main thesis to be derived from everything that we have presented in this volume is that *our principal duty is not to blame other people and tell them that they should change but to do something to help these other people ourselves.* This latter course has the added advantage of making us take our minds off ourselves and think a little more about others—something that is certainly urgently needed. We must forget such cherished notions as the existence of "free will" or the notion that all our problems arise from the sins of others and decide to lend a hand to help others succeed. If we change this attitude, we will win for ourselves that most priceless of inalienable rights—the right to the pursuit of happiness. We will achieve it by helping others to attain their own happiness. But all this requires one final ingredient.

Supervisors, Teachers, and Others Should Receive Intensive Training in Social-Science Technology.   Good will alone will get us nowhere. There have been any number of very noble movements created and promoted that have rested on the principle of "peace on earth and good will toward men." Yet, we still do not have peace on earth, and good will is in general hard to find.

We have, until very recently, lacked the knowledge with which to build the technology necessary for ending social strife; so in reality humanity cannot be blamed for not having done the right thing at certain times. But now we possess an immense amount of social-science data. This book has attempted to show how some of the most significant of these can be combined to form a technology that has actually worked in very diverse situations in solving problems that until now had seemed insoluble.

Since we now no longer have the excuse that knowledge is not available, action is necessary. In the same way that man has turned his knowledge of electricity, magnetism, steam, and atomic energy to useful purposes (and often to his own destruction), man can now utilize social-science technology to do away eventually with the destructive uses of his discoveries in other areas.

In his "Prologue or Epilogue?" which ends as if he were a pleader to some divinity for the continuation of the human race, Bertrand Russell (1962) has stated:

> . . . Do not forget that we have but lately emerged from a morass of ancient ignorance and age-long struggle for existence. Most of what we know we have discovered during the last twelve generations. Intoxicated by our new power over nature, many of us have been misled into the pursuit of power over other human beings. This is an *ignis fatuus*, enticing us to return to the morass from which we have been partially escaping. But this wayward folly has not absorbed all our energies. What we have come to know about the world in which we live, about nebulae and atoms, the great and the small, is more than would have seemed possible before our own day. You may retort that knowledge is not good except in the hands of those who have enough wisdom to use it well. But this wisdom also exists, though as yet sporadically and without the power to control events.

Russell is, of course, referring to wisdom as expressed by wise people who knew that destructive conflict is insane. He also recognizes that such persons as yet lack the power to control events. Probably every human being has felt at one time or another that war and strife are foolish, particularly when that strife has had terrible effects upon him or those he loves. In this sense, most people possess a kind of wisdom. As Russell says, the sages have taught us *what* to avoid; they have not yet shown us *how* to avoid it. Social-science technology is the discipline that will eventually achieve this most important step.

Russell, in his plea goes on to say that the sages have actually told us *more* than simply what to avoid:

> They have shown us also that it is within human power to create a world of shining beauty and transcendent glory. Consider the poets, the composers, the painters, the men whose inward vision has been shown to the world in edifices of majestic splendor. All this country of the imagination might be ours. And human relations, also, could have the beauty of lyric poetry. At moments, in the love of man and woman, something of this possibility is experienced by many. But there is no reason why it should be confined within narrow bounda-

ries; it could, as in the Choral Symphony, embrace the whole world. These are things which lie within human power, and which, given time, future ages may achieve.

But it is not a matter for future ages. Scientists have managed to transform the laser in a few years from a scientific curiosity to an instrument of unbelievably diverse capabilities. Why should a very long time have to pass before we are able to constructively apply the new paradigm introduced here? The only deterrent is a lack of the necessary education. As long as we cling to the notion that supervisors and teachers have no time to spare, then there is little hope for improvement. It has been shown, at least on a limited scale, that supervisors and teachers *can* learn and apply the relevant techniques within a reasonable period of time.

At this point, two important warnings are necessary. First, *everyone* who has dealings with people must learn to use the proper social-science techniques. This conviction is based on the author's premise that such techniques *can* be learned by able laymen. Let us illustrate with the case of a supervisor. In general, he has two jobs—one is technical (accounting, plastics manufacturing, orchestra conducting, taxing, etc.) and the other is handling the people who work for him. The author's premise is that if the supervisor is sufficiently capable of learning the technical aspects of his job, he should also be able to learn the social-science technology that enables him to handle the human element in his work. If he fails in either of these, he has no business being a supervisor.

The second warning is related to the time available for this kind of training. A supervisor cannot acquire the knowledge to run an accounting department, a plastic plant, a steel casting plant, how to conduct a large orchestra well, in a week. Neither can he learn the social-science technology necessary to run a department in a one-week seminar, no matter how intensive and well-conducted it might be. It takes time and has to be taught in assimilable doses at the place where the supervisor works.

One objection that is often raised is, "What happens if the *subordinates* know all these tricks?" In the first place, calling these problem-solving techniques "tricks" indicates a negative attitude. It can usually be countered with the question, "Would you tell a lie if by doing so you could immediately stop all racial strife in the world?" Most people give a positive reply to this. The same general question may be related to the current war or to other destructive conflict.

There is strong evidence, however, to show that the use of these psychological processes is actually aided by the awareness of their existence on the part of the subjects involved. Groups composed of individuals who are aware of the material presented in this book have been seen to move much faster than those who are naïve about the subject. Jacobson (1969) has shown that subjects who were aware of the correct positive-reinforcement contingency were able to improve performance, while those who were unaware showed no change. Zimbardo (1969) and Eriksen (1962) have found a similar result. Furthermore, we have found that in group problem solving, for example, the solutions actually appear much faster and are of a higher quality when the group is composed of people who are familiar with social-science technology. Quite often we catch one member (not the leader) saying, "Whoops! I was just about to start a win-lose conflict," or making a similar remark that shows he is aware of what is going on. This sensitivity has proved to be so useful that the decision has been taken in several departments of one company to train *all* its personnel in social-science technology, right down to the office-boy level. Two reasons have been given for this: By having this information, each employee will be able to cooperate in solving problems in the work situation *and* in his home environment. The second reason is that any one of many workers may eventually become the manager of the company, and he might as well start thinking and acting now according to the new paradigm!

This discussion of the proposed paradigm hopefully gives the reader an idea of the change that can be achieved in a relatively short time if we incorporate the new systems into our daily lives. Eventually, the new paradigm, through its use in many such sub-societies, may exert such an influence upon the total society that significant changes will begin to occur. It would then be possible to make predictions about an entirely new social system quite different from anything we know now. The courts would not have the job deciding who was to blame but would be problem-solving centers. Instead of wasting immense amounts of effort in digging into the past, they could conduct meetings designed to help those concerned decide what to do about the future. Unions would cooperate with management, and supervisors with workers at varying levels, in order to solve all kinds of problems. It should be emphasized that this would *not* be done by means of worker representation on the boards of organizations. (This would again lead to the ills that win-lose conflicts inevitably entail. Besides, most workers would still feel that their voices were not being heard.) With the new paradigm, each member, even in the largest organization, would be able to have his say in matters that lie within his area of freedom, which is the area that most concerns him and which he knows best. He would not be giving opinions in other areas about which he knows little but would trust that the decisions taken by fellow workers who are skilled and have experience in that area will be sound and not damaging to him.

In this entirely new environment the chief efforts of people would be directed toward making the best of their abilities, thereby wasting little time in useless and destructive controversy with other human beings. Even life in the home would improve. In addition, many who would otherwise become authoritarians, would very probably avoid that fate—assuming of course that authoritarianism is something that is caused by environment and not heredity. The same could be predicted of delinquency and other evils. There would still remain the problem of physiologically determined misbehavior, e.g., the cases of delinquents who have one extra chromosome, damage, should science confirm the existence of a relationship between such damage and crime, as well as those whom Schachter and Latane (1964) have demonstrated are low on adrenaline. We could then concentrate on how to eradicate even these deviations.

I have even designed a method that could be substituted for the present inadequate system for electing the representatives of the people. Two reasons deter me from explaining the proposed system here. One is that as it is so radically different from existing procedures its exposition here might be premature. The second and much more valid objection is that the new method should not be the creation of any one person but of many. Then its quality and acceptance would be much higher than what I have envisaged. Whatever the final result, it should be an improvement on our present form of democracy which was described by Winston Churchill as "the worst possible form of government except for all the others that have been tried."

CONCLUSION

Earlier, it was cited that misanthropes would find little use for the material contained in this book. It has also been mentioned that many people seem shocked at the use of what might be considered deception in some of the techniques. That is precisely the position of Alceste, the principal character in Molière's *Le Misanthrope*. He insists that one must be absolutely sincere and say nothing but what is absolutely true and comes from the heart. He detests mankind for its deceit. Philinte, his friend, of a more practical nature, says,

> There are many places where to be perfectly frank
> Would be ridiculous and little allowed.
> And often, hoping not to displease your austere honor,
> It's wise to hide what one has in one's heart.

Amelioration of social ills is possible when we tell little white lies. If everyone said immediately what he thinks of everyone else (T-group training notwithstanding), life would be horrible. Part of living in civilization is saying, "I'm pleased to meet you," or "glad to see you." We do this all the time because we have become quite accustomed to it. Yet, when there are new forms of saying things we are *not* accustomed to, we may react as Alceste does. However, it is quite probable that if we could only induce this type of character to be more civilized, his bitterness would cease.

The same occurs when people apply social-science technology. At first, there is a sense malaise, except for those who score high on Christie's Mach IV scale (Christie and Geis 1970). But as this material is learned and used, and as results are obtained, a different attitude is assimilated.

This chapter began with a Greek quotation from Aeschylus. It may have appeared quite cryptic, but in the *Eumenides* the chorus says these grand words, which I preferred to leave in their original form. Their meaning, however, could be translated as, "Consent not to live in anarchy nor under despotism." Often, in win-lose conflict, we fear that, to escape one, we must inevitably fall into the other. The history of humanity is replete with large and small examples of this absurd dilemma, but social-science technology gives us a new opportunity to use science to solve social problems and to avoid this repetition of mistakes. We may hope, therefore, that this introduction to social-science technology will eventually translate this poetic aspiration into a scientific reality. We may then visualize a world in the not-too-distant future in which social problems will be solved more with ingenuity than by using force, threat, or anarchic or despotic violence.

glossary

Here are some technical terms used in the application of social science findings to the solution of social problems. Italic terms used within a definition are also defined in this glossary.

ACTION ORIENTED: See TYPE III D.

AFFILIATION: The tendency for people to look for support from others. It is greatest when people are in a state of stress, due to fear, hunger, etc. The tendency is to be with others who are in a similar state. It has been found that those first born in a family have a greater tendency to affiliate under stressful conditions than persons born later. People who are deviant, or made to feel so, also prefer to be with others whom they feel are deviant as well.

APPROACH-AVOIDANCE
CONFLICT: The situation in which a person finds himself when he feels attracted toward some object or situation, for one or more reasons, but at the same time repelled by the same object for other reasons. An example is the case of an employee who likes his job because he likes the type of work, pay,

287

status, etc. but dislikes it because he has an overbearing supervisor who continually criticizes him in front of others and who never gives any positive recognition. A person in this situation has a tendency to reduce the anxiety caused by the conflict by showing *displaced aggression, rationalization, compensation, projection,* and/or *fixation.* The existence of approach-avoidance conflict is also indicated by errors, tardiness, and absenteeism.

APPROVAL MOTIVE:

The motive (very strong in some persons) that makes them want to seek approval from others, virtually above everything else. In employees this will, in general, take the form of not so much doing a good job but of trying to gain the approval of the supervisor. People who are high on the approval motive are those who need to make the most "show" of how good or important they are, or what excellent houses or cars they own. This may be done very grossly or more subtly depending on the person. Such people are particularly subject to yielding when placed in a *social pressure* situation. They can also reduce *dissonance* very easily when placed in a dissonance-producing situation that may affect their self-esteem. For this reason they are particularly apt to be persuaded by *persuasion by analogy* and *persuasion by successive approximation.*

AREA OF FREEDOM:

The area of action in which a particular person or group has the liberty to act. Often, when persons or groups are faced with a problem, they tend to find solutions in terms of what others should do. This proposal of freedom also refers to time. Problems are solved in the present or the future; the past is no longer available for action. Devoting time to determining who is responsible for errors means delving into the past, which cannot be changed and which is therefore outside the area of freedom. Problems are best solved when tackled within the area of freedom of the person or group, that is, in terms of what is in their power to do in the present and in the future.

ASCENDANCE:

The disposition a person has not to feel fear or anxiety when meeting a stranger, entering an entirely new type of situation, or facing a different social problem. The opposite is shyness.

ATTITUDE SCALES:

Statistically prepared instruments, usually sets of statements. A person is asked to state his degree of agreement or disagreement by making an appropriate response to each statement. This allows an expression of attitude in numerical terms, thereby making possible comparisons among persons. These scales are very useful in measuring the effects of different persuasion techniques upon different subjects.

AUTHORITARIAN PERSONALITY:	A personality type characterized by very severe and punitive attitudes toward certain minorities, coupled with subservience to a higher authority. The authoritarian also tends to be intolerant of ambiguity. He sees everything in terms of black and white, good or bad, and admits no intermediate grades or shadings. He sees relations among people more in terms of status and hierarchy than in terms of friendship. He tends to be intolerant of other people's ideas. The authoritarian is often pathologically concerned with sexual matters but frequently represses such interests.
BEHAVIORAL CONTENT:	The classification of mental abilities that deals with the behavior of people, particularly in social settings, that is, in relation to others.
CAREFREE:	See TYPE IV P.
CLASSES:	The product dimension of mental abilities that deals with sets of objects or ideas. For example, the set of all flower designs lies in the *figural* area, certain type of formulas in the *symbolic* area, classes of words and meanings in the *semantic* area, and types of behavior in the social or *behavioral* area.
COMMUNICATION NETWORK:	A term that refers to the different avenues or routes of communication that are available to a group of persons working in organizations or in a group seeking the solution to a problem. Small circles stand for persons and straight lines for the communication channels and communication "networks" (see Fig. 6.1). In the studies related to these networks, two measures have been taken (a) efficiency in problem solving and (b) satisfaction of the individuals involved. The worst network for problem-solving and the most frustrating for those involved is the "chain." (This is the usual method of communication in public offices in many Latin American Countries.) More efficient are the "wheel" and the "Y," but in both of these, only the individuals marked A are pleased. The others feel quite frustrated. The wheel is illustrated in Fig. 6.2. (See Chapter 6.) This is the usual arrangement in an organizational chart. The most efficient one of all, which also produces greatest satisfaction to all, is the "comcon," in which all participate. In group problem solving, the leader tries to create the comcon situation.
COGNITION:	The act of seeing, noticing, or recognizing something. For example, cognitive ability is used to note that a certain document belongs to a certain class in the filing system in order to file it correctly for easy retrieval when necessary.

COMPENSATION:

Turning to other types of activity for satisfaction which is not attained in a person's job. For example, a highly creative person put on a routine job which is very boring, has a tendency to compensate by devoting time to outside creative activity. This may take the form of a hobby, joining a club, or working for the union. Compensation is a frequent symptom of approach-avoidance conflict.

CONVERGENT
PRODUCTION:

The ability to find rapidly the solution to a problem when there is only one solution available. In the case of a stalled car, it is the ability to discover rapidly whether the problem is due to carburetor trouble, ignition, or merely lack of gas. Persons low in this ability may waste much time in servicing problems or diagnosing their causes.

CURIOSITY:

The motive that makes a person or animal explore his surroundings or take an interest in something, without having a definite goal in mind while doing so.

DISPLACED
AGGRESSION:

When a person in an *approach-avoidance* situation wishes to be aggressive, say, to his overbearing supervisor but does not dare to do so, he may instead express his aggression toward those having nothing to do with the problem— his subordinates, fellow workers, or his family. Such displaced aggression is an excellent symptom suggesting the existence of *approach-avoidance conflict*.

DISSONANCE:

The state in which a person finds himself when he receives two conflicting units of information. An example is the case of a person who expected a promotion and then found that someone else was appointed to the job. Another example is the case of a person expressing something opposite to what he privately believes. A third is the case of a person who works hard to achieve a given goal and then finds out that the goal is of little value. The state of dissonance is a strongly motivating one because the person feels a strong need to reduce it; this is called *dissonance reduction*.

DISSONANCE
REDUCTION:

As stated above, when a person is in a state of dissonance, he feels compelled to reduce it. There are several ways in which this can be accomplished:
(a) Changing one of the cognitions.   For example, if someone worked hard to achieve a goal that later turned out to be of little value, he cannot change the cognition that he worked hard. Consequently, he changes his evaluation of the goal, convincing himself that the goal was worthwhile after all.
(b) Derogating the source of dissonance. If a person favors a certain political party, a product or an idea, and he hears someone attacking this party, product or

idea, he may reduce dissonance by finding that the critical person is biased, unfair, etc.

(c) Seeking social support.   The person may seek out others whom he will try to persuade to his viewpoint. This behavior is typical of people who change religion, political preferences, makes of car, etc.

DYNAMIC:

This term describes a person who tends to do things fast. In general, the very dynamic person does things fast even when speed is not essential, such as when eating or engaging in recreative activity.

DIVERGENT
PRODUCTION:

The ability to think up several different solutions to a problem, e.g., to design different distributions of floor space in a building (*figural*), to solve mathematical formulae (*symbolic*), to write different texts for an advertisement (*semantic*), or to think of many different ways to train personnel (*behavioral*).

ENERGETIC:

See TYPE CO.

EVALUATION:

Refers to the ability to evaluate things, events, etc., against certain given standards. Examples are the ability to notice whether there is a difference between the print coming off a machine and the original (*figural*), whether the amounts on the invoices are the same as those on the orders (*symbolic*), whether the summary of an idea actually gives a good résumé (*semantic*), or whether the appraisal of a complex labor situation is correct (*behavioral*).

EXPLORATORY
BEHAVIOR:

See *curiosity*.

FIGURAL CONTENT:

The classification of abilities that consists mainly of figural material: designs, plans, drawings, and so forth.

FIXATION:

A mechanism whereby a person persists in a certain type of behavior despite the fact that it may be damaging to him. It is usually seen as stubbornness and often results from a severe *approach-avoidance conflict*, leading in turn to intense frustration.

GROUP PROBLEM
SOLVING:

The process in which a number of people meet together to solve a problem. The group leader uses a combination of techniques based on social science findings to obtain the best possible solution from the group; unanimous acceptance on the part of those involved should be the end result.

IMMUNITY AGAINST
COUNTER-PERSUASION:

Refers to a person's resistance to change in the direction opposite of the viewpoint which he has been persuaded to accept. Such immunity may be achieved by a variety of techniques by the persuader who produced the original change.

IMPLICATIONS:

The product dimension of mental abilities that makes a person able to see accurately the consequences of a situation, point of view, etc. For example, noting that a certain change in a product will increase sales involves ability to see a behavioral implication. Some people are very good at such implications; others are better at *figural* implications, e.g., deciding that a certain design goes well with a given fashion; still other people are skilled in *symbolic* implications, e.g., given certain formulas, others will follow from them.

INGENIOUS:

(TYPE AN.) Such an individual is flexible, looks at long range goals, enjoys feminine company, likes to get things done, and likes to be with others but not to submit to them. He can be free of tension but feels pressured if his liberty is curtailed in any way. He may feel anxious in such a situation but usually finds a way out.

INTELLECTUALLY
ORIENTED:

See TYPE II EQ.

LATITUDE OF
REJECTION:

The measure of a person's feelings or attitudes with respect to an object, person, etc. It is computed according to the number of statements a person disagrees with on a scale consisting of items differing along a certain dimension (or combination of dimensions, in some cases). Example: Attitude towards X brand shoes.

(a) X shoes are the best in the world.
(b) Although there may be a model or two of deficient X shoes, in general they are the best available
(c) X shoes have many flaws, but still they are better than average.
(d) X shoes are neither better nor worse than others.
(e) X shoes have many flaws and are a little worse than average.
(f) Although there may be occasionally good models, X shoes are in general among the worst available.
(g) X shoes are the worst in the world.

A person is asked to state how many of these statements he rejects. If he rejects all statements from (b) to (g), his latitude of rejection is 6, and therefore his attitude towards X shoes is very favorable. If he rejects only items (e), (f), and (g), his latitude of rejection is only 3; so his attitude towards X shoes is much less enthusiastic. The concept of latitude of rejection is very important in the design of persuasions by successive approximation.

MACH IV:

A scale for measuring the degree to which a person likes to manipulate others for his own use. A person high on this scale probably is a good salesman, provided he is not at the same time high in the need for approval and has the necessary mental abilities in the appropiate areas.

MEMORY: The ability to remember. There are 24 different kinds of memory. The fact that a person remembers telephone numbers, for example, does not guarantee that he will remember the events that took place with a particular client.

MENTAL ABILITIES: The various skills involved in thinking into which the general term "intelligence" has been subdivided. Initially, Thurstone described about seven separate and independent abilities. Guilford devised a new classification that indicates there are probably 120 different abilities, of which 99 have so far been discovered. These are classed under:

(a) *Operation*	(b) *Content*	(c) *Product*
Cognition	Figural	Units
Memory	Symbolic	Classes
Divergent	Semantic	Relations
production	Behavioral	Systems
Convergent		Transforma-
production		tions
Evaluation		Implications

(Separate definitions are given for each in Chapter 2.)

MOTIVATION: A generic name given to anything that causes a person to act or not to act in a given circumstance. Very obvious motivations are hunger, which makes a person want to eat, thirst, etc. Other powerful motives which social psychology has recently explored are *affiliation, approval, cognitive dissonance, curiosity, approach-avoidance conflict, positive and negative reinforcement, threat,* and *punishment.* A good understanding of the consequences of using each of these is important in obtaining the desired results in dealing with people.

NEGATIVE
REINFORCEMENT: Negative reinforcement is the name given to something disagreeable that we eliminate in order to increase the probability of the performance of an act. For example, if stopping a disagreeable noise has the effect of making a person repeat a certain action, this cessation of the noise is called negative reinforcement. A very useful application of negative reinforcement occurs in conflict resolution. In general, any conflict produces tension, which in turn is disagreeable. Every time there is progress in the solution of a conflict, there is tension reduction, which constitutes negative reinforcement. The persons involved tend to continue increasing cooperation, which is helpful in resolving the conflict, in order to continue the tension reduction.

PARTIAL
REINFORCEMENT: It has been found that the effect of *positive reinforcement* is much greater in fostering a certain habit if the reinforcement is not administered every time the desired behavior

is performed during the learning process. Any pattern of such occasional reward is called partial reinforcement.

PERSUASION BY
ANALOGY:

A method of persuasion in which a person is made to apply reasoning to a situation which is logically related but emotionally unrelated to the issue at hand. Seeing that he obtains different conclusions with the same reasoning in two different areas, produces cognitive *dissonance* which is reduced by changing his mind with respect to the emotional issue (the goal of the persuader).

PERSUASION BY
SUCCESSIVE
APPROXIMATION:

A method of persuasion in which the person's latitude of rejection is reduced one step at a time by changing his attitude first with respect to the least-rejected item. This attitude change causes cognitive dissonance, which is reduced by leading the person to change his private beliefs, one at a time, concerning several items.

POSITIVE
REINFORCEMENT:

Positive reinforcement is the name given to any stimulus that, when given to a person when he performs a certain act, increases the probability that the person will repeat that act. For example, we may give a piece of candy to a child when he puts away his toys. After doing this several times, we note that the child "gets used to" putting away his toys, and we say that candy constitutes a positive reinforcement for the child. The same positive reinforcement that resulted in putting away the toys may be used as positive reinforcement to get him to do other things.

POST-DECISION
DISSONANCE:

Every decision requires choosing between two alternatives, each having positive and negative aspects. Choosing one alternative leaves the person with the disadvantages of the chosen one and without the advantages of the rejected one. This situation causes dissonance, which is reduced by denying the importance of the chosen disadvantages and of the rejected advantages. An example is the case of a person who buys a car and tries to convince everyone how much better this car is than the other one he had in mind.

POST-DECISION
REGRET:

The discomfort a person sometimes feels after he has made a decision and is not able to reduce the subsequent *dissonance*.

PROGRAMMED
REINFORCEMENT:

Sometimes a person does not perform a desired act either because it just never occurs to him to do so or because the act is too complicated. Thus, he cannot be reinforced for performing that act. It is then possible to program or mold behavior by reinforcing every act that is a part of the total act desired. For example, if we want to have a tidy employee and feel that it is almost impossible to be thoroughly neat before he receives a positive reinforcement, we give him positive reinforcement when, for example, he has straightened out even a small portion of his papers. Hopefully, this will encourage neatness in other areas, which will be similarly reinforced. In order to be able to do this well with an employee, the supervisor must be very patient and very alert.

PROJECTION: The tendency of a person to attribute to others what is actually a major flaw in himself. An example is the soldier who says that all around him are cowards but is probably more afraid than anyone else. The person is generally unaware of the dynamics underlying his projection.

PSYCHOSOMATIC
ILLNESS: Illness provoked by severe psychological conflict. A person, attracted to his job for certain reasons but repelled because of others, may fall ill with allergies, heart trouble, ulcers, severe headaches, etc. Often a physician can find no physiological cause for the ailment. Psychosomatic illness frequently indicates *approach-avoidance conflict*. When the conflict is eliminated, the illness generally disappears.

PUNISHMENT: Punishment is the name given to something disagreeable which is administered to a person in order to get him to stop performing undesirable acts. This may take the form of reproof, suspension or threat of suspension, or dismissal from a job. Different punishments will mean different things to different persons. Punishment is, in general, very efficient in achieving an immediate reduction in the performance of undesirable acts, but it has two serious drawbacks. One of these is that in the long run there is a marked tendency to return to the discouraged behavior once the punishment is removed. For example, if an employee has been punished for tardiness by a strong reprimand, he will probably be on time, but he will eventually return to being late just as often as if the punishment had not been administered. The second drawback to punishment is that it tends to create additional undesirable effects, such as *approach-avoidance conflict*, *dissonance*, and *reactance*, with all their respective implications.

RATIONALIZATION: The use of plausible but untrue "reasons" to explain irrational action. In general, it is an excellent way of detecting the existence of *approach-avoidance conflict*. For example, the employee, who often states that his work is delayed because he lacks data, may be rationalizing, thereby hiding the true reason that he has little ability or interest for that type of work.

REACTANCE: The negative or resentful feeling a person has when he feels that his freedom to act is threatened. It can be caused by forbidding a person to perform an act, threatening him with *punishment* for doing it, and so forth. Reactance causes a person to act in ways that will tend to regain his freedom of action.

REGRESSION: The tendency of a person to act as he did many years ago, say, as a little child, when faced with a serious conflict. Regression is often another symptom of the existence of *approach-avoidance conflict*.

RETICULAR
FORMATION: Name given to a structure found at the point where the spinal cord enters the brain. Its state of excitation determines our level of consciousness, i.e., how wide awake we are. It is activated by *changes* in stimuli. In other words, it is not always loud noise that stimulates it but rather the *change* from loud to soft, from bright to dark, from color to black, and vice versa. There is an optimum state of reticular excitation for each task or stimulus a person faces, which guarantees maximum attention. If activation is very intense, as in severe *approach-avoidance conflict*, one's response is not constructive. For example, he may engage in his most accustomed behavior—aggression if he tends to be aggressive, rationalization if he has a tendency to make excuses, and so forth. Excessive excitement of the reticular formation may cause panic reaction.

SEMANTIC CONTENT: The classification of abilities that includes handling meaning and is usually expressed in the ability to deal with language.

SOCIAL PRESSURE: The influence exerted upon an individual by other persons, acting together. Such pressure reaches a maximum when 3 others agree upon, say, an opinion which is different from that held by the person in question in a particular situation, and give their opinion first. Under such conditions, group pressure often causes changes in attitudes, behavior, etc.

SYMBOLIC CONTENT: The classification of abilities that includes handling numbers, codes, letters, or names.

SYSTEM: A complex union of many interrelated elements. A meaningful sequence of events forms a behavioral system. For example, a worker spoils some work and hides it in a corner, the supervisor discovers this and reprimands the worker; this sequence of events forms a *behavioral* system. A computer program for handling credit notes, price discounts, and rebates is a *semantic* system. The plan for the design of a building is a *figural* system.

SOCIALLY ORIENTED: See TYPE IBR.

TRANSFORMATION: The product dimension in mental abilities that has to do with change. When the people in a department have been getting along well and suddenly start to have trouble, this is transformation in a *behavioral* system. Some people are very good at noticing this, while others have great difficulty.

PERSONALITY TYPES

(a) TYPE CO: A type of person who is ambitious, determined, dominating, and does not wish to be considered weak. Power and domination are very important to him. He is oriented to preserving his status, is not deferent towards others, and does not expect sympathy from others.

(b) TYPE III D: A type of person who accepts responsibility and likes to finish what he starts. He is very sure of himself, likes to control others, but at the same time, is conscious of the needs of others and can be useful to them. He characteristically gives more importance to reaching goals than to satisfying his own impulses.

(c) TYPE II EQ: A type of person who likes to achieve only in his own way. If his preferences are not in accord with higher authorities, conflict may result. If, on the other hand, supervisors treat him with understanding, he will usually prove loyal. Compared with the other types, this one is characterized by strong aesthetic appreciation.

(d) TYPE IV P: A type of person who likes to go to the aid of others in order to help and support them. He also likes to have others around him in order to be seen and heard, e.g., he likes to entertain others and be the center of a party. Rather disorganized, he feels organization curtails freedom. Not a doer, he is at heart glad that others are, so that he can lead his own carefree life while others do the work for him.

(e) TYPE IBR: A type of person who appears to be devoted to others but who is not autonomous and is excessively deferent to authority. He finds maximum satisfaction in helping the needy and does not hurt others.

TYPES OF
REINFORCEMENT: The most common and simplest reinforcement is to tell someone that he did something well, but this is not the only type. Note, for example, that *positive reinforcement* need not necessarily be logically related to the work performed. The types of reinforcement that have been identified are the following:
(a) Approval. This has to be administered judiciously, and in relation to the need for approval of the individuals involved. (Positive)
(b) Salary raise. (Positive)
(c) Recognition. (Positive)
(d) Agreement with an opinion. (Positive)
(e) Pointing out improvement. (Positive)
(f) Tension reduction. (Negative)
(g) Institution of an improvement in working conditions

	(not obtained through the employee's pressure). (Positive)
UNITS:	The product dimension of mental abilities that deals with the simplest products in any area—lines in the *figural* area, numbers or names in the *symbolic* area, words in the *semantic* area, and facial expression or body attitudes in the *behavioral* area.
UNSPOKEN LANGUAGE:	The acts, gestures, postures, and other physical attitudes that often transmit more meaning than spoken words. There are two important skills implied here: how to *use* this unspoken language effectively, and how to *interpret* the unspoken language of others.
WIN-LOSE CONFLICT:	A battle or disagreement in which each side sees no other solution than total victory or defeat. Such conflict causes people to fixate upon their chosen solution—something that stifles creativity. It also makes them invent absurd stereotypes about themselves or their opponents, and they refuse to see any merit in the solutions others propose or see flaws in their own solutions. Win-lose conflict is a very common state of affairs that is very damaging to group cooperation.

bibliography

Abelson, H. I. "Persuasion: How Opinions and Attitudes Are Changed," Springer, New York, 1959.

Abelson, R. P., Aronson, E., McGuire, W. J., Newcomb, T. M., Rosenberg, M. and Tannenbaum, P. H., eds., "The Cognitive Consistency Theories: A Source Book," Rand McNally, Chicago, 1968.

Adams, J. S. Toward an understanding of inequity, *J. Abnor. Soc. Psychol. 67*, 422–436 (1963a).

Adams, J. S. Wage inequities, productivity and work quality, *Ind. Relat. 3*, 9–16 (1963b).

Adams, J. S. Inequity in social exchange, in "Advances in Experimental Social Psychology" (L. Berkowitz, ed.), Vol. 2, Academic Press, New York, 1965.

Adorno, T. W., Frenkel-Brunswick, E., Levinson, D. J. and Sanford, R. N. "The Authoritarian Personality," Harper, New York, 1950.

Allport, G. W. and Allport, F. H. "A–S Reaction Study," Houghton, Boston, 1928.

Allyn, J. and Festinger, L. "The effectiveness of unanticipated persuasive communications," *J. Abnor. Soc. Psychol. 62*, 35–40 (1961).

American Management Association "Report No. 85," New York, 1965.

American Management Association "Report on Job Evaluation," New York, 1969.

Anastasi, A. "Psychological Testing," Macmillan, New York, 1968.

Argyris, C. "Intervention Theory and Method," Univ. of Chicago Press, 1970.

299

Aronson, E. and Gerard, E.   Beyond Parkinson's law: the effect of excess time on subsequent performance, *J. Person. Soc. Psychol. 3*, No. 3, 336–339 (1966).

Asch, S. E.   "Social Psychology," Prentice Hall, Englewood Cliffs, N.J, 1952.

Asch, S. E.   Effects on group pressure upon the modifications and distortion of judgements, in "Readings in Social Psychology" (Maccoby, Newcomb and Hartley, eds.), Holt, New York, 1958.

Backman, C. W. and Secord, P. F.   "Problems in Social Psychology," McGraw-Hill, New York, 1966.

Bandura, A. and Walters, R. H.   "Social Learning and Personality Development," Holt, New York, 1963.

Bass, B. M.   "Leadership, Psychology and Organizational Behavior," Harper, New York, 1960.

Bavelas, A.   A mathematical model for group structures, *Appl. Anthrop. VII*, 16–30 (1948).

Bennis, W. G., Schein, E. H., Berlew, D. E. and Steele, F. I.   "Interpersonal Dynamics: Essays and Readings on Human Interaction," Dorsey Press, New York, 1964.

Bergen, H. B.   Employee-employer relations in the office, in "Attitudes and Emotional Problems of Office Employees," Office Management Series no. 87, American Management Association, 1939.

Berger, R. M., Guilford, J. P. and Christensen, P. R. A factor-analytic study of planning, *Psych. Monogr. 71*, no. 435 (1957).

Berger, R. M. and Guilford, J. P.,   "Pertinent Questions Form A," Sheridan Supply Co., Beverly Hills, Calif., 1960.

Berkowitz, L.   *Sociometry 19*, 210–222 (1956).

Berkowitz, L. and Green, J. A.   The stimulus qualities of the scapegoat, *J. Abnor. Soc. Psychol. 64*, no. 6, 293 (1962).

Berlyne, D. E.   Conflict and information—theory variables as determinants of human perceptual curiosity, *J. Experi. Psychol. 53*, 399–404 (1957).

Besse, A. and Castelnau, H., De Chalambert, B., Choplin, J., and Virenque, A.   "Le Capital—Imagination," Les Editions de l'Entreprise Moderne, Paris, 1958.

Bindra, D.   "Motivation: A Systematic Reinterpretation," Ronald Press, New York, 1959.

Blake, R. R. and Mouton, J. S.   Loyalty of Representatives to Ingroup Positions During Intergroup Competition, *Sociometry 24*, no. 2, 171–183 (1961).

Blake, R. R. and Mouton, J. S.   The intergroup dynamics of win-lose conflict and problem-solving collaboration in union-management relations, in "Intergroup Relations and Leadership" (M. Sherif, ed.), Wiley, New York, 1962.

Blake, R. R. and Mouton, J. S.   "The Managerial Grid," Gulf Publishing, Houston, 1964.

Blake, R. R., Shepard, H. A., and Mouton, J. S.   "Managing Intergroup Conflict in Industry," Gulf Publishing, Houston, 1964.

Blum, M. L. and Naylor, J. C.   "Industrial Psychology," 2nd ed., Harper, New York, 1968.

Brady, J. V.   Ulcers in executive monkeys, *Sci. Amer.*, October (1958).

Bramel, D.   Selection of a target for defensive projection, *J. Abnor. Soc. Psychol. 66*, no. 4, 318–324 (1963).

Brehm, J. W.   "A Theory of Psychological Reactance," Academic Press, New York, 1966.

Brown, J. S.   Gradients of approach-avoidance responses and their relation to levels of motivation, *J. Compar. Physiol. Psychol. 41*, 450–465 (1948).

Brunner, J. S., Shapiro, D. and Tagiuri, R.   The meaning of traits in isolation and in combination in "Person Perception and Interpersonal Behavior" (R. Tagiuri and L. Petrullo, eds.), Stanford Univ. Press, Stanford, Calif., 1958.

Buss, A. H.   "The Psychology of Aggression," Wiley, New York, 1961.

Byrne, D. Attitudes and Attraction, in "Advances in Experimental Social Psychology" (L. Berkowitz, ed.), Academic Press, New York, 1969.

Carlsmith, J. M., Collins, B. D., and Helmreich, R. I. Studies in forced compliance, I: The effect of pressure for compliance on attitude change produced by face-to-face role playing and anonymous essay writing, *J. Person. Soc. Psychol. 4*, 1–13 (1966).

Carnegie, A. "Miscellaneous Writings," Country Life Press, New York, 1933.

Carpenter, Γ. and Haddan, E. E. "Systematic Application of Psychology to Education," Macmillan, New York, 1964.

Cartwright, D. and Zander, A. "Group Dynamics," Harper, New York, 1960.

Cattell, R. B. "Personality," McGraw-Hill, New York, 1950.

Cattell, R. B. "The Scientific Analysis of Personality," Penguin, London, 1965.

Christensen, P. R., Merrifield, P. R. and Guilford, J. P. "Consequences," Sheridan Supply Co., Beverly Hills, Calif., 1958.

Christie, R. and Geis, F. "Studies in Machiavellianism," Academic Press, New York, 1970.

Clay, H. The compromise of 1850, quoted in "The World's Great Speeches" (L. Copeland and L. Lamm, eds.), Dover, New York, 1958.

Cloudsley-Thompson, J. L. The Merkhiyat Jebels: A desert community in "Desert Biology," (G. W. Browns Jr., ed.), Academic Press, New York, 1968.

Cohen, A. R. "Attitude Change and Social Influence," Basic Books, New York, 1964.

Collins, B. and Guetzkow, H. "A Social Psychology of Group Processes for Decision Making," Wiley, New York, 1964.

Columbia Univ. Associates in Philosophy "An Introduction to Reflective Thinking," Houghton, Boston, 1923.

Cook, T. D. and Insko, C. A. Persistence of attitude changes as a function of conclusion re-exposure, *J. Person. Soc. Psychol. 9*, no. 4, 322–328 (1968).

Cottle, W. C. A factorial study of the multiphasic, Strong, Kuder and Bell Inventories using a population of adult males in "Worker Trait Requirements for 4000 Jobs," U.S. Bureau of Employment Service, U.S. Dept. of Labor, Washington, D.C., 1956.

Cox, D. F. and Bauer, K. A. Self confidence and persuability in women, *Pub. Opinion Quart. 28*, 453–466 (1964).

Cranberg, L. Law—scientific and juridical, *American Scientist, 56*, No. 3, 244–253 (1968).

Crowne, D. P. and Liverant, S. Conformity under varying conditions of personal commitment, *J. Abnor. Soc. Psychol. 66*, no. 6, 547 (1963).

Crowne, D. P. and Marlowe, D. "The Approval Motive," Wiley, New York, 1964.

Crutchfield, R. S. Conformity and character, *Amer. Psychol. 10*, 191–198 (1955).

Dabbs, J. and Janis, I. Why does eating while reading facilitate opinion change? An experimental inquiry, *J. Exp. Soc. Psychol., 1*, 133–144 (1965).

Deutsch, M. An experimental study of the effects of cooperation and competition upon group process, *Hum. Relat. 2*, 199–231 (1949).

Dollard, J., Doob, L. W., Miller, N. E., Mowrer, O. H. and Sears, R. R. "Frustration and Aggression," Yale Univ. Press, New Haven, Conn., 1939.

Dunnette, M. D. A note on the criterion, *J. Appl. Psychol. 47*, 251–244 (1963).

Dunnette, M. D., Campbell, J., and Jaastad, K. The Effect of Group Participation on Brainstorming Effectiveness for Two Industrial Samples, *J. Appl. Psychol. 47*, 30–37 (1963).

Dvorine, I. "Dvorine Pseudo Isochromatic Plates," Harcourt, New York, 1953.

Einstein, A. "The Meaning of Relativity," Princeton Univ. Press, 1950.

Einstein, A. and Infeld, L. "The Evolution of Physics," Simon and Schuster, New York, 1938.

El-Abd, H.   "The Intelligence of East African Students" (East African Academy Conf., September 17–21), Makerere Univ. College, Kampala, Uganda, 1969.

Elbing, A. O.   "An Experimental Investigation of the Influence of Reference-Group Role Identification on Role Playing as Applied to Business," Ph.D. dissertation, Univ. of Washington, Seattle, 1962.

Eriksen, C. W. (ed.)   Behavior and awareness: A symposium of research and interpretation. *J. Pers. 30*, 1–158 (1962).

Ewing, T. N.   "A study of certain factors involved in changes of opinion." *J. Soc. Psychol. 16*, 63–88 (1942).

Eysenck, H. J.   "Dimensions of Personality," Routledge, London, 1947.

Eysenck, H. J.   "Uses and Abuses of Psychology," Penguin, London, 1953.

Festinger, L.   "A Theory of Cognitive Dissonance," Harper, New York, 1957.

Festinger, L.   Behavioral support for opinion change, *Pub. Opin. Quart. 28*, 404–417 (1964).

Festinger, L. and Maccoby, N.   On resistance to persuasive communications, *J. Abnor. Soc. Psychol. 64*, no. 4, 359–365 (1964).

Festinger, L., Schachter, S. and Back, K. W.   "Social Pressures in Informal Groups: A Study of Human Factors in Housing, Harper, New York, 1950.

Flanagan, J. C.   The critical incident technique, *Psychol. Bull. 51*, 327–358 (1954).

Fleischman, E. A.   Dimensional analysis of psychomotor abilities, *J. Exp. Psychol. 48*, 437–454 (1954).

Fleischman, E. A. and Ellison, G. D.   A factor analysis of five manipulative tests, *J. Appl. Psychol. 46*, 96–105 (1962).

Fleischman, E. A. and Hempel, W. E., Jr.   Factorial analysis of complex psychomotor performance and related skills, *J. Appl. Psychol. 40*, 96–104 (1956).

Frederiksen, N., Saunders, D. R. and Ward, B.   The in-basket test, *Psychol. Monographs 71*, no. 9 (1957).

Frederiksen, N.   Factors in in-basket performance, *Psychol. Monographs 76*, no. 22 (1962).

Freedman, J. L. and Doob, A. N.   "Deviancy: The Psychology of Being Different," Academic Press, New York, 1968.

Freedman, J. L. and Fraser, S. C.   Compliance without pressure: the foot-in-the-door technique, *J. Person. Soc. Psychol. 4*, no. 2, 195–202 (1966).

Freeman, G. L.   The relationship between performance level and body activity level, *J. Exp. Psychol. 26*, 602–608 (1940).

Gagné, R. M.   "Human Problem Solving: Internal and External Events in Problem Solving, Research, Method and Theory," (Benjamin Kleinmuntz, ed.), Wiley, New York, 1966.

Gerard, H. B., Wilhelmy, R. A., and Conolley, E. S.   Conformity and group size, *J. Person. Soc. Psychol. 8*, no. 1, 79–82 (1968).

Ghiselli and Brown   "Personnel and Industrial Psychology," McGraw-Hill, New York, 1955.

Golembiewski, R. T.   "The Small Group," Univ. of Chicago Press, Chicago, 1962.

Grossack, M. M.   Some effects of cooperation and competition upon small group behavior, *J. Abnor. Soc. Psychol. 49*, 341–348 (1954).

Grove, E. A. and Kerr, W. A.   Specific evidence on origin of halo effect in measurement of employee morale, *J. Soc. Psychol. 34*, 165–170 (1951).

Guilford, J. P.   "Personality," McGraw-Hill, New York, 1959.

Guilford, J. P.   "The Nature of Human Intelligence," McGraw-Hill, New York, 1967.

Guilford, J. P. and Lacey, J. I. (eds.)   "Printed Classification Tests," AAF Aviation Psychology Research Program Reports, no. 5, Government Printing Office, Washington, D.C., 1947.

Haaland, G. A. and Venkatesan, M.   Resistance to persuasive communications: an examination of the distraction hypothesis, *J. Person. Soc. Psychol. 9*, no. 2, 167–170 (1968).

Hebb, H. O.   Drives and the CND' (conceptual nervous system), *Psychol. Rev. 62*, 243–254 (1955).

Haire, M.   "Psychology in Management," McGraw-Hill, New York, 1964.

Hall, C. and Lindzey, G. A.   "Theories of Personality," Wiley, New York, 1970.

Hare, A. P., Borgatta, E. F., and Bales, R. F.   "Small Groups," Alfred Knopf, New York, 1955.

Harlow, H. F.   Learning and satiation of response in intrinsically motivated complex puzzle performance by monkeys, *J. Comp. Physiol. Psychol. 43*, 289–294 (1950).

Harvey, O. J.   Some situational and cognitive determinants of dissonance resolutions, *J. Abnor. Soc. Psychol. 1*, no. 4, 349 (1965).

Heise, G. A. and Miller, G. A.   Problem solving by small groups using various communication nets, *J. Abnor. Soc. Psychol. 46*, 327–335 (1951).

Herzberg, F., Mausner, B., Snyderman, B.   "The Motivation to Work," Wiley, New York, 1959.

Hill, R. J.   A note on the inconsistency in paired comparison judgements, *Amer. Soc. Rev. 18*, 564–566 (1953).

Hoffman, L. R.   Group problem solving in "Advances in Experimental Social Psychology", Vol. 2 (L. Berkowitz, ed.), Academic Press, New York, 1965.

Hollander, E. P. and Hunt, R. G.   "Current Perspectives in Social Psychology," Oxford Univ. Press, London, 1963.

Hovland, C. I., Janis, I. L. and Kelley, H. H.   "Communication and Persuasion," Yale Univ. Press, New Haven, Conn., 1953.

Hovland, C. I. and Pritzker, H. A.   Extent of opinion change as function of the amount of change advocated, *J. Abnor. Soc. Psychol. 54*, 257–261 (1957).

Howells, L. T. and Becker, S. W.   Seating arrangement and leadership emergence, *J. Abnor. Soc. Psychol. 64*, 148–150 (1962).

Insko, C. A.   "Theories of Attitude Change," Appleton, New York, 1967.

Insko, C. A. and Schopler, J.   Triadic consistency: A statement of affective-cognitive-conative consistency, *Psychol. Rev. 74*, no. 5, 361–376 (1967).

Jacobson, L. I.   The effects of awareness, problem solving ability and task difficulty on the acquisition and extinction of verbal behavior, *J. Exp. Res. Person. 3*, 206–213 (1969).

Janis, I. L., and Guilmore, J. B.   The influence of incentive conditions on the success of role playing in modifying attitudes, *J. Person. Soc. Psychol. 1*, 17–27 (1965).

Janis, I., Kaye, D., and Kirschner, P.   Facilitating effects of "Eating-while-Reading" on responsiveness to persuasive communications, *J. Person. Soc. Psychol.*, no. 1, 181–185 (1965).

Johnson, R. E.   Smoking and the reduction of cognitive dissonance, *J. Person. Soc. Psychol. 9*, no. 3, 260–265 (1968).

Jones, E. E.   "Ingratiation," Appleton, New York, 1964.

Jones, E. E. and Gerard, H. B.   "Foundations of Social Psychology," Wiley, New York, 1967.

Kanouse, D. E. and Abelson, R. P.   Language variables affecting the persuasiveness of simple communications, *J. Person. Soc. Psychol. 7*, No. 2, 158–163 (1967).

Kiesler, C. A., Collins, B., and Miller, N.   "Attitude Change," Wiley, New York, 1969.

Koestler, A.   "The Act of Creation," Macmillan, New York, 1964.

Korman, A. K.   The prediction of managerial performance: a review, *Personnel Psychol. 21*, 295–322 (1968).

Kranzberg, M.   The disunity of science-technology, *Amer. Sci. 56*, 21–34 (1968).

Kuder, G. F.   "Kuder Preference Record: Manual," Science. Research Associates, Chicago, 1953.

Kuhn, T. S.   "The Structure of Scientific Revolutions," Univ. of Chicago Press, Chicago, 1962.

La Fave, L. and Teeley, P.   Involuntary nonconformity as a function of habit lag, *Perceptual and Motor Skills 24*, 227–234, Southern Univ. Press (1967).

La Fave, L.   Reduction of conflict to one type, *Psychol. Rep. 25*, 165–166 (1969).

Laurent, H.   The identification of management potential, in "Psychology Applied to Industry," (M. D. Dunnette, and W. K. Kirchner, eds.), presented at Amer. Psychol. Assn. Annu. Convention, St. Louis, Mo., 1962.

Lawrence, D. H. and Festinger, L.   "Deterrents and Reinforcement," Stanford Univ. Press, Palo Alto, 1962.

Leavitt, H. J.   Some effects of certain communication patterns of group performance, in "Readings in Social Psychology" (E. Maccoby, T. M. Newcomb, and E. L. Hartley, eds.), Holt, New York, 1958.

Leavitt, H. J.   "Managerial Psychology" Univ. of Chicago Press, 1964.

Lewin, K.   "A Dynamic Theory of Personality," McGraw-Hill, New York, 1935.

Lewin, K., Lippitt, R., and White, R. K.   Patterns of Aggressive Behavior in Experimentally Created "Social Climates," *J. Soc. Psychol., X*, 271–299 (1939).

Lewin, K.   Studies in group decision, in "Group Dynamics," Row, Peterson, Evanston, Ill., 1953.

Likert, R.   A technique for the measurement of attitudes, *Arch. Psychol. 22*, no. 140 (1932).

Lindsley, D. B.   Psychophysiology and Motivation in "Nebraska Symposium on Motivation" (M. R. Jones, ed.), Univ. of Nebraska Press, Lincoln, Nebraska, 1957.

Linn, L. S.   Verbal attitudes and overt behavior: a study of racial discrimination, *Soc. Forces 43*, no. 3, 353–364 (1965).

Maccoby, E., Newcomb, T. M. and Hartley, E. L.   "Readings in Social Psychology," Holt, New York, 1958.

Mackworth, N. H.   Originality, *Amer. Psychol. 20*, 51–66 (1965).

Maier, N. R. F.   "Frustration: The Study of Behavior without a Goal," McGraw-Hill, New York, 1949.

Maier, N. R. F.   "Problem-Solving Discussions and Conferences: Leadership Methods and Skills," McGraw-Hill, New York, 1963.

Maier, N. R. F.   "Psychology in Industry," Houghton, Boston, 1965.

Maier, N. R. F. and Hayes, J. J.   "Creative Management," Wiley, New York, 1962.

Malof, M. and Lott, A. J.   Ethnocentrism and the acceptance of negro support in a group pressure situation, *J. Abnor. Soc. Psychol. 65*, no. 4, 254 (1962).

Masserman, J. B.   "Behavior and Neurosis," Univ. of Chicago Press, Chicago, 1943.

McDavid, J. W. and Harari, H.   "Social Psychology," Harper, New York, 1968.

McGuire, W. J.   Cognitive consistency and attitude change, *J. Abnor. Soc. Psychol. 60*, 345–353 (1960).

McGuire, W. J.   Direct and indirect effects of dissonance-producing messages, *J. Abnor. Soc. Psychol. 60*, 354–358 (1960).

McGuire, W. J.   Resistance to counter persuasion conferred by active and passive prior refutation of the same and alternative counterarguments, *J. Abnor. Soc. Psychol. 63*, no. 2, 326–332 (1961).

McGuire, W.   Inducing resistance to persuasion, in "Advances in Experimental Social Psychology," Vol. 1 (L. Berkowitz, ed.), Academic Press, New York, 1964.

McGuire, W. and Papageorgis, D.   The relative efficacy of various types of prior belief-defenses in producing immunity against persuasion, *J. Abnor. Soc. Psychol. 62*, no. 2, 327–337 (1961).

Menninger, K. "The Crime of Punishment," Viking Press, New York, 1968.

Merhabian, A. Inference of attitude from the posture, orientation and distance of a communicator, *J. Consult. Clin. Psychol. 32*, no. 3, 296–308 (1968).

Merhabian, A. and Ferris, S. R. Inference of attitudes from nonverbal communication in two channels, *J. Consult. Psychol. 31*, no. 3, 248–252 (1967).

Miller, G. A. Psychology as a means of promoting human welfare, *Amer. Psychol. 24*, no. 12, 1063–1075 (1969).

Miller, N. E. Theory and experiment relating psychoanalytic displacement to stimulus-response generalization, *J. Abnor. Soc. Psychol. 43*, 155–178 (1948).

Moscovici, S. Attitudes and opinions, *Annu. Rev. Psychol.* 231–260 (1963).

Mowrer, O. H. "Learning Theory and Behavior," Wiley, New York, 1960.

Murray, H. A. "Explorations in Personality," Oxford Univ. Press, New York, 1938.

Newcomb, T. M., Turner, R. H., and Converse, P. E. "Social Psychology," Holt, New York, 1965.

O'Sullivan, Guilford, J. P., and de Mille, R. "The Measurement of Social Intelligence," rep. no. 34 from the Psychology Laboratory, Univ. of Southern California, June 1965.

Osborn, A. F. "Creative imagination: principles and procedures of creative thinking," New York, Scribner, 1953.

Papageorgis, D. and McGuire, W. The generality of immunity to persuasion produced by pre-exposure to weakened counterarguments, *J. Abnor. Soc. Psychol. 62*, no. 3, 475–481 (1961).

Parkinson, C. N. "Parkinson's Law and Other Studies in Administration " (Sentry, ed.), Houghton, Boston, 1957.

Pickford, R. W. "Individual Differences in Colour Vision," Macmillan, New York, 1951.

Reiss, A. E. "Occupations and Social Status," Free Press of Glencoe, 1961.

Rogers, C. "Counseling and Psychotherapy," Houghton, Boston, 1942.

Rosenberg, M. J. When dissonance fails. An eliminating evaluation of apprehension from attitude measurement, *J. Person. Soc. Psychol. 1*, 28–42 (1965).

Russell, B. "Has Man a Future?" Simon and Schuster, New York, 1962.

Sachar, E. J. "Behavioral Science and Criminal Law," *Sci. Amer.* November (1963).

Sanford, T. N. The approach of the authoritarian personality, in "Psychology of Personality," (J. L. McCraig, ed.), Grove Press, New York, 1956.

Sargent, S. G. and Williamson, R. C. "Social Psychology," Ronald Press Co., New York, 1966.

Schachter, S. Deviation, rejection and communication, *J. Abnor. Soc. Psychol. 46*, 190–208 (1951).

Schachter, S. "The Psychology of Affiliation," Stanford Univ. Press, Palo Alto, 1959.

Schachter, S. and Latane, B. "Crime cognition and the autonomic nervous system" in (D. Levine ed.) *Nebraska Symposium on Motivation, 1964*, University of Nebraska Press, 221–273, 1964.

Schachter, S., Willerman, B., Festinger, L. and Hyman, R. Emotional disruption and industrial productivity, *J. Appl. Psychol. 45*, no. 4, 201–213 (1961).

Scott, J. P. "Aggression," Univ. of Chicago Press, Chicago, 1958.

Scott, W. D., Clothier, R. C., Mathewson, S. B., and Spriegel, W. R. Personnel Management, McGraw-Hill, New York, 1941.

Schutz, W. C. "RTRO: A Three Dimensional Theory of Interpersonal Behavior," Rinehart, New York, 1958.

Secord, P. F. and Backman, C. W. "Social Psychology," McGraw-Hill, New York, 1964.

Shaw, M. E. Acceptance of authority, group structure and the effectiveness of small groups, *J. Person. 27*, 196–210 (1959).

Shaw, M. E.   Communication Networks in "Advances in Experimental Social Psychology," Vol. 1 (L. Berkowitz, ed.), Academic Press, New York, 1964.

Sherif, M., Harvey, O. J., White, B. J., Hood, W. R., and Sherif, C. W.   Norman: "Intergroup Conflict and Cooperation: The Robbers Cave Experiment," Institute of Group Relations, Univ. of Oklahoma, 1961.

Sherif, C. W., Sherif, M., and Nebergall, R. E.   "Attitude and Attitude Change, Saunders, Philadelphia, 1965.

Sherif, M.   "Intergroup Relations and Leadership," Wiley, New York, 1962.

Sherif, M. and Hovland, C. I.   "Social Judgement," Yale Univ. Press, New Haven, Conn., 1961.

Skinner, B. F.   "The Behavior of Organisms," Appleton, New York, 1938.

Skinner, B. F.   "Walden II," Macmillan, New York, 1948.

Skinner, B. F.   "Science and Human Behavior," Macmillan, New York, 1953.

Skinner, B. F.   The experimental analysis of behavior, *Amer. Sci. 45*, 343–371 (1957).

Skinner, B. F.   Reinforcement today, *Amer. Psychol. 3*, 94–99 (1958).

Smith, D. H.   Evidence for a general activity syndrome: A survey of townspeople in eight Massachusetts towns and cities, *Proc. 77th Annu. Conven. Amer. Psychol. Ass.*, 453–454 (1969).

Stagner, R.   "Psychology of Industrial Conflict," Wiley, New York, 1956.

Stein, M. I.   "Volunteers for Peace," Wiley, New York, 1966.

Stogdill, M.   "Individual Behavior and Group Achievement," Oxford Univ. Press, New York, 1959.

Stricker, G.   Scapegoating: An experimental investigation, *J. Abnor. Soc. Psychol. 67*, no. 2, 125 (1963).

Strong, E. K., Jr.   "Vocational Interests of Men and Women," Stanford Univ. Press, Palo Alto, 1951.

Strong, E. K., Jr.   Satisfaction and Interests, *Amer. Psychol. 13*, 449–456 (1958).

Super, D. E.   "The Psychology of Careers," Wiley, New York, 1957.

Swingle, P. G.   "Experiments in Social Psychology," Academic Press, New York, 1968.

Tajfel, H. "Experiments in Intergroup Discrimination," *Sci. Amer.*, *223*, 5, Nov. 1970.

Tannenbaum, A. S.   "Control in Organizations," McGraw-Hill, New York, 1968.

Tannenbaum, A. S.   Organizations and dilemmas, *Contemp. Psychol. XIV*, no. 8, 411–412 (1969).

Thorndike, R. L.   Ten thousand careers and criteria, paper presented at *Amer. Psychol. Ass.*, Chicago, September 1960.

Thurstone, L. L. and Chave, E. J.   "The Measurement of Attitude," Univ. of Chicago Press, Chicago, 1929.

Toland, J.   "Battle: The Story of the Bulge," Random House, New York, 1959.

Twain, M.   "Pudd'nhead Wilson," 1894.

U.S. Employment Service   "Worker Trait Requirements for 4,000 Jobs," Bureau of Employment Service, U.S. Department of Labor, Washington, D.C., 1956.

Varela, J. A.   "Manual del Supervisor," privately printed, Montevideo, Uruguay, 1961.

Vinacke, W. E., Wilson, W. R. and Meredith, G. M.   "Dimensions of Social Psychology," Scott Foresman, Chicago, 1964.

Walster, E.   The temporal sequence of post-decision processes, in "Conflict Decision and Dissonance," (L. Festinger, ed.), Stanford Univ. Press, Palo Alto, 1964.

Walster, E. and Festinger, L.   The effectiveness of "overhead" persuasive communications, *J. Abnor. Soc. Psychol. 65*, no. 6, 395–402 (1962).

Walster, E. and Festinger, L.   Decisions Among Imperfect Alternatives. In "Conflict, Decision and Dissonance," (L. Festinger, ed.), Stanford Univ. Press, Palo Alto, 1964.

Webster, E. C. "Decision Making in the Employment Interview," Industrial-Relations Center, McGill University, Montreal, Canada, 1964.

Weick, K. Reduction of cognitive dissonance through task enhancement and effect expenditure, *J. Abnor. Soc. Psychol. 68*, no. 5, 533–539 (1964).

Wiener, M. and Merhabian, A. "Language within Language," Appleton, New York, 1968.

Yaryan, R. B. and Festinger, L. The effects of preparatory action on belief in the occurrence of possible future events, unpublished paper cited in Festinger, L. The psychological effects of insufficient rewards, *Amer. Psychol. 16*, 1–11 (1961).

Zimbardo, P. G. Involvement and communication discrepancy as determinants of opinion change, *J. Abnor. Soc. Psychol. 60*, 86–94 (1960).

Zimbardo, P. G. "The Cognitive Control of Motivation," Scott-Foresman, Chicago, 1969.

Zimbardo, P. G. and Ebbesen, E. B. "Influencing Attitudes and Changing Behavior," Addison-Wesley, Reading, Mass., 1969.

index